The Art of Restraint

The Art of Restraint
English Poetry from Hardy to Larkin

Richard Hoffpauir

Newark: University of Delaware Press
London and Toronto: Associated University Presses

© 1991 by Assoicated University Presses, Inc.

All rights reserved. Authorization to photocopy items for internal or personal use, or the internal or personal use of specific clients, is granted by the copyright owner, provided that a base fee of $10.00, plus eight cents per page, per copy is paid directly to the Copyright Clearance Center, 27 Congress Street, Salem, Massachusetts 01970. [0-87413-378-5/91 $10.00 + 8¢ pp, pc.]

Associated University Presses
440 Forsgate Drive
Cranbury, NJ 08512

Associated University Presses
25 Sicilian Avenue
London WC1A 2QH, England

Associated University Presses
P.O. Box 39, Clarkson Pstl. Stn.
Mississauga, Ontario,
Canada L5J 3X9

The paper used in this publication meets the requirements of the American National Standard for Permanence of Paper for Printed Library Materials Z39.48-1984.

Library of Congress Cataloging-in-Publication Data

Hoffpauir, Richard, 1942–
    The art of restraint: English poetry from Hardy to Larkin/ Richard Hoffpauir.
    p. cm.
    Includes bibliographical references.
    ISBN 0-87413-378-5 (alk. paper)
    1. English poetry—20th century—History and criticism. 2. Hardy, Thomas, 1840–1928—Poetic works. 3. Larkin, Philip—Criticism and interpretation. 4. Self-control in literature. 5. Order in literature. I. Title.
PR601.H57   1991
821'.9109—dc20   89-40272
                                                                                                      CIP

PRINTED IN THE UNITED STATES OF AMERICA

Contents

Acknowledgments	7
Introduction: Sorting Out Modern Poetry	13
1 Yeats or Hardy?	29
2 Edward Thomas and the Georgians	60
3 Poets of the First World War	87
Rupert Brooke and Julian Grenfell 96	
Charles Sorley and Robert Graves 98	
Siegfried Sassoon 101	
Wilfred Owen 106	
Isaac Rosenberg 118	
Edmund Blunden 127	
Ivor Gurney 131	
4 Modern Love	139
Robert Bridges 154	
D. H. Lawrence 169	
Robert Graves 185	
5 Social Consolations	202
Edgell Rickword 215	
Elizabeth Daryush 229	
John Betjeman 241	
Philip Larkin 263	
Notes	287
Bibliography	311
Index	321

Acknowledgments

The author wishes to thank the following for permission to reproduce copyright material:

W. H. AUDEN: reprinted by permission of Faber and Faber Ltd. from *The English Auden: Poems, Essays & Dramatic Writings 1927–1937*, and *Collected Poems* by W. H. Auden, edited by Edward Mendelson; and by permission of Random House, Inc. from *Selected Poems* by W. H. Auden, edited by Edward Mendelson (1979).

JOHN BETJEMAN: John Murray (Publishers) for excerpts from *Collected Poems* and *Uncollected Poems*.

EDMUND BLUNDEN: William Collins Sons & Co. for excerpts from *Undertones of War*, and Carcanet Press Limited for excerpts from *Selected Poems*, edited by Robyn Marsack (1982).

GORDON BOTTOMLEY: Richard Lancelyn Green, literary executor for the late Gordon Bottomley for excerpts from *King Lear's Wife and Other Plays* (2nd ed., 1925).

E. E. CUMMINGS: The lines from "may i feel said he" are reprinted from NO THANKS by E. E. Cummings, edited by George James Firmage, by permission of Liveright Publishing Corporation. Copyright 1935 by E. E. Cummings. Copyright 1968 by Marion Morehouse Cummings. Copyright 1973, 1978 by the Trustees for the E. E. Cummings Trust. Copyright 1973, 1978 by George James Firmage. Also by permission of Grafton Books, a division of William Collins Sons & Co.

ELIZABETH DARYUSH: A. A. Daryush for excerpts from *The Last Man and Other Verses* (1936); and Carcanet Press Limited for excerpts from *Selected Poems from Verses I–VI* (1972) and *Collected Poems* (1976).

W. H. DAVIES: Jonathan Cape Limited for excerpts from *The Complete Poems of W. H. Davies* (1963).

C. Day Lewis: Jonathan Cape Limited for excerpts from *Collected Poems of C. Day Lewis* (1954).

H. D. (Hilda Doolittle): Carcanet Press Limited for an excerpt from *Collected Poems 1912–1944*, edited by Louis L. Martz (1984).

T. S. Eliot: Faber and Faber Limited for excerpts from "The Love Song of J. Alfred Prufrock" and "The Waste Land" in *Collected Poems 1909–1962* by T. S. Eliot; excerpts from "The Love Song of J. Alfred Prufrock" and "The Waste Land" in *Collected Poems 1909–1962* by T. S. Eliot, copyright 1936 by Harcourt Brace Jovanovich, Inc. and copyright 1963, 1964 by T. S. Eliot, reprinted by permission of the publisher.

Robert Frost: the Estate of Robert Frost, Edward Connery Lathem (editor), Jonathan Cape Limited, and Henry Holt and Company, for an excerpt from *The Poetry of Robert Frost*, edited by Edward Connery Lathem (1969).

George Grant: Mrs. Sheila Grant, executrix and sole beneficiary of George Grant's estate, and John Baxter, editor, *The Compass*, for excerpt from "Faith and the Multiversity."

Robert Graves: A. P. Watt Limited on behalf of the Executors of the Estate of Robert Graves for excerpts from *Collected Poems* (1975); from *Collected Poems* 1975 by Robert Graves. Copyright 1975 by Robert Graves. Reprinted by permission of Oxford University Press, Inc.

Thom Gunn: excerpt from "To Yvor Winters, 1955" from *Selected Poems 1950–1975* by Thom Gunn. Copyright 1957, 1958, 1961, 1967, 1971, 1973, 1974, 1975, 1976, 1979 by Thom Gunn. Reprinted by permission of Farrar, Straus and Giroux, Inc. Also by permission of Faber and Faber Limited for the same excerpt.

Ivor Gurney: Penny Ely, Trustee of Ivor Gurney Estate, Sidgwick & Jackson Limited (publishers of 1917 edition), and Carcanet Press Limited (publishers of Kelsey Thornton edition [1988]) for excerpts from *Severn & Somme*; copyright Robin Haines, Sole Trustee of the Gurney Estate 1982. Other poems reprinted from *Collected Poems of Ivor Gurney* edited by P. J. Kavanagh (1982) by permission of Oxford University Press.

Thomas Hardy: reprinted with permission of Macmillan Publishing Company from *The Complete Poems of Thomas Hardy*, edited by James Gibson. Copyright 1925 by Macmillan Publishing Company, renewed 1953

Acknowledgments

by Lloyds Bank Ltd. Copyright 1928 by Florence E. Hardy and Sydney E. Cockerell, renewed 1956 by Lloyds Bank Ltd. Also Macmillan London Limited for same excerpts.

PHILIP LARKIN: reprinted by permission of Faber and Faber Ltd. from (a) *The North Ship* (b) *The Whitsun Weddings* by Philip Larkin; also Faber and Faber Ltd. for excerpt from "Aubade" from *Collected Poems of Philip Larkin* (1988); excerpts from "To the Sea," "High Windows," "Sympathy in White Major," "Annus Mirabilis," "Vers de Société" and "Show Saturday" from *High Windows* by Philip Larkin. Copyright 1974 by Philip Larkin. Reprinted by permission of Farrar, Straus and Giroux, Inc. The quotations from "Coming," "Born Yesterday," "Next Please," "At Grass," and "Church Going" by Philip Larkin are reprinted from *The Less Deceived* by permission of the Marvell Press, England.

D. H. LAWRENCE: from *The Complete Poems of D. H. Lawrence*, edited by Vivian de Sola Pinto and F. Warren Roberts. Copyright 1964, 1971 by Angelo Ravagli and C. M. Weekley, Executors of the Estate of Frieda Lawrence Ravagli. All rights reserved. Reprinted by permission of Viking Penguin, a division of Penguin Books USA, Inc.

F. R. LEAVIS: Chatto & Windus and The Hogarth Press for excerpt from *New Bearings in English Poetry*.

LOUIS MACNEICE: the author and Faber and Faber Limited for excerpts from *The Collected Poems of Louis MacNeice*, second edition.

N. SCOTT MOMADAY: the author for an excerpt from *The Gourd Dancer* (1976).

T. STURGE MOORE: H. H. R. Sturge Moore for an excerpt from "A Sicilian Idyll" in *The Poems of T. Sturge Moore*.

WILFRED OWEN: the Estate of Wilfred Owen, Jon Stallworthy (editor), and The Hogarth Press for excerpts from *Wilfred Owen: The Complete Poems and Fragments* (1983). (Note: although some of the Owen material is in the public domain, much remains in copyright and no further reproduction of his work should take place without the prior consent of The Hogarth Press.)

BRIAN PATTEN: excerpt from "Party Piece" from *Little Johnny's Confession* by Brian Patten. Copyright 1967 by Brian Patten. Reprinted by permission of Hill and Wang, a division of Farrar, Straus and Giroux, Inc.;

also to Brian Patten and Unwin Hyman Ltd. for same excerpt from *Love Poems* (1981).

EZRA POUND: reprinted by permission of Faber and Faber Ltd. from *Collected Shorter Poems* by Ezra Pound. And from *Personae* by Ezra Pound, copyright 1926 by Ezra Pound. Reprinted by permission of New Direction Publ. Corp. and Faber and Faber Ltd.

EDGELL RICKWORD: Carcanet Press Limited for excerpts from *Behind the Eyes: Selected Poems and Translations* (1976); Sidgwick & Jackson, Limited, for excerpts from *Behind the Eyes* (1921).

ISAAC ROSENBERG: the Estate of Isaac Rosenberg and Chatto & Windus and The Hogarth Press for excerpts from *The Collected Works of Isaac Rosenberg*, edited by Ian Parsons (1979).

CHARLES SORLEY: Cambridge University Press for excerpts from *Marlborough and Other Poems* (4th ed., 1919).

WALLACE STEVENS: Faber and Faber and Alfred A. Knopf Inc. for excerpts from *The Collected Poems of Wallace Stevens*, copyright 1923 and renewed 1951 by Wallace Stevens.

WILLIAM BUTLER YEATS: A. P. Watt Limited on behalf of Michael B. Yeats and Macmillan London Limited for excerpts from *The Variorum Edition of the Poems of W. B. Yeats*, edited by Peter Allt and Russell K. Alspach; also reprinted with permission of Macmillan Publishing Company from *The Variorum Edition of the Poems of W. B. Yeats*, edited by Peter Allt and Russell K. Alspach. Copyright 1919, 1924, 1933 by Macmillan Publishing Company, renewed 1947, 1952, 1961 by Bertha Georgie Yeats. Copyright 1940 by Georgie Yeats, renewed 1968 by Bertha Georgie Yeats, Michael Butler Yeats, and Anne Yeats.

Portions of this book appeared in slightly different form as articles in various literary journals. I thank them all for permission to reprint. The Introduction first appeared in a slightly longer version as "Sorting Out Modern Poetry: A Prolegomenon," in *Sequoia* 28 (Winter 1983): 13–28; the first chapter appeared as "Yeats or Hardy?" in *The Southern Review* 19 N.S. (Summer 1983): 519–547; a section of chapter 2 appeared as "The Significance of Edward Thomas" in *Sequoia* 29 (Spring 1985): 22–35; a section of chapter 3 appeared as "An Assessment of Wilfred Owen" in *English Literature in Transition 1880–1920* 28 (1985): 41–55; another section of chapter 3 appeared as "The War Poetry of Edmund Blunden and

Acknowledgments

Ivor Gurney" in *PN Review 45* 12 (1985): 46-51; and portions of chapter 4 appeared as "Robert Bridges and Modern Love" in *The Dalhousie Review* 67 (Spring 1987): 22-39; as "The Love Poetry of Robert Graves" in *University of Toronto Quarterly* 57 (Spring 1988): 422-38; and as "The Early Love Poetry of D. H. Lawrence" in *English Studies in Canada* 14 (September 1988): 326-42 [© 1988 by the Association of Canadian University Teachers of English. Reprinted from *English Studies in Canada*, vol. 14, no. 3, September 1988, pp. 326-42, by permission of the Association].

Introduction: Sorting Out Modern Poetry

> ... the constant in all Modernism is defiance of authority. Authority can be generational or governmental, or can represent, more ambiguously, the "state" or "society," or simply, "an other." Much of the straining against authority that we find in Modernism is its effort to escape from historical imperatives.
> —Frederick R. Karl, *Modern and Modernism* (1985)

Sorting out is the general aim of this book. The motive is disappointment with the twentieth-century canon as it has gradually been defined in and for the popular and academic mind. Such a critical activity is dangerous, involving as it necessarily does both a challenge to the by now well-established reputations of poets and poems and the charting of a course between the extremes of neutral exegesis on the one hand and extraliterary polemics on the other.[1] There are poles, but they need not be so far apart: I cannot deny the value of an at least initial disinterestedness on the one hand and the inevitability of the personal act of judgment on the other. So I proceed fully aware of the difficulties but believing that there is a way of reasserting in this century the moral value of poetry while fully respecting the expressive dynamics of poetry as a distinct art form. This way will involve an initial regard for the active (and not just receptive), critical intelligence of the poet and the reader, an acknowledgment of the power of reason as something other than a calculative instrument, a proper realization of and indebtedness to our past and our strongest traditions, and finally and crucially an ethical scrutiny of the relationships of the formal and structural elements of poems to their conceptual contents. That is, it will involve a view that not all authority must be defied, that an escape from some historical imperatives diminishes rather than revitalizes poetry.

A sorting out of modern poetry on these principles must begin with a questioning of certain assumptions that have undermined the enterprise in the past, assumptions that came to be for too many the unquestioned givens of enlightened literary taste. The assumptions are of course those of modernism. Before I can turn to the promotion of a different line of poets with different assumptions, I must discuss the inadequacies of those more prevalent assumptions.[2] This introduction is devoted to that task.

The first and broadest assumption is that poetry has little to do with, if it is not actively opposed to, the intellect, that it need not be quite intelligible conceptually. This notion lurks behind Pound's slogan, "Go in fear of abstractions" and Williams's line, "No ideas but in things." What gives it particular authority in the early decades of this century is that it was repeated *as an assumption* by the two most intellectual of the early modernists, Pound and Eliot. Despite his admirable concern for economy in poetry, as part of his necessary opposition to late Victorian slush, Pound characteristically overstated the solution by too narrowly characterizing the conventional use of abstract language in verse. In 1913, defending presentation over comment, he claimed that the new poetry "is not a criticism of life. I mean it does not deal in opinion. It washes its hands of theories. It does not attempt to justify anybody's ways to anybody or anything else."[3] Notice how Arnold's phrase is deflated to mere opinion and speculation and then is guiltily associated with Milton's epically religious concern. Pound, of course, has nineteenth-century authorities for his views: behind him is Arthur Symons, who said that "Art, formal art, was the only escape from the burden of reality," and behind Symons was Walter Pater, who defied the militant moralism of the High Victorians by declaring that "Art ... is ... always striving to be independent of the mere intelligence, to get rid of its responsibilities to its subject or material." In perhaps the most complete defense of his imagist theories, the 1914 essay, "Vorticism," Pound suggests that there is indeed "thought" in the new poetry, but it is not to be confused with "argument and gibe and opinion" (his way of characterizing structured verbal thinking), but is rather a "sort of knowing," understood, of course, by the Japanese: "The image is the word beyond formulated language."[4] This can only mean that imagistic, or perceptual, thought is superior to (rather than, as most understand it, previous to) verbal or conceptual thought. He seems first to accept the romantic assertions that poetry is essentially symbolic or metaphorical and then, to economize poetic language and to reform the conventional use of images as ornaments, he simply deletes from the poem that which was ornamented, leaving the bare image, without a conceptual context, resonating and suggestive in a conceptual void. The imagist poem is then "the record of a significant glimpse,"[5] or, if it contains juxtaposed images, it becomes an equation, which he believes somehow generates a precise and particular mood or emotional state ("The image is not an idea. It is a radiant node or cluster"). So the desired exclusion of conceptual thinking from poetry that we see in the romantics' emphasis on general perception and explicit (if often imprecise) emotion is intensified in Pound's theory, with the emphasis shifting: the emotion becoming implicit and the perception precise. Concreteness, once possible in conceptual thought, comes in the twentieth century to be considered possible, theoretically at least, only in the perceptual element in poetry.

Eliot follows Pound by denigrating the importance of discursive language in poetry, as when he says of the "meaning" of Pound's *Cantos*, that it "never worries me, and I do not believe that I care. I know that Pound has a scheme and a kind of philosophy behind it; it is quite enough for me that he thinks he knows what he is doing; I am glad that the philosophy is there, but I am not interested in it."[6] Eliot qualifies this by admitting that he does not mean that poets should say nothing, for "ways of saying nothing are not interesting,"[7] but his isolation of technique from the thought in a poem does limit his criticism and his poetry. I agree with Hugh Kenner when he concludes that "Eliot deals in effects, not ideas." But although I think it is a deficiency in Eliot, Kenner appeals to what he takes to be a psychological truth, that Eliot's poems do not leave the mind, because "the mind, which grows bored with ideas ... will never leave off fondling phrases," phrases that (as he says elsewhere) resist elucidation.[8]

In his doctrine of the objective correlative, Eliot echoes Pound's emphasis on the emotional expressiveness of the image in the absence of a discursive context. Although in his later life Eliot may have become as hardily sick of the phrase as the rest of us are, the doctrine has been very influential if only to help create a climate in which later poets were encouraged to limit reference unnecessarily. In 1930, Eliot defended this "abbreviation of method" and criticized implicitly the reader's expectation of conceptual coherency: "The reader has to allow the images to fall into his memory successively without questioning the reasonableness of each at the moment; so that at the end, a total effect is produced." Eliot has enough respect for tradition, however exclusive his notion of it may be, not to want to seem to be promoting chaos, so he posits a distinction between "a logic of the imagination" and "a logic of concepts."[9] He is not concerned about explaining the distinction; those who do not understand it, he says, are incapable of appreciating poetry. I do not think it can be explained: logic is logic, and there is no reason why the imagination cannot deal with concepts. Besides, as Graham Hough says of Eliot's passage, "the device of dismissing one's opponents as unqualified instead of convincing them that they are wrong is one that works only with the very unsophisticated or the very easily scared. It has been greatly overworked by the founding fathers of modern poetics."[10] I think by "a logic of imagination" Eliot is referring to associationism, the irrational, purely emotional, or automatic setting down of the details of a poem.[11]

Before proceeding with this discussion of the theories, let us consider a few examples, all short poems written in this century and all almost totally imagistic. The first is Robert Graves's "Love Without Hope":

> Love without hope, as when the young bird-catcher
> Swept off his tall hat to the Squire's own daughter,
> So let the imprisoned larks escape and fly
> Singing about her head, as she rode by.[12]

The poem is, I suppose, just the conventional kind of metaphor to which Pound was objecting: the tenor is an abstraction, the vehicle a description, in this case of brief narrative action. Pound would have the poet either drop the first five words, leaving the reader to discern the conceptual significance or representativeness of the description; or juxtapose that perception with another, associated perception, thereby hoping to give additional fullness to the original particular. The most famous example of this is Pound's own "In a Station of the Metro":

> The apparition of these faces in the crowd;
> Petals on a wet, black bough.[13]

The first line is a vague reference to a perceptual experience; the second is a separate but much sharper perception; the comparing of the two over the semicolon suggests the poet's immediate emotional response to the first perception, the "apparition." The poem gives us neither a vivid description nor an understanding of what motivated that response; instead we have the unnecessarily impersonal statement of an emotional impression. I am not sure the emotion is defined very clearly. The theory insists that it must be: "the natural object is always the *adequate* symbol."[14] Behind this insistence, which no doubt comes from a demystified application of the French symbolist theory of correspondences, we may detect an extreme version of the pathetic fallacy—a belief that our responses to the human world can be understood in terms of our responses to the nonhuman world. In his comment on the poem, Pound said his purpose was to express the loveliness of a sudden emotion upon seeing many beautiful faces on a platform of an underground station in Paris. But, although petals are certainly and usually beautiful, against the gleaming darkness of the bough (which just may be dead) their fragility as well as delicacy may be emphasized. Are we therefore to assume the faces are sallow, just as apparitions, suggesting ghosts, are transparent? Although I cannot be sure, I have always thought the petals were fallen or scattered from a dying flower, just as the individual faces are separated by the black background of the station. This adds another ominous note to Pound's impression of beauty. How far can we go with the other suggestions in the poem: the implied oppositions of life and death, man and machine, nature and machine, the individual and the group, and the allusion (pointed out by many eager scholars who have looked ahead to Pound's first *Canto*) to Odysseus viewing the crowd of shades in Hades, also underground? Pound has both too much and too little in the poem—too much suggested, too little actually defined. This is not economical writing; it is incomplete writing. Economy is only a virtue when it safeguards precision.

Graves, on the other hand, is not fearful of abstractions, but he will allow

Introduction 17

imagery to serve them. Although Pound is concerned with impersonally recreating a private discovery, that is, "with uniqueness, with perceiving in a specialized and subjective way,"[15] Graves, in this poem at least, is concerned with defining an understanding in the *way* things are understood by relating the specific to the general. And, because he does respect the conceptual nature of language, he carefully offers fully realized perception and a definite emotion or complex of emotions, while still achieving an epigrammatic terseness that is true economy. Note, for instance, how the change from irregular meter in the first couplet to regular meter in the second parallels the move from frustration to celebration, as the grand gesture releases the boy's livelihood as well as his emotions, with his practical loss becoming a romantic compliment. Meanwhile, Graves controls the irregularity by paralleling the rhythm and partially even the syntax in the first two lines, thereby associating the hope with the tallness of the hat, which the boy's social and emotional plight causes him to misuse. Although Pound gives us suggestions and allusions instead of definitions, Graves offers us suggestions integrated into the concrete realization of a definition. Despite the heralded novelty of his methods, Pound only expresses some clichéd sentiments; Graves traditionally expresses an original wit and effectively gentle irony.

It would be unfair to criticize Pound for not doing what he did not intend to do. His purpose, in theory and practice, is accurate evocation, not analysis. My point is that his intention is too limited (if realized it can only generate very minor poems); furthermore, without the analysis the evocation remains inaccurate. He may, of course, mean accurately to evoke mysteriously unembraceable meanings, sensations and emotions "beyond language." I cannot deny the existence of such things, but I can wonder if they are as numerous as some poets suggest and if the mystery just might disappear if they thought about their sensations and emotions long enough before giving in to the urge to poeticize them. It is in some poets' interest to assume as much mystery as possible: it saves them from doing what the rest of us have to do, and it confers a special, glamorously alien status on them.

Consider two more examples. First the poem Pound held up as the ideal imagist poem, "Oread" by Hilda Doolittle:

> Whirl up, sea—
> Whirl your pointed pines,
> Splash your great pines
> On our rocks,
> Hurl your green over us,
> Cover us with your pools of fir.[16]

The poem is a plea by the spirit of a mountain to be submerged by a wind-lashed sea, which is compared to an evergreen wood that may already cover the mountain. The comparison is apt enough: the colors are not dissimilar and both trees and a whirled-up sea are pointed. But what is being evoked by the analogy? It seems to be only a desire for unity of natural elements (mountain, sea, and wood, with the wind suggesting the inspiring, plastic imagination) and for submersion in them. What human meaning can this have? The oread who speaks is a fictional projection of a need to feel that man and nature are spiritually one. The poem evokes a melodramatic pantheism. It honestly may present a subjective sensation, but it is uninteresting and naive.

In discussing imagistic poetry, Pound said that "the gulf between evocation and description . . . is the unbridgeable difference between genius and talent."[17] A poem whose perceptual accuracy and intensity probably owe much to Pound's emphasis, if not to his actual theory, is "Buteo Regalis," by the American Indian poet, N. Scott Momaday. I believe it bridges that gulf between evocation and description.

> His frailty discrete, the rodent turns, looks.
> What sense first warns? The winging is unheard,
> Unseen but as distant motion made whole,
> Singular, slow, unbroken in its glide.
> It veers, and veering, tilts broad-surfaced wings.
> Aligned, the span bends to begin the dive
> And falls, alternately white and russet,
> Angle and curve, gathering momentum.[18]

Although the abstract language is minimal here, what there is very effectively places the extremely accurate description in an intellectual context that in turn gives the perceptual language conceptual force. That is, the poem evokes a state of mind and eye capable of *this kind* of respectful acuity. The observation has status as an example, not just as an isolated experience. Unlike the solipsistic indulgences of the earlier imagistic poems, this poem is clearly by a poet who fully respects his subject, a subject that in a very significant way cannot be himself. The key word in the poem is "discrete." Just as the frailty is separated from the rodent, so the rodent is abstracted from whatever individual specimen may actually be observed, as it senses, in a legitimately mysterious way, the unheard and unseen predator. The title prepares us for this perception of the wilderness: we have no familiar English name for this particular hawk, only the austere and dispassionate Latin category. The controlled mixture of syllabic (lines 1, 3, 7, 8) and accentual-syllabic (lines 2, 4, 5, 6) meter serves that meaning by helping to separate and concretely realize the abstract motions of the rodent and the hawk: the hesitation, soaring, and confused descent. There is no sentimentality, no pathetic transformation of nature for human ends. On

Introduction

the contrary, as the last line suggests, there are physical and natural forces beyond human expropriation, and we had better understand that. Poems like the last two, which give us description and imagery almost for their own sake, can never be great poems, but they will always be insignificant if poets do not respect nature's essential separateness.

Not all modernist poets are imagists, and those who are are so only part of the time. Most poets find it difficult not to think. Eliot is an obvious example. But not far from Eliot's intellectual expressionism is Robert Frost's contention that poets, while conferring knowledge, should willfully refrain from careful thinking. This man, who most epitomizes The Poet to Americans in this century, wrote in 1949:

> Scholars and artists thrown together are often annoyed at the puzzle of where they differ. Both work from knowledge; but I suspect they differ most importantly in the way their knowledge is come by. Scholars get theirs with conscientious thoroughness along projected lines of logic; poets theirs cavalierly and as it happens in and out of books. They stick to nothing deliberately, but let what will stick to them like burrs where they walk in the fields. No acquirement is on assignment, or even self-assignment. Knowledge of the second kind is much more available in the wild free ways of wit and art.[19]

The anti-intellectualism of so much experimentalist theory in this century frees even those poets who are not fearful of thinking in their poems from having either to come to any conclusions or to come to sensible conclusions. Because knowledge comes arbitrarily and freely, it can be expressed in an equally casual way. Never have poets been so free to be intellectually irresponsible: "I am a poet, therefore what I write is poetry; being a professional poet, I am justified in being an amateur, and only an amateur, intellectual." Just as perception can be taken as a "correlative" of an emotion, so pedantry (the gratuitous display of knowledge) is mistaken for intelligence, and equivocation (usually expressed through irony) is mistaken for complexity.

Thus Pound seems learned when in the third section of "Hugh Selwyn Mauberley" he complains of the replacement of a glorious and vigorous past by the tawdry present:

> Christ follows Dionysus,
> Phallic and ambrosial
> Made way for macerations;
> Caliban casts out Ariel.
>
> (37–40)

Only easily intimidated readers will let the allusive and specialized diction prevent them from realizing the extent of underdevelopment or carelessness in the associations of Christ with Caliban and Dionysus with Ariel. Thus

Frost can seem "folksily" honest and wise in the final lines of "The Bear," in which the caged bear symbolizes rational man:

> He sits back on his fundamental butt
> With lifted snout and eyes (if any) shut
> (He almost looks religious but he's not),
> And back and forth he sways from cheek to cheek,
> At one extreme agreeing with one Greek,
> At the other agreeing with another Greek,
> Which may be thought, but only so to speak.
> A baggy figure, equally pathetic
> When sedentary and when peripatetic.
>
> (26–34)[20]

The satire is cheap because it emanates from neither a moral conviction nor a sincere misanthropy, but rather from a complacent skepticism. It is one thing to laugh at the pretentiousness and fickleness of some philosophers: it is another to reduce all intellectual endeavors to this and imply that man would be wiser and nobler if he became more like the uncaged bear of the first half of the poem.

Wallace Stevens uses the same ploy in "A High-Toned Old Christian Woman" when he opposes "the moral law" to his own favored hedonism and equates the followers of the former with the hypocritical extreme:

> Allow,
> Therefore, that in the planetary scene
> Your disaffected flagellants, well-stuffed,
> Smacking their muzzy bellies in parade,
> Proud of such novelties of the sublime,
> Such tink and tank and tunk-a-tunk-tunk,
> May, merely may, madame, whip from themselves
> A jovial hullabaloo among the spheres.
> This will make widows wince. But fictive things
> Wink as they will. Wink most when widows wince.
>
> (13–22)[21]

Stevens sounds much more iconoclastic than he really is: the dazzle hides juvenile irreverence. The part he ridicules does not stand for the whole that he wishes to challenge. This is the case with all three examples of pseudo-intellectuality; with irony and some wit they create in different ways a tone of deceptive and unearned authority. What might have begun at the turn of the century as disdain for middle-class culture and its literary conventions and developed into involved schemes to disappoint and exasperate the customary expectations of poetry readers has become an entrenched requirement that real poets have to be eccentric and obscure.

The minimizing or obscuring of reference that is sanctioned by early modernist theory, especially that defending imagism, was meant to enable poets in the new age to regain for poetry a concision lost in the long-winded and moralistic nineteenth century. They made a mistake, however, in associating accentual-syllabic meter, which is the traditional means in English of condensing poetic thought, with the discredited former century and looking for other incomplete rather than economical methods. This brings me to the other two assumptions I wish to question; one deals with poetic form and the other with poetic structure, the assumptions behind the notion that to be modern one must write free verse in some version of free association.

Behind the theory and practice of imagism, both as a specific movement, which lasted a few years in the second decade of this century, and as general ideas at the center of the characteristic poetic procedures of our time, there are two common desires: to be economical and to be immediate. The second desire became the impetus for the various experiments with *vers libre* in those revolutionary years, which in turn ironically made it more difficult for these poets to be truly economical. Eliot almost says this directly in his "Reflections on 'Vers Libre'" (1917) when he offered "the simple truth that *some* artificial limitation is necessary except in moments of the first intensity."[22] Edgar Lee Masters, therefore, requires a more rigid verse form in the *Spoon River Anthology* because his elegiac material is "reflective, not immediate; its author is a moralist, rather than an observer." What Eliot seems reluctant to say is that, all other things equal, reflection makes for more important poetry than immediate observation.

Free verse was initially part of the larger effort to liberate art from obligations toward the past and preparations for the future. The most exteme defense came from D. H. Lawrence. He called (in 1919) for a poetry of the immediate present:

> Don't give me anything fixed, set, static. . . . Give me the still white seething, the incandescent cold buring of the incarnate moment, the present, the Now. . . . We must have the seething poetry of the incarnate Now. . . . There must be haste, not rest, come-and-go, not arrival, immediacy, without beginning or end. . . . There can be no static perfection, rhythm which returns upon itself. . . . free verse depends for its rhythm upon the spontaneous utterance of the whole man. It is the soul and mind and body surging at once. Nothing is left out. They speak all together. There is some confusion, some discord. . . . Free verse toes no melodic line.[23]

Whitman, says Lawrence, is the best exponent in the past of this kind of poetry. But from these quoted lines it is also evident that the aesthetic justification comes from Walter Pater, whose famous sentence in the conclusion of *The Renaissance* ("To burn always with this hard, gemlike flame, to maintain his ecstasy, is success in life") is too close to Lawrence's "white seething . . . incandescent cold burning" not to have been a model, and behind Pater is Heraclitus's doctrine of the flux ("everything moves and nothing abides"). This fragmentary pre-Socratic philosopher is present too frequently in the poetry of this century, haunting even the ascetic Christianity of *Four Quartets*.[24]

Yvor Winters, who has written persuasively on the subject (at least as much of it as he could know in the mid-thirties), accepts that there is an advantage to free verse: because the foot is undefined, the poetic line ceases to be sharply separate from a larger rhythmic unit (a stanza or the poem itself), and the resulting frequency of run-over lines creates the effect of an unbroken rush, an emphatic continuity that is impossible to achieve any other way.[25] This is the test of any experimental device: is it able to express what could not otherwise be expressed? But it is a very specialized instrument. Just as we do not constantly live our lives with heightened intensity, so there are many other varied emotions to be communicated in verse. This might explain why the most successful free verse poems are very short.[26] The utterance may be spontaneous, but it would not be of the "whole man."

Nor can Winters agree with Lawrence's implication that traditional meter (what Lawrence calls "stereotyped movements" and "artificial conduits and canals") necessarily restricts a poet's freedom of expression—an assumption many experimentalists share with Lawrence, even if the free verse they practice differs from his. Before we proceed any further, we must clarify what is meant by free verse. Early in this century it could mean imitations of the Japanese haiku or of the experiments of nineteenth-century Frenchmen, especially Kahn and Laforgue, or a sophisticated revival of accentual measure or classical quantitative measure or the ruptured blank verse of Jacobean drama. Many poets felt that accentual-syllabic meter was too confining and monotonous (the "sequence of a metronome"), but they also believed, as Williams said, that "no verse can be free, it must be governed by some measure, but not by the old measure."[27] Subsequent poets of considerably less talent have used the term to mean the absence of all measure and, this side of Charles Olson, practically all discipline as well: what Allen Ginsberg, bringing the circle back to Walt Whitman, calls "completely free composition. ... Promethian natural measure."[28] At best we have line lengths determined by syntactical pauses, at worst by whim. At best we have highly rhythmical prose, at worst completely uncontrolled prose.

The shared assumption is mistaken because freedom is only significant and meaningful against a background of known and established order. The most intelligent experimentalists conceded the necessity of some order, but their revolutionary stance prevented them from accepting anything firmly established, either in the past or in their individual poems. But as many have argued,[29] the more firmly established the metrical norm, the more chance variations from that norm have of expressing complexities, subtleties, and nuances; the more chance that every syllable will count, will contribute to, and help control (that is, precisely define) the content of feeling in a poem.

The topic, of course, is a very complex one and one made very complicated (perhaps at times too complicated) by some prosodists. I have touched only on the most basic, but I think most essential, part of the debate. What is crucial for my larger argument here and later in this book is this possibility of a greater completeness and precision of expression in traditional meters (which need not be tainted by the bad poetry written in it in the past): "as traditional poetry tends to enrich itself with past wisdom, with an acquired sense of what is just, so the traditional meters, owing to their very subtle adjustability and suggestibility, are frequently very complex in their effects, whereas the looser meters tend to be over-emphatic and over-simple. ... a man who speaks quietly commands attention by means of a minute inflection."[30]

The varied attempts to free verse from traditional meter were part of the larger move to de-formalize the poetic voice: modern poetry had to approximate natural speech. Behind this is the assurance, which developed through the nineteenth century, that poetry is essentially dramatic. The conversational manner will naturally suit a poet who is suspicious of order; but the obvious objection is that poetry is naturally a formal statement, whereas conversation is the most careless, least formal (in this case, rhythmical), and the least premeditated of human utterance. The alternative need not be the highly artificial, inflated poeticisms found in much eighteenth- and nineteenth-century verse. A proper sorting out of modern verse must begin with a recognition that speech can be plain and direct without being colloquial and formless. (Evidence is abundant—most of the poets in this book provide much of it.)

The formless nature of immediate consciousness and conversation (along with the ever-present desire for economy) gave the poets of this century a justification for loosening their structures even further than had poets of the previous century. The result has been called "discontinuous" composition—the absence of transition from one phrase, line, image, speaker, or topic, to the next; the placing, often elliptically, of disparate units of meaning one immediately after the other. Under the aegis of modern psychological theory, those who called for and practiced it thought they were destroying the illusory principle of continuity that had been, in Hulme's words, "one of the main achievements of the nineteenth century." But they were, I think, simply combining a mystified version of the eighteenth-century doctrine of association with an impotent (that is, imitative rather than critical) response to a felt confusion and chaos in modern life. Discontinuity was said to be characteristic of modern experience, so discontinuous structures were felt to be mimetic of the character of reality in this century. Theodore Roethke, long after Hulme, offered this characteristic version of the modern poet's task with respect to structure:

> His language must be compelling and immediate: he must create an actuality. He must be able to telescope image and symbol, if necessary, without relying on the obvious connectives: to speak in a kind of psychic shorthand when his protagonist is under great stress. He must be able to shift his rhythms rapidly, the "tension." He works intuitively, and the final form of his poem must be imaginatively right. If intensity has compressed the language so it seems, on early reading, obscure, this obscurity should break open suddenly for the serious reader who can hear the language: the "meaning"' itself should come as a dramatic revelation, an excitement. The clues will be scattered richly—as life scatters them.[31]

Much of what I have been discussing so far is brought together here: the assumption that poetry expresses the immediate, dramatic, and intense, and is imitative of life's chaos. Postmodernism, of course, has sophisticated and altered these attitudes toward poetry. But during the period of English poetry I survey in this book, these were the dominant and most fashionable ideas (articulated most forcefully by—if not actually originating with—Americans, as my examples here indicate), the ideas against which the poets I promote produced their best work. They asked, as we encouraged by their example must also, do we really need to have life's chaos demonstrated to us? Should not art *order* chaos, give us understanding of experience, not just experience itself? Like understanding, after all, poetry is verbal, and immediate experience usually is not or not significantly so.

We must not, however, overlook that those new structural principles sometimes do serve economy, as in the abrupt but hardly confusing movement from the first to second stanzas of "The Love Song of J. Alfred Prufrock": "Let us go and make our visit./In the room the women come and go/Talking of Michelangelo" (12–14).[32] We could return the missing connectives ("make our visit to the room where . . ."), but the minimal gain is offset by the loss of an effective and thematically important shift in tone. In this poem we at least have the continuity of one particular consciousness. Problems arise when even that vestige of convention is removed; for instance, as we move in Eliot's poetry to the universalized persona in "Gerontion" and to the fragments of *The Waste Land*. In "Gerontion" the problem is the sudden appearance of suspended bits of dramatic action in the absence of a dramatic context (23–29), but this is not as difficult as the pretentious jumble of allusive matter in *The Waste Land*. One of the most notorious examples of this is probably the closing lines of "The Fire Sermon": "To Carthage then I came/Burning burning burning burning/O Lord Thou pluckest me out/O Lord Thou pluckest/burning" (307–11). These few words cannot do what Eliot means them to do: to evoke the presence of "eastern and western asceticism, as the culmination of this part of the poem," as he must tell us in a footnote.[33]

Conrad Aiken rightly raises the question "whether these difficulties [resulting from the compact allusions], in which perhaps Mr. Eliot takes a little pride, are so much the result of complexity, a fine elaborateness, as of confusion."[34] After all, as J. V. Cunningham said ten years after the publication of Eliot's poem, "successful formulation is clarifying, the demons disappear in the sunlight."[35] In a sense, Eliot wrote darkly to keep the demons alive. Aiken unfortunately closes his review of *The Waste Land* by repeating the fallacy that generated Eliot's method: "Its incoherence is a virtue because the *donnée* is incoherence."

Then there are critics like Cleanth Brooks who argue that although the surface of the poem is fragmentary ("the realistic surface of experience is faithfully retained"), beneath this surface is a network linking all the allusions, parodies, and ironies into a final emotional "sense of the oneness of experience, and of the unity of all periods." Eliot's deepest theme is the rehabilitation of Christian beliefs, "known but now discredited"; he therefore has to be indirect if he hopes to give new life to what have become clichés.[36] But, one may counter, if the system of beliefs has been discredited—and I am not sure it has as thoroughly as Eliot and his contemporaries seemed to think—why cannot the poet speak directly (and still poetically) to the mistakes that caused such discrediting, and argue that it should *not* be discredited. Eliot's purpose, after all, is partially moral and theological (as "What the Thunder Said" makes clear). Is there really a need for the thunder to speak Sanskrit instead of English? We have comparable fables and a more recognizable theory of the virtues. Eliot might have informed a direct confronting of reality with that shareable theory, rather than giving reality in esoterically symbolic fragments and judging that cracked reflection of reality by implicit and unsystematic reference to anthropological equations.

Countless examples of discontinuous structure could be cited; I have concentrated on Eliot because he provides some of the most famous and perhaps most important (and certainly most influential) examples. His failures are much more challenging than those by poets of less talent and daring. And it is important to remember the continual insistence on daring and novelty in those early formative decades of the century: because life is constantly and—in this century—rapidly changing, they felt art must also. As Pound advised young writers: "No good poetry is ever written in a manner twenty years old."[37] It was the Spirit of the Age. Without proper defenses, many modernists in their wholesale defiance of past authorities surrendered to the least creative authority: the demands of an isolated present.

The best poets, however, for all the reasons I have offered here, have not been slaves to the *Zeitgeist*. Because they have understood and respected the past, they have not allowed the present (or the past—or any "system" of language or conventions) to control them. For that understanding is of language not as a prison house but as the revitalizing embodiment of tradition. Our language registers the attempts of many generations to lead meaningful lives; therefore the individual use of it will be forceful and precise to the extent that it acknowledges that registering. Successful formulation *is* clarifying because that which is clarified is transferable. So, finally, the failure of the dominant poetry of most of this century has been a failure of perspective. Michael Schmidt has said, "Perspective is only achieved through form, a prime objectifying tool, or through an accurate sense of time and the effect of time upon the immediate experience, the initial response."[38] The quieter poets of this century who have worked in traditional forms, who have accepted and studied received poetic disciplines, are the true radicals, for they have had the confidence and power not to capitulate to contemporary reality; that is, to either their subject matter or their first response to their subject matter. They have come to know the world, and therefore have not rushed to embrace it. That is the nature of their restraint.

By questioning the major assumptions behind modernist poetry, I hope I have been able to indicate how a sorting out might profitably begin. We will have to stop being intimidated by reputations and the disguised impotency of the theories that created those reputations and consequently the proportions of the current canon. In the pages that follow, I will extend that questioning into more direct challenges as I offer as positive alternatives, as more than just rear guard actions, the work of a line of English poets starting with Thomas Hardy and running through to Philip Larkin,[39] who for the most part denied those assumptions and found ways of being modern without ceasing to be traditional.

The Art of Restraint

1
Yeats or Hardy?

No one who attempts to sort out twentieth-century poetry in Britain can start profitably without asking the question that gives this chapter its title. Yeats and Hardy, as poets, were contemporaries whose long careers spanned the transition from romanticism to modernism and whose work constitutes two of the most powerful dealings with that transition and those traditions. In the 1920s, Hardy was generally recognized as the greatest of England's living writers (Geoffrey Grigson could call him "the actual father of modern verse in England")[1], and younger poets as different as Ezra Pound, Edward Thomas, Siegfried Sassoon, Walter de la Mare, Robert Graves, W. H. Auden, Cecil Day Lewis, and Philip Larkin have attested to his significant influence on their work. Sir John Betjeman long after Hardy's death still can consider him "the greatest poet England has produced for a century."[2] Since the 1930s this stand has become possible only if one distinguishes England from other English-speaking countries. Dylan Thomas's response notes the shift in fashion: "Hardy was his favorite poet of the century," but he knew he ought to prefer Yeats; Yeats was in fact his chosen master.[3] Although we might forgive the *Irish Times* for being shortsighted, journalistic, and nationalistic for its conclusion on Yeats's seventieth birthday in 1935 that he was "undoubtedly ... the greatest poet writing in the English language,"[4] we cannot so easily dismiss the judgment of T. S. Eliot, who five years later said that Yeats was "the greatest poet of our time."[5] D. S. Savage could say in 1944 that "Yeats's poetry has received a greater degree of recognition than that of any modern British poet."[6] Even Donald Davie, who in some ways represents an antimodernist movement in the second half of this century, had to acknowledge in 1964 that "Yeats has already been, for good or ill, more influential than any other poet writing in English in the present century."[7] For good or ill? It is the critical necessity to answer that question that makes a comparison with Hardy continuously useful and pertinent. As Michael Alexander says in an essay surveying Hardy's reputation fifty years after his death, "while his name is held in affectionate respect, it does not raise the critical wind that has blown those of Yeats and Eliot into modern esteem."[8] Yeats's reputation shows no sign of declining, and Hardy's poetic work and that of other good poets have been incorrectly valued, minimized, or neglected because Yeats has so firmly become a standard for critics.

Considering then the course and interdependence of those reputations and influences, we are led to wider acknowledgments: that Hardy and Yeats defined the options for poets at the beginning of this century and that consequently poets have tended to divide into two distinguishable streams, variously (and unsatisfactorily) called traditional and experimental, antimodernist and modernist, discursive and visionary, plain and rhetorical. Yeats and Hardy are in modern poetry what Lawrence and Joyce, according to F. R. Leavis, are in modern fiction: "pre-eminently the testing, the crucial authors"; if you take one for a major creative writer, then you can have little *serious* use for the other.[9] This chapter is a defense of the necessity of choosing as well as a defense of a particular choice.

Previous comparisons of the two poets have been contradictory and the few helpful ones teasingly undeveloped. R. P. Blackmur in 1936 finds Yeats and Hardy committed to "disciplines," magic and ironic fatalism respectively, to neither of which "many minds can consciously appeal today."[10] Kenneth Marsden offers a version of this in 1969 but without Blackmur's misgivings: "Readers of Yeats are familiar with the fact that implausible beliefs can provide an excellent mental framework for poetry, and poems by Hardy also show this."[11] The ability of the critic to separate so casually what a poem asks us to believe from what value it has is one reason for Yeats's seemingly unassailable reputation today. One authority for such separation is, of course, Yeats himself, who simply completed the arguments begun, however inadvertently, by earlier romantic writers. Joseph Warren Beach, on the other hand, regrets that Yeats, unlike Hardy, did not "have the intellect of his time under him for support," and Philip Larkin is grateful that Hardy is "not a transcendental writer, ... not a Yeats ...; his subjects are men, the life of men, time and the passing of time, love and the fading of love."[12] But these are just hints. The most thorough consideration of the representative differences is found in Donald Davie's *Thomas Hardy and British Poetry* (1973). His thesis is that "in British poetry of the last fifty years (as not in American) the most far-reaching influence ... has been not Yeats, still less Eliot or Pound, not Lawrence, but *Hardy*."[13] To illustrate this thesis, he sets Hardy clearly against Yeats and other modernists. But except for a few undefended judgments (for instance, "In sheer *accomplishment,* especially of prosody, Hardy beats Yeats hands down"), and a very valuable distinction (only partially condoned) between Hardy's rational and judicious poetry and that by poets who claim "to have private revelations of a suprarational sort," by self-styled prophets who are above being fair-minded,[14] the contrast is too incomplete to be as persuasive as it is suggestive, and too narrow in its assessment of Hardy (however acute that often is) to be satisfying. What good was this insistence by Movement poets and their use of Hardy as "the big stick to beat the modernists with" when it leads to the patronizing confidence of these remarks in the *PN Review* (then edited by Davie):

> Attempts to construct an anti-modernist, "native" tradition in poetry with Hardy as its father-figure now look a little old hat. ... There is now no longer any need to over-stress or to hassle over his status as a major poet. One simply has to learn to balance Hardy's modernity (a voice speaking to us at the tail-end of the twentieth century) with his Victorian provincialism—those aspects of his verse which are close to us, his tragic irony, his colloquial directness, with the faded belief in scientific materialism and certain old-fashioned pieties.[15]

Although there is a greater chance in England than in North America of Hardy being granted his proper place, his reputation is not in reliable hands when the very sources of his poetic strength—his local concreteness and his rational ethic—are deflated to "Victorian provincialism" and "certain old-fashioned pieties." No one who uses such language can properly understand Hardy's value for poetic tradition in this century.

Another and more thorough attempt at a comparative assessment of Hardy and Yeats is needed. There is the always and most obviously important critical function of demanding attention for improperly respected talent. And there are the more specific and partisan functions of defending the importance of statement in poetry, defending the always vulnerable native and plain style, and defending rational and moral assessments of life wherever they appear.

1

Let us start with a specific comparison. "Neutral Tones" was written in 1867 when Hardy was about twenty-seven years old. "Ephemera" was written in 1884 when Yeats was about nineteen years old. Given Hardy's late development and Yeats's precocity, we can consider them the almost equally youthful works of two Victorian apprentice poets, dealing with the same subject—waning and lost love—in very similar dramatic situations: a man and woman by a lake in autumn or winter. The situation offers the romantic temptation to display the reciprocated sympathy of man and nature. Yeats is easily tempted.

> 'Your eyes that once were never weary of mine
> Are bowed in sorrow under pendulous lids,
> Because our love is waning.'
>
> And then she:
> 'Although our love is waning, let us stand
> By the lone border of the lake once more,
> Together in that hour of gentleness
> When the poor tired child, Passion, falls asleep.
> How far away the stars seem, and how far
> Is our first kiss, and ah, how old my heart!'

> Pensive they paced along the faded leaves,
> While slowly he whose hand held hers replied:
> 'Passion has often worn our wandering hearts.'
>
> The woods were round them, and the yellow leaves
> Fell like faint meteors in the gloom, and once
> A rabbit old and lame limped down the path;
> Autumn was over him: and now they stood
> On the lone border of the lake once more:
> Turning, he saw that she had thrust dead leaves
> Gathered in silence, dewy as her eyes,
> In bosom and hair.
>
> 'Ah, do not mourn,' he said,
> That we are tired, for other loves await us;
> Hate on and love through unrepining hours.
> Before us lies eternity; our souls
> Are love, and a continual farewell.'[16]

The poem exists for the sake of the precious and vague atmosphere of disillusionment and world-weariness and the pseudo-religious consolation in the unexpected final assertion. We hardly can expect precision from a slushy if occasionally mellifluous blank verse, in which terminal anapests soften rather than modulate (lines 1–2), and alliterations adorn rather than emphasize (lines 11, 13, 16); or from figures whose details seem to ignore visual proprieties in favor of an easy and necessarily dim connotation (the wafting and perhaps occasionally flickering movement of the falling leaves hardly resembles the steady streak of however faint meteors—Yeats probably wants the suggestion of light going out, but he gives us more). Nor can we expect it from a soft and undistinguishing diction that nonetheless insists on denoting emotional extremes ("sorrow" "weary," "passion," "mourn"), that relegates action to will-less passivities ("waning," "unrepining," "wandering"—"wandering" is indicatively one of Yeats's favorite words in his early escapist poetry), and that reaches an unearned plangency in the final, vatic stanza. Despite all this, and the distance and anonymity of the speaker, Yeats strives for a degree of immediacy: the abrupt opening and preponderance of dialogue, the otherwise unnecessary restrictive clause in line 12 (which inadvertently suggests the presence of a second man), and the awkward "once" in line 15 and "now" in line 17 disturbing the simple past tense of the narration. (Yeats, of course, was to learn how to be more efficiently dramatic.)

Contrast this with Hardy's more direct but less startling dramatics in "Neutral Tones":

> We stood by a pond that winter day,
> And the sun was white, as though chidden of God,

> And a few leaves lay on the starving sod;
>   —They had fallen from an ash, and were gray.
>
> Your eyes on me were as eyes that rove
> Over tedious riddles of years ago;
> And some words played between us to and fro
>   On which lost the more by our love.
>
> The smile on your mouth was the deadest thing
> Alive enough to have strength to die;
> And a grin of bitterness swept thereby
>   Like an ominous bird a-wing....
>
> Since then, keen lessons that love deceives,
> And wrings with wrong, have shaped to me
> Your face, and the God-curst sun, and a tree,
>   And a pond edged with grayish leaves.[17]

Yeats gives us a dialogue, but Hardy only notes that there was one ("some words played between us"), perhaps finding the words misleading ("played") beside the more revealing motions of the woman's eyes and mouth. Compare these eyes, as if moving "over tedious riddles," with those Yeats describes: "bowed in sorrow under pendulous lids." Hardy suggests a complex motive; Yeats pays homage to a Pre-Raphaelite cliché. Yeats's speaker simply records a conversation and, blending with the sentiments of the weary lovers (note especially how he picks up the woman's phrasing in line 18), blends those sentiments with the landscape. Lest we miss the point of the old rabbit with "Autumn ... over him," Yeats overtly equates the woman's eyes with the "dewy" leaves; and lest we miss that, he has her adorning herself with the leaves. The fallacy is all the more pathetic beside Hardy's deft defusing of the device: he will not deny that nature can symbolically reflect human moods, but his point is ironic because nature is essentially neutral, unsympathetic to human activity, subject in its intractable cycles to deprivation—the sod is "starving" and an anthropomorphic god cannot but curse it.

Although he gives us a much more vividly realized setting and characters, especially the woman, Hardy's drama is still: the significant *action* is the learning of the lesson off (and beyond) this particular stage. The poem is about an association of a particular event with a particular landscape and how that fares within a mental movement from particular to concrete generalization ("keen lessons") back to the inspiring particular, and how that movement, that control, cannot find validation outside of the human world (where "wrongs" can be marked). That control is how we resist the descent, through bitterness, which announces a deadness of the soul, to the prehuman survival instincts of "an ominous bird a-wing." Hardy's form expresses the distance and the control; his frequent anapests neutralize the lyrical tendency of the tetrameter quatrains, emphasizing and stilling the vision. The symmetry of the stanzas and the whole poem, framed by the "shaped" scene, embodies the control necessary for facing the impossibility of humanizing nature, the impossibility expressed in the final description by the neutral connectives: "Your face, *and* the God-curst sun, *and* a tree, / *And* a pond edged with grayish leaves."

Hardy cannot be tempted into a Yeatsian presumption or amorality. Hardy's lover learns a difficult lesson; Yeats's lover simply and inexplicably has faith in reincarnation, a faith that seemingly excuses us from ethical moderations:

> 'Hate on and love through unrepining hours.
> Before us lies eternity; our souls
> Are love, and a continual farewell.'

Even if we overlook the stylistic infelicities of Yeats's early poem (so as not to invite the charge that we are being unfair in comparing a good early poem by Hardy with a bad early poem by Yeats), there is still a procedure in "Ephemera" that is to be found in some of his most mature work; it is a melodramatic extremism topped by visionary assertions. Unlike Hardy, who draws conclusions, sometimes quite tentatively, from patient and acute observation and induction, Yeats, when not content simply with dramatically clashing contraries, gives the illusion of resolution by invoking a mystical insight. Where we must wait for guidance from revelation, energetic emotions are the only alternatives to inevitable repining: "Passion has often worn our wandering hearts."

There is this hint of determinism in both poems, but with a very important difference. Yeats implies a human weakness despite a heavy-handed insistence on nature's sympathetic identification with man; Hardy implies a human strength in the face of a nature devoid of grace and indifferent to man's social arrangements and adjustments, arrangements and adjustments all the more necessary because of that indifference. Yeats proceeds narratively and dramatically to a didactic *non sequitur* that exposes a bogus spiritualism; Hardy's poem has the structure of a mind capable of coming to a disturbing conclusion and a style capable of keeping it unobtrusive, unpretentious, and as perceptually and emotionally verifiable as possible. Hardy's poem is not perfect: the syntactical clumsiness of line 8, the rhythmic padding of the last three syllables of line 7, and the slight oddness of "chidden" in line 2 cannot be explained away as youthful indulgences; he was never to be completely free of such mannerisms. But they are minor; his thought is usually weighty and sound, while Yeats's coming eloquence cannot correct his too frequent failures of thought.

2

The question of determinism is central to any discussion of Hardy and Yeats. We might begin, however, with an instance of critical determinism. It is difficult this late in the twentieth century to deny any longer that modernism is the product of and a version of Romanticism. The argument has been made with increasing persuasiveness by, among others, Herbert Read, John Bayley, and Frank Kermode. The issue for Robert Langbaum is so settled that he wonders, in *The Poetry of Experience* (1957), "whether in the post-Enlightenment world, in a scientific and democratic age, literature, whatever its programme, can be anything but romantic...." He defines modern Romanticism as "an attempt to salvage on science's own empiric grounds the validity of the individual perception against scientific abstractions," an attempt "after the collapse of the traditional authority for values, to find and justify new values."[18] His own prose is an instance of the survival and indeed triumph of Romanticism. Why must individual perception be opposed to scientific abstractions? Besides, is there not a middle ground of individual abstractions? Just what is the "traditional authority" that has collapsed? Does it include, for instance, the moral rationalism of Aristotle and Aquinas? Can we so easily say that it has collapsed? And even if it has, does it really follow that new values are necessary and not simply newly defined authorities? The real point is that too many modern thinkers do not know how to believe in any authority, which means that they have no defenses against false authority. By discrediting reason, romanticism paved the way for our technological culture in which reason is reduced to an analytical instrument, to scientific, as distinguished from philosophic, reason. Romanticism has bred an amoral pragmatism. As George Grant has succinctly argued, "the only living morality of our society is faith in technique," and "a philosophy [pragmatism] which exalts action and life over thought cannot condemn any action as categorically wrong."[19] Attempts to oppose the authority of science or technology without returning to reason (or contemplation) can only rely on revelation. Witness the pseudo-mysticism of the new religiosity, often based on therapeutic programs, techniques authorized by psychology or by Western misapplications of Eastern beliefs. Witness W. B. Yeats, who looks helpless beside Thomas Hardy, who has shown twentieth-century poets how one can be something other than romantic in the post-Enlightenment world.

Langbaum is not an isolated case. Critics who cannot share or condone Yeats's eccentric beliefs are still able to defend him by arguing, from deterministic assumptions, either that he was an inevitable victim of some omnipotent Spirit of the Age or that a poem's value has nothing to do with its informing ideas, or both. An example of each is found in an essay by Auden from the mid-forties. On one page he says of Yeats, Joyce, and

Shaw, "we must see their reactions . . . in terms of a polemical situation in which they accepted—they probably could do nothing else—the antithesis between reason and imagination which the natural sciences of their times forced upon them." On the next page he says, "the aesthetic value of the poem is the same whether the poet and/or reader actively believe what it says or not."[20] The New Critics, who did much to inflate Yeats's reputation in the 1930s and 1940s, are largely responsible for the currency of that notion in this century. Many of them valued Yeats simply because he made the effort to create a system, a private mythology that was then imposed upon life to counter the disintegration of the traditional system. At the center of modernist poetics is what Sanford Schwartz calls a "dialectic of form and flux": "art may be associated with the recovery of immediate experience, the invention of new abstractions [forms or systems or myths], or with the interaction between the two."[21] What modernists could rarely sanction was a recovery of anything less objective on the one hand or less subjective on the other, a more central realm in which inadequate public forms (like those of the recent past) could be challenged and corrected without abandoning the possibility at least of public verifiability and communal cohesion. Because those New Critical defenders of Yeats were themselves products of modernism, any new system will do: poems, it seems, must be unified but do not have to be true or even try to be true. The fallacy of this and subsequent anti-propositional theories has been exposed fully by Gerald Graff in *Poetic Statement and Critical Dogma* (1970) and *Literature Against Itself* (1979), so there is no need rehearsing the arguments here. What is needed is a reassessment of Yeats with a full awareness that poets, like all users of language, have something to assert and that there is no good reason why choosing between beliefs, accepting or rejecting the beliefs of others, should be thought inappropriate when it appears in the criticism of poetry. We should not allow Yeats's dramatic mode to deter us from the responsibility he seems to have ignored. Richard Ellmann has been deterred as he sums up Yeats's attitude toward the question of belief in poetry:

> The only way in which poetry can be philosophical, Yeats brilliantly declared, is by portraying "the emotions of a soul dwelling in the presence of certain ideas." Without ideas at all the poet is shallow, timid, and sentimental; with ideas gripped tightly as beliefs the poet is gullible, opinionative, and biased; but with ideas as perches, or habitual surroundings, or, like the elements, symbolic counters, he is made free.[22]

Free of what? Free of restrictions to believe whatever he wants to believe, free to follow his wandering emotions. In the critical climate of this century (which has only intensified since Yeats), in which ascribing any cohesive or even intentional message to poetry is considered to be highly suspicious, it is no wonder poets, in a medium that resists not saying something, feel they can say anything, the validity of which is simply a question that rarely arises, and when it does, it is by readers who can be dismissed as dogmatic or righteous philistines or even purveyors of "old fashioned pieties." I, however, proceed on the assumption that what a poet believes affects the *way* he writes; that just as belief can affect the way we see certain things, so poetic form and content are mutually reinforcing.

3

Like his favorite romantic poet, Blake, Yeats believed that "the whole is a single organism, pursuing a single and undeviating course which has been predestined,"[23] but Yeats's determinism, much further removed from Blake's sources, was particularly rigid and couched in "pseudo-geometrical terms" to impress those of a scientific mind (whose view of the world he was opposing).[24] But if his "Vision" made the life of humanity contingent on the movement of the stars, like most people who profess a deterministic doctrine, Yeats was either wavering in his application of it or unwilling to understand its full implications. That should not, however, prevent us from recognizing the fundamental cast of his mind, which altered little throughout his long career.

Although much has been written to explain his unique system and its grab-bag mixture of astrology, magic, Jungian psychology, and historicism, to explicate his poems (and while the beliefs themselves have been rightly dismissed as "ridiculous," illogical, "something of a hoax," of no use to any other person, "Pythagorean abracadabra," embarrassing, and, as the sympathetic Harold Bloom says, "a failure in vision" that is "sometimes very unwise"[25]), few have discussed the background and foreground to this specific system, the romantic anti-rationalism that led to the amoral vitalism and stylistic imprecisions of Yeats's verse. This discussion is my answer to those who see the system, even if invalid, as somehow triumphantly giving pattern and coherence to the expression of his thought, or as an instrument only "imaginatively true" (whatever that means) for the reintegration of his personality, or as simply "the dramatic recognition of necessity"; in sum, as the provider (in the words of the voices that gave him the system) of "metaphors for poetry," metaphors whose vehicles are private schematic fantasies.[26]

We must start with what he inherited eagerly from his more extreme romantic forebears—an unquestioning disrespect for reason, the theoretic abandonment of the critical point of view. The litany would be frightening even if it came from a minor poet:

> ... reasoning from sensation, which is always seeking to reduce everything to a lifeless and slavish uniformity.
>
> ... the Reason not only created Ugliness, but all other evils.
>
> ... reason can only discover completely the use of those obvious actions which everybody admires.
>
> ... my work [is] ... the revolt of the soul against the intellect.
>
> ... a logician is a fool when life, which is a thing of emotion, is in question.
>
> [poetic thinking is] a reverie about the adventures of the soul, or of the personality.[27]

Not only is reason only seen as a utilitarian instrument, but the only alternative to that for the artist is reverie. It is that old romantic mistake of throwing out reason because it can by some be misused and replacing it with reverie because that which is out of our control cannot be misused.

Even more unfortunate is the overt presence of these sentiments in Yeats's poetry. In "September 1913" he gets dramatic and political mileage out of the facile opposition of those who have "come to sense"—the mercantile bourgeoisie "born to pray and save"—with Ireland's long-gone romantic heroes, "all that delirium of the brave." Yeats's vocabulary is in danger of tipping the poem to the other side of his intended argument (only the unsubtle irony, the title, and our knowledge of the Art Gallery controversy keep the intention before us). In addition, the failure to commit himself to a conclusion, to condone a reassessment of the past ("let them be"), is as much an indication of his disbelief in positive kind of "sense" as an instance of dramatic playfulness or political equivocation (what Ellmann calls "his being above politics").[28] If one does not have to be sensible, one can more easily "Be secret and exult," as Yeats advises Lady Gregory in "To a Friend Whose Work Has Come to Nothing," also written in 1913, and where again honor and heroism are compared to madness and are recommended. And can we doubt that Yeats approves of Tom O'Roughley, who finds intuition, and intuition only, as the way to wisdom:

> 'Though logic-choppers rule the town,
> And every man and maid and boy
> Has marked a distant object down,
> An aimless joy is a pure joy,'
> Or so did Tom O'Roughley say
> That saw the surges running by,
> 'And wisdom is a butterfly
> And not a gloomy bird of prey.'

(1–8)

But Yeats is not concerned with convincing us ("I took no trouble to convince,/Or seem plausible to a man of sense" ["The Apparitions," 3-4]); in the next stanza he has O'Roughley say that it does not matter anyway—the logic-choppers need not mend their ways (it apparently does not matter who rules the town), because we will all be reincarnated into another chance to be joyful: "What's dying but a second wind?" Yeats hides behind the irrational movement of thought here just as much as behind the persona of this mad Irish songster. But Yeats takes the ideas seriously, outside the poem. John Unterecker quotes Yeats explaining the image at the end of the first stanza: "I have a ring with a hawk and a butterfly upon it, to symbolize the straight road of logic, and so of mechanism, and the crooked road of intuition."[29] For Yeats, logic is a carnivorous mechanism; but surely an abandonment to instinct renders one a slave to stimuli, a human automaton, the saddest of mechanisms.

There is no mask and no distracting whimsy in "The Dawn," written two years before "Tom O'Roughley." There he cries out to be "ignorant as the dawn" "for no knowledge is worth a straw" (1, 13). In one late poem, "Meru," Yeats goes so far as to claim that all Western thought has been on the wrong track, or in Unterecker's uncritical paraphrase, "all man's relentless pursuit both of things and of wisdom [is] finally meaningless."[30]

Although he had little respect for the cumulative efforts of the great thinkers of our past, Yeats still had to believe that there was transferable knowledge, or more correctly, insights; if not, what was a prophet to talk about. So he theorizes a "Single Mind" and a "Great Memory." The truth then is available to those who, in effect, turn off their individual minds to be fed insights, visions, and especially symbols, which can in turn be used by the poet to "evoke" this higher reality. The poet succeeds the magician; it is his job to submit himself to his imagination, which "is always seeking to remake the world according to the impulses and the patterns in that Great Mind, and that Great Memory."[31] With this notion of the poet as serving an extra-conscious unity (during mundane intervals Yeats was content playing the courtier to Ireland's vanishing aristocracy), we have the bald consequence of poetry's fascination with associationism in the late eighteenth century.[32] Yeats was one of the "last romantics" in the sense that he was one of the last poets who needed a reason for giving up control. The procedure continues, but the faith justifying it could not continue after reaching such an esoteric dead end. Post-Yeatsian romanticism, therefore, is so often defenseless mannerism; it replaces faith with irony to continue the indulgence in the extremes of the apocalyptic and the confessional. As he grew older and knew doubt, Yeats himself plays with this option.

In the introduction to his very odd *Oxford Book of Modern Verse* (1936), Yeats declares that "The mischief began at the end of the seventeenth century when man became passive before a mechanised nature."[33] But his own alternative (the romantic alternative, as he makes clear in this essay) is a passivity before a hypothetical Great Mind. Granted there are techniques, magical ceremonies, to prepare the mind for the supernatural visitation, but they involve a lessening rather than a tightening of restraints, of mental alertness, and consequently a retreat from that which so insistently demands attention—what Yeats in his early idealistic phase variously and dismissively called "life" ("the labour of life," "the trivial game of life"), "externality," "nature," or as far as art was specifically concerned, "subject pictures."[34]

But even when life, or rather the patterns that could be made of lives in history, does later unavoidably concern him, he is still often anticipating revelation and seldom contemplating life's particulars. In "The Second Coming" (1920), between the vatic generalizations of the first stanza, with its loose and ambiguous metaphoric language expressing only a vague (but powerful) anticipation, and the description of the vision in the last ten lines, comes this excuse for not investigating and trying to understand one's own feelings:

> Surely some revelation is at hand;
> Surely the Second Coming is at hand.
> The Second Coming! Hardly are those words out
> When a vast image out of *Spiritus Mundi*
> Troubles my sight. . . .
>
> (9–13)

The motive has not been realized sufficiently to justify the insistent "Surely." And after that intense feeling, a single (and, as Bloom convincingly argues, inappropriate) phrase, "The Second Coming," triggers a visitation. The claim begins in insufficiently motivated emotion and ends with prophetic and confusing religious symbolism.[35] The language throughout is hyperbolic and powerful (Yeats is a very skilled rhetorician), but it so indirectly serves an individual understanding that it cannot hope to achieve a public one.

Just as Yeats's aesthetic encourages this structural presumption, it fails to make adequate safeguards against confusion. "I have no speech but symbol, the pagan speech I made/Amid the dreams of youth," he says parenthetically in a poem of 1917. "I seek an image, not a book," he says in another poem of the same year. The new Druidism, the belief that "the natural and supernatural are knit together," which Yeats sets against "the mechanical theory,"[36] necessitates a heavily symbolic language. Poets, unlike magicians, says Yeats, use symbols "half-unconsciously"; the symbols then cannot and should not avoid having "numberless" and "innumerable" meanings; symbolism is "the element of evocation, of suggestion" in great writers.[37]

This theory gives the poet a way of claiming significance for undeveloped images within poems and an excuse for inconsistency between poems. Yeats prints a note to "The Cap and Bells" in *The Wind Among the Reeds*: "I dreamed this story exactly as I have written it. . . . The poem has always meant a great deal to me, though, as is the way with symbolic poems, it has not always meant the same thing." A mysteriousness is claimed for a poem that alone is straightforward, simple, and minor. Ellmann knows this, but, refusing to criticize the master, retreats to a neutralizing passive: "While the significance of the poem may have changed for him, its immediate meaning was less obscure than it has been represented."[38] Almost as simple is "The Fisherman" (1916), which makes its claim within the poem. This symbol for the ideal Irish audience Yeats would like to address is described as an outdoorsman with a penchant for gray clothes and gray places and able to climb and fish. Yet we are to believe against the evidence of the poem that this man is "wise" as well as "simple," somehow able to represent the ideal alternative to the real world of cowardice, insolence, knavery, drunkenness, and hypocrisy, and somehow uniquely qualified to appreciate great art. And as for the fisherman being "Yeats's solar Mask, a Cuchulain reborn," as Unterecker wants,[39] we only can be confused by Yeats's arrogant dismissal of the scholars in a poem by that name in the same volume as "The Fisherman," because he seems to need scholars to complete some of his poems for him. Yet Yeats cannot simply be demanding a coherence realized only by the entire body of his work, for here his theory intervenes to condone symbolic inconsistencies between poems. The hawk, which in Yeats's note to "Tom O'Roughley" symbolizes mechanical logic, symbolizes the proud freedom of nature that resists encagement by utilitarians two years before in a poem titled "The Hawk." There are the multiple and conflicting meanings of the Sato sword and its scabbard (in "Meditations in Time of Civil War," "A Dialogue of Self and Soul," and other poems).

Finally there is just plain sloppiness: the loose structure of "Easter 1916," for instance, suggests that the stone in the midst of the living stream symbolizes a "terrible beauty" suddenly born. The metaphysical indolence of Yeats's determinism led him to a theory that partly justifies stylistic indolence.

But if the mind is passive, the emotions are not. The poet who uses symbols half-unconsciously composes ideally in what Yeats called a "fit."[40] For him, exaltation is the proper mood, extravagance the proper result. In his early Pre-Raphaelite phase, the emphasis was on aesthetic pleasure and retreat from social responsibility. If by 1917 the pleasure principle is less obtrusive, the extravagance continues. The famous change in Yeats's poetry is more a change in emphasis and tone than in essential method: he remained a romantic, a determinist, and an extremist throughout his life. Always a believer in the autonomy of the imagination and therefore of the artist, Yeats simply moves from a view that poetry is an alternative to real life to a view that poetry is (almost) all there is to life; from the view of the poet as hypersensitive aesthete to the view of the poet as prophet. Both views are anti-social.

Yeats's aesthetics is, as he says, "the religion of the wilderness";[41] it is religion separated from ethics. For example, take this sentence from his essay "At Stratford-on-Avon," in which he attacks Shakespeare's Victorian critics for daring to think Shakespeare a moral poet:

> The Accusation of Sin produced its necessary fruit, hatred of all that was abundant, extravagant, exuberant, of all that sets a sail for shipwreck, and flattery of the commonplace emotions and conventional ideals of the mob, the chief Paymaster of accusation.[42]

This comes at the end of a section in which Yeats, with almost Blakean gusto, equates reason, sin, the commonplace, convention, and the mob and opposes them to the equally synonymous abundance, extravagance, exuberance, individuality, and eccentricity.

He consequently has a particularly childish view of evil and sin. It is simply a late and extreme version of Shaftesburian naturalism, with a Godwinian equation of evil with social restraint and a Blakean equation of good with pure energy. But with no sufficient understanding of evil, there can be no sufficient safeguards. Note, for instance, his inability to blame Maud Gonne, in "No Second Troy," for bringing misery to him and inciting violence in others. Because she had great beauty and a simple mind, we are to forgive her and blame the age: "in an age like this / . . . . what could she have done, being what she is?" (9, 11). There is his attitude toward war: Hone tells us that, against his father, "Willie" in about 1889 agreed with Maud Gonne "that there was something a little grey in the prospect of a perpetual Victorian peace."[43] We also have his own words from 1936: "If war is necessary, or necessary in our time and place, it is best to forget its suffering."[44]

For Yeats, then, the poet should be a reckless[45] exhibitionist: he must have "strength of personality," be a creature of impulse with a strong and rough energy of expression, even careless, "never too observant, too professional."[46] The theory, in other words, requires the poet to be loud and imprecise:

> The intellect of man is forced to choose
> Perfection of the life, or of the work,
> And if it take the second must refuse
> A heavenly mansion, raging in the dark.
>
> ("The Choice," 1–4)

"Forced to choose" by whom or what? The dynamics of the Platonic Year or the determinants of the Primum Mobile? (In "Vacillation," he says that poets "play a predestined part.") The idea that a good poet cannot be a good man is patently absurd, and if anyone other than Yeats had said it, more people would disagree with it.

Yeats once told Symons early in his career, "if we had felt a tendency to excess we would be better poets."[47] In his fifties he confessed openly, with little or no regret, his tendency to overstate, his desire to vex, startle, confound, and confuse.[48] His extremism as he grew older usually found expression in his desire for ecstasy (the sexual and spiritual often confused) rather than pleasure; and although he did attend more to this world, his dichotomizing habit intact, he saw alternatives as violent opposites, recognizing "no human mean between the supernatural and the bestial"[49] except perhaps dullness.

As one might expect, his verse is not always as extreme as his prose declarations would have it. One thinks, for instance, of the quiet opening stanzas of "The Wild Swans at Coole." But his theories (and here we cannot separate the aesthetic from the moral) do seriously damage much of his poetry. That his amorality has in it an element of naivety and immaturity is clear from such admired poems as "A Prayer for My Daughter" and "An Irish Airman Foresees His Death," the sentiments of which are hopelessly inadequate to the very serious and almost religious occasions. In the first poem Yeats, at a seemingly apocalyptic time ("The storm is howling"—she was born one month after he wrote "The Second Coming"), prays that his daughter will be beautiful, but not too beautiful, charming and courteous, unopinionated, radically innocent, and married to an aristocrat. The Irish Airman goes to meet his fate, to kill or be killed, totally without moral compunction, for the sheer selfish delight of it all:

> Nor law, nor duty bade me fight,
> Nor public men, nor cheering crowds,
> A lonely impulse of delight
> Drove to this tumult in the clouds.
>
> (9–12)

Dudley Young finds "marvelous" this poetic recommendation of what he calls "a playfulness beyond good and evil."[50] The position is reprehensible whether it comes from Robert Gregory or Yeats, or both. If it is only Gregory's attitude, then we must regret Yeats's inability to judge it. But I think the attitude is completely Yeats's.

The amorality of his poetry breeds in turn egotism, irresolution, and, again, imprecision. There is never modesty in Yeats's voice. Whatever self-criticism we may occasionally detect usually serves the dramatics of his self-regard rather than a sincere introspection. The melodramatic scarecrow that appears so often in his later verse is a case in point. When he is sincere, he is quite pleased with himself (and we should not let his quotation marks or his various masks deceive us). He could, with no sense at all of conflict, freely publish all his work, yet place himself above and beyond the reading public, which at times seems for him to be made up only of knaves and dolts. After reading "Against Unworthy Praise," in which he instructs his "proud" heart to be impervious to public responses (because his poetry, written "for a woman's sake," is "a secret between you two"), one wonders why he could not have just sent her the manuscript, as traditional courtiers did. He can at times place himself in the same circle with serious moralists, like Landor, Donne, and St. Anthony ("To a Young Beauty" and "Demon and Beast") and at other times place himself above morality, as when he says he is

> ... content to follow to its source
> Every event in action or in thought;
> Measure the lot; forgive myself the lot!
> ("A Dialogue of Self and Soul," 65–67)

Whether this is "pure and beautiful solipsism" or "ecstatic and reductive solipsism" (as Bloom labels it), it is still pride, and pride is a sin, against whatever we believe we belong to.

It is this egotism, and not impersonal and just estimation, that turns his friends into mythic heroes. It is all part of the same drama of the self. The annoying insistence that Maud Gonne is like Helen of Troy is never justified beyond the simple and apparent fact that both were beautiful. Maud Gonne was a minor but active instigator of violence; Helen was not. Helen, as the daughter of Leda, can be said to have indirectly destroyed a civilization, but Maud Gonne cannot by any stretch of the historical imagination. The mythic equation is one way of avoiding having to criticize her: like most of Yeats's blameless heroes and heroines, she has "the purity of a natural force" having "not lived in thought but deed"—she simply has bad luck, while those against her are ignorant and evil, dishonest drunkards and pilferers ("The People"). I think the best way to see Yeats's poetic obsession with Maud Gonne is as a kind of extended, latter-day Petrarchanism: a combination of exaggerated compliment and self-pity. There are never enough qualifiers in Yeats's poetic diction. Yeats seems to be saying: if the emotion is large enough, any analogy is justified. Considering, for instance, the ease with which his political indignation generated the mythic hyperboles of "Parnell's Funeral" and his failure to deal responsibly with the events of "Easter 1916," his retreat there into pathetic and disorganized questions and finally propagandistic chant, can we really doubt that Yeats, even for a poet, had a surprisingly undeveloped political intelligence? The point is that he thought that as a poet he need not bother. The deprivation is quite voluntary.

The prophet, after all, is above being fair-minded. With enormous confidence he asks us to believe, among other things, that "*All* that was said in Ireland is a lie," "the best lack *all* conviction," "*all* neglect / Monuments of unaging intellect," and "*all* [scholars] think what other people think." These statements and the violent oppositions that invigorate so much of his poetry are further indications of the incompleteness of his thought. Irresolution is acceptable, but not preferable, when it comes after a clear and disinterested attempt to acknowledge the full complexity of the subject matter. What is preferable is a defended resolution; that is, a rational understanding, however tentative and conjectural it has to be, because of *unavoidable* human limitations. More often than not, Yeats creates the limitations, to which he succumbs dramatically. As he "developed" in his career from a Pre-Raphaelite into a modernist poet, Yeats simply exchanged dramatic apostrophes for dramatic dialogues, or highly personal views of others in dialectical terms. Whether the choice is of creators over thinkers (in "Ego Dominus Tuus"), or "clean and sweet" horsemanship over "bitter" politics (in "On a Political Prisoner"), or intellectual souls over sensual bodies (in "Sailing to Byzantium"), or admirers of tragic joy over hysterical women (in "Lapis Lazuli"), or heroes, peasants, and aristocrats over everyone else, the dialectics are facile and the polarization (and the thereby created tension) artificial. When he is not denying by omission more moderate alternatives, he seems to be suggesting, by the very width of the gap, that he has considered unstated intermediate alternatives—the authority implied is rarely earned.

Occasionally, as in the Crazy Jane poems, he seems to be striving for a union of opposites. Within a hyperbolic vision in which churchmen are coxcombs and deformed beasts and half-wits are wise with lust, old Jane asserts that "Love is all / Unsatisfied / That cannot take the whole / Body and soul" ("Crazy Jane on the Day of Judgment," 1-4) and "Fair and foul are near of kin, /. . . . For nothing can be sole or whole / That has not been rent" ("Crazy Jane Talks with the Bishop," 7, 17-18). In practical terms, this amounts to little more than an excuse to seek out intensities for their own sake. Such union of opposites, according to Balachandra Rajan, expresses a "sense of wholeness";[51] but certainly this is the wrong kind of wholeness—a mechanical acquisition of experiences lived to the hilt for the sake of some dimly sanctioned eclecticism. The union is a violent yoking rather than a resolving of contraries. True wholeness involves a fullness of being, which allows one to comprehend fully and therefore to deal rightly with experience, to choose creative rather than destructive experiences.

The aging Yeats openly acknowledged his fanaticism, but at the same time refused to accept the blame, in a poem whose title is more ironic than he intended, "Remorse for Intemperate Speech." In the first stanza he says he cannot rule his "fanatic heart." In the second stanza he says with characteristic overstatement, that his aristocratic friends turned his "hatred into sport." In the final stanza, he assumes himself representative of the Irish:

> Out of Ireland have we come.
> Great hatred, little room,
> Maimed us at the start.
> I carry from my mother's womb
> A fanatic heart.
>
> (11–15)

If that is the curse of being Irish in the present age, then the blessing lies in a curious, untameable quality that needs to be revived, which has something to do with the prevalence in the past of

> Hard-riding country gentlemen,
> The holiness of monks, ...
> Porter-drinkers' randy laughter ...
> [and] lords and ladies gay.
>
> ("Under Ben Bulben," 75–78)

After advising Irish poets to turn to these things, he concludes this list of commonplaces of the past with the hollow pomposity of these summarizing lines:

> Cast your mind on other days
> That we in coming days may be
> Still the indomitable Irishry.
>
> (81–83)

No wonder Yeats can only be fanatical when the only alleviating past that attracts him is so trivial.

4

Yeats's view of Hardy, one contemporary poet who was attracted to a substantial past, is predictably slight. This hater of the contemplative English and enemy of the objective and natural and promoter of inspired carelessness, found Hardy an interesting balladeer, who despite a "mastery of the impersonal objective scene," "lacked technical accomplishment."[52] When he selected modern poetry for his Oxford anthology, he included only four poems by Hardy: "Weathers," "The Night of Trafalgar" (from *The Dynasts*), "Former Beauties," and "Snow in the Suburbs." The first two are simple, musical pieces; the third a nostalgic yearning for lost youth and beauty; only the fourth with its fine observation and slight moral suggestion is of much value. Yeats was clearly unable to appreciate Hardy.[53]

Hardy's references to Yeats are even scarcer, but more accurate. The most suggestive is his comment to Vere Collins in December 1920: "I don't suppose [Yeats] believes in Sinn Fein. I don't suppose he knows what he believes."[54] I do not know if Hardy had in mind the irresolute political poems recently published in *Responsibilities* and *The Wild Swans at Coole*, but I would like to think so.

The issue of Hardy's beliefs is perhaps approached best by examining briefly "Snow in the Suburbs," which suggests the context for Hardy's beliefs, a context that Yeats probably could just agree with. After two eight-line stanzas describing snow-laden trees, streets, pavements, and fences, and then a lone sparrow initiating a small avalanche in a tree, the four-line final stanza quietly (with an unobtrusive "and") takes us to an interior, human refuge:

> The steps are a blanched slope,
> Up which, with feeble hope,
> A black cat comes, wide-eyed and thin;
> And we take him in.
>
> (17–20)

Nature, although not ominously threatening here, is nevertheless inhospitable and arbitrary. The insistent "every" and opening trochees of the first four lines intensify the suggestion of a scene heavy with disturbing potential. This is balanced by the inadvertent comedy of the bombarded bird in the next stanza and the marvelous delicacy of the realized movement in lines five and six:

> Some flakes have lost their way, and grope back upward, when
> Meeting those meandering down they turn and descend again.

Against this natural waywardness, the human observation is steady and productive, moving from the general and various to an isolated particular, from tree to wild animal to domesticated animal to humans, and as a result of the observation there is action.

Both Hardy and Yeats find nature mostly unsympathetic to man, but Yeats will advise a dreamy escape to either fairyland or The Great Mind, whereas Hardy will illustrate a dignified resistance and adjustment within the real world. I say dignified, because although he acknowledges that man is a part of nature and even speculates on a Universal Will, of which man is a subservient part, he recognizes the possibility of free will.[55] Darwin had taught Hardy that the law of evolution was a better "provisional view of the universe" that any "idea of omnipotent goodness." So while Yeats offers us a vision of a higher reality beyond or behind a nature that he rarely observes very carefully, Hardy, as a result of his acute scrutiny of those appearances, offers us personal and narrative instances of man's responses to the obdurate neutrality of nature. Yeats goes elsewhere for the grace that Darwin denied Wordsworth's nature; Hardy assents to that divesting and takes us back to that pre-eighteenth-century view of nature as nonrational; but because he had Darwin between himself and those disillusioned Renaissance Christians, he saw not evil but only unconsciousness in nature. If Hardy had stopped with this, he would have been no better than all the other nihilists of the late nineteenth century. Instead he went on to build a practical but not pragmatic ethic upon this base. He wanted to be a Christian, found it impossible, but refused to be a relativist; to William James's dictum that "Truth is what will work," Hardy in 1925 responded, "A worse corruption of language was never perpetrated."[56]

Hardy's dealings with reality, when he is successful, and he very often is, are almost always moral. Never a transcendentalist, he also could never only be an objective observer. If the cosmic questions could not be answered, he insisted at least on resolution in questions of human conduct. He found modern literature "insincere" because "half its utterances are qualified, even contradicted, by an aside and this particularly in morals and religion."[57] Honest doubt was one thing, playful evasion quite another. Although he could sometimes seem to be dogmatic in his philosophical speculations (for instance, "Before Life and After" and "The Unborn"), he was rarely morally dogmatic. I see him in the tradition of George Crabbe; both were modest, anti-romantic moralists; each, as Hardy says of Darwin, "saying his say / In a quiet way" ("Drinking Song"). In "Lying Awake," from *Winter Words*, he visualizes very vividly what can be seen outside on this night, and the order of his list is significant: a steady-eyed Morningtide Star, beeches engraving their thin twigs on the sky, a meadow white with a counterpane cover of dew, and finally a churchyard with the names on the tombstones "creeping out everywhere." As his imaginative eye moves literally down to earth, he also moves away from the symbolic temptations of the star down to the significance of human time—the threat of death and the hold the past can have on us. Contrast this with the opposite movement (the one Yeats almost always took) in another but much weaker poem from *Winter Words*, "'I Am the One,'" in which he starts with ringdoves and hares and ends with the stars commenting on him and deciding not to scathe him: "'He is one with us / Beginning and end.'" A similar subject is treated much more successfully in "Afterwards." Hardy is at his observant best here, noting the qualities he hopes to be remembered for, and again the order is significant: he "notices" the smallest details of nature so often that they are "familiar" sights and to the extent that he tries to protect innocent creatures; he even lifts his gaze to "the full-starred heavens," for he has "an eye for such mysteries"—not an enclosing and defining system, but simply an eye for the cosmic mysteries. Fortunately the poem has another stanza: he also "notices" bells of quittance—the passing of men's lives under those steadfast stars. The whole poem is quietly informed with the sense of passing time, signalled by the definition of life as a "tremulous stay" in the opening line. There is the movement from spring to winter and from day to dusk to night; and every image, except "the full-starred heavens that winter sees," is precarious: "delicate-filmed" wings, the dewfall-hawk's flight "like an eyelid's soundless blink," the "furtively" moving hedgehog, and the "crossing breeze." Hardy answers with his sympathy such transience in the natural and the human world. (Is not that exactly what morality does for mortality?) In "Drinking Song," after surveying the decline of superstitions as great minds offer solutions to the riddle of existence, a progress Hardy is grateful for but not really comforted by, he comes to this:

> So here we are [after Einstein], in piteous case:
> Like butterflies
> Of many dyes
> Upon an Alpine glacier's face:
> To fly and cower
> In some warm bower
> Our chief concern in such a place.
>
> (73–79)

The survey has been punctuated by a chorus suggesting a response not unlike that of Hardy's ancestors in "Night in the Old Home" ("'Enjoy, suffer, wait: spread the table here freely like us, / And, satisfied, placid, unfretting, watch Time away beamingly!'" [15–16]): "Fill full your cups: feel no distress; / 'Tis only one great thought the less!" The poem ends with this refrain, with an extra line: "We'll do a good deed nevertheless!"

Despite his occasional speculations on larger issues, Hardy, unlike Yeats, rarely allows himself to wander far from a full acknowledgment of the limits of our individual lives and the strengths of our human tradition. It is a modesty that should not be confused with what Davie, in regretting Hardy's lack of romantic ambition, calls "just so many glosses" on reality.[58] Hardy has a keen sense of present difficulties, a strong memory, and an essentially Christian ethic lacking spiritual authority but not appeal.[59]

It is therefore more helpful to think of Hardy not as a determinist but as a realistic pessimist who never gave up wanting to believe in a traditional Christian god. The problem for someone searching for a label is that Hardy's theories were always, as he himself said, "tentative," and they changed slightly as he attended closely to and reacted against the events of his age. He seems to have started as a moderate Victorian progressive, whose natural pessimism intensified as a result of World War I, then in later old age wavered between meliorism (a belief that the world might be getting better, the Universal Will more conscious of itself) and skepticism. But always he was an opponent of romantic optimism. This is what bothered an Edwardian reviewer of *Poems of the Past and the Present* who found Hardy acceptable ("genial" is his word) as long as he was only melancholic and not disillusioned.[60] I believe Hardy's strength is that disillusionment; it made him careful to keep his vision clear and his emotions restrained.

The temptation to let go is often there for Hardy—he did, after all, live in a romantic culture. He comes close to the edge sometimes, as in "Thoughts of Phena," in which he consoles himself with the thought that his idealized memory of Tryphena Sparks "may" be better than the reality he does not know, or in the sentimental excesses of "A Singer Asleep," an elegy to Swinburne, or in the rather Wordsworthian poem, "Dream of the City Shopwoman," which uncritically employs the old pastoral opposition of city and country. There are also Wordsworthian echoes in "Wagtail and Baby" and "'Sacred to the Memory,'" but the former carries the light-heartedness that saves some of the Lyrical Ballads and the latter the simple poignancy of some of the Lucy poems.[61] Most often, however, he acknowledges the temptation but backs off. "Shut Out that Moon" is representative. Each of the first three stanzas opens with a command:

> Close up the casement, draw the blind,
> . . . .
> Step not forth on the dew-dashed lawn
> . . . .
> Brush not the bough for midnight scents.
>
> (1, 7, 13)

If the order were reversed, we would have a dramatic presentation of a backing into a room. By shutting the window first, he avoids the direct view that would tempt him to indulge in nostalgia and raise memories of irretrievable pleasures with his father, mother, and first wife. The memories are there in each stanza but are kept at a distance; after all, the moon can steal our hard-won composure. This is the fourth and final stanza:

> Within the common lamp-lit room
> Prison my eyes and thought;
> Let dingy details crudely loom,
> Mechanic speech be wrought:
> Too fragrant was Life's early bloom,
> Too tart the fruit it brought!

The rhyme scheme here, for the first time in the poem, is strictly *a b a b a b* (there are two deviations in the first stanza, and one each in the next two stanzas), paralleling the achievement of acceptance over simple avoidance. The acceptance comes with the expression in the last two lines of the motive for the avoidance. He is avoiding not the past but only the associations with extremes of pleasure and pain. The key word is "common." (The fourth line there is uncharacteristically overstated.) He says elsewhere, "I only need the homeliest/Of heartstirrings" ("'Any Little Old Song,'" 11-12).

Limits, boundaries, and order are important for Hardy. They not only help men assert their significance and provisional meaning against an indifferent universe but also prevent men from losing control of their own humanity. That is, Hardy's pessimism, much regretted by so many readers, made him into a moral poet. He says this explicitly in his "Apology" to *Late Lyrics and Earlier* (1922):

> ... what is to-day, in allusions to the present author's pages, alleged to be 'pessimism' is, in truth, only such 'questionings' in the exploration of reality, and is the first step towards the soul's betterment, and the body's also.[62]

And betterment he thought definitely necessary, as he observed in 1920: "people are not more humane ... than they were in the year of my birth. Disinterested kindness is less."[63] In 1902 he defined pessimism as "playing the sure game.... Having reckoned what to do in the worst possible circumstances, when better arise, as they may, life becomes child's play."[64] Again, in 1918, he says, "As to pessimism. My motto is, first correctly diagnose the complaint—in this case human ills—and ascertain the cause: then set about finding a remedy if one exists."[65]

I admit to finding Hardy's attempt to find moral stability in a mediating alliance between religion and "complete rationality," more difficult now than during his lifetime, a courageous and necessary one; which is not to say, however, that full concurrence with his belief in every detail is necessary to praise and promote his best poetry. There are, I think, three possible relations between a reader and the informing ideas in literary works: (1) substantial agreement; (2) substantial respect for ideas in works usually written before our time, which means that we have good reason to believe that many other people have believed these things and that such ideas have seriously affected human thinking and feeling and that these ideas represent the best and fullest belief possible at the time they were held; and (3) disagreement with ideas that we consider and can defend as wrong or foolish whenever they are held. Hardy only occasionally takes us into the third category; Yeats rarely takes us out of it. Hardy is not a profound philosopher in his verse (although I would not go so far as Leavis and Winters and call him naive), but he is a sound moralist; Yeats is too often a foolish philosopher, in and out of his verse. Hardy does not need a mechanical schema to explain his poems. What Jon Silkin says of Dr. Johnson applies to Hardy: his "surety ... comes not from intellectual arrogance but from a perception of what can be shared";[66] which is to say that Hardy respects reason and trusts in the efficacy of contemplation.

Hardy "tells the truth," as Howard Baker so rightly said in 1940.[67] Hardy himself says, "Let there be truth at last,/Even if despair" ("Between Us Now," 7–8). He was careful, however, not to be labelled a rationalist; he was too empirical for that. It is safe to say he wanted rationality and reasonableness to prevail, but he realized with some regret the price that had to be paid. The sound of the breeze against "A Cathedral Façade at Midnight"

> ... seemed sighings of regret
> At the ancient faith's rejection
> Under the sure, unhasting, steady stress
> Of Reason's movement, making meaningless
> The coded creeds of old-time godliness.
>
> (17–21)

"The sure, unhasting, steady stress/Of Reason's movement" aptly describes the structure of many of Hardy's poems. This movement calms and controls yearnings, desires, and frustrations that cannot be denied.

This brings us directly to the consequences of his beliefs: the centrality, accuracy and precision, moderation, and formality of his poetry. The poetry is, first of all, seldom without a social perspective on immediate and personal concerns. Even in his little parable, "Winter in Durnover Field," in which the assertion of a present debility by the Rook ("Throughout the field I find no grain") frames the poem and even interrupts the Starling and Pigeon with a desperate "No grain!", we have a reminder by the sensible Starling that "patient pecking" is only *now* vain—it was not so in the near past—and an explanation by the sociable pigeon that they must wait until the rain or "genial thawings loose the lorn land." Although he will not condone personal escapes to "some fancy-place/Where pain had no trace" ("At the Piano"), he understands the need for self-protection. Most moving is the psychological situation of "The Shadow on the Stone": he decides that to "keep down grief" he must not "unvision" that which he knows to be an illusion, yet he "wanted to look and see/That nobody stood at the back of me." We might contrast this with Yeats's ready acceptance of his visions. Hardy is not a simple debunker of dreams. He is profoundly aware of the need for some carefully controlled illusions, but he never doubts their invalidity ("yet abides the fact" ["Your Last Drive"]); he does not want to have to believe that there are ghosts. He understands the need for some romantic indulgences, but in the context of a broad and gentle skepticism.

A more constructive sign of this self-protection is Hardy's provincialism. Compared with the scope of his modernist contemporaries, especially the transplanted Eliot and unplantable Pound, Hardy seems very narrow, but as Irving Howe correctly says, "His range is limited, but his penetration deep."[68] His inability to match the cultural heterogeneity of the early modernists allowed him to transcend their evasive ironies and achieve an uncommon responsiveness. So rooted in the Englishness of Wessex, he could respond all the more surely and precisely. He knew he was part of a proud and threatened tradition; he was consequently more sensitive to the destructions and accumulations of passing time. This explains his symbolic method: whereas Yeats will burden an object with a multitude of esoteric meanings, Hardy will discover what R. W. King calls the "significant anecdote,"[69] a single fully realized event that is meaningful as it is placed in time and as it instances an enduring state of mind or feeling. There are constants, things that "will go onward the same / Though Dynasties pass" ("In Time of 'The Breaking of Nations'"), but they are in danger of being overlooked or undervalued. There is no Wordsworthian moment of eternity. In the absence of a Great Memory, we must rely on our individual memories. We have a duty to be vigilant and remember, and that memory, says Hardy, that "loved continuance," can give us "world-awakening scope" ("The To-Be-Forgotten").

His concern, with its mediating political, social, and psychological realism substantiated by a singular rootedness in place and time, and the attendant respect for tradition, for human and humane continuity, in turn makes possible accuracy and precision in the description of the present, which is always in danger of slipping away as "unadjusted impressions." There is no need here to document Hardy's descriptive precision; it is everywhere in his verse and is the one quality of his art all of his commentators agree on, even, grudgingly, Yeats. It ranges from the almost photographic observation of "A Sheep Fair," "Throwing a Tree," and "No Buyers," to the delicate acuity of "Afterwards," to the unambiguous evocations of the atmospheric "Nobody Comes." Less widely noted is his ability to describe complex but not uncommon emotional states. No one has described the mixture of grief and different kinds of relief that immediately follows the death after a lengthy illness of a loved one as does Hardy in "After the Last Breath (J. H. 1813–1904)."

> The lettered vessels of medicaments
> Seem asking wherefore we have set them here;
> Each palliative its silly face presents
>   As useless gear.

> And yet we feel that something savours well;
> We note a numb relief withheld before;
> Our well-beloved is prisoner in the cell
>   Of Time no more.
>
> (9–16)

Only a master of descriptive language and tone could draw such unexpected expressiveness out of words like "silly" and "savours," could have so deftly avoided the potential portentousness of "the cell/Of Time" by a simple but perfect line division. It is a poem that should be better known.

First and foremost, Hardy is a poet of tone. In an age when ambiguous ironies and sophisticated sarcasms were replacing the sweet plangencies of late Victorian poetry, Hardy was almost alone with his clarifying moderations. The best way to illustrate his extraordinary control of tone is to point to examples of his handling of modes that in the hands of most other poets, especially Yeats, seem to accommodate immoderation—the dramatic and the confessional.

Hardy has many poems in which he speculates that God either does not exist or is limited. One such poem is "God-Forgotten," an imaginary dialogue between himself and God. This is directly followed in *Poems of the Past and the Present* by "The Bedridden Peasant to an Unknowing God," in which the speaker is a fictive character also talking to God, but this time God does not reply. Considerably less fanciful, this poem immediately seems more authoritative even though the speaker comes to a very different conclusion than the skeptical Hardy does. In addition, the qualities of the speaker in this second poem partially substantiate the conclusion: he is one of those unsentimental, stoical, usually uncomplaining, men of the soil whom Hardy greatly respected (see "Night in the Old Home"). The homely wisdom of this peasant is suggested by the plainness and economy of the ballad form—a form that, as Thom Gunn argues in one of the best essays yet written on Hardy's poetry, gives that poetry much of its native strength.[70] The opening stanza realizes a tone poised between anxiety and resignation. Whatever desperation the situation might anticipate is quickly muted:

> Much wonder I—here long low-laid—
>   That this dead wall should be
> Betwixt the Maker and the made,
>   Between Thyself and me!
>
> (1–4)

The exclamation is moderated by the ruminative opening, "Much wonder I," by the repeated internal balancing of lines three and four, and by the placement of the exclamation mark after what is already the most emphatic syllable of the stanza. The exclamation mark, like the self-conscious desire not to repeat "Betwixt," can suggest that the speaker is perhaps almost amused at finding himself so seriously pondering issues beyond his ken. He continues with some rustic hypothesizing ("For, say one ..."), moving from premises only highfalutin thinkers like Hardy would not take on faith ("Thou art mild of heart" [16]), through some plain speaking (might God but do what any man would do), to a resolve that Hardy, but not the speaker, finds attractive but untenable:

> Then, since Thou mak'st not these things be,
> But these things dost not know,
> I'll praise Thee as were shown to me
> The mercies Thou wouldst show!
>
> (29–32)

Resolve only can come by mixing a New Testament faith that God is merciful with an empirical conclusion that God is imperfect, which contradicts biblical teaching. Hardy is not making fun of the alternative to his view but quietly testing it, and therefore his own. Too often the dramatic mode (with for instance Browning and Yeats) is a way of avoiding judgment; for Hardy it is a way of refining judgment.

In two companion love poems, "Lost Love" and "The Walk," he manages a delicate balance of honesty and courtesy. Both poems are about the loss of love and Hardy's walks without and away from his wife. The first (probably written before his wife's death), although spoken by her, is as confessional as it is dramatic. The obvious sadness of the speaker is checked by the symmetrical six-line stanzas, four dimeter lines framed by trimeter lines, with monosyllabic rhymes emphasizing the closure of each one-sentence stanza: $abbcca$. The emotion is thereby controlled, and the meter is held back from being too inappropriately musical by the frequent anapests. But music is suggested: the woman is attempting unsuccessfully to recapture his affections by playing and singing "the airs he knew / When our love was true" (2–3). The rhyme is slightly disruptive in the first stanza with the too insistent "balk" and "walk," but in the last and by far most emotional stanza, the hold is masterful:

> So I wait for another morn,
> And another night
> In this soul-sick blight;
> And I wonder much
> As I sit, why such
> A woman as I was born!
>
> (13–18)

The emotion is genuine but not indulged: the retracting phrases, "And another night" and "As I sit," prepare for the double meaning of the last clause: "why such/A woman as I was born!" She seems to be concomitantly censuring herself for her part in the estrangement and complaining of mistreatment. These attitudes are not contradictory. Few poets would have the combination of modesty and skill to write a poem sympathetic to a woman they no longer loved without self-defensively trying to explain their side. When he does give his side of the story in "The Walk," the courtesy is even more poignant:

> You did not walk with me
> Of late to the hill-top tree
>   By the gated ways,
>   As in earlier days;
>   You were weak and lame,
>   So you never came,
> And I went alone, and I did not mind,
> Not thinking of you as left behind.
>
> I walked up there to-day
> Just in the former way;
>   Surveyed around
>   The familiar ground
>   By myself again:
>   What difference, then?
> Only that underlying sense
> Of the look of a room on returning thence.

The form here echoes that of the earlier poem, but each stanza is imperfectly symmetrical. The opening rhyme is not repeated, and the final couplet in each stanza is a foot longer than the opening couplet. In these slower closing couplets, Hardy unobtrusively calls attention to his private feelings, his past insensitivity and his present sense of loss. The calmness of the poem is then the result not of insensitivity but of an intensely sensitive attempt to come to terms with an experience that would have reduced weaker poets to mannered laments. Thom Gunn writes of the final lines:

> ... in such trivia the whole of loss may be contained. The image at the end is almost casual, almost flat, almost not there, it is so commonplace. Yet, after all, it is precisely and terribly there, terribly because it is part of everybody's daily experience. There is no drama, no ghost: only the acknowledgment of a loss you have to live with, as everybody has to live with his losses—and it is as ordinary as a room.[71]

If we need an early twentieth-century example of the power of the plain style, we have it in this poem.

The direct approach and subtle tone are made possible by extreme formality. Hardy is important to modern poets because he shows them how expressive restraint can be. Against experimentation in the direction of formlessness, he still could be highly individual and inventive without ceasing to be formal. Just as he was unable both to believe in the old certainties and to give up the need for certainty, so, except for a few sonnets and may variations on the ballad, he replaced the old forms and their particular associations with new ones. These new forms were often highly elaborate, reflecting the intensity of his desire to remain formal. His meters are traditional throughout. Some defenses had to be maintained against what he saw in the 1920s as "the barbarizing of taste in the younger minds ..., the unabashed cultivation of selfishness in all classes, the plethoric growth of knowledge simultaneously with the stunting of wisdom."[72]

One of the many things that Emma meant to Hardy after her death was a kind of impulsive informality that he had difficulty accommodating. The theme is explicit in "Without Ceremony": her death, he says, was characteristic of her "swift style," her tendency in life to "vanish without a word" and "career/Off anywhere" suddenly. As he describes these instances in the first two stanzas, he introduces more and more anapests into his trimeter lines. But when he comes in the third and final stanza to a direct interpretation, he deliberately refuses swiftness. There is a general slowing of the rhythm that suggests slight disapproval. The spondee in the last foot of the second line signals the perfect iambic movement thereafter and the very slow final line:

> So, now that you disappear
> For ever in that swift style,
> Your meaning seems to me
> Just as it used to be:
> 'Good-bye is not worth while!'

(11–15)

The lack of the most rudimentary ceremony is faintly and perhaps unnecessarily unsettling. But if he is slightly disapproving here, Emma's restlessness is set in approving light in "Lament," where her love of parties, "gaying," "junketings," her "ardours unfeigned," her eagerness, are seen as simple vitalities against the "infinite rest" of her death. Perhaps in this poem he is mildly reproving his own preference for repose.

In several poems she is the romantic counter to his reserve, often associated with the sea, a powerful romantic symbol of the energy, flux, and creative source into which romantics desire or are tempted to submerge their identities. In "Beeny Cliff," the western sea is described as "wandering," ceaselessly "babbling," the bulking shore of which is "wild" and "weird." In a poem in which the title might just contain a relevant pun, "I Found Her Out There," Hardy wonders if in taking Emma away from Cornwall he robbed her of her earlier, almost child-like, vitality, a vitality that is yet associated with an ocean that "breaks," "beats," "smites," and "swells and sobs," with "blind gales" and hurricanes that shake "the solid land." He wonders finally if her shade "will creep underground / Till it catch" the sound of the sea, "And joy in its throbs / With the heart of a child" (34–35, 39–40). This is a dangerous attraction for the innocent and unprotected. Hardy's forms are his protection against such crude threats to being and refinement—it is what he called, in commending the highly structured art of Anatole France, "the force of reserve."[73]

When critics like Donald Davie, then, praise Hardy for breaking the rigid symmetry of the form in "The Voice" to be faithful to his feeling, they mistake for "honesty" what I think Hardy would have considered a momentary, if poignant, weakness. Davie goes on to cite Winters's judgment, to him wholly unacceptable, that "The Haunter" is "by far the better poem."[74] For Davie,

> "The Haunter" is an imperiously symmetrical piece in four eight-line stanzas, the rhyme words of the even lines in the first stanza reproduced exactly in each of the stanzas that follow. Winters does not tell us what he finds wrong with "The Voice"; in view of his preference for "The Haunter" one may suspect that he likes just that rigid symmetry which I have called technological, a symmetry which "The Voice" departs from, whereas "The Haunter" presses it home relentlessly.[75]

"Relentlessly"? Surely Davie is mistaken. But let us start with "The Voice." It is a fine poem, moving and sincere. But what does it amount to? Hearing a sound, Hardy wants immediately to believe it is the voice of Emma returned in the ghostly form of the young woman he fell in love with, the form that her death reminded him of.

> ... not as you were
> When you had changed from the one who was all to me,
> But as at first, when our day was fair.
>
> (2–4)

The effective use of the negative and the fluid telescoping of the four time periods (the present, near past, distant past, and time of change in between) are only marred slightly by the loose denotations of "all" and "fair." The next stanza asks the question that is central to the poem: is the voice really Emma's? If so, this stanza continues, show yourself as you were "at first." The third stanza entertains the possibility that it is only the breeze, and then we have the much-acclaimed breakdown:

> Thus I; faltering forward,
> Leaves around me falling,
> Wind oozing thin through the thorn from norward,
> And the woman calling.
>
> (13–16)

Hardy is rarely so immediate. He has not waited long enough. The questions that gave structure to the two previous stanzas are either not taken seriously or are unanswerable. The verse and Hardy's usual, sensitive resolve falter. If he cannot immediately answer the questions, he will have it both ways: the wind *and* the woman calling. We do indeed discover and the poem's movement discovers the speaker's feeling—a rather nostalgic need for a woman he knew more than forty years before. But the need has not been understood fully enough: he has stopped too soon, betraying the initial structure. He has not gone through the emotion; he has not achieved what Irving Howe calls "the salvage of poise."

After the explicitness of "The Voice," "The Haunter" might seem too playful and fanciful, not nearly immediate enough. The fact that the speaker is the fictive ghost of Hardy's first wife might at first compromise the seriousness of the poem. But this is part of the poem's power: we know it is a projection of his guilt and revived love. There is a moral perspective here missing in the other poem. The concern in "The Haunter" is not with the personality or motive of the speaker, the ghost, but with the meaning of the projection—the need to be and the fear of being haunted. He needs to be comforted and he fears the censure of the incompleteness, partly his fault, of their relationship. The last two lines of each of the first three stanzas point to different kinds of failures: no response to words spoken, not seeing what one speaks to, nearness without the ability to speak. In the crucial second stanza, Hardy directly criticizes his own insensitivity to her overtures. Having the ghost say these things and also assure us that she is "a good haunter," ready to ease his grief, is Hardy's way of acknowledging, accepting, and dealing with the inevitability of such incompleteness. The last two lines of the last stanza have the moral authority that they do and are not empty optimisms because of the symmetry of their form.

> Tell him a faithful one is doing
>   All that love can do
> Still that his path may be worth pursuing,
>   And to bring peace thereto.
>
>   (29–32)

The appeal to a central humanity, the unswerving sense of limitations, the strength to go on living intelligently despite those limitations, and the need for patience and composure—these lines give us the essence of Hardy's accomplishment.

In this brief discussion of the weaknesses of Yeats's poetry and the strengths of Hardy's poetry, a discussion in which so much has had to be left out, I only mean to illustrate the possibilities for sanity, order, sensitivity, and moral integrity in the twentieth century, a century in which too many poets have taken their cue from W. B. Yeats and too few from Thomas Hardy. Those few deserve more of our attention.

2
Edward Thomas and the Georgians

The Georgian poets and their critics have done much to misdirect our understanding of the verse of the second decade of this century. The Georgian movement started as a crusade to popularize poetry by opposing the sentimentality, rhetoric, and facile patriotism of late Victorian and Edwardian poetry with aggressive realism and directness; but it ended in the 1920s as the epitome, in many influential minds, of reactionary and pallidly agreeable retreat. As always, the lines of cause and effect are difficult to define; but we can with some certainty say that a combination of events (including Edward Marsh's failure of will or taste, the propagandizing of brash coteries of avant-gardists, a brutalizing and desensitizing war, the premature deaths in that war of some of England's brightest young poets, and a particularly narrow and ill-tempered progressivism increasingly informing the Spirit of the Age) deflected and obscured the reputations of Thomas Hardy and those younger poets who legitimately shared, as most of the Georgians did not, his poetic interests. The best of these younger poets was Edward Thomas.

Although there have always been admirers of Thomas, most of the attempts by professional critics to secure his reputation have had to argue either that he is, in his unassertive manner, a Keatsian romantic simply better than the Georgians with whom he is grouped or that he anticipates the sensibilities of the experimental modernists of the 1920s. Here I would like to promote a third alternative, one that has been made difficult to recognize.

To provide a sufficient context for this reassessment of Edward Thomas, I begin with a brief review: first of the currents of taste and fashion in the eleven years spanned by the popular Georgian anthologies and second of the salient features of Georgian verse itself. The survey I propose suggests that the two popular views of Thomas are not as clearly distinct as some would have it, that the Georgians have more essentially in common with their experimental contemporaries than with Hardy or Thomas. The Georgians were more cautious than the experimentalists on the Left, and that caution, we are told, was the cause of their eventual decline. Robert Ross says it bluntly, "the new poets [the modernists] were fighting on the winning side, for they were fighting with, not against, the spirit of the age."[1] That view needs to be further refined. The Georgians failed not simply because they could not respond vitally enough to the demands of a radical present, but also and more importantly because they could not offer a substantial enough traditionalism to counter the louder and brasher calls for novelty and experiment. Therefore, it is not that traditional literary values could not survive in a progressive twentieth century but that the Georgians were not capable of properly defending or even fully understanding the strengths of the literary past. That is, both the major tendencies of the 1910s began as reactions to late romantic excesses but in two different ways were unable to go back farther than the early romantics for innovative models and sources of inspiration: one simply settled complacently back into romantic habits of feeling; the other violently pushed and developed romantic habits, assumptions, and theories to their logical and necessarily reductive conclusions.

1

A sampling of the literary pronouncements of influential poets and promoters in the year before and the year after publication of the first *Georgian Poetry*, which appeared in December 1912, reveals two gradually appearing tendencies. What all had in common is a call for directness and vitality, not unlike a call by Wordsworth in 1800 for a natural poetry that "in liveliness and truth" offers "the image of man and nature." Harold Monro, in the first issue of *The Poetry Review* (January 1912), in an essay significantly called "The Future of Poetry," called explicitly on young poets to complete Wordsworth's task: there were in the past "some reactions, as that of Wordsworth," to the artificial poetic jargon and the consequent supersession of poetry by prose; "it is now at last absolutely necessary for the fetters of stereotyped poetic language to be shaken off." He sounded even more broadly romantic when he argued that modern poetry must express "the real aspirations of life," and this can be done only "when the soul shall authoritatively and finally rule the body."[2] A note of caution and a specific reference to "the experiments of Whitman," who with his imitators has "shirked the problem by simply dispensing with metre," are the only indications that Monro was aware of another, more radical way of dealing with the problem.

When John Drinkwater published "Tradition and Technique" six months later in Monro's journal, he could actually define two "camps," two ways of dealing with the dead end of Swinburne's example, and although he admitted that each was acting as a corrective on the other, he clearly preferred the less adventurous poets, those who "refused to deny their inheritance altogether." After all, he reminded his reader, "worthily to continue a tradition is at least as difficult as to invent one." The "tradition," however, for him is that defined by the early nineteenth century, and we realize just how thin Drinkwater's caution is when we find him saying that "Collins and Gray and Blake emancipated poetry from the bondage of the eighteenth-century couplet."[3]

The experimentalists spoke out more boldly, especially after Marsh's first collection appeared. Harriet Monroe, in a May 1913 editorial in *Poetry: A Magazine of Verse*, characterized the diffference between the two camps as that between the strong and the weak, those "who can stand alone" and those "who need protection." To make her point she too neatly defined the enemy's "tradition" as that of "external form rather than the larger [and more acceptable] tradition of spiritual motive."[4] One detects a positive regard for Whitman when she adds spontaneity to directness as the necessary modern poetic qualities and praises those poets "with whom popularity is poison." Pound makes the same point in an essay published in *The Egoist* that same year ("The Serious Artist"). The anti-intellectual strain in the avant garde becomes more evident. It is one thing not to pander to popular taste; it is quite another condescendingly to disregard altogether the reading public and its expectations. Pound is narrowing the debate, of course: art is an image, not an argument; it "never asks anybody to do anything, or to think anything, or to be anything. It exists as the trees exist." He rightly calls for precision, energy, and "true reports," but in this context such reports undermine community and true seriousness: "From the arts," he says, "we learn that man is whimsical, that one man differs from another."[5] Although Wordsworth never would have agreed with these statements, the theoretical simplicities of early romanticism, deprived (as they came to be in the later nineteenth century) of a substantiating if irrational doctrine, cannot but have aided the individualistic and democratic strains that are given such incautious expression in Pound's early manifestos.

The call for change is even narrower in Ford Madox Hueffer's speculations on "Impressionism" in August and September 1913, again in *Poetry*. Directness is central ("It is, in fact, better to be vulgar than affected"); the almost neutral relativism is there (poetry's aim should be "to register my own times in terms of my own time"); spontaneity is a given (verse "just comes"); and "Impressionism" is an early and perhaps mistaken term for what is essentially imagism:

> ... the putting of the one thing in juxtaposition with the other, that seems to me to be much more the business of the poet of today than setting down on paper what he thinks about the fate of Brangaene, not because any particular "lesson" may be learned, but because such juxtapositions suggest emotions.[6]

The images must be of "the Crowd" and distinctly urban. When a definition of adequate poetry becomes this limited, we suspect that behind the vigor of the opposition to Victorian sentimentality is an even shorter-sightedness than Drinkwater's.

The force of the belief in the need for a new poetry and the prevailing spirit of liberalism began to cause even such a defender and benefactor of the Georgians as Harold Monro to muddle the positions. Less than two years after that 1912 call to return poetry to life and especially to the spirit, he offered with almost Poundian gusto his own brand of English futurism, the first principles of which are

> I. To forget God, Heaven, Hell, Personal Immortality, and to remember always the earth.
> II. To lift the eyes from a sentimental contemplation of the past, and, though dwelling in the present, nevertheless, always, to *live*, in the future of the earth.[7]

The caution is still there, but only in the dismissal of Italian futurism as "no more than frenzied Whitmanism," and gone is the moral purposefulness and even a mention of the possibility of an unsentimental contemplation of the past. Of course, as Robert Ross argues (in chapter 3 of *The Georgian Revolt*), Monro was more sympathetic to modernism than Marsh and the other Georgians, but he was also a self-proclaimed and extremely influential defender of the Center against overeager literary leftists and stolid conservatives, and his case typifies the shallowness of the defense of tradition by this group.

Using this quick sampling, I wish to indicate the extent of the narrowing, at least in theory, of poetic aims in both camps. Alan Pryce-Jones correctly places the Georgians when he argues that finally "it is to the nineteenth century that most of them belong," but although he rightly sees them holding the opposite position to that of the private visionaries and didacticists of the 1930s, he does not develop the implications of his dichotomy: "they adopted a common attitude which aimed at percipience, not at intellectuality."[8] We should not confuse intellectuality with the esoteric allusiveness and cryptic strategies of the modernists, and therefore we should realize that the separation of percipience from intellectuality (and the defense of the obvious or the clichéd with realistic images is still a separation) is common to most poetry of the second decade and has its roots in romantic philosophy. The seeming difference between a philosophizing Wordsworth and a symbolizing Frenchman was only a temporary bifurcation of an inevitable development through the nineteenth to the twentieth century. The Georgians differ from the modernists simply in the ways they reflect that development. The real alternative is found in those rare poets who could truly dignify the few positive achievements of the previous century by being intelligent and percipient, concrete and universal, and personally and socially moral rather than egocentrically didactic.

Such poets are rare because, as the decade progressed, the opportunities for a fuller poetry became scarcer. The war tended to further separate the camps: its harsher realities, although briefly recorded by Sassoon, Owen, and Rosenberg, undermined the optimism of the surviving Georgians, many of whom retreated into what Ross calls "exotic moon-drenched landscapes." But insipidity is natural if the initial realism is founded on an unchallenged philosophical base no stronger than romanticism. Meanwhile the experimentalists with their French-inherited ironies and cynicisms were invigorated by post-war disillusionment: the *Zeitgeist* was forming in their favor. With imagist and especially vorticist theories sounding abroad more loudly, they could no longer be dismissed as promoting frenzy and formlessness (as were the pre-war futurists): their writings stressed form as well as energy, hatred of sentimentalizing about the future as well as the past, and a tradition was being invoked, however eccentric and un-English. But the talk of form had more to do with music than language, and there was a continuing disrespect for conventional syntax, discursive structures, and abstract diction. So the concern was still with registering images and suggesting emotions, and not with communicating complex understandings as well.

Nevertheless, the tide was beginning to run with the modernists. T. S. Eliot, for instance, in two attacks on the Georgians in *The Egoist* in 1917 and 1918,[9] could with more journalistic ease than usual and a minimum of actual argument assume that specifically English contents, patriotic and moral, were damaging to poetry. Notice the insidious "even" in this: "The Georgian poets insist upon the English countryside, and are even positively patriotic," and the underhanded denigration of provincialism in this praise of Monro:

> he is also less a Little-Englander, and deserves a public not purely insular. Often he employs the same tone of infantile simplicity . . . but the total effect of his last volume is not one of prettiness.[10]

Some of the Georgians, especially the later ones, may be guilty of complacency and vagueness, but Eliot's tone here suggests a smug disregard for the concern for and love of anything local and native. His major complaint is that Georgian poetry is "inbred": "the serious writer of verse must be prepared to cross himself with the best verse of other languages and the best prose of all languages." He then too quickly opposes "Georgian emotions" to "human ones"; therefore, not to be an internationalist is not to be human. He seems to have picked up Pound's curious notion of seriousness when he declares the second *Wheels* "a more serious book" than the third Georgian anthology, on the grounds that the former "as a whole has a dilettante effect, refreshing after the schoolroom."[11] Ross is right to charge Eliot here with distortion and willful confusion,[12] but of more concern is Eliot's implicit deprecation of moral content in verse and blindness to the possibility that a poet might be concrete if he stays in and fully understands his own language and traditions.

The fatal blow came with Middleton Murry's review of *Georgian Poetry 1918-19* in *Athenaeum* (5 December 1919).[13] According to Ross, "His forthright statement of the postwar anti-Georgian position merely summed up what many other poets and critics were thinking, but no one put the case quite so cogently,"[14] including apparently Eliot, whom Murry echoes. Both are concerned with being "serious" in a muddled age; both find the Georgians unserious because of their simplicity (Murry finds it "false," Eliot "infantile"), their vague emotions, and their public morality. Murry is upset by their "fundamental right-mindedness":

> You feel, somehow, that they might have been very wicked, and yet they are very good. There is nothing disturbing about them ... they are kind, generous, even noble.[15]

It seems that to be a serious poet in 1919 one cannot display too much stability and civic virtue.[16] Murry does differ from Eliot in being more irritated with the "false sophistication" of *Wheels*, which Eliot found "refreshing." But he ends the review with this:

> There is the opposition. Against the righteous man, the *mauvais sujet*. We sympathize with the *mauvais sujet*. If he is persistent and laborious enough, he may achieve poetry. But he must travel alone.[17]

Edward Marsh's anthology needed to be toppled from its pedestal, but not by such sympathies. Such sympathies also could cloud the accomplishment of Edward Thomas and cause those who wanted to salvage him from the Georgian wreck to try to read him as a modernist.

2

Now let me indicate more directly why Georgians in their verse could not offer a substantial threat to their opposition and did not learn enough from Hardy and the native tradition behind him to invigorate and extend the conventions of that tradition in this century. It will help us better recognize the alternative offered by Thomas. Even if we restrict our view to the early anthologies, in which most critics agree the best poetry of the entire series can be found, we still detect weaknesses arising from an uncritical acceptance of early romantic procedures and motifs as the most frequent manifestation of their anti-Victorianism. I call attention specifically to four weaknesses: an incomplete concern for form that results in ornamental rather than functional structures; realistic and dramatic textures that promote a simple, revived primitivism; anti-intellectualism; and, often because of the previous three, a lack of moral firmness.

If, as the *TLS* reviewer of the first volume claims, the newness of these poets is their intensified "desire . . . to clarify and shape experience, rather than to sit receptively awaiting its impact,"[18] then the clarifying amounts to little more than an eagerness to use colloquial and previously unpoetic diction—as when Rupert Brooke describes the contents of his vomit in "A Channel Passage" (not included in the anthology), or the notorious song of the old woman who comes to lay out King Lear's dead wife in Bottomley's play in the second anthology:

> A louse crept out of my lady's shift—
> Ahumm, Ahumm, Ahee—
> Crying "Oi! Oi! We are turned adrift;
> The lady's bosom is cold and stiffed,
> And her arm-pit's cold for me."

(II, 41)[19]

Shaping had less to do with rational and moral principles (with understanding) than with superficial aesthetics. The word "beauty" was still being used broadly and loosely in this decade. That is, to escape the poetic enervation of the aesthetes of the 1890s, the Georgians offered material that was direct, immediate, and dramatic; to avoid the formlessness they saw in their less cautious and often American contemporaries, they imposed forms onto unreconciled, sometimes still raw material. The problem is evident even in what is certainly one of the best poems in all five anthologies, Walter de la Mare's "The Listeners." The poem is a frustrated ballad in form and content. Although there are no dividing stanzas, four-line groupings are established by syntax and the *a b c b* rhyme scheme, with the second and fourth lines iambic trimeter and the first and third, if somewhat irregular, at least almost always containing four primary stressed syllables. The feminine endings of the unrhymed lines complement the abbreviated narrative in the creation, which is the poem's principal accomplishment, of a tone of sinister simplicity and delicate mystery. The poem offers what seems an episode in a larger, but ungiven, story: a traveller, honoring some pledge, knocks three times on the door of a lone house in the midst of a forest on a moon-lit night, but only unstirring "phantom listeners" now dwell there. It ends with the listeners hearing the rider remount and ride away, "And how the silence surged softly backward,/When the plunging hoofs were gone" (I, 71–72). The poem is most directly about the disturbance and re-emergence (that wonderful penultimate line) of silence, and the poem's restraint is its success. But it is perhaps too suggestive of a plot that does not exist, and when the narrative elements are extracted from the poem, we are left with an imagistic fragment. The poem is suspended between an old-fashioned and a modern mode, being neither one nor the other. The mysterious atmosphere depends a little too much on expectations raised and then unsatisfied in the reader.

In poems of considerably less control, the problem is more damaging, as in Wilfred Gibson's "The Gorse," in which a strict pattern (pentameter quatrains rhyming *a b a b*) serves almost no function at all. There are neither visual breaks between stanzas nor syntactical units defined by them: sentences begin and end and are structured irrespective of the poetic form. It is useless to speak of counterpointing; the poem's simple subject and pathetic tone do not support such complexities. The pattern is superfluous. Then there is the sheer meaninglessness of the formality of Ralph Hodgson's much acclaimed "The Bull"; four-stress lines with painful regularity fill up six-line stanzas (*a b b a c c*) that somehow have to move the narrative over stilted couplets such as this from the very first stanza: an old bull, "sick in soul" is alone, "Banished from the herd he led, / Bulls and cows a thousand head" (II, 137). Not only does the form not function here, it positively undermines whatever pathos exists in this sentimental and silly attempt to record the consciousness of a dying bull. Again we wonder about the meaning of *serious* in this decade when a *TLS* reviewer (quite possibly Gosse) could single out for high praise Hodgson's treatment of his subject: "He treats it seriously, and it seems to be a poem about a bull written by a bull with the gift of poetry."[20] I should mention in fairness that there is some formal dexterity in these early Georgian poems, notably G. K. Chesterton's deftly written little ballad, "The Song of Elf," the firm blank verse serving a significant theme in T. Sturge Moore's "A Sicilian Idyll," and of course John Masefield is almost always felicitous if nothing else, or at least he seems so after the ponderous incongruities so frequent elsewhere in the volumes.

One thing the Georgians shared with the futurists was a desire to return to the brutal and primitive; less extreme than their Italian contemporaries, they had simply to bring an English romantic convention up to date. Ross quotes Fletcher quoting Synge: "poetry, to be human again, must first learn to be brutal."[21] Synge got as far as the Aran Islands and Rupert Brooke actually voyaged to the South Pacific, but most poets took Wordsworth's example, together perhaps with a reserved fascination for the recent vagabondage of W. H. Davies, and turned to the unfortunates among England's lower classes as well as to the old staple, children. Edward Thomas noted the breadth of this concern in his reference in a review in The

Daily Chronicle (14 January 1913), to "the modern love of the simple and primitive, as seen in children, peasants, savages, early men, animals, and Nature in general."[22] But if they spread their sympathies around and added many realistic and dramatic surface details, the poems rarely realize enough context for these portraits to rise from Wordsworthian idealisms to the kind of pointed social criticism and moral penetration of a true realist like George Crabbe. The sympathy is never more complex than this from Davies's encounter with a London madman:

> Was it a man that had
> Suffered till he went mad?
> So many showers and not
> One rainbow in the lot;
> Too many bitter fears
> To make a pearl from tears.
> ("The Heap of Rags," I, 62)

There are Wordsworthian echoes throughout Davies: "The Mind's Liberty" is very like "The Reverie of Poor Susan," and a dramatic narrative on the death of a prostitute reminds us more of Wordsworth's simplicities than, for instance, of Hardy's dialectal directness in "The Ruined Maid":

> "Nell Barnes was bad on all you men,
> Unclean, a thief as well;
> Yet all my life I have not found
> A better friend than Nell."
> ("The Bird of Paradise," II, 73)

Then there is Gibson overhearing a "wild song" by a widowed bride ("Devil's Edge") who reminds us of the several abandoned women in the *Lyrical Ballads*.

Such renewed glorification of the low and simple is part of a larger resistance in most Georgians to intellectual sophistications. Wishing to eschew the decadent academism of a previous generation, they also kept themselves from questioning the assumptions of the naturalist philosophy they recalled naively. On the simplest level there is the ready faith in instinct and emotion. Davies praises a sheltered girl this way:

> Sweet Well-content, sweet Love-one-place,
> Sweet, simple maid, bless thy dear face;
> For thou hast made more homely stuff
> Nurture thy gentle self enough;
> I love thee for a heart that's kind—
> Not for the knowledge in thy mind.
> ("Sweet Stay-At-Home," II, 71)

This has little to do with the mature localism of Hardy and Thomas. We have the frequent fascinations with the enchanted and magical, engaging in the work of de la Mare and too often cloying elsewhere: in the unstructured celebrations in Edmund Beal Sargant's "The Cookoo Wood" and in the cutesy tale of Welsh magic by Francis Ledwidge, "The Wife of Llew." Masefield's "The days that made us happy make us wise" (from "Biography") suggests a Wordsworthian passivity, and there is more than a hint of pantheism in Harold Monro's address to the landscape around "Lake Leman": "Dwell as a spirit in me, O one/Sweet natural presence" (I, 134). A similar unitary life is suggested in Hodgson's pathetic fallacies and Blakean celebrations of nature: he hears, in "The Song of Honour" (II, 149), "the whole/Harmonious hymn of being roll/Up through the chapel of my soul." Blake, or at least the legend of Blake, is invoked in the opening of James Stephens's "In the Poppy Field": "Mad Patsy" tells the speaker that he has visions of angels walking on the sky and running to see poppies in the sun. And this madman must be wiser than the pragmatic and mundanely sane speaker: he can counter the latter's suggestion that the poppy is a "devil weed" with the pointed reply, "The devil has not any flower,/But only money in his power" (I, 181). Here primitivism spreads into pantheism. Walter de la Mare's claim that "the aim of these poets is as alien from that of 'The Prelude' as it is from that of 'Prometheus Bound,'" makes sense only if he means to dismiss these sentiments as merely decorative, which, of course, he does not. But I must agree with him when half a page earlier he says, "Those who seek in poetry ethical solace and edification, or demand of it a reasoned criticism of life, are unlikely to be won over."[23]

This edification and criticism need not be overt and should not be platitudinous. I am not agreeing with the reviewer for *The Spectator* who is disappointed by "Milk for the Cat" because Monro "has not moralized his lay."[24] That reader was looking for agreeable tags. Having said this, I can now lodge my final complaint against these Georgians: the absence of a firm moral base to their poetry. Nature worship, of course, could not provide such a base, and some Georgians understood this but could answer the defeated optimism of the Victorians and the ethereal escapism of the aesthetes with nothing better than a vigorous hedonism, often arising out of cynicism or vague nihilism. These responses are as anti-intellectual as the more positive ones, and none is an advancement over the nineteenth century. For example, the vague lament of Ronald Ross's "Hesperus" mixes Tennysonian diction with the often motiveless remorse of Shelley and Keats; addressing the "sweet silent star," Ross says,

> How many a one hath watched thee even as I,
> And unto thee and thy receding ray

> Poured forth his thoughts with many a treasured sigh
> Too sweet and strange for the remorseless day.
>
> (I, 165)

There is a motive for Robert Trevelyan's "Dirge," but it is so general that it makes us suspect that he is moved by fashion rather than felt experience. Earth is a wilderness, we are told; belief in life after death is a vain attempt to cheat an inevitable despair:

> Trust not fond hope,
> Nor think that bliss
> Which neither seems,
> Nor is,
> Aught else than grief.
>
> (I, 195)

With these lines, Marsh concludes his first very popular anthology, an anthology "issued in the belief that English poetry is now once again putting on a new strength and beauty," to help lovers of poetry "realize that we are at the beginning of another 'Georgian period'" ("Prefatory Note to First Edition"). This is another Georgian period, sharing and often intensifying the weaknesses of the earlier one.

Rupert Brooke best exemplifies the depressed pleasure seeker. The depression sometimes seems to be the result of his inability to share the unconsciousness of lesser animals; while the fish

> Sans providence, sans memory,
> Unconscious and directly driven,
> Fades to some dank sufficient heaven,

man must live consciously in a human world full of "the strife of limbs" and "sightless clinging," "where hope is fleet and thought flies after" ("The Fish"). And like many romantics he seeks mindless pleasures in exotic places:

> Hear the calling of the moon,
> . . . .
> And in the water's soft caress,
> Wash the mind of foolishness,
> Mamua, until the day.
> Spend the glittering moonlight there
> Pursuing down the soundless deep
> Limbs that gleam and shadowy hair,
> Or floating lazy, half-asleep.
> . . . .
> Well this side of Paradise! . . .
> There's little comfort in the wise.
>
> ("Tiare Tahiti," II, 52–53)

In "The Great Lover," he brings Shelley and Pater together ("Love is a flame;—we have beaconed the world's night," "Nothing remains") to provide a shadowy authority to his catalogue of pleasures, which may be more modern but is no more adequate for including "the keen/ Unpassioned beauty of a great machine" or "the benison of hot water." His eclecticism indicates just how superficial and desperate he is.

Sturge Moore seems to give us a dramatic portrait of a similar sensibility in "A Sicilian Idyll." Having had his optimism and rebelliousness dampened by experience, the still youthful but now "realistic" Delphis rejects civilization and the difficulties of living in it and takes the solitary way, giving himself to the moment because he cannot be an optimist:

> ... wearied peoples each in turn awake
> From virtue, as a man from his brief love,
> And, roughly shaken, face the useless truth;
> No answer to brute fact had e'er been found.
> . . . .
> A vagabond I shall be as the moon is.
> The sun, the waves, the winds, all birds, all beasts,
> Are ever on the move, and take what comes;
> . . . .
> Not even Memory shall follow Delphis,
> For I will yield to all impulse save hers,
> Therein alone subject to prescient rigour;
> . . . .
> Free minds must bargain with each greedy moment
> And seize the most that lies to hand at once.
>
> (I, 160–161)

We have here, as in Brooke and others, a post-Paterian version of what Morse Peckham once called "negative romanticism" ("a period of doubt, of despair, of religious and social isolation, of the separation of reason and creative power," a period frequented by the young Byron[25]). Moore, who was never properly a Georgian, by age and temperament, gives us reason in this long dramatic narrative to think he does not necessarily approve of Delphis. The same cannot be said, however, of Lascelles Abercrombie, one of the most respected of the Georgians. In his verse playlet, "The Sale of Saint Thomas," which opens the first anthology, he speaks through a "Stranger," who seems to be God and who has the last word in the play, to attack prudence:

> ... prudence is the deadly sin,
> And one that groweth deep into a life,
> With hardening roots that clutch about the breast.
> For this refuses faith in the unknown powers
> Within man's nature; shrewdly bringeth all
> Their inspiration of strange eagerness
> To a judgment bought by safe experience;

>   Narrows desire into the scope of thought.
>   . . . .
>   But send desire often forth to scan
>   The immense night which is thy greater soul.
>
>   (I, 20–21)

The advice is too inflated appropriately to conclude a poem about the cowardly Saint Thomas's reluctance to take Christianity to barbarous India. Abercrombie has been carried away. Just as Emerson does not mix well with Christianity, so these Georgians with no more than an incongruent formality and the ragged ends of Romantic thought and morality, regardless of their much professed sincerity, could not possibly defend any worthy tradition in the early twentieth century.

3

The anti-intellectual base of romantic philosophy and modernist technique and the morally incautious preference for isolated emotional experience have caused critics to mistake Edward Thomas's unassertive manner for either romantic or modernist instability. Not understanding that moral firmness need not be expressed as the kind of overt and static moralizing one finds in bad Victorian and Edwardian verse, they are too ready to find Thomas insecure, directionless, irresolute, uncommitted, restless, and tension-ridden. Because the dichotomy for them is so clear, these are terms of praise. In an early essay on Thomas, Theresa Ashton argues that he is too contemplative, too clear of vision, too quiet, and too gentle to properly be called a poet:

> Edward Thomas' apprehension of objectivity was the apprehension of a long mature imagination; and his nature was above all contemplative. The still clarity of the vision of such an imagination has its attendant risk of failure; for too keen a sense of eternity may hold back creation. . . . such detailed uniformly focussed attention belongs more properly to prose.[26]

His best poems are the less detailed, "more lyrical" ones in which, in Ashton's words, "he found poetic freedom." The less clear the vision, the more successful the poem. An example of the strength of the assumption is found in Ralph Lawrence's generally sensible appreciation: praising Thomas's "dispassionate accuracy of observation," and claiming that because of this he "was no sentimentalist; not even a romantic," Lawrence nevertheless goes on to find and commend in Thomas's poetry "mysticism," "ecstasy," and "self-communing reverie."[27] Extremes are still the stuff of true poetry.

Then there are Hugh Underhill and Maire Quinn[28] who published essays on Thomas a year apart in the early 1970s, one to prove Thomas a romantic, the other to prove him a modernist: both cite "Over the Hills" as evidence. Here is Thomas's interesting but minor poem:

> Often and often it came back again
> To mind, the day I passed the horizon ridge
> To a new country, the path I had to find
> By half-gaps that were stiles once in the hedge,
> The pack of scarlet clouds running across
> The harvest evening that seemed endless then
> And after, and the inn where all were kind,
> All were strangers. I did not know my loss
> Till one day twelve months later suddenly
> I leaned upon my spade and saw it all,
> Though far beyond the sky-line. It became
> Almost a habit through the year for me
> To lean and see it and think to do the same
> Again for two days and a night. Recall
> Was vain: no more could the restless brook
> Ever turn back and climb the waterfall
> To the lake that rests and stirs not in its nook,
> As in the hollow of the collar-bone
> Under the mountain's head of rush and stone.[29]

Underhill is intent on finding similarities between Thomas and Keats: "the kind of passive extinction of self in the experience of the moment," "embracing of death," and a reconciliation with reality after an attempted escape. This poem, he claims, is an instance of such a reconciliation. The memory (2–8), he says, is "of the poet's restless and impossible quest"; the "loss" suggests "the extinction of self in the moment of release as well as the failure to recover the moment"; and the final image is an acknowledgment that fulfillment constantly eludes the poet. Thomas's own diction is never as inflated as that of some of his readers intent on making him more intense than he is. One wonders, if the memory is of "an inward quest for fulfillment or self-extinction, for 'sanctuary' or rest," why the quest lasted no more than "two days and a night," a detail that should warn us against too eager a symbolic reading. Surely the "loss" is less private and extreme than Underhill would have it: it can quite satisfactorily refer to the simple fact that the past cannot be recovered; the memory of it, however, can be rediscovered: "I ... saw it all/. ... It became/Almost a habit ... for me/To lean and see it and think to do the same/Again. ..."

Quinn, who like Leavis wants to set Thomas against Hardy, whose

"Victorian 'solidity'" and confidence in the value of the personal past the younger poet lacks, also ignores this passage (10–14), because she wants the distinction clear: in Thomas, remembering brings "dulled consciousness." Nothing could be farther from the truth, as I shall insist later. Quinn emphasizes the last six lines of the poem: the "image of the brook points to the irreversibility of life and also equates recall with regression," the lake being natal and womb-like. The key word for her is obviously "restless"; her thesis in the essay is that Thomas's poetry "reflects the subjectivity and incertitude of the modern mind." Thus this poem's tone is "restless dissatisfaction" and frustration. There is tension everywhere, even at the source: she wants "rush" to suggest "rapid forward movement." She does not explain what that could mean about the lake that "rests and stirs not." The phrase "irreversibility of life" is also too eager given the quieter tone than Quinn recognizes. Besides, and this both critics have overlooked, the personal loss is not of a personal past but of a social one. What he remembers is not action (questing or journeying) but things, social things: "the day," "the path," the "inn"—even the "pack" of clouds is communal. The curious detail in line 4 ("half-gaps that were stiles once in the hedge") indicates that even when he first made his trip by foot "to the new country," the once well-travelled path he followed had fallen into disuse. The loss then, as so often in Thomas's poetry, is of a rural life of hospitable strangers, well-worn paths, and a productive harmony with nature (it is harvest time), a life that he has seen threatened since his youth and that he fears the war will help to end.

Having mentioned Leavis, I should pause over his influential assessment of Thomas in *New Bearings in English Poetry*. Emerging in 1932, it did much to encourage readers of Thomas by disassociating him from the Georgians, who were then suffering their lowest reputation. Unfortunately, in his concern to promote the poetry he then thought related most vigorously to the modern world, Leavis overstated the case for Thomas's modernity. The mistake develops from an inadequate assessment of Thomas Hardy: a true Victorian who "inhabits a solid world," a naive poet of simple attitudes and outlook, attitudes characterized by a "naive conservatism" and "precritical innocence," a poet whose "rank as a major poet rests upon a dozen poems," who cannot and should not be very influential. Thomas, then, "a very original poet who devoted great technical subtlety to the expression of a distinctively modern sensibility" is, in his lack of certainty, continual questioning, "negativeness," and recordings of "modern disintegration" and "relaxed and undirected consciousness," directly opposed to "Hardy's Victorian solidity":

> Only a very superficial classification could associate Edward Thomas with Mr. Blunden, or with the Georgians at all. ... Mr. Blunden's poems are frankly

'composed', but Edward Thomas's seem to happen. It is only when the complete effect has been registered in the reader's mind that the inevitability and the exquisite economy become apparent. A characteristic poem of his has the air of being a random jotting down of chance impressions and sensations, the record of a moment of relaxed and undirected consciousness. The diction and movement are those of quiet, ruminative speech. But the unobtrusive signs accumulate, and finally one is aware that the outward scene is accessory to an inner theatre. Edward Thomas is concerned with the finer texture of living, the here and now, the ordinary moments, in which for him the 'meaning' (if any) resides. It is as if he were trying to catch some shy intuition on the edge of consciousness that would disappear if looked at directly. Hence, too, the quietness of the movement, the absence of any strong accent or gesture.[30]

I do not disagree with much of this, and the characterization does indeed fit some of Thomas's poems, but not the best or the most representative. My disagreement is with Leavis's emphases. First, there may be a surface ease and sense of spontaneity in some of the poems, but the "inevitability" and "exquisite economy" are only possible, Leavis fails to add, because Thomas's consciousness is anything but relaxed and undirected. He was a mature writer when he began writing poetry, and his poems (as Pound similarly said of Hardy's) are the harvest of having written thirty books of prose first. Leavis does not adequately stress or explain the "seem" and "has the air of" and "as if." Second, the movement of Thomas's verse *is* quiet, but more often because of a certain assuredness and seriousness than because he was trying to sneak up on "a shy intuition on the edge of consciousness." The signs accumulate inevitably and unobtrusively because he deals with the centers of consciousness, with agreed truths and expectations. The dealing itself may be personal, but his themes and concerns are mostly social.

These misemphases have been repeated by subsequent critics: H. Coombes stresses "an almost ever-present sense of an elusive element in consciousness" and Thomas's lack of "solid views"; William Cooke finds Thomas "another of those 'rootless moderns'" and skeptical next to the confident Frost; John Danby takes this into the age of the New Critics by emphasizing the tensions and polarities in his verse stemming from a lack of commitment and his sense of a present discontinuous with the past; Roland Mathias will go so far as to call him a relativist and nominalist ("his solitary impression" was "all that he cared for"); J. P. Ward sees him as one of the bleaker existentialists, as "privatized, inner and alienated," and his poetry "reflexive" and absorbed with the elusive; Jan Marsh talks of his "endless, unsatisfied searching"; Andrew Motion finds the varying stress patterns reflecting "a mind actually engaged in the act of thinking, rather than offering its concluded thoughts"; W. J. Keith contrasts Wordsworth to Thomas, whose poems bear witness to the "uncertainty of comprehension and significance of any experience."[31] These readers have much to say about Thomas that is useful, but these frequent echoes are damaging and often lack the undeveloped qualifications of Leavis's initiating comments.

In perhaps the best of the book-length studies to appear so far, *The Imagination of Edward Thomas* (1986), Michael Kirkham goes some way to resolving the problem of Thomas's placement within the romantic and modernist traditions. He argues that Thomas is better read as an uncertain romantic, clearly in the conversational-meditative tradition fostered by Wordsworth and Coleridge, but without the certainty of personal vision and pseudo-religious purpose of those early romantics, and with some of the restlessness of many sensitive inhabitants of the bewildering and faith-destroying twentieth century. One side of Thomas's achievement is still unaccounted for, however. Kirkham cannot see Thomas's possible links with an older tradition than romanticism and is himself rather too restricted by New Critical assumptions about poetry, especially the one that sees poetry as essentially paradoxical, ambivalent, and tension-ridden.[32] Kirkham is too keenly in search of subtlety, pushing delicate, poised complexities of statement over the edge into mysteries and paradoxes, what he calls the "shimmer of uncertainty" and the "inconclusive openness" of Thomas's verse.[33] The best poems, I contend, were written by Thomas when he transcended his melancholia and despair to satisfy what R. George Thomas calls his "urgency to convince."[34] His wife, Helen, has said, "Edward was always a truth teller," but he could only have been truly satisfied with telling the truth, not of our inevitable uncertainty, but of the country creed he defended so eloquently in his most mature and assured work, when he achieved what he himself called "a deep ease and confidence ... underneath that unrest." Again he said: "It is not, however, to a man walking for pleasure that we shall go for a sense of roads, but to one like Bunyan. *Pilgrim's Progress* is full of the sense of roads."[35] The man who wrote that could not be satisfied with the man Kirkham or most of the other recent critics find in the poems.

This leads me to my final general point about Thomas's reputation. William Cooke, who is not as insistent as is Leavis or even Kirkham in arguing Thomas's modernity, characterizes one poem as "overheard rather than heard."[36] Other critics have recently picked up the figure, expropriated by Cooke from J. S. Mill, and applied it more generally to Thomas: Edna Longley refers to Thomas's "inner 'soliloquy'"; W. K. Keith says, "we feel we are overhearing Thomas"; Andrew Motion contends that "while Frost addresses his audience confidently, Thomas's poems seem to be overheard."[37] My point can best be made by looking at the poem that gave rise to Cooke's original comment:

>   Tall nettles cover up, as they have done
>   These many springs, the rusty harrow, the plough

> Long worn out, and the roller made of stone:
> Only the elm butt tops the nettles now.
>
> This corner of the farmyard I like most:
> As well as any bloom upon a flower
> I like the dust on the nettles, never lost
> Except to prove the sweetness of a shower.

The poem *is* an undertone, as Cooke says, especially compared with Frost's epigram, "The Wrights' Biplane." But this does not mean it is overheard. People, even poets, do not talk to themselves this way. Thomas is quietly talking to us. Public statement need not be loud and assertive, as are the puns and anecdotes in Frost's poem. Thomas's undertone could be a sign of quiet assurance just as Frost's tone of "all-round confidence" could be a sign of private insecurity. "Tall Nettles" is a reminder of how the less conventionally beautiful can sharpen as well as reorder our conventional sense of the beautiful. I call particular attention to the care Thomas takes, and this is *very* characteristic, to place the experience in time ("as they have done/These many springs"); this prevents the impression that the experience is unique. The more experiences are understood as caused *in time*, the less unique they seem; the less unique they seem, the more available they are. The poem records not a private impression but an understanding and a recognition. It is this sense of time and traditional country knowing in Thomas's verse that has not been recognized fully enough.

To deny that there are hesitations and uncertainties in Thomas's poetic voice would be foolish, but there are firmer contexts and bases to the surface equivocations than are acknowledged by critics; the restlessness so often detected is a misreading of a desire to inquire into and even correct some conventional and tempting notions about certainty. Thomas is modern in the sense that Hardy is modern: he is against the philosophical pretensions of the early romantics and the complacencies of the later romantics, but at the same time he has a firm sense of time and place and human tradition that prevents him from being skeptical or amoral. It is understandable that he is often compared to Keats, the most obervant and least philosophical of the romantics, but the comparison can be misleading: Thomas is more reserved and more mature than Keats.

"The Trumpet" was written at the Royal Artillery Barracks, Trowbridge, in late September 1916. In a letter to Eleanor Farjeon introducing the poem, Thomas wrote, "you can see I have some ease, because I have written some verses suggested by the trumpet calls which go all day. They are not well done and the trumpet is cracked, but the Reveille pleases me (more than it does most sleepers). Here is the result."[38] The poem hints at a slight advantage in forgetfulness (one remembers Keats's "Ode to a Nightingale"), but is more concerned with mounting defenses against the night; the clearer advantage is an acute awareness of stages in time's passage. The first stanza, almost half the poem, economically places the scene in time:

> Rise up, rise up,
> And, as the trumpet blowing
> Chases the dreams of men,
> As the dawn glowing
> The stars that left unlit
> The land and water,
> Rise up and scatter
> The dew that covers
> The print of last night's lovers—
> Scatter it, scatter it!
>
> (1–10)

As it is natural for the light to follow the darkness, so men must expel their "unlit" dreams. Thomas parallels the set of three natural phases, in lines 4–6 (the night's blackness, the dawn's glowing, the day's lighting) with a second set of three phases, this time involving human action, in lines 7–9 (the print of the night's lovers, the dew cover, the scattering of the dew). The next and last stanza opens with a commitment to clarity—the only forgetting that is advised is of illusions (dreams and the insufficient star light):

> While you are listening
> To the clear horn,
> Forget, men, everything
> On this earth newborn,
> Except that it is lovelier
> Than any mysteries.
>
> (11–16)

The poem closes then with the reversal of a Petrarchan figure and a reminder of immediate duty:

> Open your eyes to the air
> That has washed the eyes of the stars
> Through all the dewy night:
> Up with the light,
> To the old wars;
> Arise, arise!
>
> (17–22)

"Old wars" certainly introduces a complexity: Thomas is no compliant patriot, but the first stanza's suggestion of a past continuous with the present and the repeated imagery in both stanzas of cleared perception invest that phrase with more than just cynicism toward the cant of "a war to end war." Thomas's nature, unlike Keats's, does not call to escape, and unlike Brooke on the one hand and Sassoon and Owen on the other, Thomas is both committed to and realistic about this war (see, for instance, "No Case of Petty Right or Wrong"). There is a similar mixture of national pride and regret in Hardy's war poems. I disagree with William Cooke, who finds in the final lines "a note of weary resignation rather than joyful acceptance."[39] The word "old" does qualify the exclamation point of the next line, but the tone, which has been carefully prepared for earlier, is of firm and realistic, but not joyful, acceptance. Cooke's alternatives are too simple. He says, "It was as if he had to pervert his own nature to adapt himself to the war." Actually, it is the strength of that nature, refusing to be and always aware of the dangers of being misled, that allows him to realize daily necessities and to adapt.

Although correcting, Thomas is careful not to give the impression that he has final answers. The absolute worries Thomas as much as it does Hardy. In the last lines of his fine poem "The Path," he says that there is no easy access to the truth, whether it be by means of the road (the adult, "level" place where "men and women / Content themselves" [6–7]), or the wood (nature and specifically for Thomas the unknown and perhaps death), or the path (between the human and the natural, frequented by fanciful children).[40] The poem could serve as a critique of de la Mare:

> But the road is houseless, and leads not to school.
> To see a child is rare there, and the eye
> Has but the road, the wood that overhangs
> And underyawns it, and the path that looks
> As if it led on to some legendary
> Or fancied place where men have wished to go
> And stay; till, sudden, it ends where the wood ends.
>
> (16–22)

Life is surrounded by the unknown ("the wood that overhangs / And underyawns") and there is no escape—the path does not guide one through the wood to anything or anyplace beyond. Like Hardy, Thomas is acutely aware of human limitations. Man's attempt to share fully in nature's efficiency is impossible, he says in "For These." After three stanzas describing the ideal life of the Back-to-the-Land movement of the late nineteenth century, he concludes:

> For these I ask not, but neither too late
> Nor yet too early, for what men call content,
> And also that something may be sent
> To be contented with, I ask of fate.
>
> (13–16)

Thomas's unobtrusive moral concern is in the qualification of the first and second lines: content at the right time is a just reward, perpetual ease is both impossible and, if possible, stagnating. In "Interval" he admits he cannot share the comfort of the "woodman's cot," but such "unwavering" comfort is only possible if one is oblivious to the subtleties of the scene, awareness of which might just be more legitimately if less immediately comforting. The interval is a brief twilight respite between a wild day and a wilder night. The road is "firmly soaked" and the beeches "keep/A stormy rest" (5, 9–11). These oxymorons prepare for the general one that closes the poem and that suggests more than just a natural atmosphere: "This roaring peace" (32). Another interval observed and felt keenly is described in "Sowing," in which he celebrates man's productive use of nature and slightly regrets the end of that practical interchange.

> A long stretched hour it was;
> Nothing undone
> Remained; the early seeds
> All safely sown.
>
> (9–12)

Richer examples of this concern are "As the Team's Head-Brass" (with its obvious echoes of Hardy's "In Time of 'The Breaking of Nations'") and "Haymaking."

Now perhaps we can have a better perspective on Thomas's famous melancholy, which should not be confused with modernist disillusionments and cynicisms. As the biographers make clear, it was a minor psychological disorder: it was, as Thomas said of Hardy's pessimism, neither literary nor insincere.[41] Because it was a problem seen as a problem, its presence in the poetry as distinct from the life is rarely indulgent. Even in the bleakest of his poems, "Rain," the "love of death" (17) is quickly qualified in the last two lines; the quietening intelligence rather than the extreme emotion has the last word: "If love it be towards what is perfect and/Cannot, the tempest tells me, disappoint" (17–18). In "Liberty," written just more than a month before, he is more explicit about the need to resist the temptation to escape to some illusion of perfection. Here the Keatsian echo is ironic: "And yet I still am half in love with pain,/With what is imperfect" (24–25). Escape, he says earlier in the poem, would be into inertia and irresponsibility:

> ... There's none less free than who
> Does nothing and has nothing else to do,
> Being free only for what is not to his mind
> And nothing is to his mind.
>
> (12–15)

Meaningful life, he understands, occurs in responsibility. "Rain" could do with more of this consolation; two lines, however well-placed, are not enough. It is curious but not surprising that so many consider such an unwholesome poem to be one of Thomas's best.

We now can turn to the more positive notes in Thomas's poetry. The staying power as expressed in his healthiest poems is based on his thorough knowledge of and trust in traditional continuities, especially seasonal change and rural man's productive accommodation to it. Jeremy Hooker, in one of the best essays yet written on Thomas's verse, makes the relevant point:

> Like our major 'nature' poets Edward Thomas knows that Nature is not picturesque, not a pastoral tapestry the poet can unpick to adorn his own fancy, or only a neutral source of imagery, but first and foremost the 'maternal stone' of a civilization, and the home of the society which tends it. This knowledge is a shaping influence on his poetry.[42]

Unlike Wordsworth, however, Thomas has no illusions about a spiritually animated and responsive nature. Thomas is in a sense an elegist not just of the tradition of rural England but of Natural Law itself. His love is for the England of Shakespeare when a natural order was still believed in. (One of Thomas's favorite poems was Ben Jonson's "To Penshurst.") Wordsworth Protestantized nature; he is an elegist of his own youthful communings with the landscape, not of a realistic social adjustment. Thomas's less private view results in a specificity, both temporal and geographical, rarely found in Wordsworth. It is a substantial rather than impressionistic specificity because of his respect for memory and continuity. Because they start with precisely defined times and places, some of his best poems are able to move securely toward general statements. In poems like "The Manor Farm," "Haymaking," and "Adlestrop," the outward scene is accessory to more than just an inner theatre.

"The Manor Farm" begins with the poet's eye moving from "a thin gilding beam" of briefly unfrozen mud to a farm house with pigeons nestled in its roof, a church and yew tree opposite, and the sound of cart-horses swishing their tails against a solitary fly. Only when he comes to the manmade scene can he properly value this interval between winter and spring as "more than a pretty February thing." The atmosphere of cooperative order is enhanced by the balancing and enclosing in the structure of these lines:

> ... I came down to the old Manor Farm,
> And church and yew-tree opposite, in age
> Its equals and in size. Small church, great yew
> And farmhouse slept in a Sunday silentness.
>
> (7–10)

One can understand why Leavis would claim that Thomas's poems "seem to happen," but surely the stress must be on "seem"—the lines are very carefully composed. The details are accessory to a public statement, they secure the generalizations:

> The Winter's cheek flushed as if he had drained
> Spring, Summer, and Autumn at a draught
> And smiled quietly. But 'twas not Winter—
> Rather a season of bliss unchangeable
> Awakened from farm and church where it had lain
> Safe under tile and thatch for ages since
> This England, Old already, was called Merry.
>
> (18–24)

Thomas's attentiveness to the transitions between the seasonal divisions allows him to solidify the moment to authenticate and revitalize the abstraction (the cliché) of the last line. That is, by not denying that it is only a passing moment, he can emphasize man's success in steadying such passing ("Safe under tile and thatch for ages").

The structure of "Haymaking" is similar. The opening couplet announces the procedure in an image:

> After night's thunder far away had rolled
> The fiery day had a kernel sweet of cold.
>
> (1–2)

The darkness and the storm are not only not forgotten, they are responsible for the crispness of the otherwise hot day. The cold "kernel" prepares us for the value abstracted in the final lines and "fiery day" for the reminders of activity and transience (uncurling clouds, tumbling mill-foot water, birds singing and shrieking, travelling scents of woodbine and hay) surrounding the stilled center where the haymakers rest, and it is literally a center:

> The team, as still, until their task was due,
> Beside the labourers enjoyed the shade
> That three squat oaks *mid-field* together made
> Upon a *circle* of grass and weed uncut,
> And on the hollow, once a chalk-*pit*. . . .
>
> (26–30, emphasis mine)

But even among the earlier images of transience, there are seeming permanencies: the clouds are compared to "the first gods before they made the world/And misery, swimming the stormless sea," and the birds sing "unceasingly." Time and timelessness cannot be divided clearly. We never forget that that which is being held is only a moment, and that it is being held to understand its relation to its past and future:

> The men leaned on their rakes, about to begin,
> But still. And all were silent. All was old,
> This morning time, with a great age untold,
> Older than Clare and Cowper, Morland and Crome,
> Than, at the field's far edge, the farmer's home,
> A white house crouched at the foot of a great tree.
> Under the heavens that know not what years be
> The men, the beasts, the trees, the implements
> Uttered even what they will in times far hence—
> All of us gone out of the reach of change—
> Immortal in a picture of an old grange.
>
> (32–42)

"About to begin, / But still," "All was old, / This morning time." The time is seemingly permanent because it is renewable, as recorded by those mentioned in the fourth line. The order of the items in the eighth line is natural, and the rhythm of the last line, with "picture" in the middle of three light and rapid feet and the "old grange" drawn out into a near spondee, takes the emphasis away from the artifact and places it back not on nature but on man's (literal) accommodation to and with nature. And we had to move from the particular to the general to secure it. The moment has been held by the secure understanding of the stability of such human action adjusted to non-human constraints. The poem defines and illustrates the tradition itself.

"Adlestrop" is another held moment, this time more concerned with individual memory. At first the poem is about an association of a place name, a permanent abstraction, with details of the transitory sights and sounds Thomas experienced while momentarily and unexpectedly stopped at a small rural station. The association seems initially to be colored by a pervading sense of isolation:

> The steam hissed. Someone cleared his throat.
> No one left and no one came
> On the bare platform. What I saw
> Was Adlestrop—only the name
>
> And willows, willow-herb, and grass,
> And meadowsweet, and haycocks dry,
> No whit less still and lonely fair
> Than the high cloudlets in the sky.
>
> (5–12)

But finally the isolation gives way to a sense of continuity:

> And for that minute a blackbird sang
> Close by, and round him, mistier,
> Farther and farther, all the birds
> Of Oxfordshire and Gloucestershire.
>
> (13–16)

The bold rhyming and the controlled enjambments and caesurae leading to the grand sweep of those final multisyllabic county names hold and calm the feeling; Thomas has recognized relatedness, not discovered uniqueness. This feeling of a larger continuity has nothing to do with pantheism but rather with knowledge of the typical, the type—and the security that comes with such knowledge.

These poems do not offer us timeless revelations; they are about the meaningfulness of moments in time, about the persistence of the past into the present, and about how, to the diligent and perceptive, knowledge of the past can stabilize to a limited extent the insecure present. The man who wrote the poems could not have thought that remembering brings dulled consciousness, as Maire Quinn claims in her effort to make Thomas not sound like Hardy.[43] Besides, why was Thomas often so distressed by the difficulties he had remembering thoroughly enough? In saying that the past should not be turned away from, he was not saying that it was easy to remember much less bring back the past, especially his own. "Old Man" is the most poignant instance of this and one of Thomas's most moving poems.

> I have mislaid the *key*. I sniff the spray
> And think of nothing; I see and I hear nothing;
> Yet seem, too, to be listening, lying in wait
> For what I *should*, yet never can, remember.
> (32–35, emphasis mine)

The problem is summed up in "Two Houses":

> And the hollow past
> Half yields the dead that never
> More than half-hidden lie.
> (25–27)

Understanding the dangers of ignoring the past, Thomas was also careful that his attachments were sound. There is no regressive longing for a lost innocence, maternal coziness, or primitive exoticism. "We have been robbed," he wrote in *The Country*, "of the small intelligible England of Elizabeth and given the word Imperialism instead."[44] One might add, remembering Hardy's preference, "the word British instead." It has to do with historical as well as geographical limits. "Tears," written the same day as "Adlestrop," parallels the phrases "English Countrymen" and "British Grenadiers" and seems to regret the transformation of the one into the other. A combe symbolizes, in a poem with that title, the "dark, ancient and dark" past; its mouth is stopped with "bramble, thorn, and briar," it shuts out "the sun of Winter" and "the moon of Summer," and it houses "that most ancient Briton of English beasts, the badger." The precivilized past has almost as many dangers as a present uninformed by the past.

The acuteness of Thomas's descriptions and the cautiously assured tones result naturally from his keen sense of location in time and place. They are the compensations for the relative lack of adventurousness and ambition in his style. That style is the most telling evidence of Thomas's resistance to anything that might threaten his hard-won selfhood. Helen Thomas repeatedly tells us of his reserve. He used to make fun of her bohemian friends with their "serious cults of purity and freedom and nakedness," finally convincing her that their "unconvention" was almost as intolerant as her parents' convention. When she taught for a while among progressive schoolteachers, she says, his "quick eye for superficiality was never taken in" by their liberal experiments. He even corrected her enthusiasm for free love, "telling me that [it] was only another bondage, a new-thought-out idea with no tradition of human wisdom behind it."[45]

The reader is surprised then to come upon a poem like the very popular "Lights Out." Despite its control of movement and exactness of statement and despite Thomas's circumstances when it was written, in November 1916 (critics have alluded to both), the quietness with which he longs for death ("The unfathomable deep/Forest where all must lose/Their way" [2-4]) gives undue solidity to an immature emotion.

> Its silence I hear and obey
> That I may lose my way
> And myself.
>
> (28-30)

Our sympathy for Thomas about to be sent to France cannot take the place of a critical attitude toward the temptation.

The plainness that characterizes Thomas's style[46] so much of the time promotes honesty and courage. The minimal metaphoric cover entails a greater responsibility for the soundness of thoughts and feelings. As Thomas's descriptive accuracy often validates his move to general conclusions, so his plainness allows him to capture with precision movements of abstract thought. We see it in many of the poems and passages already quoted, especially "Liberty" and "For These." The style is the perfect vehicle for this honest and completely unpretentious expression of love for his wife:

> I would give you back yourself,
> And power to discriminate
> What you want and want it not too late,
> Many fair days free from care
> And heart to enjoy both foul and fair,

>   And myself, too, if I could find
>   Where it lay hidden and it proved kind.
>
>   ("Helen," 16–22)

It even exposes an undeveloped talent for epigrammatic statement:

>   When he should laugh the wise man knows full well:
>   For he knows what is truly laughable.
>   But wiser is the man who laughs also,
>   Or holds his laughter, when the foolish do.
>
>   ("When He Should Laugh")

Discussing in 1938 the decline in quality of the last two Georgian anthologies, Herbert Palmer implicitly summed up a set of literary and social values that allowed for the triumph of modernism, and for the misemphases of Edward Thomas's admirers. Palmer remarks that the moon-worship of the later Georgians "meant that passion was dying, that it was thought better that it should die ... henceforth poets must seek strength in complete escape.... The sun, the old life-giver, had gone corrupt; the moon, the new life-giver, was to be the symbol of the new serene order in the world of poetry, of art, of human life. Suppression! Resignation! Restraint!"[47] By being so easily linked with resignation and suppression, restraint drops into disrespect. Yet it is the possibility of restraint *not* to resign, to clarify rather than suppress emotions that marks the significance of Edward Thomas. He is not a profound poet, but, in his quiet and realistic defense of a rural tradition that even the non-English cannot allow to die, a valuable poet, in an age that lost its perspective amidst nostalgic imitations and aggressive experiments.

3
Poets of the First World War

Both Jon Silkin in *Out of Battle* (1972) and Paul Fussell in *The Great War and Modern Memory* (1975) begin their influential and well-received studies of the poetry of World War I with chapters on Thomas Hardy, the former complaining of Hardy's failures in his war poetry to continue with the antiwar emphasis of his earlier Boer War poems and *The Dynasts*, while the latter, concentrating on *Satires of Circumstance* (published in November 1914), commends Hardy's clairvoyance just as a war was beginning that was to be "more ironic than any before or since."[1] These distortions are characteristic of the two tendencies in recent critical dealings with the war poets. Those few critics, such as Silkin, who are willing openly to confront and assess the ideas of a poem, are almost always looking for early twentieth-century formulations of their own post–World War II and Vietnam antiwar sentiments. Most other critics, such as Fussell, those still uncomfortable with political or moral ideas in verse, are no less liberal but stop short with explicit applications of modernist criteria, especially that of irony. The comfortable hindsight of such critics not only misplaces this phase of Hardy's work but also almost consequenty disallows an appreciation of the less radical younger poets of 1914–18. I want to suggest a different set of criteria and poets of a wider and I think more mature perspective on the horrors and waste of that war. I am disagreeing with the critics not about the nature of World War I, but only about what may constitute an adequate poetic response to it.[2]

We begin with Hardy's war poems. As so often with the verse of the early decades of this century, a standard is set by Hardy.[3] Of the two critics I have mentioned, Silkin is more unjust to Hardy: while Fussell simply ignores Hardy's unironic "Poems of War and Patriotism" in *Moments of Vision and Miscellaneous Verses* (1917), the volume that followed *Satires of Circumstance*, Silkin looks directly at those later poems and misrepresents them. First of all, of the seventeen poems in the group, he names only four, emphasizing the two least characteristic, "Men Who March Away" and "A Call to National Service," as if they were the most characteristic, and thereby generalizes freely: "Hardy's poems of the First War are neither indictments of war, nor ... tentative gropings," but are "mainly distortions," "deceitful" and "declamatory propaganda," no better than "recruiting songs." He grudgingly mentions two other poems, "Often When Warring" and "In Time of 'The Breaking of Nations,'" as momentary defections from "blind patriotism" that are nonetheless "simplistic."[4] Secondly, he fails to acknowledge qualifying complexities in those first two poems he does treat.

"Men Who March Away" was first published as "Song of the Soldiers" in *The Times* of 9 September 1914, and is often cited as exemplifying the intensely patriotic fervor of those early months of the war (Silkin remarks snidely that "Hardy was quick off the mark"). There is nothing, of course, inherently wrong with agreeing with a popular sentiment, but Hardy as usual gives us more. The poem is not a "braggadocio boast" as Silkin implies, but more quietly a defense and explanation of their motives by soldiers answering cynical intellectuals who claim the soldiers are ignorant pranksters. The first two stanzas are slightly indignant questions: "What of the faith and fire within us ...?" and "Is it a purblind prank, O think you,/Friend with the musing eye ...?" The last three stanzas directly answer the charges, with the last stanza a more assertive version of the first ("Hence the faith and fire within us"). The third and fourth are quoted most often:

> Nay. We well see what we are doing,
>   Though some may not see—
>   Dalliers as they be—
>   England's need are we;
> Her distress would leave us rueing:
> Nay. We well see what we are doing,
>   Though some may not see!
>
> In our heart of hearts believing
>   Victory crowns the just,
>   And that braggarts must
>   Surely bite the dust,
> Press we to the field ungrieving,
> In our heart of hearts believing
>   Victory crowns the just.
>
> (15–28)

One can object to the cliché in the middle of the fourth stanza and to the easy equation in the third stanza of particular ruling politicians' (honorable or dishonorable) objectives with "England's need,"[5] but not even Hardy, hardly less Jon Silkin, could in 1914 have foreseen the coming indecisiveness of Asquith, incompetence of Kitchener, and inflexibility of Haig. The poem after all is expressing dramatically the selfless (if perhaps innocent) resolve of those early recruits; what it objects to is not worldly wisdom but selfish cynicism. There are braggarts in the poem, but they are

Prussian militarists, not the faithful English soldiers. The poem is rhetorically defensive, not aggressive. In addition, further qualifications come with the recognition by the soldiers that they are "Leaving all that here can win us" (suggesting the difficulty and the necessity of their decision—they temporarily give up what is worth saving), and with the refrain in the third and fourth lines of the opening and closing stanzas:

> ... the faith and fire within us
> Men who march away
> Ere the barn-cocks say
> Night is growing gray,
> Leaving. ...

I do not know where the "jaunty rhythms" are that Silkin finds in the poem, but they are certainly not in these lines: the persistent enjambments dampen any potentially emphatic regularity and press us toward that important condition, "Leaving," that emphasizes the strength of their "faith." They are not joining up when victory seems likely, hoping to share in the subsequent glory. With victory (the light) not yet in view, they act out of belief in the absolute value of justice. In this darkness, however, it is not they who are "purblind," but the "hoodwink[ed]" skeptics. The Spirit Sinister of *The Dynasts*, we remember, is allowed to work only as long as the Will is unconscious. These soldiers insist that they know ("see" is their word) what they are doing—that is the poem's emotional impulse. Hardy is simply dignifying their dedication.

Silkin thinks it "surprising" that Edward Thomas liked Hardy's poem, but it is not in the least surprising. Thomas, a mature soldier as well as poet, had a similar faith: England, he says in "This is No Case of Petty Right or Wrong,"

> ... is all we know and live by, and we *trust*
> She is good and must endure, loving her so:
> And as we love ourselves we hate her foe.
>   (24–26, emphasis mine)

Silkin tries to offset Thomas's praise and not to rely too obviously on his own advantageous hindsight by recalling Charles Hamilton Sorley's contemporary criticism of the poem. Sorley, much younger than Thomas, although refreshingly detached early in the war from the facile and self-serving patriotism of many of his contemporaries, still had little of Thomas's subtlety and complexity of insight. In a letter, Sorley says the poem is "arid" and singles out "Victory crowns the just" as "the worst line [Hardy] ever wrote, ... and unworthy of him who had always previously disdained to insult Justice by offering it a material crown like Victory.[6] I do not think Hardy is saying that the victorious are always the just or that the just are always victorious. The strongest stress in the line falls on "Crowns" (because of the two preceding unstressed syllables). The soldiers justify their going to war by their belief that their victory will validate justice and invest it with the power to dominate human affairs. That is not to insult Justice but simply to want it to be realized and honored in this world. Sorley's idealism will not allow him to appreciate Hardy's cautious expression of a soldier's innocent faith in the possibility of human action having earthly significance and of things improving.

But between the two poems to which Silkin objects ("A Call to National Service" was published on 12 March 1917), Hardy was writing poems of regret and protest. Long before the Somme disasters changed the mood of the trench poets, Hardy was writing poems sympathizing with the victims of the war, especially the Belgians ("On the Belgian Expatriation," dated 18 October 1914, and "An Appeal to America on Behalf of the Belgian Destitute," dated December 1914). In 1914 and 1915 he wrote poems lamenting the destruction by militarists of "Teuton genius" ("England to Germany in 1914" appeals for less rancor between the two countries, and "The Pity of It" is a reminder of the shared linguistic heritage of the two countries). Four of the poems in the group, all written in 1915, echo a contention in *The Dynasts* that warring is part of man's nature: far from glory, Hardy sees in war only "Empery's insatiate lust of power" ("In Time of Wars and Tumults"), a human cockfight that swells the already "swollen All-Empery plans" of "gambling clans" ("'I Met a Man'"), simply "more Famine and Flame/More Severance and Shock" ("A New Year's Eve in War Time"). And, as the well-known "In Time of 'The Breaking of Nations'" makes clear, his perspective is much too broad for any reader to think mistakenly he is only criticizing Germany. When he does directly blame the national enemy, in "Cry of the Homeless: After the Prussian Invasion of Belgium," his anger still manages an almost Socratic temper. A curse on the "instigator of the ruin" richer than reciprocated suffering is

> 'That compassion dew thy pillow
> And bedrench thy senses all
> For thy victims,
> Till death dark thee with his pall.'
>
> (21–24)

It is worse being a victimizer, and fully conscious of it, than being a victim.[7]

But even if warfare is no better than a "game with Death," and this particular war the "sly slaughter" of "innocents," there is still for Hardy, the famous pessimist, a respect for honor and courage. In the elegiac "Before Marching and After" the lament is finally

> For him who had joined in that game overseas
> Where Death stood to win, though his name was to borrow
> A brightness therefrom not to fade on the morrow.
>
> (19–21)

How different the sentiment is here from that in Sorley's poems (for instance "Such, Such is Death"). In "Then and Now" the lament is for the loss of a different kind of warfare, a "chivalrous sense of Should and Ought," when "Honour is some reward," when men fought by "honourable rules."

This is hardly jingoistic patriotism, but critics such as Silkin cannot distinguish a respect for honor from shrill and deceitful propaganda. At the end of the chapter, Silkin does mention Hardy's recognition of the horror and pity of war in "And There Was a Great Calm," written at the Armistice in November 1918. "But why," he asks, "does this recognition come so late?"[8] My point has been that it came much earlier, but not in terms Silkin could recognize. Silkin's touchstone is "The Soldier's Death" by Anne Finch, Countess of Winchilsea, which entreats "dejected men of war" to cease sacrificing themselves "to your mistaken shrine, to your false idol Honour." In these "Poems of War and Patriotism," Hardy neither condones the war nor is shocked by man's inhumanity to man; rather he is concerned with defining a way of getting on intelligently and responsibly, which means moving through and beyond outrage and pity to moral understanding.

If we want shrill propaganda, we find it more in the avant-garde poetry of the time. Another noncombatant, Ezra Pound, offers his poetic commentary on the war in sections IV and V of *Hugh Selwyn Mauberley*, and Pound's obsessive interests create this nearly hysterical deviation from the quatrains, themselves barely controlled, of the rest of the poem:

> Died some, pro patria
> non "dulce" non "et decor" ...
> walked eye-deep in hell
> believing in old men's lies, then unbelieving
> came home, home to a lie,
> home to many deceits,
> home to old lies and new infamy;
> usury age-old and age-thick
> and liars in public places.
>
> (71–79)

This same poet, who years earlier urged many of his friends to join up, offers this adolescent summary of the false ideals of the war:

> There died a myriad,
> And of the best, among them,

> For an old bitch gone in the teeth,
> For a botched civilization,
>
> Charm, smiling at the good mouth,
> Quick eyes gone under earth's lid,
>
> For two gross of broken statues,
> For a few thousand battered books.
>
> (88–95)

The prophetic sweep and self-consciously shocking images here expose the shallowness of Pound's political and moral intelligence. So many of the experimentalists are so far from an understanding of the traditional virtues that impiety becomes a substitute for intellection in a poem. Ford Madox Ford deals with the complex problem of private and public responsibility in wartime in "That Exploit of Yours" and can only declare "duty to Society and the Fatherland" a "cliché." And F. S. Flint in "Lament" reduces the same problem to this:

> The young men of the world
> Are condemned to death.
> They have been called up to die
> For the crime of their fathers.
>
> (1–4)[9]

This is as simple-minded and sentimental as the pro-war poetry of Rupert Brooke and Julian Grenfell.

If Silkin and Fussell begin their books with Thomas Hardy, Bernard Bergonzi begins his (*Heroes' Twilight: A Study of the Literature of the Great War*, 1965) with William Shakespeare and especially notions of heroism in *Henry the Fourth*. His thesis in the book is that World War I marked the final deflation for our century of the heroic ideal and that the best poetry of the war expresses the anti-heroic protest. Consequently, he begins with Shakespeare's play and with a dichotomy he sees in Hotspur, representing traditional heroism, and Falstaff, representing the "biological virtue of cowardice" and the "scoffing, sceptical intellect." He talks rather freely of "the old absolute distinction between 'heroism' and 'cowardice,'" and claims that although Hotspur's view dominated in the Renaissance, in the nineteenth century anti-heroic views began to challenge the older view, and that since World War I the Falstaffian view has prevailed.[10]

Bergonzi is like many critics of war poetry in not being able to find value in honor and courage. It is present, for instance, in the readiness to characterize all pro-war poetry as "adventurous romance" (as does J. M. Gregson in *Poetry of the First World War*, 1976) or as the last gasp of the English puritan tradition (as does V. de S. Pinto in *Crisis in English Poetry*

1880–1940, 1967), and to characterize antiwar poetry as sincere, realistic, and truthful. Paul Fussell is easily the most extreme: he approvingly quotes Hemingway in *A Farewell to Arms*: "abstract words such as glory, honor, courage, or hallow were obscene beside the concrete names of villages, the numbers of roads, the names of rivers, the numbers of regiments and the dates." He speaks snidely of the "system of high diction" of the pre-war years (in which "Friendship" is called "fellowship," "Bravery considered after the fact" is "valor," "Obedient soldiers" are "the brave," and "Cowardice" is "dishonour"); this "essentially feudal language" indicates, he asserts condescendingly, an age of pitiful and conspicuous innocence. The sophisticated, experienced view is apparently nihilism: referring to the recruiting poster depicting a worried father of the future being asked by his children, "Daddy, what did *you* do in the Great War?" Fussell says, "Today, when each day's experience seems notably *ad hoc*, no such appeal would shame the most stupid to the recruiting office."[11]

The Great War, as Fussell wants to argue, may mark the real birth of modernism; certainly another popular motif in the criticism dealing with this period (and one of the stylistic assumptions of modernism) is that the war forced poets to devise new techniques to deal with it, and that there was nothing in traditional poetry to allow poets to express the extreme violence, brutality, baseness, and destruction of this first "modern" war. It is the central contention, for example, of J. M. Gregson's book, but his logic is particularly shortsighted: the poetic techniques fashionable in the immediate prewar years, he argues, were not adequate for the new material of the war.[12] He does not attempt to look back further than the immediate prewar years for adequate techniques. This is surprising, because the "new" style of the most lauded and seemingly successful war poets amounts to little more than a combination of directness, simple and colloquial language, and occasionally half-rhymes and irregular rhythms. Only the last two qualities point toward modernists' experiments of the 1920s, and are foreshadowed by formal slackness and imprecision in much nineteenth-century verse.[13] Directness and simple and colloquial diction have been part of our native literary tradition since Chaucer and Langland, and although this plain style tradition was out of fashion in the century before the war, it was revived and kept vigorously alive by Thomas Hardy. But the traditional plain style also is the moral style. When the presentation is plain, inadequate thought is readily exposed; there are no aesthetic contrivances to hide behind. The moral principles that inform the greatest poems in our native tradition are classical and Christian. What "technique" can Sassoon or Owen offer that will give us a sharper exposure *and* condemnation of the corruptions of war than that offered over three hundred years before by George Gascoigne:

>   And such I counte the happe of *Haughty hart*,
> Which hunts (nought els) but honor for to get,
> Where treason, malyce, sicknesse, sore and smarte,
> With many myschieves moe his purpose let,
> And he means while (which might have spent it bet)
> But loseth time, or doth the same mispend,
> Such guerdons gives the wicked warre at end.
>   I set aside to tell the restlesse toyle,
> The mangled crops, the lamed limbes at last,
> The shortned yeares by fret of fevers foyle,
> The smoothest skinne with skabbes and skarres disgrast,
> The frolicke favour frounst and foule defast,
> The broken sleepes, the dreadfull dreames, the woe,
> Which wonne with warre and cannot from him goe.
>   ("The Fruites of Warre")
>
> He cannot climbe as other catchers can.
> To leade a charge before himselfe be led,
> He cannot spoile the simple sakeles man,
> Which is content is feede him with his bread.
> He cannot pinch the painefull souldiers pay,
> And sheare him out his share in ragged sheetes,
> He cannot stoupe to take a greedy pray
> Upon his fellowes groveling in the streetes.
> He cannot pull the spoyle from such as pill,
> And seeme full angrie at such foule offence,
> Although the gayne content his greedie will,
> Under the cloake of contrarie pretence.
>   ("Gascoignes Woodmanship")[14]

What Gascoigne has and what modern war poets and their critics usually do not have is a commitment to more than sympathy and pity for suffering humanity. What it finally amounts to is an ability to express man's dignity,[15] something modernism has difficulty expressing. Dignity can be claimed only for and by the virtuous and therefore only for and by those who believe in the virtues. The war experience did encourage a new technique, but it usually was no more than a new mixture: an intensification of the realism already present in the nineteenth-century novel, Edwardian drama, and the avowed aims of the prewar Georgians, and romantic, sentimental morality. The satire one finds in Sassoon and occasionally in Owen, and the private mythologizing of Rosenberg, for instance, were hardly innovative, the one coming straight from Byron and the other from Blake.

But we require more than a broader literary perspective. This brings us back to Bergonzi's historical view of heroism and his reading of *Henry the Fourth*. There is another reading, a much more convincing one that takes into account Shakespeare's understanding of Aristotle's *Ethics*, still in Renaissance England the most influential account of the virtues. This reading was argued by William B. Hunter, Jr. in a 1951 essay.[16] He calls attention to Prince Hal's crucial place in the moral argument of the play as an alternative to Hotspur and Falstaff's opposing attitudes toward honor. Whereas Hotspur asserts extravagantly the nobility of personal honor, a feudal code that finally destroys him, Falstaff will have none of it, concerned as he is (superficially and egocentrically) with his own reputation. Here is his speech before he enters the Battle of Shrewsbury (I quote it because several of the Great War poets and critics make similar points):

> What is honour? A word. What is that word honour? Air. A trim reckoning! Who hath it? He that died a Wednesday. Doth he feel it? No. Doth he hear it? No. 'Tis insensible then? Yea, to the dead. But will [it] not live with the living? No. Why? Distraction will not suffer it. Therefore I'll none of it. Honour is a mere scutcheon—and so ends my catechism.
>
> (V, i, 132–139)

If Hotspur's attitude is excessive, Falstaff's is obviously deficient. This naturally suggests Aristotle's theory of virtuous action as a mean between two extremes, both of which are vicious. The mean in the play is surely represented by Prince Hal, who openly recognizes and rejects both extremes (whatever his motives): he laughs at Hotspur's excessive concern for honor and proves Falstaff selfish. Hal is (or at least allows himself to be publicly recognized as) the moderate alternative to another related set of extremes as well: his actions at Shrewsbury emphasize his courage, in contrast to Falstaff's cowardice and Hotspur's rashness. As Aristotle reminds us, the motive of courage is the sense of honor, and honor is the end of virtue.[17] What is particularly relevant to the twentieth-century use of the terms are Aristotle's qualifications: that fear is an expectation of evil and therefore to fear some things is right and noble (disgrace, for instance); that death in itself is not evil, but the thought of it is painful for the truly virtuous man, because "life is best worth living for such a man, and he is knowingly losing the greatest goods, and this is painful. . . . he is none the less brave, and perhaps all the more so, because he chooses noble deeds of war at that cost"; and that choice and motive are essential for true courage (the man who is brave under compulsion rather than because it is noble to be so, or who is driven by passion rather than honor is not truly brave). Of the three kinds of fighting men—the critizen-soldier (or enlistee), the conscript, and the professional soldier—the courage of the first is most likely to be true, because the citizen-soldier is more likely to act out of desire of a noble object (honor) and not out of fear of punishment or hope for a share of the spoils.[18] (These are the men who sing Hardy's marching song.) Let those who would dismiss "honor" and "courage" as the feudal cant of armchair patriots or unsophisticated recruits, as old-fashioned aims rendered absurd or obscene by World War I, speak directly to Aristotle's argument and not just to the obvious misuse of those patriotic appeals in one particularly grotesque war.

I spend this time reviewing the best classical formulation of the most important virtue of warfare for several reasons: to suggest that our understanding of the traditional notions of honor and courage may be distorted (especially if Hotspur can be regarded as their embodiment; the Falstaffian view may prevail today, but I see no reason to be pleased about it or to mistake it for sophistication); to offer an ethical context for understanding and placing the poetic commentaries of the Great War that is more secure than that provided by late twentieth-century nihilism or even liberalism; and to suggest some criteria for assessing individual war poems, for surely poets with the widest, sharpest, and most rational moral perspective on the war will, with the necessary verbal mastery, have the greatest chance of writing successful and more than simply topically relevant poems on man's most self-destructive but not always avoidable activity. Style and content, as always, are interdependent here: moderation is not just a program for virtuous living but a stylistic aim and strength; restraint is the best means of expressing the fullest and most mature emotional and intellectual responses to the war. As sincerity is authorized by judicious commitment, so realistic exposure and emotional intensity do not constitute argument by themselves. I proceed on the assumption that "war poetry" is naturally didactic.

Critics have conventionally divided the English poetry of World War I roughly into two periods: the early pro-war, patriotic period from the outbreak of the war to about the Battle of the Somme in 1916; and the later, antiwar protest period from 1916 to the Armistice.[19] This agreeable bifurcation supports the over-simple ethical view and the biases I referred to earlier. I believe there is a stronger middle ground or phase than the critics have allowed, a poetry neither blatantly pro-war nor blatantly antiwar. It is not to be found in as yet undiscovered poets so much as in certain undervalued or misread poems or parts of poems by the major writers, poems in which the emotionalism of either patriotism or protest did not deflect the intellect from considering the complex moral (but not necessarily political) questions raised by service in war (even an unusually brutalizing, badly managed, and perhaps unnecessarily extended war).

Rupert Brooke and Julian Grenfell

I am not suggesting that we should value the early patriotic poets more highly than they deserve, but that we should be careful to recognize their real weaknesses. Feelings of intense patriotism hardly can be held against any Englishman living in the summer of 1914, but what makes for weak and ephemeral poetry is the insubstantiality of the moral conviction and the subsequently weak abstract expression.[20] It may be ironic that for so many years during and after the war the prototypical "war poet" should be one whose only poems dealing with the war are five sonnets written while he was training, and also who, except for a brief glimpse of the chaotic Belgian retreat (which he found "thrilling"), saw no action. But it is not his lack of battle experience that makes the patriotism of Rupert Brooke's sonnets so insubstantial. He can give the "glory" of a soldier's sacrifice an effective concreteness, as in the final lines of the fourth sonnet, "The Dead":

> ... And after,
> Frost, with a gesture, stays the waves that dance
> And wandering loveliness. He leaves a white
> Unbroken glory, a gathered radiance,
> A width, a shining peace, under the night.
>
> (10–14)[21]

"Gathered radiance" is particularly fine, but it could give more intellectual significance to the metaphor if its context could do more than gesture complacently to the lost life as "wandering loveliness." We are asked to mourn the loss of individual sensuousness, not of potentially valuable lives, and to believe that the mere fact of death rather than its motive or purpose confers honor. The octave says little more than that before they died (those dancing waves of the imagistic sestet), they were sensuously alive in the Keatsian sense: "Washed marvellously with sorrow, swift to mirth. /. ... Felt the quick stir of wonder; sat alone." Nor, I think, does the anglicizing of "the eternal mind" as well as French soil in "The Soldier" provide the kind of memorial ("If I should die, think *only* this of me") that the dedicated soldier would relish.

Such facile mysticism is more than a hint and is even less social in Julian Grenfell's most anthologized poem, "Into Battle." We are far from Hardy's soldiers' complaint against cynics and dalliers and Hardy's own consideration of the Unconscious Will when we have a military adventurer assert in thumping tetrameter lines that "he is dead who will not fight" and bolster his own confidence with "Nor lead nor steel shall reach him, so / That it be not the Destined Will" (41–42).[22] We see what happened to the ancient Greek notion of courage in the mind of an overeager professional soldier in a romantic culture. Aristotle had agreed that "brave men are excited in the moment of action," but stressed their preparatory collectedness, their awareness and complete knowledge of the situation, and their justifiable fear of death. There is no cost for Grenfell's predatory professional. He looks forward to battle as the fulfillment of his natural being (in fighting the soldier follows the direction of nature and shares in its glory). His "comradeship" is not with his fellow soldiers but with stars, trees, birds, and horses (stanzas two through seven). The moment of action promises a willful ignorance:

> And when the burning moment breaks,
>   And all things else are out of mind,
> And only joy of battle takes
>   Him by the throat, and makes him blind,
>
> Through joy and blindness he shall know,
>   Not caring much to know, ...
>
> (35-40)

It is difficult finding anything patriotic in this poem; it is both self-serving and amoral and not much different in its sentiments from that of Yeats's one true war poem, "An Irish Airman Foresees His Death."

Charles Sorley and Robert Graves

Two poets who are much less sentimental in their advocacy of service are Charles Hamilton Sorley and Robert Graves. Sorley, as a comparison with Graves makes clear, although more realistic than Brooke and Grenfell, is not necessarily more mature. Consider, for example, Sorley's attitude toward death in his sonnet, "Such, Such Is Death," and Graves's in "The Leveller." Here are the last eight lines of Sorley's formally unconventional sonnet:

> Victor and vanquished are a-one in death:
> Coward and brave: friend, foe. Ghosts do not say
> 'Come, what was your record when you drew breath?'
> But a big blot has hid each yesterday
> So poor, so manifestly incomplete.
> And your bright Promise, withered long and sped,
> Is touched, stirs, rises, opens and grows sweet
> And blossoms and is you, when you are dead.
>
> (7-14)[23]

There is some disagreement over the meaning of the last three lines. John Press says the poem expresses "a willing acceptance of death both as a great leveller, and as the prelude to a richer life"—the blossoming Promise therefore taking place in Heaven.[24] Silkin prefers to think that the potential remains "sweet" for those who survive and speculate on what might have been achieved.[25] The lines are unnecessarily ambiguous, and I am unable to decide between the two readings or to offer a third. But the attitude is deficient whichever interpretation we accept, and the deficiency is prepared for by the first sentence in the quoted passage. What is humanly significant is neither what the dead think of themselves in some afterlife nor what the survivors think might have been had they not died. A finished life is important publicly as a moral example and only to those still alive. Sorley seems to be confusing the fact of death (in which he says there is no inherent glory) with the circumstances of the death (in which there can be glory, to the extent that the man was brave for the right reasons). The poem is arguing either that one should accept death as the way to a more egalitarian and fulfilling future; or (echoing Falstaff) that because the dead do not care about bravery and cowardice, neither should the living.

Graves offers a clearer and more focused answer to Grenfell. "The Leveller" relates the death of two men by the same shell: the pale, thin, girlish eighteen-year-old, who was "not too bold, / . . . The shame and pity of his platoon," died "cursing God with brutal oaths"; the other, an older, experienced foreign soldier who "had known death and hell before / In Mexico and Ecuador," died childishly calling for his mother. But the more significant irony comes when old Sergeant Smith sends the same "accustomed funeral speech" to "the women folk of each":

> 'He died a hero's death: and we
> His comrades of "A" Company
> Deeply regret his death: we shall
> All deeply miss so true a pal'.
>
> (ll. 21–24)[26]

Officialdom, not death, is the great leveller. Graves is concerned about the war's assault on moral distinctions, and Sorley is trying to deny the final value of such distinctions. By restricting his scope and controlling his form (and therefore his tone), Graves clarifies a more inclusively relevant attitude.

Neither poet had any illusions about the war, and Sorley in one of his letters offers a very sensible criticism of Rupert Brooke and the egocentric strain in the early patriotic verse:

> He is far too obsessed with his own sacrifice, regarding the going to war of himself (and others) as a highly intense, remarkable and sacrifical exploit, whereas it is merely the conduct demanded of him (and others) by the turn of circumstances, where non-compliance with this demand would have made life intolerable.[27]

One wants, however, to know precisely how to read that "merely," and whether there is any resentment in those references to an external "demand." Although he could be insensitive to Hardy's "Men Who March Away," he shared with Hardy a sense of man's self-destructive tendencies ("the blind fight the blind," he wrote in "To Germany") and of nature's indifference to human deeds (in "All the Hills and Vales Along"). We know that Hardy was one of his favorite poets, and there are few better guides for the stern stoicism that Robert Nichols detects in the young man,[28] or the "desire to follow the truth" that John Press finds in the letters and poems. But there is almost always a slackness in the thinking and the verbal expression, exposing a lack of resilience in the moral gestures. "When You See Millions of the Mouthless Dead" exemplifies the limits of the achievement. He is right in advising us to "Say not soft things as other men have said" (including, of course, Brooke), but his alternative instruction, admirable in its plainness, is only a little less insulting:

> Give them not praise. For, deaf, how should they know
> It is not curses heaped on each gashed head?
> Nor tears. Their blind eyes see not your tears flow.
> Nor honour. It is easy to be dead.
> Say only this, 'They are dead.' Then add thereto,
> 'Yet many a better one has died before.'
>
> (5–10)

His iconoclastic eagerness muddles the thought: if the dead are blind as well as deaf, how can they know that there is anything going on that they can misinterpret as curses? And if "honour" is not a viable notion, by what do we judge as "better" those who have died before? The sentiment here echoes that of "Such, Such Is Death," and both remind us of Falstaff's irrelevant comment on the insensibility of honor to the dead.

What we hope Sorely refers to is the debased notion of honor so prevalent in the war rhetoric of 1914 and 1915. We do not have to hope when reading Graves. This poet, capable of as much realistic, impersonal accuracy as Owen and Sassoon (in "Dead Boche" he offers as "a certain cure for lust of blood" the forceful but unpathetic picture of a German corpse), is also careful when attacking false courage in "Big Words" and foolish courage in "Goliath and David" not to attack courage itself. A man may seem brave, as Aristotle says, but not always be brave.

We should probably honor Graves's desire to suppress his war poetry, and I admit there is a certain jauntiness of tone and what Bergonzi calls "the always-possible retreat into myth"[29] that together sometimes compromise the seriousness of his poetic commentaries on the war. But I do not so much want to present Graves as a great war poet as to commend the glimpses of some moral complexity one occasionally has reading his early verse. (He is, as I shall argue in the next chapter, a great love poet.) A sense of honor could survive even in this war, but it had little to do with patriotism and religion, as Graves remarks in *Goodbye to All That*:

> ... we all agreed that regimental pride remained the strongest moral force that kept a battalion going as an effective fighting unit. ... Patriotism, in the trenches, was too remote a sentiment, and at once rejected as fit only for civilians, or

prisoners. ... Hardly one soldier in a hundred was inspired by religious feeling of even the crudest kind.[30]

Not quite Aristotle, but a much more concrete form of that not uncommendable comradeship and communal loyalty appealed to so easily and vaguely by such popular poets as John McCrae and Alan Seeger. But although Graves could not understand "the war-madness that ran wild everywhere, looking for a pseudo-military outlet" in the England he returned to in 1916, at the same time he could not abide the pacifism of men like Bertrand Russell, who once asked him if he had to lead a company of men to break a strike of munition makers would he order his men to fire. Graves recalls the exchange:

"Yes, if everything else failed. It would be no worse than shooting Germans, really."
He asked in surprise: "Would your men obey you?"
"They loathe munition-workers, and would be only too glad of a chance to shoot a few. They think that they're all skrim-shankers."
"But they realize that the war's all wicked nonsense?"
"Yes, as well as I do."

The passage ends with Graves saying of Russell, "He could not understand my attitude."[31]

Siegfried Sassoon

Unlike Sorley, Graves and the more overtly protesting poets lived through the disillusionments of 1916 and the consequences of what became obviously by 1917 a war of attrition. But although we can understand why the broad, usually personal, romantic glorifications of battle should give way to narrow, more impersonal, realistic exposures of the horrors of war, why the mood should more often be anger than enthusiasm, and the mode more often pathos than celebration, we can still require adequate moral perspectives. As frustration, weariness, and desperation increased, however, the poets usually sought blunt rhetorical weapons that finally kept their poetry from reaching a didactic plane higher than an immediately satisfying and emotional propaganda. What must be remembered is that despite much realistic description in their verse, Siegfried Sassoon and Wilfred Owen are not realists but rather disheartened idealists. It is not surprising that Sassoon, the most clearly propagandistic of the two, after the war became an active communist and later converted to Roman Catholicism. Graves comments on his friend's "unconquerable idealism [which] changed direction with his environment: he varied between happy warrior and bitter pacifist."[32] (Graves quietly notes that he himself was "both more consistent and less heroic than Siegfried.") Sassoon's avowed purpose as a war poet was not just to convey the suffering of soldiers but also to shame those at home, to attack the apathy and complacency that to some extent allowed the war to continue; thus his weapons were direct and sometimes brutal description, irony, and satire. With few exceptions, each weapon, because of his usually unrestrained anger, is loosely handled and imprecisely aimed. Although he was the oldest of the major trench poets— he was twenty-eight when he enlisted—his verse is, I think, the most youthful in its effects.

"At Carnoy" (dated 3 July 1916) is a good example of a movement (all too frequent in his poems) from an overabundance of details to a bathetically angry close:

> Down in the hollow there's the whole Brigade
> Camped in four groups: through twilight falling slow
> I hear a sound of mouth-organs, ill-played,
> And murmur of voices, gruff, confused, and low.
> Crouched among thistle-tufts I've watched the glow
> Of a blurred orange sunset flare and fade;
> And I'm content. To-morrow we must go
> To take some cursed Wood ... O world God made![33]

The all too obvious juxtaposition of pastoral expectations with mundane realities ("hollow"—"Brigade," "mouth-organs"—"ill-played," "murmur" and "low"—"gruff" and "confused," "sweet"—"blurred," "content"—"cursed") does little to justify or give subtle meaning to the final exclamation. "Counter-Attack," justly called by Silkin "one of Sassoon's most relentless poems,"[34] contains one of his most uncompromising and graphic pictures of battle experience:

> The place was rotten with dead; green clumsy legs
> High-booted, sprawled and grovelled along the saps
> And trunks, face downward, in the sucking mud,
> Wallowed like trodden sand-bags loosely filled;
> And naked sodden buttocks, mats of hair,
> Bulged, clotted heads slept in the plastering slime.
> And then the rain began,—the jolly old rain!
>
> (7–13)

There are no artificial juxtapositions here, but in his attempt to draw some statement from the raw details, which for his purposes must remain as raw as possible (meaning that the first sentence must remain a list), he overburdens the verbs: "grovelled," "Wallowed," and "Bulged" suggest movement where he wants to emphasize absolute lifelessness. Although they may be used somewhat metaphorically to prepare us for "slept," the misdirection of the sense is not worth the flat irony of the euphemistic "slept." As a result, the effect is slightly dulled, and for the wrong reason we welcome the return to colloquial directness in the final line of the passage: "the jolly old rain!" is not quite as intrusive as "O world God made!" or as it would have been had the descriptive passage been more successful. The rest of the poem focuses on one soldier and his death (not unlike Owen's "Dulce Et Decorum Est"), and passes through an unnecessarily direct imitation of blurred confusion—

>   ... Bullets spat,
> And he remembered his rifle ... rapid fire ...
> And started blazing wildly ... then a bang,
>
> (31–33)

to a summary statement ("The counter-attack had failed") that is trying too hard to be ironic. Significantly Sassoon is most successful when he does not prejudice the details with angry protest in those poems that rely heavily on description. "Falling Asleep" is a poignant atmospheric piece wherein the details are sharper because the tone is quieter and the voice less caustically colloquial:

> Out in the night there's autumn-smelling gloom
> Crowded with whispering trees; across the park
> A hollow cry of hounds like lonely bells:
> And I know that the clouds are moving across the moon;
> The low, red, rising moon. Now herons call
> And wrangle by their pool; and hooting owls
> Sail from the wood above pale stooks of oats.
>
> (4–10)

It is a poem about the war but written after the Armistice when he was back in England but not free of his memories.

In those poems (often narrative) that depend mostly on irony, he has a tendency still to close awkwardly: "To-night he's in the pink; but soon he'll die./And still the war goes on—*he* don't know why" ("In the Pink," 17–18). Too often the irony is cheap, as in "Lamentations," in which after observing a soldier's uncontrolled grief over the death of his brother, the speaker concludes, "In my belief/Such men have lost all patriotic feeling" (9–10). This simplifies unjustly a complex matter, because instead of attacking the type of person who would have such an attitude it attacks the value of patriotism itself. "Does it Matter?" intends to criticize the insensitivity of those who try to cheer up the wounded, but manages also to insult those who do care:

> Does it matter?—losing your sight? ...
> There's such splendid work for the blind;
> And people will always be kind,

>   . . . .
> For they'll know you've fought for your country
> And no one will worry a bit.
>
> (6–8, 14–15)

In both these poems, Sassoon has not controlled the irony enough—he hits more than his target.

But the irony is not always so imprecise. "Dreamers" is one of his best war poems: by being less pretentious and less shrill, it is more serious. The seriousness is established in the octave of the sonnet in which there is neither irony nor shocking details, but a series of definitions of soldiers that moves from the public to the private: "Soldiers are citizens of death's grey land"; "Soldiers are sworn to action"; "Soldiers are dreamers" (1, 5, 7). There is some inflated diction here ("time's to-morrows," "the great hour of destiny," "fatal climax"), but also a fine individualizing line: "Each with his feuds, and jealousies, and sorrows." The sestet develops the third definition:

> I see them in foul dug-outs, gnawed by rats
>   And in the ruined trenches, lashed wih rain,
> Dreaming of things they did with balls and bats,
>   And mocked by hopeless longing to regain
> Bank-holidays, and picture shows, and spats,
>   And going to the office in the train.
>
> (9–14)

In pointing to the mundane objects that crowd their dream world, Sassoon corrects a false view of soldiers, humanizes them without making them seem unheroic or mundane. Few other ironic poems are as controlled as this one; elsewhere we must be satisfied with a few scattered lines (such as the parenthetical last five lines of the fourth stanza of "To Any Dead Officer," in which the target is effectively narrowed to military euphemisms).

Sassoon is most ambitious and takes on the most responsibility when he attempts to write satire. I have to disagree with Bergonzi who with his modernist bias thinks that the satiric approach is inherently inferior to the ironic: the ironic, he claims, recognizes the complexities of actual experience; the satiric reduces them to "a single satisfying gesture."[35] This may be true of bad satire, but in the best poets satire can be the completion of the ironic view—if irony recognizes complexity, satire judges it. But Sassoon is no Alexander Pope, and his satiric targets are often too easy (such as the journalistic stereotypes of "Base Details," "Memorial Tablet," and "The General"). This is also true of his postwar sketches of English social life, such as "Concert-Interpretation," which with its audacious rhymes and attack on obvious hypocrisy and cant reminds us of the English satirist he most resembles—Lord Byron. In "Villa d'Este

Gardens" he confesses as much: "My intellect (though slightly in abeyance)/Functioned against a Byronistic background" (13-14). Like Byron and unlike Pope, he is less concerned with defending a moral center by exposing deviations from it than with savagely lampooning those who disagree with his own unpopular views. Those views may be correct at times, but he does not have the skill or inclination to defend them persuasively while satirizing the opposition. "'They'" offers in the first stanza a humorless satire of a bishop's defense of the war (and thereby the Church's complicity in prolonging the war) and in the second stanza an explicit rebuke, but the poem itself is irrational:

> The Bishop tells us: 'When the boys come back
> They will not be the same; for they'll have fought
> In a just cause: they lead the last attack
> On Anti-Christ; their comrades' blood has bought
> New right to breed an honourable race,
> They have challenged Death and dared him face to face.'
>
> 'We're none of us the same!' the boys reply.
> 'For George lost both his legs; and Bill's stone blind;
> Poor Jim's shot through the lungs and like to die;
> And Bert's gone syphilitic: you'll not find
> A chap who's served that hasn't found *some* change.'
> And the Bishop said: 'The ways of God are strange!'

The argument turns on two different meanings of "change," but although the physical change referred to by the soldiers may add to the clergyman's perspective, it does not cancel or deny the latter's reference to possible spiritual or psychological change. That is, a more intelligent Bishop could have better answered the soldiers. Sassoon no doubt wants the Bishop to represent the Church, but this caricature of an incompetent can represent little beyond itself, and so the satire is as impotent as the argument is incomplete. Sassoon (even if inadvertently, that is, even if he only meant to contrast the pomposity of the cleric with the down-to-earth cares of the soldiers) has contributed almost as much as the Bishop to the demeaning of the serious moral concepts of justice and honor. There is too much harsh fervor in Sassoon's wartime satires. He is only able to be pointedly incisive and persuasive when he has calmed down a bit, as in the hardly profound but amusing and precise postwar poem "On Reading the War Diary of a Defunct Ambassador." The portrait does manage to be representative, and one line even hints at a Popian antithesis ("And gossiping on grave affairs of State"), and the final couplet is as good as the best Byron: "The visionless officialized fatuity/That once kept Europe safe for Perpetuity" (36-37).

Hardy was one of Sassoon's favorite writers. He read *The Return of the*

Native at the Front, hoping not to die before finishing it.[36] Hardy's *Satires of Circumstance* was the only literary source he could suggest for the satirical war poems that made him the best-known "new poet" in 1920.[37] His understanding of Hardy's power is evidenced in "At Max Gate": the chatty, sociable old man, who "wore an air of never having heard / That there was much that needed putting right," is not, says Sassoon, "Hardy, the Wessex wizard" (5-7). But the real Hardy of the novels and poems is not an ostentatious reformer either, but rather the contemplative man who later during the visit with Sassoon sits "Silent, the log fire flickering on his face." "Here," declares Sassoon, "was the seer whose words the world had known" (10-11). We might, however, compare Hardy's "'And There Was a Great Calm' (On the Signing of the Armistice, Nov. 11, 1918)," in which the pity is never maudlin and the recognition of man's potential evil never cynical, with Sassoon's Armistice poem, "Reconciliation," in which the tone is still arrogant and the matter sentimental, or with "Ancient History," another postwar reflection, in which the most penetrating analysis of the causes and psychology of war he can offer is a speculation that Adam preferred Cain to Abel. Sassoon could recognize but never emulate Hardy's quiet strength, just as he could acknowledge the "quiet-toned persistence" and "sober skill" of some eighteenth-century poet ("To an Eighteenth Century Poet"), but too often allow his anger and frustration rather than his weighing intellect to motivate his own sincere persistence.

Wilfred Owen

Although Sassoon was an older and more experienced poet than Wilfred Owen, whom he met in August 1917, and although Owen was for a while almost Sassoon's disciple, Owen's most accomplished verse is only slightly broader and more complete in its moral treatment of the war. If the emotional response is less strident, it is also more diffuse. If the realism is more richly sensuous, it is also more aesthetically indulged. Although there is more to the emotion, as Owen tempered his anger with compassion, it is still as unrefined as Sassoon's. And there is little advance in intellectual complexity.

There is no doubting Sassoon's influence: there is the same colloquial directness, caustic irony, and quick indignation directed at insensitive and complacent staff officers and civilians ("Inspection" and "Smile, Smile, Smile"). "The Dead-Beat," written consciously in Sassoon's style and very like Sassoon's "'They,'" instances a similar debasing of moral language but in a context that does not realize fully enough the poet's own reaction to the debasement. All we get is a final line that is embarrassingly crude and awkward. A soldier has a mental breakdown during a strafe:

> ... A low voice said,
> 'It's Blighty, p'raps, he sees; his pluck's all gone,
> Dreaming of all the valiant, that *aren't* dead:
> Bold uncles, smiling ministerially;
> Maybe his brave young wife, getting her fun
> In some new home, improved materially.
> It's not these stiffs have crazed him; nor the Hun.'
>
> (8–14)[38]

He is sent to the field hospital, unwounded, and suspected of malingering. The poem closes with "Next day I heard the Doc's well-whiskied laugh: / 'That scum you sent last night soon died. Hooray!'" (18–19). What C. H. Sisson says of this poem applies to many of Owen's (as well as Sassoon's) explicit protest poems: "It is the voice of protest, but protesting against an attitude no adequate mind would defend."[39]

On at least two memorable occasions, Owen is able to broaden a Sassoon-like protest with the addition of a quiet poignancy. In "The Send-Off" the statement is obvious, but expressed with delicacy, due partly to the somewhat halting rhythm of alternating pentameter and dimeter lines and to a seamless structural movement from a detached description of soldiers boarding a train on their way to France to concerned speculation about the future of those soldiers. The third and fourth stanzas prepare curiously for the transition to a more personal voice by retreating momentarily through the view of the porters and a tramp to the animated but completely unemotional signals and lamp:

> Dull porters watched them, and a casual tramp
> Stood staring hard,
> Sorry to miss them from the upland camp.
>
> Then, unmoved, signals nodded, and a lamp
> Winked to the guard.
>
> (6–10)

When comment comes in the next line, it is tentative and cautious and moves to an assured, but subtle and effective close, so unlike Sassoon:

> So secretly, like wrongs hushed-up, they went.
> They were not ours:
> We never heard to which front these were sent;
>
> Nor there if they yet mock what women meant
> Who gave them flowers.
>
> Shall they return to beatings of great bells
> In wild train-loads?
> A few, a few, too few for drums and yells,

> May creep back, silent, to village wells,
> Up half-known roads.
>
> (11–20)

The thought of the second stanza here is perhaps too easy (see Sassoon's "Glory of Women"), but this is a minor blemish on a finely poised poem. In "S. I. W." the situation is slightly more complex, and the expression more intense and (perhaps therefore) more uneven. An early reference to "disgrace" is undeveloped by a stereotyped context:

> Patting good-bye, doubtless they told the lad
> He'd always show the Hun a brave man's face;
> Father would sooner him dead than in disgrace,—
> Was proud to see him going, aye, and glad.
> Perhaps his mother whimpered; how she'd fret
> Until he got a nice safe wound to nurse.
>
> (1–6)

The narrative of the poem does, however, finally deal ironically but still not adequately with the reference: the boy would rather commit suicide than give himself "a blighty one":

> He'd seen men shoot their hands, on night patrol.
> Their people never knew. Yet they were vile.
> 'Death sooner than dishonour, that's the style!'
> So Father said.
>
> (21–24)

That last line is a fine qualification, but is not enough to prevent the poem from dismissing the idea of the previous line rather than the misapplication of it. And Owen cannot resist a Sassoon-like close: "With him they buried the muzzle his teeth had kissed,/And truthfully wrote the mother, 'Tim died smiling'" (36–37). But at least Owen, in that section somewhat pretentiously called "The Poem," investigates the motive for the suicide (as Sassoon in "Suicide in the Trenches" does not). The blame is not grandly and sweepingly left at "this world's Powers who'd run amok"; there was in addition and more immediately "the reasoned crisis of his soul/Against more days of inescapable thrall," and against the "Slow grazing fire, that would not burn him whole/But kept him for death's promises and scoff" (20, 29–30, 33–34).

In those poems that distinguish Owen from Sassoon, there is, of course, the famous pity, which D. S. R. Welland attributes to an emotional, romantic vision of "the tragic beauty of human suffering"; which Paul Fussell credits to a "de-sexed extension" of his earlier homoerotic tendencies; and which led Jon Silkin to claim that "Owen must appear as one of the most authentic voices of compassion in English poetry."[40] But, as these characterizations indicate, the pity is too often an end in itself, isolated from larger, less personal, social commitments. That is, there is a tendency rarely absent even in Owen's later poetry to concentrate too exclusively on the emotion. The tendency is evident, for instance, in the very early prewar poem, "To Eros," and persists even into one of his most admired war poems, "Greater Love," cited by Welland as a clear indication of his rapid maturation at the Front. "To Eros" is a protest against idealized love, and although one thinks immediately of the tradition of anti-Petrarchanism in the later Elizabethan period, Owen's sonnet has more to do with the disillusionment of a Byron than with the moral strictness of a Fulke Greville. The octave describes the intensity of his past dedication to the idea of love ("I sacrificed./All of most worth I bound and burnt and slew") and includes an amusing and perhaps ironic simile: "Glory I cast away, as bridegrooms do/Their splendid garments in their haste of joy" (2–3, 7–8). The joy of a bridegroom may, of course, yield progeny, not the least important of the memorials one can hope to have (in one version of the poem "Glory" is more specifically "Fair fame"). We get in the sestet the expected correction but unsubstantiated by an alternative: a laughing Eros pushes away the worshipping poet and retreats; without hope, the poet "starkly" returns "To stare upon the ash of all I burned" (14). The poem rests on the rejection, on the emotion of disillusionment. The self-pitying perhaps is kept in abeyance by the slight note of modest humor, but the judiciousness is still incomplete.

"Greater Love" also alludes to literary love conventions, but there is a more defined alternative. In a letter of May 1917, Owen writes, "Christ is literally in no man's land. There men often hear His voice: Greater love hath no man than this, that a man lay down his life—for a friend."[41] Owen's poem specifies the compassion: the love of conventional love poetry is measured against the love of soldiers for each other. The poem is a simple list: red lips are not so red as "the stained stones kissed by the English dead," the kindness of heterosexual lovers "seems shame" next to the "pure" love of fellow soldiers, and so on. The list, however, is arbitrary (lips, kindness, eyes, attitude, voice, heart, and hand), and the statement tautological. Owen wants to shock his reader by contrasting the artificial and sentimental with the real and horrific. And that limited intention forces awkwardnesses, such as the crude self-conscious rhyming of the second stanza:

> Your slender attitude
>   Trembles not exquisite like limbs knife-skewed,
> Rolling and rolling there
> Where God seems not to care;

> Till the fierce love they bear
> > Cramps them in death's extreme decrepitude.
>
> > > (7–12)

(The fourth line of this stanza, incidently, is gratuitous.) The theme of love has indeed widened to include pity, but the poet is still concentrating with rather forced intensity on the emotional response.

Just how limited this advance is can be realized if we compare "Greater Love" with a lesser known poem by the less famous Ivor Gurney. Here is the first and last stanza of "To His Love":

> He's gone, and all our plans
> > Are useless indeed.
> We'll walk no more on Cotswold
> > Where the sheep feed
> Quietly and take no heed.
> . . . .
> Cover him, cover him soon!
> > And with thick-set
> Masses of memoried flowers—
> > Hide that red wet
> Thing I must somehow forget.
>
> > > (1–5, 16–20)[42]

Although Gurney's lines are metrically less accomplished than Owen's, his less emphatic and obtrusive rhymes (helping to close and shape each stanzaic sentence while not calling attention to themselves) combine with the numerous trochaic openings to keep the tone reserved *and* forceful. This more elegiac tone is appropriate to the wider consideration of the topic of death and sacrifice in war. Gurney perhaps is more securely universal by referring more concretely to a representative single "he" than is Owen, who is content with a generalized "they." Owen sets real horrors against artificial conventions; Gurney sets war's consequences in a context of past plans and future adjustments. The structure of Gurney's poem is much more complex: the indifference of nature off-handedly referred to at the end of the first stanza gives significance to the image in the second stanza of human effort ("on Severn river / Under the blue / Driving our small boat through")—there is no Romantic wandering with the current—and that opposition prepares for the more explicit one in the last half of the poem, in which an almost sentimental gesture ("cover him over / With violets of pride") is quickly qualified by the realistic imperative of the last stanza. The horror is no less intense for being less graphic: "that red wet / Thing." But characteristically Gurney refuses both to discredit the notion of noble dying and to close with the startling detail. It is not so much an opposition of patriotism and realism as an attempted fusion, and this places the final emphasis on the need to deal with the death ("I must somehow forget"), not just expose its gruesome nature and pity its victim. I return to Gurney at the end of this chapter.

The central problem for most of the later, protesting war poets was how to give significance to the experiential details they knew they had to present as vividly as possible, how to do more than what responsible war correspondents and journalists (had there been any free of censorship) would have done. Owen, like the rest, was consciously and avidly a propagandist. "All a poet can do to-day is warn," he wrote in the preface to his proposed collection of war poems.[43] But effective warnings must be more than emotionally charged details. Owen could distance himself from the recorded experiences and even from the initial outrage and loathing, but not from the emotion itself. The didactic demands of his poetic situations are rarely met by his poems. When he structures a poem as a rational argument, when he tries to be less personal and more political, as in "Dulce et Decorum Est," he falters. Silkin says, contrasting Owen with Sassoon, that "Owen doesn't allow his censoriousness or didactic impulse to dominate his sensuous life."[44] Perhaps he should have in this instance. There is no denying the skill with which Owen describes the man dying of gas poisoning in the first sixteen lines of the poem. But although the details continue in the last section of the poem (17–28), the section offers itself as a rational statement of the effect of the scene on the sensitive reader. *If* you too could see and hear what I have seen and heard, *then*

> My friend, you would not tell in such high zest
> To children ardent for some desperate glory,
> The old Lie: Dulce et decorum est
> Pro patria mori.
>
> (25–28)

The poems tries to score didactic points too easily. It simply does not follow that because death in war can be horrible one should not die for one's country. Would he argue conversely that it is right to die for one's country as long as the death is clean and swift? The physical manner of death does not itself prove Horace's sentence a lie. But an unjust war with illegitimate and dishonorable aims led by incompetent or corrupt officers and politicians would prove it a lie, or more accurately prove it inapplicable in such a case. But Owen says nothing of this. Welland generalizes that "the only call to which Owen answers is not that of the church but of human suffering. It is human suffering rather than abstract morality that determines his ethical position."[45] That is, I think, too simple. Owen himself seemed to realize that the simple recording of suffering was not enough. But as this poem indicates, when he tried to place the descriptions within signifying moral contexts, his own intellectual limitations were exposed. (One is remined of the problems his beloved Keats had with the intellectual epic, *Hyperion*.) Morality is not itself the recognition of human suffering, although that may be where and how it begins; it is the set of defensible principles guiding our active (not just emotional) response to that suffering.

In "Futility," however, he adds sound organizing thought to the graphic details and subjective responses:

> Move him into the sun—
> Gently its touch awoke him once,
> At home, whispering of fields half-sown.
> Always it woke him, even in France,
> Until this morning and this snow.
> If anything might rouse him now
> The kind old sun will know.
>
> Think how it wakes the seeds—
> Woke once the clays of a cold star.
> Are limbs, so dear achieved, are sides
> Full-nerved, still warm, too hard to stir?
> Was it for this the clay grew tall?
> —O what made fatuous sunbeams toil
> To break earth's sleep at all?

The poem is not much more than a complex mixture of tones, but it is unusual in Owen's work for being personal without being too subjective and for keeping the descriptive details plain and relatively bare. The organizing thought is simple yet precise and important; it is similar to Wordsworth's "A Slumber Did My Spirit Seal," one of his finest lyrics for the same reasons Owen's little poem is noteworthy. Just as Wordsworth's poem moves from a past delusion about Lucy's immortality to a present realization (after her death) of her mortality, Owen's moves from an uneasy hope fed by past recurrences to a controlled bitterness, with frustration growing as his thought moves through the temporal divisions of the first stanza (from the distant past, to the near and then very near past, to a future prospect), and then in the second stanza through a series of rhetorical questions. We are given the motive and the appropriate and complex emotional response; and although large philosophical questions are asked, they are not pretentious (as "fatuous" brilliantly indicates). They are asked within the confines of carefully and intricately formed stanzas to define the emotion, not to present the poet as a professional thinker. That is, while the context is broader, the poem is successful because Owen does not try for more than he is capable of, unlike the narrower "Dulce et Decorum Est" that pretends to do more than it can.

But, as with most poets, it is the most aesthetically ambitious and least plain poems that attract the most critical attention and praise. With a young poet like Owen, however, we are sent to his weakest poems: the thought is still immature, so the literary devices are all the more obvious: the visionary melodrama of "The Show," the ponderous symbolism of "Hospital Barge at Cérisy," the inflations of "Six O'Clock in Princes Street," the earnest and repetitive ironies of "Anthem for Doomed Youth," and the stiff archaisms of "The Parable of the Old Man and the Young." The three most praised poems by Owen cannot so easily be set aside. Not one is free from the intellectual and emotional limitations we have been tracing, but they are richer and more interesting than most of his other poems. Let us examine briefly each in turn: "Exposure," "Insensibility," and "Strange Meeting."

"Exposure" is predominantly a descriptive poem; Dominic Hibberd judges the first six stanzas "perhaps Owen's finest piece of descriptive writing."[46] But the description is directed by a thematic opposition (nature and war), and in one nondescriptive stanza (the seventh) that opposition is briefly (too briefly) expanded into an abstract defense of the necessity for a Christ-like sacrifice. It is one of the few times that Owen seems to defend his involvement in the war. The main problem is one of proportion: too much space is devoted to description, which is allowed to become too sensuous, and not enough to the defense, which remains ambiguous and unclear.

The poem is in a sense a commentary on the opening line: "Our brains ache, in the merciless iced east winds that knive us..." For the first five stanzas the commentary reservedly goes no further than the Hardyesque suggestion that nature in its indifference to man's plight can occasionally aggravate that plight: "Watching, we hear the mad gusts tugging on the wire, / Like twitching agonies of men among its brambles" (6–7). This metaphor introduces the idea by comparing the wire's barbs to a country hedge's brambles. In his figurative eagerness, Owen perhaps animates nature too much, for he begins to hint at an active malevolence in addition to the indifference: "Dawn massing in the east her melancholy army / Attacks once more in ranks on shivering ranks of gray" (13–14). A mention of the snow flakes' "wandering" and the wind's "nonchalance" (19) is followed two lines later by "Pale flakes with fingering stealth come feeling for our faces." One may defend the confusion by pointing to Owen's attempt to capture a collective sense of confusion and anxiety among the soldiers (there is no "I" in the poem, only "we"), but one thereby simply points to an inherent weakness in the dramatic mode; it explains the confusion, but does not justify it. Another minor confusion is caused by Owen's carelessness with possessives: is "the poignant misery of dawn" (11) the misery delivered by the dawn or the misery felt by the dawn? The most serious problem with the descriptive stanzas is the tendency to aestheticize the scene of suffering soldiers with too insistent alliteration.

Line 16, 18, and 21, for example, are too arty not to interfere with their primary requirement to clarify.

In the sixth stanza, the commentary comes forward and leaves momentarily the descriptive language behind. The soldiers, in that very fine phrase from the fifth stanza, "back on forgotten dreams," their "ghosts" (an unfortunate word) "drag home," where they imagine cozy fires, jingling crickets, and a late night house taken over for a few hours by innocent rejoicing mice. This movement to an imagined scene of nature and man in temporary harmony, a harmony denied the warring men on the front, ends in obvious symbolism: "on us the doors are closed,—/We turn back to our dying."

The seventh stanza then offers what seems syntactically a rational sequence; but again, because of careless expression, and I suspect incomplete thinking, it is far from being rationally clear.

> Since we believe not otherwise can kind fires burn;
> Nor ever suns smile true on child, or field, or fruit.
> For God's invincible spring our love is made afraid;
> Therefore, not loath, we lie out here; therefore were born,
>   For love of God seems dying.
>
>   (31–35)

Jon Silkin offers an exhaustive reading of these lines, claiming that "an extremely complex set of ideas is explored," but he can finally only find multiple interpretations for the first, third, and fifth lines. He may be right that the secular and religious possibilities of the first and third lines "could be carried together without any contradiction,"[47] but definitive and thorough expression of such important (even if complex) matters is preferable to a simple absence of contradiction. Despite the eccentric punctuation, I believe the "Since" clause of the first line modifies the last line of the previous stanza, rather than the fourth line of this stanza: the first two lines here then explain why they turn back to the realities of the war instead of dreaming on about home fires, because the war must be fought to preserve the values symbolized (rather sentimentally perhaps) by those fires. Silkin suggests that the first line can be read as an independent clause by pausing after "believe," with an implied "in God." I find this a little forced, even if it makes sense of Owen's punctuation. The poem has not prepared us for such a sudden declaration of religious faith, but it has for a tentative psychological and patriotic justification—we expect such a contemplative poem to answer the earlier question, "What are we doing here?" (10). Owen was not given to the abrupt jumps that Silkin's alternative reading assumes. But Silkin needs to find as many references to God as possible to make sense of the fifth line of the stanza and the seeming statement in the next stanza that God punishes those who make war (and is therefore on Silkin's side). He can find bitterness in the last stanza and justify it, as he sums up what he proposes is Owen's major, "complex" point: "We had originally, but mistakenly, thought that war was a moral act because it was committed to moral objectives, but it is immoral and we must now bear God's retributive wrath in the form of hostile nature."

Hibberd is closer to the mark in his brief comment on this seventh stanza: it is "the fullest statement in a major poem of the belief that men must die, like Christ, in order that humanity may be purified."[48] "Purified" is too strong, however. The "love" referred to in the third line is of those home values. (Owen rarely localized his dim patriotism beyond the "sad shires" of "Anthem for Doomed Youth"). That third line is ambiguous, but the best possibility is: our love is made afraid, that is, defensive, so that we can have the same assured hope of renewal and growth as nature has after this harsh winter. For these soldiers, "nothing happens." But I cannot be sure of this reading, mostly because of "For" at the beginning of the line (it could, as Silkin hopes, mean "on behalf of," or better yet, "because of"; but this so unsupportedly complicates the sense that I prefer my suggestion). The "for" in the fifth line is not dealt with so easily (Silkin says nothing about it), nor is "love of God." If "for" is right, then "love of God" should be "man's love of God": that is, this generation was born to be sacrificed to halt the spread of godlessness. But this (Hibberd's emphasis) is not the reason declared in the previous lines of this and the sixth stanza. If "for" should be "but" (which I suspect), then the thought is: although we have a sense of our destined sacrifice, our immediate experience (so vividly recorded in the early stanzas) detects no loving God directing that destiny, and we return to that more frightening sense of nature's indifference. The soldiers desperately need some support for their faith in the rightness of their cause or some sign of God's mercy, but none comes. There is no sacrificial glory in the eyes of the dead, only ice, and "nothing happens." I am not disagreeing radically with other critics so much as trying to find the clearest sense of a badly written stanza in the context of the rest of the poem and even of Owen's other poems. "Inspection," for example, which Hibberd says satirizes the belief expressed in "Exposure," does not seem so different if "Exposure" is read as a dramatic expression of attempted but difficult belief. "Inspection" is an attack on those whose faith in God's support of their cause is unshakable, those who have not been exposed. I have gone on at length about this poem and what the critics have said to suggest that we should not confuse complexity with ambiguity and should expect real complexity to be accompanied by clarity. "Exposure" is written in a loose accentual meter: six stresses in each of the first five lines of each stanza, and two stresses in the fifth lines (with the exception of line 35). One wonders if a tighter form would have encouraged a more disciplined expression (as it did in "Futility"); the accentual line does little more than encourage the distracting alliterations.

"Insensibility" is a clearer statement about a more complex issue: wartime stoicism. The poet moves from sympathy with the forced insensitivity of frontline soldiers to criticism of the self-imposed stoicism of civilians. The first four sections comprise a catalogue of various kinds and causes of insensibility in soldiers (a lack of compassion for others, a cessation of feeling for themselves, unimaginativeness, inexperience). The fifth section is a somewhat indeterminate and unironic acknowledgment of the advantages of these deficiencies, and in its last two lines ("He cannot tell/Old men's placidity from his") acts as a transition to the sixth section, which declares such "happy" insensibility to be a curse if not forced on one, as it is not on noncombatants:

> But cursed are dullards whom no cannon stuns,
> That they should be as stones.
> Wretched are they, and mean
> With paucity that never was simplicity.
> By choice they made themselves immune
> To pity and whatever moans in man
> Before the last sea and the hapless stars;
> Whatever mourns when many leave these shores;
> Whatever shares
> The eternal reciprocity of tears.
>
> (50–59)

The inadequacy here is not confusion but more obviously a limitation of the thought; this treatment of civilian insensitivity is too easy, a mere indignant gesture. With his disordered list, his loose, expansive, and undefining emotional rhythm of syntactical repetitions ("Happy are ..." throughout the first four sections, and in addition "Their ..." throughout the third section), and his piecemeal sensuosity, he finally only laments a loss of emotional responsiveness, of an emotional sense of tragedy ("the eternal reciprocity of tears"), which reminds one of the melodramatic generalization by the equally young Keats: "Here, where men sit and hear each other groan" ("Ode to a Nightingale" [24]). Owen regrets only the inability to respond sympathetically to the moaning; a more mature poet also would regret the loss of that which allows one to deal with the suffering and perhaps, limited as such actions are, do something about it. I am not simply talking about a socialist revolution (as Silkin does when he finds the compassion in Owen's poem "a factor contributory to desired change"[49]), but about an effort at least to limit those restrictions (self-imposed but self-defensive) that deny or undermine being, definition, and fulfillment. It is a question not so much of freedom as moral survival.

Most critics consider "Strange Meeting" Owen's greatest poem, but they also admit grudgingly that it obviously remains unfinished. The praise is based on that post-Romantic emphasis in this century on visionary intensity (even in the absence of finished thought) as the essence of poetic achievement. "Strange Meeting" is one of a small group of poems including the almost surreal "The Show" and the two fanciful sonnets, "The Next War" and "The End." Owen was more successful when he found intensity in accurate pictures of the real war and its consequences (such as "Mental Cases," "Disabled," "Spring Offensive," "The Chances," "À Terre," and "Miners"), poems that may not rise above responsible journalism, but for the most part avoid pretentious prophecy. Young men should never try to be prophets. It was not a mode Owen was comfortable with, and although "Strange Meeting" is the best of the small group, the discomfort shows, however potentially powerful the imaginative situation is. Compassion for the common German soldier is not original with Owen, of course; one remembers Hardy's "Often When Warring" and Graves's "Dead Boche." But what distinguishes Owen's poem and unfortunately also restricts its significance is that the poet is not sorry he has killed another human being, but only sorry he has killed a fellow romantic poet.[50]

The poem has two parts; lines 1 to 13 narrate a visionary descent into hell that is effectively described as a permanent version of a World War I tunnel ("long since scooped / Through granites which titanic wars had groined"). The only problem here is the concept of hell, which is unconventional without reason: why are the dead smiling in hell (9–10), and why would the visiting poet who knows this is hell think there is no cause for mourning (14)? Is not hell perpetual mourning for the loss of heavenly bliss? The poet seems to be confusing the state of being dead with the more specific state of being forever damned. The second part of the poem (14–44) is a dialogue or perhaps a monologue, because the poet only speaks one line and the rest is the dead man's reply. The German soldier mourns the loss of hope, both his own and what his poetry would have given others had he lived to write it; not a hope for moral understanding or social stability or fullness of being, but for aesthetic extremes:

> ... Whatever hope is yours,
> Was my life also; I went hunting wild
> After the wildest beauty in the world,
> Which lies not calm in eyes, or braided hair,
> But mocks the steady running of the hour,
> And if it grieves, grieves richlier than here.
>
> (16–21)

Welland has established Shelley's *The Revolt of Islam* as a source of the poem, and Hibberd has suggested Keats's *Endymion*, Dante's *Inferno*,

Sassoon's "Rear-Guard," and even one line by Oscar Wilde. These particular lines, however, most suggest Shelley's "Alastor," that long record of a pathetic search by a poet for an unobtainable vision of fiery beauty. The fourth line of the passage even recalls the Shelleyan poet's rejection of the calm and sacrificing Arab maid. The next line, of course, echoes Marvell's promise to his coy mistress of sexual fireworks and the next the glutted sorrow of Keats's "Ode on Melancholy." In the lines that follow, Owen quickly and inexplicitly equates beauty with truth and truth with pity, and thereby outdoes Keats. Meanwhile the speaker suggests strongly that if poets had not been killed in the war the nations would not, as he prophesizes they will, "trek from progress." One therefore wonders about the nature of the "wisdom" he claims for himself, and what "mystery" means in this context:

> Courage was mine, and I had mystery,
> Wisdom was mine, and I had mastery:
> To miss the march of this retreating world
> Into vain citadels that are not walled.
>
> (30–33)

He seems to be saying, contrary to what he said earlier about preventing the retreat, that as a poet he will be uncontaminated by the inevitable decline of civilization, and only later ("Then, when much blood had clogged their chariot-wheels") would he

> ... go up and wash them from sweet wells,
> Even with truths that lie too deep for taint.
> I would have poured. ...
>
> (35–37)

The sudden shift of tense (from "I would go" to "I would have") also makes the passage very difficult to follow. The poem ends with the dramatic revelation that this fellow poet is the enemy killed by the narrator. The only thing that justifies "my friend" is their shared view of the poet's function. The pathos is not as sharp as it should be, because it comes after such immature and inflated claims. If we are at least to respect Owen's capacity for pity and compassion and therefore his limited advance over Sassoon's anger, we had best not invoke "Strange Meeting" as representative of his best efforts.

Isaac Rosenberg

Although we hope for a wide enough perspective in war poetry so that neither the patriotism nor the protest (in themselves not uncommendable social virtues) have an authority more persuasive than the emotional convictions of the individual poet, and especially soldier-poet, we also should ask that that width not carry the poet too far away from the reality of his participation in this war and the moral significance of *that* reality. The perspective should be anchored somehow in concrete details and publicly responsible (that is, rational) structures. Aristotle's conception of honor and bravery, I have contended, is still as effective a moral ballast as even twentieth-century poets can hope for; but by itself it is perhaps too abstract and distanced from modern life to be realized readily; a historical mediation is always necessary, and at its sincerest it usually takes the form of an intelligent and highly localized patriotism, a full sense of what one is fighting for and why it is necessary to fight for it. Contemporary political abstractions like "freedom" and "democracy" were even in 1917 and 1918 too variously interpretable (especially after the Bolshevik Revolution), and "the English way of life," although more discernible, offered little more solid justification for the mass killings. Something even more particular was necessary, and with poets like Edmund Blunden and Ivor Gurney, we see the possibilities.

Before we look at those poets, both of whom survived the war, we must, after having traced the development from Sassoon to Owen, note the extension of that development in the original work of Isaac Rosenberg. It is a development into a wider response to the war, but in Rosenberg we see clearly the disadvantages of such a breadth (what Bottomley called his "ample sweep") in the absence of an anchoring moral commitment of some sort. Rosenberg tried (as did David Jones more thoroughly and eccentrically later) to give a mythic dimension to the war experience and thereby distance the experience, not to judge it in central, human terms and give it intellectual vitality, but to shape it into an aesthetic object detachable from the demands of everyday life.

This was clearly his intention. Although in the last two years of his life he came to value precision and definition (to which his letters and later poems testify), he was never free of his early aestheticism and particularly his Romantic desire for the "ungraspable." In a letter of around 1910, he acknowledges his debt to Rossetti and Swinburne and his preference for what he calls "the poetical subject"—his examples include Coleridge's "Kubla Khan," Francis Thompson's "The Mistress of Vision" and "Dream Tryst," and works by Poe and Verlaine: "Here feeling is separated from intellect; our senses are not interfered with by what we know of facts: we know infinity through melody."[51] In his 1914 lectures on art to a South African audience, he echoes Shelley's idealism: "Science explains nature physically by atoms; philosophy explains life morally, but art interprets and intensifies life, representing a portion through the laws of unity that govern the whole."[52] The problem (*the* romantic problem) is encapsulated here: in trying for too much he ignores the stabilizing center; poetry is allied with a monistic philosophy but divorced from morality, giving itself a broad perspective but a very limited ability to interpret life in any significantly human way. And so the intensification (almost by default) is for its own sake. Believing that the unique, private imagination could achieve greater visions than those offered by others, which he saw as limited by race, culture, or morality, he moved closer to a Blakean celebration of unrestraint and energy. In "Moses," written in 1915, as D. W. Harding says, he "accepts violence because it seems a necessary aspect of any effort to bring back the power and vigour of purpose which he felt the lack of in civilized life."[53] Moses proclaims:

> Egypt was in the way; I'll strike it out
> With my ways curious and unusual.
> I have a trouble in my mind for largeness,
> Rough-hearted, shaggy, which your grave ardours lack.
> Here is the quarry quiet for me to hew,
> Here are the springs, primeval elements,
> The roots' hid secrecy, old source of race,
> Unreasoned reason of the savage instinct.
>
> (ii, 445–452)

He complains of a "rotting God" and his priests in words that could have been written by Blake:

> Who has made of the forest a park?
> Who has changed the wolf to a dog?
> And put the horse in harness?
> And man's mind in a groove?
>
> (i, 146–149)

For Rosenberg, a war was both an opportunity for his art and material for his myth of the interdependence of violence and creativity. He wrote to Lawrence Binyon in late 1916: "I am determined that this war, with all its powers for devastation, shall not master my poeting.... I will not leave a corner of my consciousness covered up, but saturate myself with the strange and extraordinary new conditions of this life, and it will all refine itself into poetry later on."[54] His first response "On Receiving News of the War" is chillingly amoral and primitivistic:

> O! ancient crimson curse!
> Corrode, consume.
> Give back this universe
> Its pristine bloom.
>
> (17–20)

Even the realities of the front could not compromise his dedication to his own art, mostly because his commitment to non-artistic values was relatively weak and certainly secondary. Jean Liddiard, Rosenberg's biographer, documents the development in this East End Jew born of immigrant parents of a sense of alienation and single-minded independence; like Yeats, he was in but not strictly of English culture. Unlike the Georgians, he felt no emotional commitment to England of the kind expressed through love of the English countryside. Although he may have been influenced by the Tolstoyan views of his Russian father and the pacifism of many of his close friends, certain practical considerations overcame his idealistic hatred of war. He wrote to Edward Marsh soon after enlisting in October 1915:

> I never joined the army from patriotic reasons. Nothing can justify war. I suppose we must all fight to get the trouble over. Anyhow before the war I helped at home when I could and I did other things which helped to keep things going. I thought if I'd join there would be the separation allowance for my mother.[55]

There also was half of his seven shillings a week, which he sent home to his mother. Perhaps more importantly, as Liddiard speculates, there was "the chance of directly fulfilling 'the fierce desire for virility, and original action.'"[56]

We can detect a concomitant development in his verse style. In "Marching (As Seen from the Left File)" we note in the second stanza some animated generalities that set aside the potential for local definition in the first, descriptive stanza, in favor of a prophetic gesture:

> We husband the ancient glory
> In these bared necks and hands.
> Not broke is the forge of Mars;
> But a subtler brain beats iron
> To shoe the hoofs of death
> (Who paws dynamic air now).
> Blind fingers loose an iron cloud
> To rain immortal darkness
> On strong eyes.
>
> (8–16)

In the absence of such a context, "ancient glory" is cheaply sarcastic, the violent fusions in lines 14 and 15 are insistently ambiguous, and the political suggestiveness of line 11 is frustratingly undeveloped. The vague impressiveness of this develops into the detached symbolic concerns of "Returning, We Hear the Larks." The potential of the opening lines, describing the combined anticipation of rest and sense of the night's "sinister threat" in fatigued soldiers returning to camp, is dissipated by the final similes into a mere pointing out (Liddiard is wrong, I think, to call it an examination) of the power and danger of beauty:

> But hark! joy—joy—strange joy.
> Lo! heights of night ringing with unseen larks.
> Music showering on our upturned list'ning faces.
>
> Death could drop from the dark
> As easily as song—
> But song only dropped,
> Like a blind man's dreams on the sand
> By dangerous tides,
> Like a girl's dark hair for she dreams no ruin lies there,
> On her kisses where a serpent hides.
>
> (7–16)

The emotional exclamations of lines 7 and 8 are as artificial as the poem is incomplete. The war may be providing Rosenberg with material for his art, but his art is not providing us with significant feeling and thinking about the war.

It is then but a short step to the overtly mythologic and Blakean "Daughters of War," which took Rosenberg a year to write and which he then considered his best poem. Here the abstruseness of "Marching" combines with the amoral detachment of "Returning, We Hear the Larks": the only advance is toward an eccentric mythologic vision that has none of Blake's political and social relevance. The poem rests on an ideological fiction: a possible plane of living reached only through the sacrifice of man's defective humanity. D. W. Harding claims, perhaps rightly, the immortality represented by the Amazonian spirits, who wait for the spirits of "the sons of valour" killed on the battlefield, is "no more than the immortality of the possibilities of life."[57] But these possibilities are difficult to discern in a poem that dismisses explicitly life as "the doomed glee / And hankering of hearts," and that suggests implicitly that war is a first backward step toward the primitive sources of life: the spirits dance

> By the root side of the tree of life,
> (The underside of things
> And shut from earth's profoundest eyes).
>
> (3–5)

The ancient virtue of courage thus has been cheapened into a vague program for decivilizing a life that Rosenberg himself only experienced as despotic, oppressive, and mundane.

Rosenberg, like Owen, is most successful when he is least conceptually or formally ambitious. "Break of Day in the Trenches" is notable for the extent to which the attention is anchored and kept on the three subjects: the rat, the poppy, and the soldiers. Only in the last half of the poem does he wander into some unnecessarily inflated metaphors, as he describes the men:

> Less chanced than you for life,
> Bonds to the whims of murder,
> Sprawled in the bowels of the earth,
> The torn fields of France.
>
> (15–18)

One suspects that the obscure "whims of murder" is there primarily to oppose "Bonds"; and although the next two lines are not difficult to understand, the metaphors ("bowels" and "torn") are mutually distracting: as the poem intensifies, Rosenberg gives way to quick and unhomogenized clichés. The next three lines seem to develop another easy opposition, but this time not just for its own sake but to bring together all the elements of the poem into a central thematic statement:

> What do you see in our eyes
> At the shrieking iron and flame
> Hurled through still heavens?
>
> (19–21)

"Still heavens" can only suggest that nature (including the rat and poppy) is not in sympathy with man's destructive activities ("torn fields" prepares for this). The rat on behalf of nature then mocks the "haughty athletes" with its sardonic grin and "cosmopolitan sympathies." As it stands it is only a romantic commonplace; Hardy, for instance, would have denied nature this function as a moral measure and placed man's evil against potential *human* standards. But this is the worst the poem does. The opening and closing lines are particularly fine, with the crumbling darkness of the first line echoed by the white dust of the final line, and the reference to the sunrise as "the same old druid Time," with its connotation of the false security of pagan superstition and perhaps even blood sacrifice, preparing for the sarcastic security of the penultimate line referring to the plucked poppy, "But mine in my ear is safe." Except for those unfortunate four lines (15–18), Rosenberg gives scope to his subject without abstracting his immediate attention.

An uncharacteristic control of diction, rather than a strict meter, is just able, except for a few lines and because the poem is short, to define a consistent tone in "Break of Day in the Trenches." In "Dead Man's Dump," there is a more regular iambic rhythm, but the lack of any stanzaic ballast, with somewhat random groupings of tetrameter and trimeter (with a few pentameter) lines, and occasionally wayward diction destabilize the tone. Awkwardness is evident from the very beginning:

> The plunging limbers over the shattered track
> Racketed with their rusty freight,
> Stuck out like many crowns of thorns,
> And the rusty stakes like sceptres old
> To stay the flood of brutish men
> Upon our brothers dear.
>
> The wheels lurched over sprawled dead
> But pained them not, though their bones crunched,
> Their shut mouths made no moan,
> They lie there huddled, friend and foeman,
> Man born of man, and born of woman,
> And shells go crying over them
> From night till night and now.
>
> (1–13)

Rosenberg begins immediately with an exaggerated comparison—the limbers with their load of wire may seem from a distance like crowns of thorns, and the stakes like old sceptres. The juxtaposition of "crowns of thorns" with "sceptres" introduces an irony (the true king was crucified) that cannot continue into the next two lines, especially the sixth, or else the poem itself becomes rather callous. Yet such a direct patriotic sentiment (the Germans are "brutish," the English are "brothers dear"), made more cloying by the inversion in the sixth line, and the extra stress that falls on "dear" because the line is unexpectedly short, is very uncharacteristic of Rosenberg and indeed of the rest of the poem (see, for instance, line 10).[58] It is very difficult to know how to read this first stanza and precisely what is meant; if no irony is intended, then it is not easy to avoid concluding that the speaker sees the English cause as a holy war against the barbaric Germans. But if this is the case, what do we do with the de-glamorizing diction in the first two lines ("shattered," "racketed," "rusty")? This problem of tone is compounded when we move to the seventh line and the artificial pronunciation of "sprawled" as two syllables, forced by the iambic regularity that precedes it. The second stanza continues with an unnecessary reminder that dead men do not feel pain or moan, and then with a sudden rhyme (the first in the poem) that tempts one to read "woman" as "woe-man." Surely the rhyme is unnecessary; line 10 is better with "foe" rather than "foeman" and line 11 is better as "Man born of woman, and born of man." The rhythm is thereby undisturbed and, I think, the emphasis more subtle (moving away from rather than toward the cliché "born of woman"). But I suppose Rosenberg wants "woman" last to draw out the secondary, maternal meaning of "crying over" in the next line, which adds blunt (and this time obvious) irony to earlier rhythmical incongruity.

This is a poor introduction to the next section of the poem; lines 14 to 38, like those weak lines in "Break of Day in the Trenches," move away from concrete detail to more intense speculation on the meaning of the scene. Such speculative passages should be prepared for carefully by firmly defined attitudes toward the immediate, inspiring scene, but here they are not. The syntactical awkwardness continues (for example, "Immortal seeming ever" [35]), as do the inappropriate metaphors: "When the swift iron burning bee / Drained the wild honey of their youth" (30–31). Too attached to the force of "drained" and the idea of the third stanza that nature is eager for man's death, Rosenberg overlooks the fact that a bee's motion is not at all similar to that of a bullet or bomb and that a bee does not destroy the flower it collects from. Only the fact of mortality can account for the personification of an eager Earth, "fretting for their decay," in that third stanza, but it is not an unjustified device and certainly not as pretentiously handled as it is in "The Daughters of War."

The fourth stanza introduces questions about immortality, and so far the movement of thought is rational. But the thought here is a little unclear: why must he assume that the souls of the dead have gone into the earth and not into a conventional heaven, because a few lines later he does acknowledge human continuity as originating in God (the dead body is the "soul's sack / Emptied of God-ancestralled essences")? There appears to be an unorthodox view at work here, but it is not explained sufficiently or even exposed. The fifth stanza continues this line of thought, simply and unhelpfully adding that no one saw the souls leaving the bodies, so they must have passed into the earth. Since when have the faithful depended on empirical evidence for their belief in heaven and in the transcendence of souls?

The sixth stanza digresses with an overstated comment on the unconsciousness of mortality in the living:

> What of us, who flung on the shrieking pyre,
> Walk, our usual thoughts untouched,
> Our lucky limbs as on ichor fed,
> Immortality seeming ever?
>
> (32–35)

"Us" obviously includes the poet, the same poet who has just been speaking of mortality, death, and decay, whose little fiction in the third stanza is an expression of his intensified awareness of mortality. Does Rosenberg expect us to believe that the "us" represents the average soldier, that the average soldier does not fear death, does not have his usual thoughts touched by the destruction and death around him?

The speaker then returns to the external scene, and except for some rather forced dramatics in the seventh stanza ("Till the shrapnel called 'An end!'"

[44]), there is clarity and calmness.[59] The rest of the poem (48–79) is impressive in its precision and pathos. Stanza eight is especially effective:

> A man's brains splattered on
> A stretcher-bearer's face;
> His shook shoulders slipped their load,
> But when they bent to look again
> The drowning soul was sunk too deep
> For human tenderness.
>
> (48–53)

The potential sensationalism is defused by the controlled and functional alliteration: the *s*'s at first emphasize the slippage, and then after being suspended for a line are used to soften the voice, as the sentence ends and is anchored in "tenderness."

The undeveloped religious suggestiveness re-enters briefly in line 55 ("Stretched at the cross roads"), but this is a very minor flaw in a renewed rational movement from the very recent dead to the older dead (stanzas 8 to 10), which provides the frame for the final sustained focus on "one not long dead" and the poignant recreation of his last moments of conscious life as he hears the limbers (with which the poem began) nearing. The final lines are moving not so much because of the earlier conceptual assertions or because of the obvious irony of this particular situation (he dies just before the wiring party reaches him), as because of the constraint in those last stanzas, which define an unsentimental tenderness:

> Even as the mixed hoofs of the mules,
> The quivering-bellied mules,
> And the rushing wheels all mixed
> With his tortured upturned sight,
> So we crashed round the bend,
> We heard his weak scream,
> We heard his very last sound,
> And our wheels grazed his dead face.
>
> (72–79)

The poem finally finds its tone, but only after it restricts its compass.

Rosenberg was the most romantic and the most experimental of the major war poets, but "Break of Day in the Trenches" and "Dead Man's Dump" are his most nearly successful poems, because some of the lines at least expose a native talent free of his damaging aesthetic theories. But his accomplishment, I believe, is a limited one. Near the end of her biography, Jean Liddiard offers this summary statement:

> As an artist he was outside any tradition, and this gave him significance in an age which has found its traditions invalid. He was a victim several times over of his

own rootlessness, of the social structure, of established cultural attitudes, and finally of the war itself. This was the source of his failure and his success, and because of it his achievement has a resonance and poignancy that transcend the brief facts of his life and the incompleteness of his work.[60]

The complacency behind that first sentence is my central concern in this study. There were strong creative traditions available to those intelligent and mature enough to discover them. In the absence of such discovery, the poet can easily become the victim of his own detached and eccentric imagination. But so many of the critics are preoccupied with victims. Jon Silkin goes so far as to say that "the proper focus in a poem about war is on man as man's victim."[61] Again, my concern here is with the principles and moral strengths that allow the soldier, be he a poet or not, to try to avoid being a victim.

Edmund Blunden

What Bergonzi says of Edmund Blunden could apply to Ivor Gurney as well: his "war poems are neither traditionally heroic nor radically antiheroic. They are the products of a gentle mind intent upon preserving its defenses; not, in such conditions, an ignoble aim." That last qualifier is unnecessary: such preservation is never ignoble. But Bergonzi, like most of the critics, is ill at ease with the traditional qualities of both poets: he finds Blunden "anachronistic" and Gurney "conventional," and classifies both, along with Edward Thomas, as poets of pastoral retreat, "evading the conditions of the Front."[62] "Evading" is a very misleading term; they may not often be successful, but at least they are attempting to find significance in, and not just to record (or mythologize), their war experiences. If this is a "retreat," it is from the absorption in immediate events (and consequent anger and sometimes pathos) of Sassoon and Owen into the kind of judicious perspective one occasionally finds in Hardy and Graves. Both Blunden and Gurney were indebted significantly to the tradition of regional poetry, the "tradition of the essentially rooted writer," as Michael Thorpe puts it,[63] and such indebtedness authorized their attempts at a widened perspective. Blunden's failed attempt highlights all the more Gurney's accomplishment.

What strikes one about Blunden's war poetry (most of which was printed as a supplement to his prose memoir, *Undertones of War*[64]) is the frequency with which he deals with lulls in action, such as "The Guard's Mistake," "A House in Festubert," "Gouzeaucourt: The Deceitful Calm," "Battalion in Rest," "La Quinque Rue," "At Senlis Once," and "Concert

Party: Busseboom." These situations provide Blunden with the opportunity to observe with his admirable clear-sightedness the details of nature (especially those disturbed by war): his most persistent themes are warring man's devastation of nature and nature's ability to calm, if not cure. The themes are not original in Blunden, only more persistent. Unfortunately, he rarely does anything with them: he broadens the perspective only to leave the moral implications undeveloped. Billeting behind the lines in a house in Festubert, Blunden only offers a Sassoon-like sarcasm:

> A hermit might have built a cell
> Among those evergreens, beside
> That mellow wall: they serve as well
> For four lean guns. Soft, hermits, hide,
> Lest pride display you.
>
> (16–20)

In "Illusions," he almost justifies Bergonzi's criticism:

> Trenches in the moonlight, allayed with lulling moonlight,
> Have had their loveliness; when dancing dewy grasses
> Caressed us stumping along their earthy lanes;
> When the crucifix hanging over was strangely illumined,
> And one imagined music, one ever heard the brave bird
> In the sighing orchards flute above the weedy well.
> There are such moments; forgive me that I throne them,
> Nor gloze that there comes soon the nemesis of beauty.
>
> (1–8)

Too many times the nature he juxtaposes to the war is sifted through a self-satisfied, "literary" sensibility that feels no need to do more than point out the ironic contrasts. His juxtapositions are gentler than Sassoon's but no more probing. "Vlamertinghe: Passing the Chateau, July, 1917" opens with "'And all her silkin flanks with garlands drest'—/But we are coming to the sacrifice." The pastoral tradition is kept literary rather than real by the allusions to Keats's "Ode on a Grecian Urn," and so the perspective is widened but hardly clearer for the effort. The abrupt colloquialism in the final couplet, referring to the "gay carpet" of flowers ("But if you ask me, mate, the choice of colour/Is scarcely right; this red should have been duller") only calls attention to the status of the intellectual background to the poem as little more than a cliché.

Blunden's problem was that he was reading not only Keats in the trenches but more avidly Young's *Night Thoughts*, so his style as well as his thinking suffered. There are the exclamatory outbursts ("Such a gay carpet!" in "Vlamertinghe"), the proliferation of adjectives, often in monotonous arrangements (as "brave bird," "sighing orchards," and "weedy well" in lines 5–6 of "Illusions"), the awkwardly packed verbals ("blossoming trees robed round" from "A House in Festubert," and "East then and west false dawns fan-flashed" from "Trench Raid near Hodge"), the inevitable inversions ("And iron seeds broadcast he threw" from "Rural Economy"), the pretentious personifications ("Then war brought down his fist" from "Pillbox"), the poetic diction (instead of the sky we have "the blue profound" in "Recognition"), the obtrusive alliteration ("Pale sleep in slimy cellars scarce allays / With its brief blank the burden" from "Preparations for Victory")—all so annoyingly present that they suggest that the defenses sought by Blunden were as much stylistic as pastoral. He so flaunts his eloquence that nature in his war poems in little more than a pastoral artifice.

On one of the few occasions when he tries to confront violent experience directly in his verse, as in the praised "Third Ypres," his style clashes with the dramatic intention, and the result is an impressionistic rush constantly tripping over its own expression. Like the mid-eighteenth-century poets he admired, he gives us second-rate Miltonisms rather than defined experience. The poem opens:

> Triumph! How strange, how strong had triumph come
> On weary hate of foul and endless war
> When from its grey gravecloths awoke anew
> The summer day.
>
> (1–4)

Action is anticipated by the sound of the enemy changing his positions:

> The hurrying batteries beyond the masking hills
> For their new parley setting themselves in array
> In crafty forms unmapped.
>
> (15–17)

He is surprised that the guns do not stop when the rain starts: "And those distorted guns, that lay past use, / Why—miracles not over!—all a-firing!" (38–39). Amidst the intensified bombardments the next day, he constructs a semi-precious metaphor: "the clay dances / In founts of clods around the concrete sties" (86–87). The attack is "wrath's oncoming," and men chatting in a pillbox to keep up their courage are "skirting the abyss of madness with light phrases" (91). Toward the end of the poem, Blunden gives us six lines of plain speaking (the officer—Blunden himself—speaks to headquarters by phone); the intrusion is refreshing and calls more attention to the stilted language:

> ... "For God's sake send and help us,
> Here in a gunpit, all headquarters done for,
> Forty or more, the nine-inch came right through,
> All splashed with arms and legs, and I myself
> The only one not killed nor even wounded.

You'll send—God bless you!"

(111–116)

We are tempted to overvalue this because of what surrounds it—and the relief is too short. The poem continues immediately with "The more monstrous fate/Shadows our own, the mind swoons doubly burdened" (116–117), and thus to its inflated close: "But who with what command can now relieve/The dead men from that chaos, or my soul?" (125–126).

Blunden is most palatable, or least objectionable, and certainly most readable, when on too few occasions he sounds like Sassoon and is content with plain diction and simple ironies, as in "Two Voices," "The Welcome," "Escape," and "Concert Party: Busseboom." Contrary to the critical commonplace about most of his fellow trench poets, the war temporarily made Blunden into a bad poet: its destructive enormity called out his most pompous poeticisms. This is not the kind of broadened perspective that I want to defend. Fortunately without the war to inflate him, he could (but again on too few occasions) find strength in firmer, better understood, experiences. In "The Recovery" from 1931, he manages to sound more like a mature Wordsworth than Edward Young, finding "temperate sense" returning as he keeps his eyes away from a Shelleyan sky:

> The meadow-stream will serve
>   For my refreshment; that high glory yields
> Imaginings that slay; the safe paths curve
>   Through unexalted fields.

(21–24)

Blunden is at his observant, quiet, English best in a poem like "Winter: East Anglia" (1926), in which he uses a stylistic device in the final lines, in this case a triplet rhyme, that is functional rather than decorative, forceful rather than literary:

> But the cornered weasel stands his ground,
> Shrieks at the dogs and boys set round,
> Shrieks as he knows they stand all round,
>   And hard as winter dies.

(15–18)[65]

Unfortunately either his immaturity, or the war, or both delayed his appreciation of the power of such plainness. Even when his mind returned to the war, the memory was enough to reinflate his style: the sight of Ypres' battlefield in 1929 causes him to generalize loosely and almost mythologically how

>   Man in our time . . .
>   . . . struck the Sun,
> And for a season turned the Sun to blood;
> Many such nights as this his Witch and he
> Unmasked their metal, and with poisonous blasts
> Broke the fair sanctuary of this world's rest
> And circumvented God.
>
> ("Return of the Native," 22–28)

In most of Blunden's postwar poetry, it is very evident that he was too committed to a soft Romanticism to give his war experiences the precise definition they required.

Ivor Gurney

Ivor Gurney also had trouble with his style (his structures are weak and his syntax often "gnarled," to use Blunden's word), but it is because of a failure to revise (for whatever reasons, one of which was the mental instability that kept him in an asylum for many years) and not because of a failure of literary or moral understanding. Edmund Blunden also says in the introduction to the 1954 edition of Gurney's poems that "the invincible love of his county [Gloucestershire] which Gurney's experiences as a child and as a youth implanted may be said to have acted at length almost as a tyranny over his poetical character and range."[66] Blunden, I suppose, escaped such "tyranny" by anchoring his patriotism in nothing more specific than an eighteenth-century tradition of English landscape poetry. But "tyranny' could not be more wrong; because Gurney's love of England was more localized, his patriotism more personal, it could allow for a more complex and more qualified attitude toward the war. For instance, in "De Profundis" (from 1919 volume *War's Embers*) he says that a living tradition is clarity:

>   We are stale here, we are covered body and soul and mind
>   With mire of the trenches, close clinging and foul,
>   We have left our old inheritance, our Paradise behind,
>   And clarity is lost to us and cleanness of soul.
>
> (9–12)

But "Paradise" is not, as it was to Georgians like Blunden, some generalized and all too often poetic "English countryside," but a particular part of England, as the last stanza asserts:

>   Hard it is for men of moors or fens to endure
>   Exile and hardship, or the northland grey-drear;

> But we of the rich plain of sweet airs and pure,
> Oh! Death would take so much from us, how should we not fear?
>
> (25–28)

This is a slightly unconventional way of expressing love of one's homeland, but the patriotism is no less substantial, and perhaps more so, than the more public and abstract declarations by Brooke and others. Rather than glorify the sacrifice of men for their country, Gurney vivifies the sense of loss that is the direct motive for the sacrifice. Only that which is valuable is worth missing.

But as I have said, his patriotism was qualified. On the one hand, he had a sense of public duty. In an undated letter written soon after he volunteered (early in 1915) for the 2nd/5th Gloucesters, he justified his decision: "It is indeed a better way to die; with these men, in such a cause: than the end which seemed near me and was so desirable only just over two years ago [reference probably to a nervous breakdown in 1913]. And if I escape; well, there will be memories for old age; not all pleasant, but none so unpleasant as those which would have come had I refused the call." On the other hand, he had no illusions about military life: in a letter of about the same time he said, "The aim of training troops is to make them as tired as possible without teaching them anything." Later from the Front he wrote, "when I return to England I am going to lie in wait for all men who have been officers, and very craftily question them on several subjects." And on 27 July 1917, he defined his kind of patriotism:

> though I am ready if necessary to die for England, I do not see the necessity; it being only a hard and fast system which has sent so much of the flower of Englands [sic] artists to risk death, and a wrong materialistic system; rightly or wrongly I consider myself able to do work which will do honour to England. Such is my patriotism, and I believe it to be the right kind.[67]

There are hints of this complex patriotism in the often crude and derivative poems in his first volume, *Severn and Somme* (1917). "The Fire Kindled," the first poem in the collection, begins with "God, that I might see," and the next nineteen lines catalog Gloucestershire places, but the sixth and final stanza adds a note of disillusionment to the nostalgia:

> Here we go sore of shoulder,
>   Sore of foot, by quiet streams;
> But these are not my rivers. . . .
>   And these are useless dreams.
>
> (21–24)[68]

In "Strange Service" he vows service to the England that bore him "under the Cotswold hills," but in the final stanza there is an unsentimental reversal:

> Think on me too, O Mother, who wrest my soul to serve you
> In strange and fearful ways beyond your encircling waters;
> None but you can know my heart, its tears and sacrifice;
> None, but you, repay.
>
> (17–20)

Of all the war poets, Gurney has the greatest talent for closure. One may be dissatisfied with the turns in thought before the end of the poem, but one must be impressed by Gurney's ability to conclude so firmly.[69] "The Strong Thing" is a much slighter poem, but is touching and amusing in its final characterization of heaven as Gloucestershire:

> And on the Day of Days, the Judgment Day,
>   The Word of Doom awaiting breathless and still,
> I'll marvel how sweet's the air down Framilode way,
>   And take my sentence on sheer-down Crickley Hill.
>
> (5–8)

The volume ends with five sonnets "To the Memory of Rupert Brooke" that may not be as verbally accomplished as Brooke's, but with sentiments that complete and correct his. "Pain" gives us a realistic picture of what Brooke never saw:

>   ... Grey monotony lending
> Weight to the grey skies, grey mud where goes
> An army of grey bedrenched scarecrows in rows
> Careless at last of cruellest Fate-sending.
>
> (5–8)

It ends with: "The amazed heart cries angrily out on God." "Home-Sickness" defines home as the knowable as well as the familiar. "Servitude" criticizes of servitude of "this brass-cleaning life," but nonetheless finds a place for one kind of courage:

> Only the love of comrades sweetens all,
> Whose laughing spirit will not be outdone.
> As night-watching men wait for the sun
> To hearten them, so wait I on such boys
> As neither brass nor Hell-fire may appal,
> Nor guns, nor sergeant-major's bluster and noise.
>
> (9–14)

This comradeship that Gurney discovered in the army gave him, however briefly, a sense of security and perhaps even purpose. There is surely respect rather than irony in that admirable passage in "First Time In ('The Captain addresses us ...')" in which he comments on how the experienced soldiers advised the inexperienced ones of life "in the Line":

> Never were quieter folk in tea party history.
> Never in 'Cranford', Trollope, even. And, as it were, home
> Closed round us. They told us lore, ...
> . . . .
> ...—all necessary
> Common-sense workmanlike cautions of salutary
> Wisdom—the mechanic day-lore of modern war-making,
> Calm thought discovered in mind and body shaking.
> The whole craft and business of bad occasion.
>
> (30–32, 37–41)

Much of the rage of his madness in the years after the war stems from his own sense of betrayal. Michael Hurd talks rather condescendingly of "the world of happy warriors ... falling apart and leaving him,"[70] but Gurney put it better toward the end of "First Time In":

> What an evening! What a first time, what a shock
> So rare of home-pleasure beyond measure
> And always to time's ending surely a treasure.
>
> Since after-war so surely hurt, disappointed men
> Who looked for the golden Age to come friendly again.
>
> (50–54)

His rootedness, his love and thorough-going knowledge of his native Gloucestershire, also was the source of his much-prized but seldom achieved serenity of mind. He preferred Bach to Milton: "the tolerant admiration on the one side and the slightly contemptuous fatheadedness on the other! Milton is one of the great men not worth crossing the street to speak to. Bach was worth a hungry pilgrimage to see."[71] He disliked the mannerism of rhythm and diction in Rupert Brooke's poetry, which he thought was caused by Brooke's soaking in immediate events too quickly.[72] It is not difficult to determine his attitude toward the Victorian aesthetes: he describes in a September 1917 letter the old gas: it "had a heavy hothouse Swinburnian filthy sort of odour—voluptuous and full of danger."[73] And of course there is his high regard for Ben Jonson,

> ... labouring like the great son he was
> Of Solway and of Westminster—O, maker, maker,
> Given of all the gods to anything but grace.
>
> ("Townshend," 15–17)[74]

The letters and poems indicate that Gurney was not overwhelmed by the horrors of the war he experienced. He achieved a certain detachment, perhaps a certain "kind of stoic irony" (as Hurd calls it). When he complained of the war, it was in terms different from those of the more emotional poets: "You simply dont know what France means, not in horror, but in everyday trial."[75] It is quite mistaken I think to try to see him, as does Leonard Clark, as a poet of the antiwar protest: "The poetry is in the agony rather than in the pity."[76]

It may be true that Gurney was to some extent influenced by Whitman and Hopkins, as many critics point out, but this influence had little effect on his best and sanest work. He seems to have equally valued Hardy and Edward Thomas. Walter de la Mare certainly saw it when he wrote in 1937 of Gurney's poems:

> The paramount effect on the mind after reading these new poems is a sense of supreme abundance. One has ascended to the top, as it were, of some old Gloucestershire church tower, and surveyed in a wide circuit all that lies beneath it. And then, as with the reader of *The Dynasts*, one sinks unjarred to earth again; and all that is now so close and precise reveals why the distant seemed so lovely, so lovely, and brimful of grace.[77]

"A sense of supreme abundance"—Blunden tells us in his book on Hardy of C. E. Montague who, while serving on the Western Front during World War I, turned to Hardy's books again, and was more than ever impressed by the bigness of the author in comparison with his contemporaries.[78]

The abundance can be noted when we set the Thomas-like delicacy of "The Awakening" (written two or three years after the war) next to "The Canadians," which deals directly with the war. The one is quiet and contemplative:

> In the white painted dark lobby
> The rosy firelight is thrown,
> And the mat is still moisted with fresh mud
> As I work at my task alone.
>
> The murmuring of the kettle soothes me—
> As those above sleep on still.
> I love that dear winter-reflection ...
> Gone truant from loving too well.

The other, equally detailed, is angry but also almost philosophical in its secure handling of the abstract summary lines:

> We marched, and saw a company of Canadians,
> Their coats weighed eighty pounds at least, we saw them
> Faces infinitely grimed in, with almost dead hands
> Bent, slouching downwards to billets comfortless and dim.
> Cave dwellers last of tribes they seemed, and a pity
> Even from us just relieved, much as they were, left us.
> Lord, what a land of desolation, what iniquity
> Of mere being, of what youth that country bereft us.
>
> (1–8)

That "iniquity of mere being" carries more mature judgment than all the irony, pathos, and myth-making of Sassoon, Owen, and Rosenberg.

The abundance, or what I prefer to call a broad and defensible moral perspective, finds expression as intelligent caution in one of Gurney's finest war poems, "The Silent One." Hurd refers to it as "this most truthful report from the battlefield,"[79] but it is considerably more than a report. Here Gurney's local and qualified patriotism, his sense of comradeship with his fellow soldiers, his fear of excess and of threats to security are all present. The title must be part of the first sentence:

The Silent One

Who died on the wires, and hung there, one of two—
Who for his hours of life had chattered through
Infinite lovely chatter of Bucks accent:
Yet faced unbroken wires; stepped over, and went
A noble fool, faithful to his stripes—and ended.
But I weak, hungry, and willing only for the chance
Of line—to fight in the line, lay down under unbroken
Wires, and saw the flashes and kept unshaken,
Till the politest voice—a finicking accent, said:
'Do you think you might crawl through there: there's a hole.'
Darkness, shot at: I smiled, as politely replied—
'I'm afraid not, Sir.' There was no hole no way to be seen
Nothing but chance of death, after tearing of clothes.
Kept flat, and watched the darkness, hearing bullets whizzing—
And thought of music—and swore deep heart's deep oaths
(Polite to God) and retreated and came on again,
Again retreated—and a second time faced the screen.

There is neither Falstaffian revolt here nor Hotspurian heroism, but there is common sense, and a sense of duty. The poem notes the foolish but sincere nobility of the man who died on the wires, criticizes the polite officiousness of the unrealistic officer, and expresses a desire to fight *in the line*, not in front of it. "Butchers and Tombs" is another poem that treats honor and service realistically and without irony:

After so much battering of fire and steel
It had seemed well to cover them with Cotswold stone—
And shortly praising their courage and quick skill
Leave them buried, hidden till the slow, inevitable
Change came should make them service of France alone.
But the time's hurry, the commonness of the tale
Made it a thing not fitting ceremonial,
And so the disregarders of blister on heel,
Pack on shoulder, barrage and work at the wires,

> One wooden cross had for ensign of honour and life gone—
> Save when the Gloucesters turning sudden to tell to one
> Some joke, would remember and say—'That joke is done,'
> Since he who would understand was so cold he could not feel,
> And clay binds hard, and sandbags get rotten and crumble.

These poems are not only two of Gurney's best, but as good as any and better than most written about World War I.

We should close this discussion of Gurney with two poems that seem to have been inspired by Hardy's "In Time of 'The Breaking of Nations'" and, like that poem, display Gurney's broad but stable moral perspective on this and perhaps most other wars. "Between the Boughs" combines that delicacy I spoke of earlier with an acknowledgment of cosmic mysteries, but there are no vatic pretensions:

> Between the boughs the stars showed numberless
> And the leaves were
> As wonderful in blackness as those brightnesses
> Hung in high air.
>
> Two lovers in that whispering silence, what
> Should fright our peace?
> The aloofness, the dread of starry majesties,
> The night-stilled trees.

If there is an American influence here, it is surely Emily Dickinson and not Walt Whitman. "Brown Earth Look" begins with the burning couch grass from Hardy's poem and broadens in the second stanza to a sense of the historical continuity in the practice:

> Brown the sense of things, the light smoke blows across
> The field face, light blue wisps of sweet bitter reek
> Dear to the Roman perhaps, so old seems the dross
> Burning of root, grass, wheat, so near, easy to seek.
>
> (5–8)

It ends with the best gloss of Hardy's theme that I know:

> And all the tales of far Europe that come on one,
> The sense of myriads tending the needings of life,
> Are more to one than the near memory of battle gun.
> Peace with its sorrow blots out the agonies of strife.
>
> (13–16)

Donald Davie, in his review of Kavanagh's edition of Gurney's poems, rightly says that "great poetry is greatly sane, greatly lucid." There are signs of nervous disorder in most of the poems written by this man who survived the war only to spend the last fifteen years of his life in a mental hospital. In a few poems, however, one detects a superior and deeply moral sanity and lucidity that testifies to at least the possibility of an alternative to the aestheticized response of Blunden or to the emotional protest of the more popular poems emerging from the Great War.

4
Modern Love

In the introduction to the *Faber Book of Love Poems* (1973), Geoffrey Grigson laments that "our own time, for various reasons, is stingy with love poems or poems about love, stingy in fact with the cadences of poetry."[1] The connection between cadences and love, he goes on to explain, is the need of the poet to solace himself, "in the chaos of being in love, by firmly enclosing as much of it as he can in measure." And he quotes Donne: "For, he tames it, that fetters it in verse" ("The Triple Fool"). The connection is even broader than Grigson allows. Love is that poetic subject most demanding of formal flexibility; not the deceptive flexibility of open or nonexistent form that so cherishes incoherence and therefore selfishness, but the true flexibility of a controlled and moderating measure that can define and hence allow for variety, extension, and deviation while communicating the full consciousness and understanding of them. The loosening and abandonment of form in the early decades of this century was not so much rebellion against authority as part of the general suspicion of possibility, of creative communal order, therefore of claims of physical and spiritual union, of fullness and fulfillment in human love. In stressing the failures, discouragements, and isolations of "modern" desire, the "modern" poets questioned the very capacity for that highest form of human sympathy and most complex form of self-sacrifice. As James McFarlane says in "The Mind of Modernism," because of the fusing of the mechanistic and the intuitive, the growth of faith in positivistic science *and* its opposite (occultism and anarchism), and the acceptance of Nietzsche and promotion of a climate of shrillness, frustration, and irreverence, "the custody of life's integrities began to pass from society to the individual."[2] Where concern is with the individual (and the stress is on his alienation), with the eccentric, with the vanity of endeavor, then the mixture of impersonality and generalizing power necessary to express otherness *and* indeed the very knowledge of the other (the foundation of mature love) is consequently undervalued, and the stinginess Grigson speaks of is almost inevitable.

I say almost. There were a few poets who although no less "steadily refusing to be comforted" (as I. A. Richards said in 1925 of Thomas

Hardy[3]) were able within the decades dominated by modernists' doubts and attacks on traditional moral positions and language to write mature, full, and sometimes even great love poems. I have already discussed those of Thomas Hardy (especially the "Poems of 1912–13"), and of Edward Thomas (especially "And You, Helen"); in this chapter I investigate the love poetry of Robert Bridges (whose lyrical love poems do not really belong in a discussion of twentieth-century verse, but who provides an exemplary introduction to the standards we should expect our more modern poets to meet), and of D. H. Lawrence and Robert Graves. All three were in very important senses independent of contemporary trends and fashionable sensibilities, and the last two were almost rare in their strength of character and extraordinary persistence in the immediate post-war years, which were, as William Pritchard says, "not the easiest ones to be a poet in."[4] But before looking closely at the love poetry of these three poets, let us consider more fully our general topic and the challenge facing the poets of the age, the challenge that so many failed or ignored and so few met.

One can, of course, overemphasize the change in the attitude toward love in the early twentieth century. Both Grigson in his Faber collection and Jon Stallworthy in his Penguin collection of the same year organize their material thematically, collecting love poems from all ages and placing them side by side under such headings as "Love Expected," "The Plagues of Loving," "Persuasions," and "Reverberations," Stallworthy reminding us with some justice "of man's changeless responses to the changeless changing seasons of his heart.[5] But I wonder if before this century such anthologists would have spent, as does Stallworthy, so much more space on poems dealing with "Aberrations," "Separations," and "Desolations" than on those dealing with "Celebrations." Looking more closely, one can detect (outside of the steady stream of directly erotic poetry) a tradition declining gradually in strength and, from the late eighteenth century especially, an increasing number of poems undermining and narrowing the definition and expectations of love that supported that tradition.

The Great War seemed to accelerate the change. In *The Long Weekend*, Robert Graves and Alan Hodge, charting the social history of Britain from 1918 to the Second World War, summarize the particular force of the application of Einstein's theory of relativity and of Freudian psychoanalysis to ethical contexts:

> Relativity dismissed Christianity as a take-it or leave-it hypothesis. So long as one acted consistently in accordance with one's personal hypothesis and was not ashamed of what one did, all was well. . . . To [the followers of Dr. Ernest Jones] men and women were not thinking beings of independent judgment, but behaviouristic animals whose natural modes of behaviour had been interfered with by superstitious moral codes.[6]

So if the war intensified the questioning of the virtue of courage and the aims of honor, the 1920s broadened that assault, bringing further into doubt the absoluteness and reasonableness of many more moral categories and distinctions, including love and lust. Sexual and homosexual promiscuity were defended publicly more and more; mental health was equated with an uninhibited sex life; to be well and happy, one must obey one's sexual urges (the age was reminded of Oscar Wilde's dictum, "Never resist temptation"). The most popular fictional character among the lowbrow public of the twenties was "Tarzan of the Apes," and the most popular compelling fiction was the sex-problem fiction of Aldous Huxley, Michael Arlen, and D. H. Lawrence.

But it would be wrong to associate Lawrence too closely with this popular movement or at all with the vogue of bohemianism of the time, nicely characterized by Graves and Hodge as "a gay disorderliness of life, cheerful bad manners, and no fixed hours or sexual standards."[7] Rather than rehearse any further these well-known traits of the "Careless Twenties," I would rather point to the counter view still alive and able to be profoundly embodied only a few years earlier in *The Rainbow*, Lawrence's most historically rooted and English novel. Although the central theme of the novel, as Leavis so convincingly argues, is "the urgency, and the difficult struggle, of the higher human possibilities to realize themselves" and "'fulfillment' in the individual as the essential manifestation of life," this theme carries with it a corollary: "it is only by way of the most delicate and complex responsive relations with others that the individual can achieve fulfillment."[8] It is this corollary and its wonderful enactment in chapter 5, "Wedding at the Marsh," that I would like to attend to now. In this chapter and especially in the inspired speech on marriage by Tom Brangwen, whose earlier life had left him knowing that "mere satisfaction of the sexual impulse—was not what he wanted, and could not, in fact, bring him satisfaction,"[9] we find, if only in powerful suggestion, the criteria of a fully satisfying conception of love, as that conception has crystallized from thousands of years of human history (the pressure of which we ignore at our peril) into the communal ceremony that gives a structure to chapter 5.

The opening sentence places the ancient ceremony within a mirroring natural setting: although winter, "It was a beautiful sunny day for the wedding, a muddy earth but a bright sky."[10] This suggests more than just the potential for emergence from the sucking mud. In chapter 1, Lawrence established the symbolic duality that the ceremony merges: the men working on and living close to the rich land were most content facing "inwards to the teeming life of creation, which poured unresolved into their veins." This "drowse of blood-intimacy" was also on the women, but they "were different," they "looked out from the heated, blind intercourse of farm-life to the spoken world beyond." The men's faces were "always turned to the heat of the blood, staring into the sun, dazed with looking towards the source of generation, unable to turn around," while the women "faced outwards" to "the far-off world of cities and governments and the active scope of man, the magic land ..., where secrets were made known and desires fulfilled" (pp. 7-9).[11] In the wedding of man with woman, those (male) preverbal instincts of generation are brought up through the (female) articulation, which is the acknowledgment, to a community (only within which it can have meaning), of a mutual and scrupulous responsibility of one toward another. In the complex symbolic distinctions of this novel, the wedding ceremony is a feminine form. The "spoken world" that the couple thereby enter makes fulfillment possible: "where secrets were made known and desires fulfilled." Those distinctions of chapter 1 are still present 124 pages later in that same opening paragraph of chapter 5. Tom and Anna, the father and mother of the groom, are described: he in "grey trousers," she in "dark grey silk with lace," but his coat is black, while she has "a touch of peacock-blue in her bonnet" (p. 133). In addition, he is "hearty but troubled," and she is "very sure and definite."

Within that natural enclosure is the gathering of the villagers, and even closer the family of the bride and groom. At the center of the narrated events and of the group is Tom, who "becoming roisterous" and confident with drink, initiates a toast, then a little later, "in his solid fashion ... letting himself go at last," makes a speech on the joys and virtues of married love. I agree completely with John Baxter in his discussion of the episode of the toasts as an illustration of both the plain style and J. V. Cunningham's notion of "the ethics of character," in which the most intensely individual actions of characters carry a powerfully extra-personal significance.[12]

> 'Lift your glasses up,' shouted Tom Brangwen from the parlour, 'lift your glasses up, an' drink to the hearth an' home—hearth an' home, an' may they enjoy it.'
> 'Night an' day, an' may they enjoy it,' shouted Frank Brangwen, in addition.
> 'Hammer an' tongs, and may they enjoy it,' shouted Alfred Brangwen, the saturnine.
> 'Fill your glasses up, an' let's have it all over again,' shouted Tom Brangwen.
> 'Hearth and home, an' may ye enjoy it.'
> There was a ragged shout of the company in response.
> 'Bed an' blessin', an' may ye enjoy it,' shouted Frank Brangwen.
> There was a swelling chorus in answer.
> 'Comin' and goin', an' may ye enjoy it,' shouted the saturnine Alfred Brangwen, and the men roared by now boldly, and the woman said 'Just hark, now!'
>
> (136-137)

Baxter comments: "Intensely individual, each toast sums up what marriage has meant to each of the Brangwen brothers; taken together, they represent the potentiality, the range of possibilities in marriage open to Anna and Will who, by choosing to marry, are committed absolutely to these ways of creating significance in marriage."[13] I add, further to help me use this passage to discuss some modern love poems, the prior point that the commitment of public marriage (and this chapter is very public—we rarely get close to the bride and groom) itself creates significance for their love. Or as Ian Robinson has said, "marriage guarantees the possibility of significance. ... We have to retain our judgment [even when in love]; and marriage is the great guarantee that judgment is possible."[14] (Another guarantee, he continues, giving me my larger critical point, is the imaginative language of love in the great love poems and novels.) It is this possibility that Tom Brangwen discusses in his speech after the feast.

But before looking at that I would like to note the structure of the narration of the toasts. The first three, more personal but not directed at the couple ("may *they* enjoy it") are, like the second three, ordered temporally: domesticity can aggravate differences, which can lead to conflict. The last three, coming also in order from the serious Tom, then the ironic Frank, then "the saturnine" and cynical (and, as Lawrence notes later, "unseeing") Alfred, less personal but now directly addressed to the couple ("may *ye* enjoy it"), reinterpret the possibilities in a more positive or at least ambiguous light: a more emphatic domesticity ("Hearth *and* home" rather than "Hearth an' home"), procreation (only possible because of biological differences), and "comin' and goin'," which might imply, after "hammer an' tongs," the inconstancy and promiscuity that can follow marital discord, but actually denotes (as Baxter says) "the eternal process of Providence that orders men's lives" (27): birth and unexpected death. Of course, the wedding party reacts openly to the implication: "the men roared by now boldly and the woman said, 'Just hark, now!'" But we have the advantage and can respond more fully. The passage has the tightness, economy, and expressive breadth of a poem. These toasts with this movement from home through birth to death and from personal to public (death is the most public of facts) prepare for the almost philosophical speech (called variously a "conundrum" and "discourse" by the narrator) that follows.

This man of the soil, who had "faced inwards to the teeming life of creation," is by his participation in this ceremony turned outwards "to the spoken world beyond": "For the first time in his life," we are told, "he must spread himself wordily." Lawrence is careful at the beginning of the speech to establish a tone for it that, as we shall see, has long been held to be the most appropriate for love itself: "he was deeply serious and hugely amused at the same time." The speech contains two arguments. The thesis of the first is that "Marriage ... is what we're made for," and runs like this:

1. "'A man ... enjoys being a man: for what purpose was he made a man, if not to enjoy it?' ... 'And likewise, ... a woman enjoys being a woman. ...'"
2. "'Now, ... for a man to be a man, it takes a woman,' ... 'And for a woman to be a woman, it takes a *man*.'"
3. "'Therefore we have marriage.'"

In his homely and unsophisticated way Tom Brangwen is offering a narrower, sexual version of ancient Greek and particularly Aristotelian propositions: man is a rational animal; what distinguishes him from other animals is his capacity for thinking, knowing, and understanding. The final cause of human existence must be the fulfilling or completing of his distinguishing nature. Because happiness is the satisfaction of desires and man naturally desires to perfect his own nature, the way to the greatest happiness will be the completing of one's nature by living intelligently (or in Brangwen's terms, finding the best way of being a man or a woman—marriage).

The second argument extends that second proposition in the first argument to show how perfecting one's nature moves one closer to Perfection, or God. It extends the secular into the spiritual: both arguments are fundamentally teleological. It runs like this:

1. Human beings strive to be angels, but amongst angels "'there is no such thing as a man nor a woman.'"
2. But an angel can't simply be "'the soul of a man *minus* the man,'" because "'then it would be less than a human being.'"
3. Since an angel's "'got to be more than a human being, ... an Angel is the soul of man and woman in one: they rise united at the Judgment Day, as one Angel. ... when a man's soul and a woman's soul unites together—that makes an Angel.'"

The speech ends with Tom answering the objections of his two brothers, with what amounts to a much more interesting program of soul-making than the young Keats ever proposed:

> 'I dunno about souls. I know as one plus one makes three, sometimes,' said Frank. But he had the laugh to himself.
> 'Bodies and souls, it's the same,' said Tom.
> 'And what about your Misses, who was married afore you knew her?' asked Alfred, set on edge by this discourse.
> 'That I can't tell you. If I am to become an Angel, it'll be my married soul, and not my single soul. It'll not be the soul of me when I was a lad: for I hadn't a soul as would *make* an Angel then.'

How different from and how so very much more human and satisfying is this than the definition of marriage not so much offered as assumed, with a detached and self-flattering rhetoric, by Michel Foucault: "It will be granted no doubt that relations of sex gave rise, in every society, to a *deployment of alliance*: a system of marriage, of fixation and development of kinship ties, of transmission of names and possessions."[15] Foucault's language is completely unable to give any meaningful significance to this or any human institution. But his *is* sadly the prevalent intellectualists' view. That other contemporary French guru is more bluntly dismissive: for the eclectic aesthetician of freedom, Roland Barthes, marriage is "the silliest of spectacles," but then it is meaning itself that he wants to be liberated from: also in *Roland Barthes* he quotes himself from a 1971 article: "'What is difficult is not to liberate sexuality according to a more or less libertarian project but to release it from meaning, including from transgression as meaning.'"[16]

To emphasize further that inadequacy and the strength of the connection between the language and views of Lawrence, this most modern yet not untraditional writer, and to draw out the full suggestive force of this passage in *The Rainbow*, we can go back to the seventeenth century and what is arguably the greatest love poetry in the language.[17] In Book IX of *Paradise Lost*, when Adam learns of Eve's fall, he decides on the instant, without having to think, that he is lost with her. He first speaks to himself:

> ... with thee
> Certain my resolution is to Die;
> How can I live without thee, how forgo
> Thy sweet Converse and Love so dearly join'd,
> To live again in these wild Woods forlorn?
> Should God create another *Eve*, and I
> Another Rib afford, yet loss of thee
> Would never from my heart; no no, I feel
> The Link of Nature draw me: Flesh of Flesh,
> Bone of my Bone thou art, and from thy State
> Mine never shall be parted, bliss or woe.
>
> (906–916)[18]

With such resolution he is "recomforted"; "in calm mood" he turns to Eve and, after a weak attempt to put the best light on the situation, back to a resolute avowal:

> However I with thee have fixt my Lot,
> Certain to undergoe like doom; if Death
> Consort with thee, Death is to mee as Life;
> So forcible within my heart I feel
> The Bond of Nature draw me to my own,
> My own in thee, for what thou art is mine;

> Our State cannot be sever'd, we are one,
> One Flesh; to lose thee were to lose myself.
>
> (952-959)

"These lines mean *love*," says A. J. A Waldock.[19] They are notable for being very plain within the Miltonic grandiloquence, and this fact and the firmness of the movement of verse reinforce their ability to mean as they do. Adam falls through love: far from being "fondly overcome with Female charm" (999), he has experienced the most selfless and therefore truest kind of love. I send you to Mr. Drummond's essay for a full and brilliant commentary on the difficulty Milton has making this compatible with the narrative and theological demands of the poem. My concern is with the essential qualities of the fullest human experience of love manifest here. There is the attachment to that which is readily acknowledged and *known* as independently itself ("another *Eve*," much less simply another woman, could not replace her, and it is "sweet Converse" with her, whereby they can continue to know each other, that he cannot forgo). There is the refinement of thought as well as the enlargement of emotion that the dedication sustains and enhances (Adam has come to understand his own *human* nature—"Our State"—and emphatically to make, as Drummond says, a "decision of his whole being."[20] And there is the force of both of these in drawing the lovers closer to their *natural* selves ("I feel/The Bond of Nature draw me to my own,/My own in thee"), and thus only by mutually and reciprocally completing their human beingness ("to lose thee were to lose myself") do they make themselves angels, as Tom Brangwen would say, that is, worthy of God—but perhaps not Milton's God, who condemns them for this knowledge and this completion.

That Milton's portrayal of human love could so overwhelm his religious doctrine so that what he justifies successfully are not God's but man's ways[21] is evidence of the power of a cultural understanding in the seventeenth century; that Lawrence's rustic echo of that understanding should seem so out of place and "unmodern" even in 1915 attests to a serious decline that only the most independent of literary geniuses could resist in our "enlightened" century. Milton could say it despite himself and Lawrence and a few others (including Robert Bridges and Robert Graves) despite almost everything except themselves.

Let me be more specific about the decline. We must not be taken in by the usual stance of rebelliousness in early twentieth-century dealings with love, mistaking for a daring and honest dismissal of rigid and debilitating Victorian strictures what is more essentially a too-ready acceptance of a Romantic dichotomy, with a shift of preference: the separation of love from sex and the early nineteenth-century idealization of the former and the late nineteenth-century idolization of the latter. The separation was made possible by sophisticated confusions like this one by George Granville, one of Pope's early friends:

> Love is begot by fancy, bred
> By ignorance, by expectation fed,
> Destroyed by knowledge, and, at best,
> Lost in the moment 'tis possessed.
>
> ("Love")[22]

We should, of course, substitute "sexual attraction" for "love" here, but the urbane appeal of the poem depends on our not making such discriminations. The failures of Neoplatonic and other transcendental faiths in the nineteenth century gave rise to one of the polar reactions typical of that age, what C. S. Lewis calls "a ludicrous and portentous solemnisation of sex."[23] It is the move from Shelley's pathetic aspirations:

> The worship the heart lifts above
> And the Heavens reject not,—
> The desire of the moth for the star,
> Of the night for the morrow,
> The devotion to something afar
> From the sphere of our sorrow,
>
> ("To _____," 9–16)

to Crazy Jane's love, who has "pitched his mansion in/The place of excrement." Like C. S. Lewis, I believe that "the highest does not stand without the lowest,"[24] but this is not Yeats's point; he is interested more in asserting his geriatric virility than in thoroughly investigating the bishop's commonsensical advice, which is not far from Shakespeare's "ripeness is all" or Lawrence's attention to "comin' and goin'."

In "The Temperaments," Ezra Pound reduces modern love to a deadpan list of immoral acts (Florialis's "Nine adulteries, 12 liaisons, 64 fornications and something approaching a rape"); the only alternative, in this detached and amused (but not very funny) play on the old appearance vs. reality motif, is the example of Bastidides, who, while he

> ... both talks and writes of nothing save copulation,
> Has become the father of twins,
> But he has accomplished this feat at some cost;
> He had to be four times cuckold.
>
> (5–8)

Here Pound seems interested totally in repugnant extremes (illicit sex and faithless marriage), with the title deflecting the blame from each character and with irony that is impossible to detect because the lack of measure renders mundane what is originally all too prosaic: there is no life in the voice. A final and summary example of this dichotomizing habit is in Herbert Read's "Ritz: Love Among the Ruins": the varieties of lovers, just wakening at sunrise in their rooms at the Ritz, are contained in two ruinous extremes: "the abattoirs and coy fanes of love" (14). These sophisticated experimental poets of the early modernist era seemed intent on actively denying significance to love, for their "advanced" insights could only at best uncover the possible sordidness sometimes beneath Romantic illusions.

Cynical, sarcastic, world-weary, disillusioned modern voices are really no better instruments for discovering or even creating meaning than the inflatedly solemn Romantic ones. They all reveal the poet's discomfort with a subject he has not made much of an effort to master. Many critics have mentioned the necessity for mixing the comic and serious in love poetry: "making love serious . . . is what love poets always do," says Ian Robinson, but "there is something wrong with a totally uncomic love poetry."[25] The presence of the comic element (which can range from simple lightness and informality to the ludicrous) convinces us of the seriousness of the treatment of love, because it is the result of a comprehensive search for a normative perspective. But even more than indicating fine discriminations and placements (the ludicrous, after all, is a measurement against a norm), the comic is also the consequence of a refusal to be immersed. If marriage is the judgment of love, levity is a judgment of the inseparable sexual expression of love.

> The fact that we have bodies is the oldest joke there is. . . . Lovers, unless their love is very short-lived, again and again feel an element not only of comedy, not only of play, but even of buffoonery, in the body's expression of Eros [that kind of love lovers are "in"]. And the body would frustrate us if this were not so. It would be too clumsy an instrument to render love's music unless its very clumsiness could be felt as adding to the total experience its own grotesque charm—a sub-plot or antimasque miming with its own hearty rough-and-tumble what the soul enacts in statelier fashion. . . . For indeed we require this relief. . . . When natural things look most divine, the demoniac is just around the corner.[26]

This attitude is possible only for those who recognize the dangers of such immersion in the physical and the impulsive, an attitude that is not as common as it should be in our century, so many of whose poets found their liberating examples in Emerson and Whitman and their validating premises in popularized psychoanalysis, as Auden solemnly records "In Memory of Sigmund Freud" (1939), of one who "is no more a person/Now but a whole climate of opinion":

> One rational voice is dumb: over a grave
> The household of Impulse mourns one dearly loved.
>   Sad is Eros, builder of cities,
>   And weeping anarchic Aphrodite.
>
>   (67–68, 109–12)

Thomas Wyatt very lightly defines a joyous moment of past surrender in the middle stanza of "They Flee from Me":

> When her loose gown from her shoulders did fall,
> And she me caught in her arms long and small,
>   Therewith all sweetly did me kiss
>   And softly said, 'Dear heart, how like you this?'
>
> (11–14)

One must smile with Wyatt when reading that last line, and the bitterness of the last stanza is more substantial because that scene had its place in a larger scheme of obligations and expectations. His keen sense of justice, not his suffering libido or damaged male pride, lead him to question the appropriate response to the present "fashion of forsaking" ("But since that I so kindly am served,/I would fain know what she hath deserved"). Four hundred years on, Brian Patten's protagonist, looking to bed a bird in "Party Piece" (1967), can contain neither his language nor his impulses. After the other guests have left the party, he says (in his substitute for the witty gymnastics of Renaissance seduction poems), let's "make gentle pornography with one another," as "the dawn creeps in,/Like a stranger," and then he restates the proposition:

>   'Let us not hesitate
>   Over what we know
>   Or over how cold his place has become,
>   But let's unclip our minds
>   And let tumble free
>   The mad, mangled crocodile of love.'
>
> (8–13)

The cool snideness of the poet's conclusion ("And all there was between them then/was rain") is as inadequate as the seducer's sentimentalized selfishness, which is to say that that judgment of the seducer is ours, not the poet's.

Some will argue that the wit and humor of Renaissance love poems, the absence of which in most modern love poetry I am lamenting, is merely an artificial convention that the poet indulges in to show off his intellectual agility, and that we should be grateful for the sincerity and direct honesty of recent poets. I question the depth and motive of that show of sincerity. Modern seriousness is too often pretentious. The poet wants us to admire his anti-idealistic insight and his detachment, which he presents as a superior capacity to resist emotional involvement in his subject. As in so much modernist art, he minimalizes his subject to emphasize what in pre-nineteenth-century verse was already present, but not so emphatically, in a richer context of social and moral concerns. That older poet, usually because of his greater intellectual range, also was more emotionally present in the lines. We as readers could engage with a fuller being, fuller certainly than those pious reporters satisfied with cynical observations of the misunderstandings and failures of love relationships. Poems such as Eliot's "Portrait of a Lady" or Ransom's "Piazza Piece" are directly structured to reveal those gaps that almost seem inevitable to the world-weary poets. Although having some value as mildly satirical recreations of "a world of revealing reticences," as George Williamson calls it,[27] the perplexities, hesitations, and indecisiveness of the personae of such poems so narrowly and intentionally serve only an atmosphere that they suggest a moral paralysis within the poet as well.

But a deficient tone is only one consequence of these limited views of love. The discomfort I spoke of earlier also is present in the distrust of generalities that lies behind the imagist enterprise. As impulse is preferred or at least given undue attention, so immediate consciousness becomes the primary aim of the poem, and unalloyed, suggestive images its primary expression. As usual, Archibald MacLeish can simplify a modernist dictum and unintentionally expose its absurdity. In "Ars Poetica," he concludes a poem full of abstract language with "a poem should not mean / But be"; and in "'Not Marble Nor the Gilded Monuments'" his naive nominalism targets the old and especially Elizabethan notion that in praising his beloved in verse, the lover can immortalize her. "These were lies," the modern poet confidently asserts and decides to replace all that praise ("the undying glory of women") with some deathless snapshot of a young, fair-skinned woman who "stood in the door and the sun was a shadow of leaves on [her] shoulders / And a leaf on [her] hair." But the praise that seems so ephemeral and artificial to MacLeish was more than just a requirement within a poetic convention. In exercising the convention, those older poets were acknowledging a fund of human understanding within which their private experience could make public sense. The power of a generalized language is just that dedication to public meaning and to a retrievable coherency in the past and a possibility of significance in the future. MacLeish's physical emblem, the "shape of a leaf," carries no more than an obscure association in his mind at the moment of writing the poem. Thus, loss with the abstract language is a belief in some permanence, and when that goes so goes the mode of the dedication, the pledge, the vow that usually motivated the praise.

That mode generated a rich store of metaphors drawn from the worlds of religion, commerce, and the law, helping the poet both to vivify his own complex sense of the mutual obligations arising from honorable promises and, depending on the cleverness and extent of the analogy, to provide the necessary comic relief. The Earl of Rochester advises Phyllis to fling her prayer book away and be merciful to her fellow man, especially this one:

> ... to calm the angry powers
> And save my soul as well as yours,
> Relieve poor mortals from despair,
> And justify the gods that made you fair.
> ("Written in a Lady's Prayer Book," 10–13)

One of the most powerful and poignant (but hardly funny) responses to a lady's cruel rejection of a lover she once encouraged is in Wyatt's "To His Lute":

> Vengeance shall fall on thy disdain,
> That makest but game on earnest pain:
> Think not alone under the sun
> Unquit to cause thy lover's plain,
> Although my lute and I have done.
>
> Perchance thee lie withered and old
> The winter nights that are so cold,
> Plaining in vain unto the moon:
> Thy wishes then dare not be told:
> Care then who list! for I have done.
>   (21–30)

Love cannot be just a frivolous indulgence, a "gentle pornography," an imprisonment by either the senses or the impulses, or even an emotional compulsion, when the breaking of bonds can have such consequences, or when the hedonistic seducer must still defend himself within the moral categories:

> We have done no harm; nor was it theft in me,
>   But noblest charity in thee.
>   (Abraham Cowley, "Dialogue After Enjoyment")

However insincere and manipulative he may be, he still can be seen to be such. He cannot be outside the standards that inform his own language.

Perhaps I can best make my various points about a debased sense of love, the replacement of humor by pretentious irony, and the stylistic imprecisions that have resulted from a cruder tone, obsession with images, and loss of a sanctioning diction, by showing you these variations on a timeless pleasure: a man touches the body of the woman he "loves," and it echoes thusly down the centuries:

> What arms and shoulders did I touch and see,
> How apt her breasts were to be pressed by me.
>   (Marlowe's translation of Ovid's "Elegy 5," 19–20)

How blessed am I in this discovering thee.
To enter in these bonds is to be free,
Then where my hand is set my seal shall be.
                (Donne, "To His Mistress Going to Bed," 30–32)

On her soft breasts my hand I laid,
And a quick, light impression made;
They with a kindly warmth did glow,
And swelled, and seemed to overflow.
. . . .
O'er her smooth limbs my hands did stray;
Each sense was ravished with delight,
And my soul stood prepared for flight.
    (Anonymous 18th-century poet, "I Gently Touched Her Hand," 7–10, 14–16)

[A woman says to her lover]
Lie closer, lean your face upon my side,
Feel where the dew fell that has hardly dried,
  Hear how the blood beats that went nigh to swoon;
The pleasure lives there when the sense has died.
                    (Swinburne, "In the Orchard," 11–14)

(may i touch said he
how much said she
a lot said he)
why not said she
. . . .
(cccome? said he
ummm said she)
you're divine!said he
(you are Mine said she)
            (E. E. Cummings, "May I Feel Said He," 5–8, 29–32)

Although ostensibly a straightforward erotic poem, the unexpected "apt" of Marlowe's translation gives more emphasis to "by me" at the end of the couplet, helping those two words draw out more intensely the suggestion of mutual appropriateness that is the first recognition on the way to a more than momentary physical bonding. Donne makes the transition in his lighthearted persuasion: the religious sense of "blessed" is secondary, but it is there, as is the pledge, which in a sense sanctions the jesting. Something is beginning to go wrong in that anonymous eighteenth-century poet who means only to please himself (whatever response there is in the woman is *hers alone* as well). "Soft," "impression," "warmth," "swelled," "overflow," "smooth"—the diction is insistently physical, overpowering whatever faint possibilities we may hope for in "kindly." Certainly the "and" connecting lines fifteen and sixteen is woefully inadequate if "soul" here is to be more than a summary term for all those sensations merging in orgasm. But even that seems preferable to Swinburne's self-satisfied plangencies, in which the pleasure is narrowed even further than the physical into the aesthetic. Cummings's reaction is a shallow cuteness that only can literalize and cheapen a once highly expressive commercial metaphor (dealing with the complex notion of possessiveness in love) in order to deny a religious one. The thought of the poem remains clichéd while playing with clichés.

The qualities that make the most satisfying love poems, I believe, are contained in this definition of love offered by George Grant: noting that the word "has lost its clarity in contemporary language," he says,

> 'Love' is attention to otherness, receptivity of otherness, consent to otherness. ... When we love other human beings, we know those human beings because we have paid attention to them, have received something of what they are, and consented to what they are as good. Indeed in this example, consent is easily joy, because of our obvious need of people close to us; whereas consent may not easily be joy in the more difficult reaches of love. The interdependence of love and knowledge is most clearly manifest when we try to understand what it is to love justice—(and it must be remembered that the love of justice is what all human beings are primarily called to).... In our daily attempts to be just the central fact about human love is made plain. Love is only love in so far as it has passed through the flesh by means of actions, movements, attitudes which correspond to it. If this has not happened, it is not love, but a phantasy of the imagination by which we coddle ourselves.[28]

Poetry that would deal with love in this complete sense must have formal means, first, of acknowledging otherness, so we would expect a degree of impersonality; second, of articulating more than just sensory knowledge, so we would expect a directness, plainness, and respect for generalities, that is, for ideas in verse; and, third, of expressing a range of emotional states, from consent to joy, from need to satisfaction, from levity to seriousness, so we would expect the textural control provided only by a flexible and precise metrics. Most importantly we require the presence of a mature mind capable of completing the vision of love, of recognizing the limitation of isolated experiences and the lack of self-sufficiency in lovers, and therefore the need of something to secure the feeling—be it as simple as decency and common sense or as complex as goodness and the whole moral life, be it the public pledge of constancy or the love of something larger than our or some other human self. We see it in George Crabbe, still able in an age that spent much of its imaginative energies lamenting lost, frustrated, or worn passion, to write this:

> The ring so worn as you behold,
> So thin, so pale, is yet of gold:

> The passion such it was to prove;
> Worn with life's cares, love yet was love.
>
> ("A Marriage Ring")

We also see it in Tom Brangwen who wanted so desperately at his son's wedding to talk about angels.

Robert Bridges

Robert Bridges also could talk about angels, but with an ease and lofty assurance that neither Tom Brangwen nor even D. H. Lawrence had. It might appear odd to bring into a discussion of modern love the old laureate who is for so many the arch-Victorian. But I wish to add my voice to those of Albert Guerard and Donald Stanford in defending the relevance to our and indeed any century of this in fact most independent, unrepresentative, and much underrated poet. He was so independent of literary fashions that he was not given a chance to influence many younger and later poets, unlike the slightly less independent Hardy whose lifespan is almost the same. But criticism should not suffer: at his best in his shorter and often lyric love poems, he can provide us with a standard more recent than the Renaissance poems I appealed to in the previous section, a model of poetic possibilities in an age that has had difficulties expressing a full experience and understanding of love.

Bridges had that broader view. In sonnet 35 of *The Growth of Love* sequence, written at different times from the 1870s to 1898, he presents in solid and clear generalities the ideal of a teleological love:

> All earthy beauty hath one cause and proof,
> To lead the pilgrim soul to beauty above:
> Yet lieth the greater bliss so far aloof,
> That few there be are wean'd from earthly love.
>   Joy's ladder it is, reaching from home to home,
> The best of all the work that all was good;
> Whereof 'twas writ the angels aye upclomb,
> Down sped, and at the top the Lord God stood.
>
> (1–8)[29]

But he was no romantic idealist (despite his "embarrassing enthusiasm for Shelley"[30]); the difficulty of attaining this ideal is stressed in the more personal sestet:

> But I my time abuse, my eyes by day
> Center'd on thee, by night my heart on fire—
> Letting my number'd moments run away—
> Nor e'en 'twixt night and day to heaven aspire:

> So true it is that what the eye seeth not
> But slow is loved, and loved is soon forgot.
>
> (9–14)

Bridges confronts, acknowledges, and even laments the failure, but he remains calm; there are no histrionics. His sadness is more sincere and convincing because it remains when soberness returns, that is, when he speaks these lines. The only deviations from the steady iambic norm are the mildly emphatic trochees opening lines 10 and 11 and the unusually slow anapests closing lines 12 and 13. The return to generalized statement in the couplet further defuses any potential for an emotional display of disillusionment.

How different this is from the following "sonnet" from George Meredith's 1862 sequence *Modern Love*, which has invited comparisons with Bridges's sequence:

XXIX

> Am I failing? For no longer can I cast
> A glory round about this head of gold.
> Glory she wears, but springing from the mould;
> Not like the consecration of the Past!
> Is my soul beggared? Something more than earth
> I cry for still: I cannot be at peace
> In having Love upon a mortal lease.
> I cannot take the woman at her worth!
> Where is the ancient wealth wherewith I clothed
> Our human nakedness, and could endow
> With spiritual splendour a white brow
> That else had grinned at me the fact I loathed?
> A kiss is but a kiss now! And no wave
> Of a great flood that whirls me to the sea.
> But, as you will! we'll sit contentedly,
> And eat our pot of honey on the grave.[31]

Exclamations and questions, enjambments and broken lines—all intensify the tone here as Meredith indulges *his* (or his persona's) disappointment: there are seven *I*'s in the poem, and only one in Bridges's. The indulgence takes the added, pseudo-sophisticated step of half mocking itself with melodramatic diction and posturing, especially in the fourth quatrain. He is lamenting the loss of what is now recognized as only a defensive illusion in the past ("That else had grinned at me the fact I loathed"), so we cannot even credit the proffered emotion. There is reason to regret the influence of Shelley on Bridges, but we can be thankful for Bridges's native reticence and prudence when we see the extent of Shelley's influence on other Victorians.

Bridges was capable of fevered passion, of course, but he rarely gives us those uncomfortable moments directly in his poems; he more characteristically comments on them, trying to understand them before he speaks to the reader, thus with other safeguards trying to reestablish repose. In sonnet 37 he recalls headlong rushes on horseback toward goals that nearness proves illusory, so he stands

> as one who sees the source
> Of strong illusion, shaming thought to force
> From off his mind the soil of passion's gust.
>
> (6–8)

Meredith would stop with the revelation of the vision as an illusion and milk its emotional possibilities. Bridges not only shames his thought but can find a social recovery: "with slacken'd speed" he gives "good heed" to "kind salutation" and can ride on "And seek what cheer the village inn provides" (9, 11, 14).

Not only does he go beyond the mere imitation of immediate emotional experience, he also offers that ability itself as proof of his devotion. Arthur Symons complained in 1901 that Bridges "has put into his poetry the peace and not the energies of life, the wisdom and not the fever of love."[32] My first response would be that because most of us know the fever and very few attain the wisdom, we should be grateful for that much. But the matter is more complicated, because the control that makes the understanding possible is itself part of his service to the beloved. "Behold me, now," he says at the end of the first sonnet in *The Growth of Love*, "Master of the art which for thy sake I serve." His art is not for his or art's sake but for her. It is no compliment to her if he has no mastery, that is, no comprehension of the meaning of his love. His love is all the more substantial and constant for surviving the understanding. And he can make great poetry of calm assurance:

> And when we sit alone, and as I please
> I taste thy love's full smile, and can enstate
> The pleasure of my kingly heart at ease,
> My thought swims like a ship, that with the weight
> Of her rich burden sleeps on the infinite seas
> Becalm'd, and cannot stir her golden freight.
>
> (sonnet 5, 9–14)

The heart is best after all, he says in sonnet 11, "when most / 'Tis sober, simple, true, and fancy-free" (13–14). And it needs company. Love tops the list of crew members of the ship of life in sonnet 15, which very cleverly develops the conceit; the keel is health, "whereto the ribs of mirth are wed," and the rest of the company includes diligence, wit, justice, courage, temperance: "And at her helm the master reason sit[s]" (2, 14).

If moderation deepens Bridges's love, excess cheapens that of Meredith's protagonist. He has so isolated his passion ("self-caged Passion" he calls it) that, in turning to "other joys of life" in IV, he finds nothing can satisfy: "high Philosophy" is "cold as a mountain" and more foe than friend. His closing generalization is so clichéd and wrong that it seems more an excuse than a regret:

> Oh, wisdom never comes when it is gold,
> And the great price we pay for it full worth:
> We have it only when we are half earth.
> Little avails that coinage to the old!
>
> (11–14)

He echoes that almost comfortable despair in XIX:

> If any state be enviable on earth,
> 'Tis yon born idiot's, who, as days go by,
> Still rubs his hands before him, like a fly,
> In a queer sort of meditative mirth.
>
> (13–16)

This has its roots in romantic philosophy, but it also looks forward to both the overstatements of Yeats and the shallow cynicism of many modernist writers.

It is not surprising that for Meredith's speaker, love is only "a thing of moods" (X), and at best a "crowning sun" whose light distracts us momentarily from recognizing the "shadow of the tomb" (XXX). His "crime," as he calls it in that former poem, was to hope for constancy, for "loyal Life" in "Love's deep woods." We should learn from nature, he says in XIII (reversing a Wordsworthian lesson) not to pledge ourselves to anything ("'I play for Seasons; not Eternities!'" he has Nature declare). Bridges, on the other hand, in contemplating betrayal in love, will not descend to a display of personal grief. Instead he turns a somewhat exaggerated compliment into a moral caution, a rhetorical move reminiscent of Wyatt and Gascoigne. Her encouragement has bred his constancy, which in turn obliges hers. This could have been written any time since the early sixteenth century, its plainness testifying to its universality:

> ... since I am sworn thy slave, and in the bond
> Is writ my promise of eternity;
> Since to such high hope thou'st encouraged me,
> That if thou look but from me I despond;
>
> Since thou'rt my all in all, O think of this:
> Think of the dedication of my youth:

> Think of my loyalty, my joy, my bliss:
> Think of my sorrow, my despair and ruth,
> My sheer annihilation if I miss:
> Think—if thou shouldst be false—think of thy truth.
>
> (sonnet 54, 5-14)

Meredith's discussion stays at the level of frustrated sexual impulse ("a thing of moods"), but Bridges means to stretch the continuum. At the end of his life, in *The Testament of Beauty* (1929), he went so far as to separate the bond of marriage from "mere impulse of sex," however strong that is ("from animal mating/to the vision of Dante"). If breeding ceased, he speculates, men and women would continue to mate:

> Happiness, which all seek, is not composable
> of any summation of particular pleasures;
> the happiness in marriage dependeth for-sure
> not on the animal functions, but on qualities
> of spirit and mind that are correlated therewith.
>
> (III, 850-54)

So Bridges is not simply a Victorian optimist blinded to the darker realities uncovered by the more "modern" and fatalistic Meredith. "I see no sin," the protagonist says late in Meredith's sequence,

> In tragic life, God wot,
> No villain need be! Passions spin the plot:
> We are betrayed by what is false within.
>
> (XLIII, 14-16)

Bridges would answer that allowing the passions to "spin the plot" is itself the sin. A betrayal from within is just as blameworthy as one from without. And most importantly, it can be remedied. But it means daring to love, which is to be vulnerable. The alternative to a breakable heart is an impenetrable, irredeemable one. C. S. Lewis said: "The alternative to tragedy, or at least to the risk of tragedy, is damnation."[33] One does not have to be a Christian or even religious to understand that damnation is most pertinently a neglect of the need to fulfill one's being. For all his later joyous acceptance of the idea of evolution of life as a process of becoming, for all the so-called personalism and "psychological insight"[34] of *Modern Love*, Meredith displays little understanding of personal responsibility. F. R. Leavis's summary judgment is perhaps only slightly overstated: "*Modern Love* seems to me the flashy product of unusual but vulgar cleverness working upon cheap emotion: it could serve later poets, if at all, only as a warning."[35] Unfortunately it did not. Bridges's significantly titled *Growth of Love*, perhaps not as narratively dynamic as Meredith's sequence, because it is devoid of dramatized passion and despair, investigates possibilities beyond the commoner pleasures and pains of love. Not all of the sonnets are successful—only a handful are first rate—but in their lucidity *and* depth of statement they are unlike any in that century.

Bridges's poems after *The Growth of Love* continue to assert his belief in the worth of moral effort and his trust in life's chances. Not always to my liking, the emphasis often is on a Platonized Beauty, but on significant occasions it is also on human love. He never denies that effort is necessary, even if it is solely intellectual. He had a fortunate, almost aristocratic life, and this is part of the reason why less privileged twentieth-century poets found it easy to ignore his example. Only a few of his poems reveal a pressure of personal, deeply felt experience behind his usually generalized concerns with life's struggle.

> I laugh to have learned
> That joy cannot come
> Unless it be earned;
>
> For a happier lot
> Than God giveth me
> It never hath been
> Nor ever shall be.
>
> ("Fortunatus Nimium," 22–28)

That is from a collection published in 1920. In a poem published thirty years earlier, in *Shorter Poems* (1890), he details his "happier lot" as a ready access to both a simple, unambitious rural life and the urban pleasures of good company, music, literature, and philosophy. But the peace of mind he enjoys is "hard-won": "health our toil rewards,/And strength is labour's prize." The threats to his gratitude (in 1890) are still fashionable ones:

> But think not I can stain
> My heaven with discontent;
> Nor wallow with that sad,
> Backsliding herd, who cry
> That Truth must make man bad,
> And pleasure is a lie.
>
> ("Spring: Ode II," 35–40)

Because there are no poeticized autobiographical crises, no dazzling mannerisms, no challenging flights into darkness, because there is "a deliberate reticence, a sedulous restraint, a hatred of revelations",[36] a cheerfulness and discretion, a conscious intention, an "equable and steady poetic flight",[37] we must not, as have so many,[38] conclude with Yeats that his magnificently crafted poems are empty[39]—Yeats, after all, could not appreciate Hardy either. (Bridges, we might note, was very impatient with

Yeats's irrational occultism.[40]) A literary culture dominated by the assumptions of nominalism will have difficulty recognizing, much less accepting, the substance and import of Bridges's moral and philosophical generalities, but they are there nonetheless. The trust and effort to maintain that trust that his best poems plead for could not be more relevant, central, or rife with potential significance.

The effort is against many things. It is against complacency and the temptation to escape: in "Nightingales" (one of his most successful experiments in accentual verse), a Keatsian poet longs to "wander" among the beautiful mountains, fruitful valleys, and starry woods where the nightingales must have learned their song. The birds' response is that great art originates in a longing that contradicts Keats's desire for flight from human suffering:

> Nay, barren are those mountains and spent the streams:
> Our song is the voice of desire, that haunts our dreams,
> A throe of the heart,
> Whose pining visions dim, forbidden hopes profound,
> No dying cadence nor long sigh can sound,
> For all our art.
>
> (7–12)

The effort is against melancholy, not just the sadness that usually accompanies the frustration of such flight, but also the dejection that comes from more mature motives: "love dishonoured," "friendship slighted," memory of "loving hearts, that gone before / Call their old comrade to the grave" ("Dejection," 7–12). One is reminded of Tennyson's "Tears, Idle Tears," but Bridges's poem goes on, as Tennyson's does not:

> O soul, be patient: thou shalt find
> A little matter mend all this;
> Some strain of music to thy mind,
> Some praise for skill not spent amiss.
>
> Again shall pleasure overflow
> Thy cup with sweetness, thou shalt taste
> Nothing but sweetness, and shalt grow
> Half sad for sweetness run to waste.
>
> O happy life! I hear thee sing,
> O rare delight of mortal stuff!
> I praise my days for all they bring,
> Yet are they only not enough.
>
> ("Dejection," 13–24)

The emphatic repetition of "sweetness" (that emotional workhorse of nineteenth-century verse) points ironically to a deficiency in his facile removal from dejection, so quietly but poignantly emphasized by that "only" of the last line. He is disillusioned at the end, but the dealing with the problem is assured; there is progress, not from pessimism to optimism but from immaturity to maturity. How unlike those romantic poets who so often, not seeing the chance of complete salvation, fall back upon their initial melancholy, falling upon the self-created thorns of an adolescent vision of life, bleeding poetical blood in public in a woefully unplatonic present. Bridges's view is not a dialectical opposite of a romantic one, but rather simply a broader, more inclusive, more mature, more effortful one.

Perhaps less personally intense but as important for others is the effort against the tyranny of either instinct or analytical reason. "To Robert Burns: An Epistle on Instinct" repudiates Rousseauistic primitivism. Man must choose his "pleasurable ways" carefully in order "to find / Severe perfection" (29–30); true pleasure attends moral good; pleasure, therefore, is "not well-being's end, / But its fruition" (35–36), a very Aristotelian point. Reason tames our instincts. But we must grant, he goes on, that we owe a great deal to the instincts as they function in primitive man:

> Want of analysis
> Saved them from doubts that wreck the Will
> With pale paralysis.
>
> (82–84)

Then the argument moves back to Aristotle, bringing instinct and reason together in the larger net, or "lodgement":

> Tho' Science hide beneath her feet
> The point where moral reasonings meet,
> The vicious circle is complete;
>   There is no lodgement
> Save Aristotle's own retreat,
>   The just man's judgement.
>
> (91–96)

A more chilling exposition of the predicament, of the ever-present attacks on Reason (philosophical, not scientific), is "Low Barometer." A house is flailed by gale winds,

> ... Air has loosed
> Its guardian grasp on blood and brain,
> . . . .
> And Reason kens he herits in
> A haunted house. Tenants unknown
> Assert their squalid lease of sin
> With earlier title than his own.
>
> (5–6, 9–12)

A hundred-year-old way of thinking out these matters is powerfully subverted in this poem, to no small extent by the tone of qualified respect for and subdued horror of these uncivilizing and subconscious forces.

Although an uncivilized past may threaten, a nearer civilized past that is lost forever has more ambiguous claims on him, as in this poem:

Ghosts

> Mazing around my mind like moths at a shaded candle.
>   In my heart like lost bats in a cave fluttering,
> Mock ye the charm whereby I thought reverently to lay you,
>   When to the wall I nail'd your reticent effigys?

Life's chances are severely circumscribed by cultural and historical changes to which even the retiring bard of Boar's Hill is acutely sensitive. Although not a love poem in the strictest sense, "Elegy: The Summer House on the Mound" powerfully expresses a love for a past childhood, home, and heroic age no longer possible in an industrialized and mechanized empire. The lament is made subtly in contrasting descriptions of the great wooden sailing ships of old and the new steam dreadnoughts. First the older vision:

> That sea is ever bright and blue, the sky
> Serene and blue, and ever white ships lie
> High on the horizon steadfast in full sail,
> Or nearer in the roads pass within hail,
> Of naked brigs and barques that windbound ride
> At their taut cables heading to the tide.
>
> (31–36)

The repeated "ever" suggests the temporal depth of this direct ("naked") confrontation of "steadfast" human effort with the "serene" forces of sea and wind, and the firm and grave movement of the iambic rhythm across the restraining couplets (especially in the enjambments of the first two lines and the move from the end of the second line to the trochee that fronts the third, and the near pyrrhic to spondee opening of the last line slowing the rhythm in mid-line, then dropping off easefully in the last four syllables) emphasizes the tenuous, but achieved, and respectful mastery of those forces. But this was all before "our iron age" and "the engines of a mightier Mars"

> Clipp'd their wide wings, and dock'd their soaring spars.
> The gale that in their tackle sang, the wave
> That neath their gilded galleries dasht so brave
> Lost then their merriment, nor look to play
> With the heavy-hearted monsters of to-day.
>
> (68–72)

Modern Love

The respect is replaced by brutal (potentially guilty) assertions of control (the wind need no longer cooperate). As a child he watched from the Kent shore as Napier's fleet sailed past on its way to the Baltic:

> ... round Saint Margaret's cliff mysteriously,
> Those murderous queens walking in Sabbath sleep
> Glided in line upon the windless deep:
> For in those days was first seen low and black
> Beside the full-rigg'd mast the strange smoke-stack,
> And neath their stern revolv'd the twisted fan.
>
> (76–81)

"Black" replacing "white," "twisted" replacing "taut": in this context Bridges strives to maintain human dignity with love.

At other times, he even wonders (with Hardy) how responsive nature is. Just seven poems after the "Elegy" in *New Poems* one finds "The Sea Keeps Not the Sabbath," in which the "loving fancy" of two lovers ill suits the "sadness of the clouded sky, / The bitter wind, the gloomy roar" (7–8). There is little evidence of a providential God in a "nature that doth half consent / That man should guess her dreary scheme," man being "so fugitive a part / Of what so slowly must expire" (15–16, 21–22). On the other hand, the poem concludes, nature, in addition to "mocking alike hope and despair," can "mock our praise" by enchanting us on "her brighter days," days "fit for the gaiety of Mozart" (25–27, 31). Nature finally defies our human conclusions, and therefore, in providing little comfort for the lover, necessitates resilience. This poem, written before "The Sea Keeps Not the Sabbath," closes Book III of *Shorter Poems* and is one of Bridges's most moving poetic meditations, and brings us squarely back to our theme of love:

> The evening darkens over
> After a day so bright
> The windcapt waves discover
> That wild will be the night.
> There's sound of distant thunder.
>
> The latest sea-birds hover
> Along the cliff's sheer height;
> As in the memory wander
> Last flutterings of delight,
> White wings lost on the white.
>
> There's not a ship in sight;
> And as the sun goes under
> Thick clouds conspire to cover
> The moon that should rise yonder.
> Thou art alone, fond lover.

Thus the effort is against an indifferent nature as well as the allure of escape, melancholy, an isolated instinct, scientific reason, the survival of a dehumanizing past, and an uncivilizing present. But the struggle bears fruit; despite all, he can believe in a god of love. The final achievement is summarized in "The Affliction of Richard." It is a hard-won choice. He is fully aware that he may not attain the ideal at which he aims: "Though I must fear to lose" (5)—"must" in an unemphatic position quietly insisting on the consequences of his own imperfection. He has had to overcome the loss of an original and perhaps too easy faith:

> Though thou, I know not why,
> Didst kill my childish trust,
> That breach with toil did I
> Repair, because I must.
>
> (9–12)

The second, more emphatic "must" suggests the strength and willed determination necessary to reestablish his trust on maturer grounds. Then there were the attacks of "frighting schemes,/With which the fiends of Hell/Blaspheme thee" (13–15), variously interpretable as Victorian science, or the Old Testament conception of God and damnation,[41] or, as I prefer to believe, any allegedly inclusive system of thought that frightens away our hope (including notions of a merciless deity and a purposeless universe). The poem begins with the rather bitter and certainly ironic question, "How can I love too much?" (4) and ends this way:

> What am I that complain?
> The love, from which began
> My question sad and vain,
> Justifies thee to man.
>
> (21–24)

This could be from a wise and disillusioned Adam directed at Milton's God.

We come then to "Eros," written in 1899, almost a decade after the publication of "The Affliction of Richard" but in many ways a companion piece. If the earlier poem contemplates the hazards of a strictly Christian faith, this one questions the sufficiency of a conception of strictly physical love. The actual title is the Greek EPΩΣ: this is, as Donald Stanford says, no mischievous Roman god,[42] but a powerful and proud "king of joy." The poem, through its tetrameter couplets and expressive rhyme ("words that earn their emphasis," say Robert Beum[43]), is a controlled investigation of the quality of that power:

> Why hast thou nothing in thy face?
> Thou idol of the human race,
> Thou tyrant of the human heart,

> The flower of lovely youth that art;
> Yea, and that standest in thy youth
> An image of eternal Truth,
> With thy exuberant flesh so fair,
> That only Pheidias might compare,
> Ere from his chaste marmoreal form
> Time had decayed the colours warm;
> Like to his gods in thy proud dress,
> Thy starry sheen of nakedness.
>
> (1-12)

The poem opens with a question that seems to grow out of the answer to a prior inquiry as the poet gazes into the face of what is probably a statue of Eros, searching for a meaning. The tone is of critical disappointment just as the expected awe is declining. It grows into defiance in the next two lines: we expect more of our gods. This only can be a false god, an impostor, yet, despite the absence of divine depth, it is able to attract the passionate devotion of the whole "human race," so powerful in its ability to deceive. But we expect more of ourselves as well. Willingness to idolize that which rules absolutely, unrestrained by law, over the "human heart" (the repeated "human" insisting on the generality of the statement—this is no mere personal lament or confession) is a sin against being itself. Before the sentence ends, however, and as the appositional phrases seem to continue (each emphatically contained within its own line), the poet abruptly qualifies his criticism, suggesting the possible benefit of Eros's pervasive influence over us. I say that the appositional phrases *seem* to continue: it is not until the end of line four that we realize that "flower" is not in direct series with "idol" and "tyrant," but rather the object of a restrictive clause modifying the compound subject "idol" and "tyrant" (thou idol and tyrant that art the flower and that standest ...). What may at first appear to be an unnecessary inversion, then, in line four, is there to give us the full force of an abrupt change of tone ("idol" to "tyrant" to "flower" in exactly the same place in each of these consecutive lines), to account partially at least for the almost inevitably enslaving attraction, without denying the proper, more complex, modifications. That is, Eros is not sometimes idol, sometimes tyrant, and sometimes flower of youth; he is primarily the idol and tyrant who is also the image in this awesomely base form of an eternal truth. Robert Beum makes the point succinctly:

> The point of view is far from anything like a barren Puritanism. After all, Eros is a "king of joy", even "An image of eternal Truth" (a phrase delicately ironic but also literal). In sensuous beauty are the beginnings of heavenly beauty, and Bridges' own worship was a worship of Beauty—though as a means to the highest evolution of mind and soul, not as an end in itself. This contemplation of physical beauty gives rise to an awareness of the existence—and, vaguely, intimations of the quality—of heavenly beauty.[44]

The highest does not stand without the lowest. I would simply emphasize that Bridges is careful to give (however subtly) grammatical precedence to the unregenerate ("shameless," he says later) victimizer. The charitable manner that Beum and later Stanford detect in the poem is there, but it is secondary to the firm moral criticism of isolated physicality. In following the ephemeral "flower" with "youth," and then repeating that word in the next line, Bridges reinforces the grammatical point.

We are still only half way through the sentence. Line 7 sums up, in "exuberant flesh," the dual attitude, the first word giving and the second taking away. This prepares for the reference to Pheidias, perhaps the greatest ancient sculptor, who could capture god-like beauty and power in "marmoreal" forms, but such forms are finally and only polished surfaces and lifeless bulk, imitations (as Eros is only an imitation) of true divinities.[45] But there is also a submerged dissimilarity between this statue of Eros and those of Pheidias (no Pheidian Eros is known) brought to the surface by the opposition of "chaste" in line 9 and "nakedness" in line 12. Pheidias's statues are usually draped with "proud dress," and, most significantly, have good reason to be proud (his most famous statues are the Athena in the Parthenon and the Zeus made for the temple at Olympia). Eros's nakedness is his badge of singular power, and he wears it proudly; but to emphasize his lack of mind (all too present if we recall Athena), Bridges describes the "starry sheen" of his naked body, a lustrous *surface* only, and reminds us in line 10 of Time's inevitable effects even on marble bodies. The implicit warning is to the human worshippers of this god of sensuous experience.

The second stanza begins by answering the question that opened the first stanza, summing up the full implications of the intervening lines:

> Surely thy body is thy mind,
> For in thy face is nought to find,
> Only the soft unchristen'd smile,
> That shadows neither love nor guile,
> But shameless will and power immense,
> In secret sensuous innocence.
>
> (13–18)

His thoughtlessness means that he has neither the wits to beguile others nor the sympathetic knowledge to love another. The pre-Christian and unsanctified smile, then, is without consciousness of guilt and simply reveals raw will and power. The "sensuous innocence" is "secret" perhaps because it is a pure state that man cannot know. But man, who can will his own incompleteness, can be evil if he makes Eros an idol and tyrant.[46]

The final stanza develops the notion of Eros as essential and innocent, inquiring after whatever thought such a body-mind can have:

> O king of joy, what is thy thought?
> I dream thou knowest it is nought,
> And wouldst in darkness come, but thou
> Makest the light where'er thou go.
> Ah yet no victim of thy grace,
> None who e'er long'd for thy embrace,
> Hath cared to look upon thy face.
>
> (19–25)

Bridges speculates on what it is to be powerful and conscious of one's own mindlessness: one consequence is a certain shyness before one's devotees. Bridges thereby meshes myth and common reality: sexual activity tends to intensify at night (perhaps because of a latent sense of shame in the participants themselves). The paradox of darkness and light calls to mind the fallen Prince of Light in the dark flames of Milton's Hell. And Satan did provide Adam and Eve with the "light" of forbidden knowledge. Eros is not a Satanic figure in any significant sense, but he does provide the context for the evil of others. He can only make the light for others, not bring it for them: Bridges's meaning seems to be (and here I disagree somewhat with Beum who says light becomes in the stanza "a metaphor of sense experience") that those whom Eros visits often feel or want to believe that sexual passion is a good in itself—the light is their delusion of the adequacy of physical love. Like Eros, the light is false. They become victims (there is no equivocation in these final lines) of their desire; that is the only blessing ("grace" must be a pun) conferred on them. And, like the partially conscious Eros, they know there is nothing in his face and agree to remain in joy in darkness. Although not a conventional love poem that declares love from one to another, it is nonetheless Bridges's greatest poem about love, and, I believe, one of the greatest in our language. The insights are not original, but they have never been so succinctly, honestly, and powerfully expressed. It is the poem we should have in mind as we read love poems.

It is evident in a poem like "Rondeau" (from Book I of *Shorter Poems*) that Bridges could be playful with this subject. Cupid replaces his Greek original here. There's that wonderful descriptive line telling us that after dipping his "shafts" in "juice of plants that no bee sips," he goes out hunting, "Hanging his quiver at his hips" (2, 5). The rest of this short poem centers on a witty turn. If a maiden but "Suck from the wound the blood that drips,/And drink the poison from the wound" (11–12), a remedy is found that strips the shafts of "their deadly terror"—only the terror, not the consequences of the poison. But that is hardly a characteristic Bridges love poem. With the effort behind him, the battle engaged and won or at least the dangers fully and deeply acknowledged, he is capable, like few others of the age that ushered in our cynical self-conscious one, of light and joyous love poems. Commentators frequently see similarities with Elizabethan lyricists, especially Shakespeare, Campion, and the song writers. There is that most delicate "My Spirit Kisseth Thine," which appears to blur the transition from love of woman to love of God:

> My spirit kisseth thine,
> My spirit embraceth thee:
> I feel thy being twine
> Her graces over me.
>
> (1–4)

Rarely distant from his expressions of love (physical and spiritual) are reminders of the superiority of mature over youthful love. "Let truth be told," he says in "So Sweet Love Seemed," "love will change in growing old." In the end we will forget "the pleasure that was all in all." The sentiment is not unlike that of Crabbe's "The Wedding Ring."

> His little spring, that sweet we found,
> So deep in summer floods is drowned,
> I wonder, bathed in joy complete,
> How love so young could be so sweet.
>
> (13–16)

The maturity of his view also encompasses gratitude:

> Since now I see in the measure
> Of all my giving and taking,
> Thou wert my hand in the making
> The sense and soul of my pleasure;
>
> The good I have ne'er repaid thee
> In heaven I pray be recorded,
> And all thy love rewarded
> By God, thy master that made thee.
> ("Since Thou, O Fondest and Truest," 9–16)

It is (again) an Aristotelian, not just a Christian, point: loving is more of the essence of friendship than being loved.[47] And mutual loving is the reward:

> When my love was away,
> Full three days were not sped,
> I caught my fancy astray
> Thinking if she were dead.
> ("When My Love Was Away," 1–4)

But Bridges can go further than Wordsworth, further than his own feelings. The lover rides quickly to her, and she is also tearful. The poem ends with her words:

> O now thou art come, she cried,
> 'Tis fled: but I thought to-day
> I never could here abide,
> If thou wert longer away.
>
> (17-20)

A line near the end of "La Gloire de Voltaire" says it simply and profoundly: "But man's true praise, the poet's praise, is love."

Of all the major poets of the late nineteenth and early twentieth century, Bridges is probably the one least read and valued today. The causes are not difficult to detect: his reputation, false but persistent, as an unadventurous classicist, and the preference of our century for personal dramatics and cryptic or exotic intellectualisms in its poetry. But the poems I have discussed here, especially "Eros," "The Affliction of Richard," "Elegy: Summer House on the Mound," "The Evening Darkens Over," "Low Barometer," and "So Sweet Love Seemed that April Morn" rank with the best poems of that period. That is not a new claim, nor does my list differ significantly from that of the few readers who have studied and written about his work, but the claim is one whose frequency has dropped markedly since the 1920s. It is our shame and our and poetry's loss. We miss part of own possibilities when we ignore a great artist. More specifically, and this has been my emphasis here, the poems dealing with the efforts and satisfactions of mature love make a particularly strong case for Bridges's modernity, for his recuperative value late in our century, a century with an impoverished tradition of love poetry.

D. H. Lawrence

A welcome caution to all the scholars trying to extract a visionary or even mystical theory from the writings of D. H. Lawrence is this direct statement by Frieda Lawrence a few years after his death (possibly 1939):

> When he speaks of blood consciousness that so many smart ones find so ludicrous, it was no theory with him but the voice of his race, of his own English common people in him, something beyond the intellect that I had to respect whether I understood it or not, or disliked it even. It was always somehow real and genuine. He loved his fellow men often with an exasperated angry love. But it was always love. Love is really the key to Lawrence. When I said, like a woman does: 'But why do you bother about other people? You have me, isn't that enough?' he replied: 'Yes, it's a lot, but it isn't everything.' His voice was not for me alone but for the many.[48]

This "voice of his race" is not racial pride so much as an intensely sensitive responsiveness to the cultural continuity of English life, to the rooted Englishness in him. What such continuity means for an artist is the giving of oneself with critical attitudes and moral and social preoccupations, to life; the same dedication grounded the novels of the great English writers who could abandon the continental picaresque form as well as deflect the more recent irresponsible tendencies of either playing technical games or putting together fictions to illustrate an arbitrary literary theory. The Englishness of the English novel, as Q. D. Leavis argues so powerfully, is that "radical and responsible enquiry" into the extra-literary human condition, "a profound sense of obligation to humanity," "the English fully human, sympathetic and yet critical interest in *people*."[49] This responsibility and interest for the greatest twentieth-century English novelist amounted to love, not sex but "always love." And for Lawrence as the inheritor of Shakespeare and "the Shakespearian 'fullness of life,'"[50] that love must include sex.

So much has already been written of Lawrence and sex and of the relationship of love and sex in his works, I will not try to add to that but rather take my cue, for the limited purposes of this section of this chapter, from E. M. Forster's broadcast talk of 30 April 1930, less than two months after Lawrence's death. Stressing Lawrence's dislike of contemporary civilization, Forster adds,

> He does believe in individuality ... and, illogical as it sounds, he even believes in tenderness. I think here that the memory of his mother counts. Theirs was an attachment which cut across all theories, and glorified other relationships when she died. Tenderness is waiting behind the pseudo-scientific jargon of his solar plexuses and the savagery of his blood-tests.... It is the Morning Star, the Lord of Both Ways, the star between day and the dark.[51]

It is to this dimension of his love poetry that I wish to speak. Such an investigation will take us, after a very brief review of the problems with his poems of sexual love, to the poems on his mother from 1910–1911. All are love poems, but some in the latter group are perhaps his best and most mature.

Let me say initially that Lawrence is not, I think, a great love poet. His poetic expressions of love to young women and even to Frieda are not on the whole his best—some very far from being his best—poems. We must go to his novels for an unsurpassable literature of love: in his greatest novels, *Sons and Lovers*, *The Rainbow*, and *Women in Love*, he inquires more thoroughly perhaps than any other writer into just what love can, should, and should not be in our century. But in the poetic response to the dying of his mother, we see the germs of that novelistic achievement, the enactment of an essential attentiveness, respect, and care.

Critics of Lawrence's poetry usually either lament his lack of craftsmanship and sophistication (such as Blackmur, Savage, Squire, and Eliot) or praise his disorder, his vision, his daring to strip the mask off the present (such as Rexroth, Alvarez, and de S. Pinto). Too much of his verse is weak in execution, is really not poetry but poetic sketches, and often inspired prose fragments, but surely there are better ways of praising him, of finding a place for him in literary history, than to commend the source of his weakest verse. In a few poems at least (as I hope to demonstrate) we see an accomplishment that, however briefly in his career as a poet, shows his affinity with a native English style older and richer than that of Whitman. To consolidate our findings we recall his 1911 comment to Catherine Carswell: "The essence of poetry with us in this age of stark and unlovely actualities is a stark directness, without a shadow of a lie, or a shadow of deflection anywhere. Everything can go, but this stark, bare, rocky directness of statement."[52] As late as 1928 we find him saying, "The essential quality of poetry is that it makes a new effort of attention."[53] "Directness of statement" (not image) and the "effort of attention" "without a shadow of a life": here is neither an Imagist nor a Georgian, but a poet who could, with such aims and those few poems, understand Hardy, his clarity, his tact, his tenderness.

Part of the problem in the poems to and about "Miriam" (Jessie Chambers), Helen Corke, and Louise Burrows is that there was never an adequate reciprocation in the affairs, no basis for a thoroughgoing respect and care, and therefore tenderness. They are for the most part poems of fevered desire and psychological studies of failure. He has Paul Morel sum up the problem in the penultimate chapter of *Sons and Lovers*: "'That's how women are with me,' said Paul [to Baxter Dawes], 'They want me like mad but they don't want to belong to me.'"[54] The poems are full of lines like these:

> Against the haystack a girl stands laughing at me,
>   Cherries hung round her ears.
> Offers me her scarlet fruit: I will see
>   If she has any tears.
>
> ("Cherry Robbers," 9–12)[55]

> I suffocate in this intimacy
>   In which I half love you;
> . . . .
> Yet closely bitten in to me
> Is this armour of stiff reluctancy,
>   And my dream is ill-founded.
>
> ("Excursion Train," 17–18, 26–28)

> ... but the body of me
> Closing upon you in the lightning-flamed
> Moment, destroys you, you are just destroyed.

> Humiliation deep to me. ...
> ("Lilies in the Fire," 36–39)

> I watch her ward away the flame
> Yet warm herself at the fire— ...
> ("Passing Visit to Helen," 38–39)

> ... to me she's the same
> Betrothed young lady who loves me, and takes good care
> Of her maidenly virtue and of my good name.
> ("The Hands of the Betrothed," 42–44)

Very often they end in real, anguished questions:

> Am I doomed in a long coition of words to mate you?
> Unsatisfied! Is there no hope
> Between your thighs, far, far from your peering sight?
> ("These Clever Women," 16–18)

> ... And is that evil?
> ("Come Spring, Come Sorrow," 45)

> Will you open the amorous, aching bud
> Of my body, and loose the essential flood
> That would pour to you from my heart?
> ("Excursion Train," 40–42)

Delicacy and subtlety are rarely possible without calm, so in these poems of unfulfillment, tenderness is expressed only when he can see the end of his yearning and feel only regret, as in the two moon poems about his rejection of "Miriam" in 1911, "Aware" and "A White Blossom," or only when he can step away from his own disappointment and criticize himself as well, as in "Last Words to Miriam" (for all its final hardness: "I should have been cruel enough to bring/You through the flame"):

> Yours is the sullen sorrow,
>   The disgrace is also mine;
>   . . . .
> Body to body I could not
>   Love you, although I would.
> We kissed, we kissed though we should not.
> You yielded, we threw the last cast,
>   And it was no good.
> (1–2, 11–15)

Unfortunately, the time when he did find a soul-mate and could enjoy a mature, fulfilling, and reciprocated love coincided with the time he determined to reject traditional forms and to experiment with "the unrestful, ungraspable poetry of the sheer present."[56] He first explicitly proclaimed his aim in the introduction to the American edition of *New Poems* in 1920, but the program is obviously well under way in *Look! We Have Come Through!*, published three years earlier, the sequence dealing with his elopement and travels with Frieda. The relative lack of formal precision in what are mostly loose sketches and discursive outbursts (the first of what he called "unrhyming poems") may be a way of expressing "the crisis of manhood" and "the conflict of love and hate [that, seemingly necessarily] goes on between the man and the woman," as he says in the "Forward" to and "Argument" for the volume.[57] His theory of immediacy certainly allows him to indulge an unmanly desire for oblivion when all does not go *his way* ("And Oh—That the Man I Am Might Cease to Be—"). And it allows for undigested "thoughts" to come to light prematurely:

> You are the call and I am the answer,
> You are the wish, and I the fulfilment,
> You are the night, and I the day
> . . . .
> Strange, how we suffer in spite of this!
>
> ("Bei Hennef," 14–16, 21)

When the desire is too strong or the moment too pressing for articulation, then the possibilities of care and regard finding a place in his mind, much less in verbal form, are slim. But there was a period between the passions of his heterosexual affairs and the chaos of his early time with Frieda when a grimmer force from without forced attention on him, forced a serious calm in which he could find and nurture tenderness, could find with his words a love and a way of dignifying that love. This was the long dying, the lingering grief for, and the gradual adjustment to the death of his mother. In the poems in that time, he manifested the promise of his own fullness of character, that which made the novels of 1913, 1915, and 1920 possible. Into the novels, not into the subsequent poems, this fuller sense of love's meaning went and grew even further.

I count about sixteen poems dealing with the death of his mother and his bereavement, placed roughly together in volume one ("Rhyming Poems") of the 1928 *Collected Poems*.[58] With the exception of "Remainder," which first appeared in 1913 in *Love Poems and Others*, all were first published in *Amores* (1916). Lydia Lawrence announced to her son that she had cancer in late August 1910, and she died in December. There is little reason not to believe that the poems were written immediately after her death, or in the three or four months after. Harry T. Moore speculates that they "were written as direct expressions of Lawrence's feelings, and written perhaps at the moment of experience."[59] I would not emphasize that last phrase; the best of the poems certainly do not show signs of having been written in haste. The best poems in the group, I think, are "Suspense," "The Bride," "Sorrow," "Silence," "Brooding Grief," and "Troth with the Dead." I will disscuss them in that order, the order of their appearance in both *Amores* and *Collected Poems*.

Graham Hough contends that "the poems on the death of the mother belong mostly to the class that cannot stand on their own; without their biographical context they are painful and eccentric."[60] It is difficult to know just how much biography Hough needs. It is, of course, an issue that has bedeviled Lawrence criticism. He regarded his poetry as "so personal that, in their fragmentary fashion, they make up a biography of an emotional and inner life."[61] But he goes on in that same preface to say generally that "no poetry, not even the best, should be judged as if it existed in the absolute, in the vacuum of the absolute. Even the best poetry, when it is at all personal, needs the penumbra of its own time and place and circumstance to make it full and whole."[62] He may here be promoting not so much a closely biographical criticism as a simple philological responsibility on the part of the reader to understand the past in its own terms, in its own spirit. Besides, although it was a powerfully unique life, it was not so different, and certainly the death of the mother was not so different (in kind at least) as to make his poetic response to it unavailable. Also, this is not a case of pseudo-reference, as we find so often in the works of his more experimental contemporaries, that is, the reference to a nonexistent plot: his life was real and to a large extent, especially after his death in 1930, public. Let us not underestimate our historical advantage for the sake of some New Critical prejudice: we have the life (in many accounts, including his own transformation of it in his prose writings). But, I would insist, the experiences behind the poems are universal, and the formal qualities of the best ones help to overcome whatever not unreasonable dependence they have on the now available personal context.

A further point needs to be made. R. P. Blackmur was not entirely wrong when, in his famous attack on Lawrence's poetry in 1935, he said,

> [Lawrence] was in contact with the disorder of life. In his novels and tales the labor of creating and opposing characters, the exigencies of narrative, all the detail of execution, combined to make his works independent, controlled entities to a great extent. But in his poetry, the very intensity of his self-expression overwhelmed all other considerations, and the disorder alone prevailed. . . . Art was too long for Lawrence; life too close.[63]

Without slighting the very real, if limited, accomplishment of some of the later formally less precise poems, I want to argue that when he did write poems in accentual-syllabic meter, often in intricate stanzaic patterns, occasionally those restraints clarified the intensity and allowed him and us to understand the experience. But the experience itself and therefore the possibility of understanding would not have been his had he not been close to life, closer than perhaps any writer of our century. One of the first reviews of his first volume of poetry remarks on this quality, "an unmistakable and impassioned *yea-saying* to actuality."[64] Lawrence himself said in "Education of the People," "Nothing will excuse us from the responsibility of living: even death is no excuse. We have to live. So we may as well live fully."[65] He lived so fully that he seemed to Jessie Chambers "a symbol of overflowing life."[66] We might regret the too immediate expression of the overflow, but the energy, range, and fullness of the living must impress us. Surely it is better to be too close than too distant from life. He gave himself to life more than to art, and his art triumphs because of it. And sex, for him, this hater of Freudian psychoanalysis, is simply and importantly the presence of the "life-flame"; so living our lives in love means "we should be kindled and full of zest in all kinds of ways and for all kinds of things."[67] So many of Lawrence's poems are weak not because he had not aestheticized his material enough, but because he had not let it *live* enough before he set it to paper: we too often get impressions and outbursts instead of settled recreations and conclusions.

Before looking directly at those six poems, let us place in mind passages from two much later poems:

> Oh leave off saying I want you to be savages.
> Tell me, is the gentian savage, at the top of its coarse stem?
> Oh what in you can answer to this blueness? .
>
> ("Flowers and Men," 7–9)

> They say that reality exists only in the spirit
> that corporal existence is a kind of death
> that pure being is bodiless
> that the idea of the form precedes the form substantial.
>
> But what nonsense it is!
> . . . .
> Even the mind of God can only imagine
> those things that have become themselves;
> bodies and presences, here and now, creatures with a foothold in creation.
>
> ("Demiurge," 1–5, 8–10)

In attacking the idealists, Lawrence is insisting on the interdependence of body and mind, of perception and intellection. We deny our "coarse stem" at our peril while we urge our souls into bloom. Although these were written fifteen or more years after the poems on his mother's death, we can detect in the earlier writings a similar concern. It is there clearly at the very end of *Sons and Lovers*. After the death of his mother, Paul Morel finds himself in a "void," with no place in life, all holds on him gone, but consciousness of his own physical self draws him back:

> But yet there was his body, his chest, that leaned against the stile, his hands on the wooden bar. They seemed something. ... On every side the immense dark silence seemed pressing him, so tiny a spark, into extinction, and yet, almost nothing, he could not be extinct. Night, in which everything was lost, went reaching out, beyond stars and sun. Stars and sun, a few bright grains, went spinning round for terror, and holding each other in embrace, there in a darkness that outpassed them all, and left them tiny and daunted. So much, and himself, infinitesimal, at the core a nothingness, and yet not nothing. ... But no, he would not give in. ... He walked towards the faintly humming, glowing town, quickly.
> (420)

In the poems as well, a physical reality of some sort is set against (and saves him from) a darkness. In the weaker poems he can only indulge the tension; in the better ones he acknowledges *and* resolves it.

"Suspense" is the first in the series and concerns the tension in him as he waits in the south for news of her death coming from the north. Lawrence was living in London, teaching at a Croydon school through the autumn of 1910, getting away on alternate weekends to see his mother in Eastwood, Nottinghamshire. But that information is really incidental to our understanding of the poem.

> The wind comes from the north
> Blowing little flocks of birds
> Like spray across the town,
> And a train roaring forth
> Rushes stampeding down
> South, with flying curds
> Of steam, from the darkening north.
> (1–7)

It is one of the most perfectly symmetrical stanzas he ever wrote. The crucial rhyming word is "north" in the first line and last line, with the stanza pivoting on "forth" in the middle, fourth line. The rhyme scheme itself is a mirror image, $abc/a/cba$, which offers a formal expression of the reflective forces of the wind and train, the latter aided by the former, and which coincides with a somewhat symmetrical arrangement of details in this primarily descriptive stanza: the "blowing little flocks" of line 2 echoed in the "flying curds" of line 6, and the spraying action of line 3 echoed in the stampeding action of line 5. A stampede usually suggests a headlong rush and spray of a mass of frightened animals or people. Saying that the single, massive train can stampede gives that image an ominousness not present in the wind, which simply and naturally "comes." Thus the rhyme scheme suggests a comparison (lines 3 and 5), only to highlight a subsequent more important difference (the clumps of steam, after being belched from the more frightening train will be dispersed by the same wind that dispersed the birds). The train is more frightening because it is a man-made force seemingly out of man's full control ("stampede"). This development of a fearful mood is aided by the development from the opening to the closing phrases: "from the north" to "from the darkening north."

To these two forces from the cold north, natural and mechanical, both non-human, the poet must be attentive, but unlike them he is still.

> Whither I turn and set
> Like a needle steadfastly,
> Waiting ever to get
> The news that she is free;
> But ever fixed, as yet,
> To the lode of her agony.
>
> (8–13)

Now the rhyme scheme, as if to announce this almost resisting position, is simpler and steadier, with more, slightly harder terminal sounds in the rhyme words. The irony of line 11 is enforced by the wonderfully apt but unexpected "lode" of line 13 (almost Hardyesque here). Yes, death will set her free from her pain and her suffering body, but then she will be nought. His complex mood is contained here: desire for that which will erase her pain but also her being. With her release and loss will come his relief and pain. The metaphor "lode" has several cooperating meanings: first, of course, it is an ore deposit and an abundant store, like the pervasive weight *and value* of her pain (which attests to her living consciousness); second, it is (in dialect English) a waterway, suggesting more vividly the branching growth of the cancer; third, there cannot but be a pun on "load" to intensify the primary denotation, but also we must think of the lode-star, which fixes the compass needle of his attention (line 9). He is turned north, because from there will come news of her death *and* because there is the object of his love. That it is love is made clear by the refusal only to sympathize with her agony and wish her a speedy end: it is *another* that he loves. He moves beyond identification with the common experience of pain (the force of "But" in line 12) to acknowledgment of her separate being: "*But* ever fixed, *as yet,* / To the lode of her agony." In these final lines there is a note of withstanding, standing against the inevitable rushing forces from the north bringing darkness. He knows he must accept, he even relishes the relief for her as well as for himself, but still he must pay for the relief with a loved life. It is the tension between "ever" and "as yet."

In *Amores* this poem was significantly titled "Patience," what he sets against the provoking haste of the wind, train, and death. The poem that follows it in the *Collected Poems* is "Endless Anxiety," on the same subject, but whose title promises less than the previous poem. There is a train and birds, but none of that conjoined southward movement, and there is a redundant if more immediate "telegram-bicycle" approaching and passing. But although the double response is still there (relief that she is not dead *and* regret that she suffers still), the quality of that relief is, in the substitution of "deeper bruise" for "the lode," mundane and commonplace:

> He has passed us by; but is it
> Relief that starts in my breast?
> Or a deeper bruise of knowing that still
> She has no rest.
>
> (9–12)

Here the desire for release gets the last word, not so in the less humane but more human "Patience."

In *Sons and Lovers*, Mrs. Morel in the days before her death is often described as looking "like a girl," "lying on her side, like a child," "her blue eyes smiled . . . like a girl's" (384–85), and when she lay dead finally,

> she lay like a maiden asleep. . . . The mouth was a little open as if wondering from the suffering, but her face was young, her brow clear and white as if life had never touched it. He looked again at the eyebrows, at the small, winsome nose a bit on one side. She was young again. Only the hair as it arched so beautifully from her temples was mixed with silver, and the two simple plaits that lay on her shoulders were filigree of silver and brown. . . . Still she dreamed her young dream. But she would be cold.
>
> (399–400)

"The Bride," the poetic rendering of this, is a much plainer poem than "Suspense," with no complexly resonant metaphors, almost simply a subdued lyric description—almost. Certainly the first stanza is in a lyric measure, alternating tetrameter and dimeter lines, with only the short lines rhyming.

> My love looks like a girl to-night,
> But she is old.
> The plaits that lie along her pillow

>   Are not gold,
>   But threaded with filigree silver,
>   And uncanny cold.
>
>   (1–6)

In this poem the tension is between the appearance of youth and the fact of age and death, and in this stanza the form participates in defining the opposition: in the first two sets of two-line units the long lines begin to offer the illusion but the short ones quickly deny it; and in the last set, although furthering the denial of line 4, the short line is much blunter than the preceding long line. The two anapests in the second and third positions of line 5 and the defective fourth foot resist the iambic march established earlier (despite the line break, lines 3 and 4 are really six emphatic iambs), but they only set us up for extra stress on "cold," created by the alliteration and the delay, through three unstressed syllables ("-ver, / And un-") before the first "c." The "But" of line 2 is driven home gently but unequivocally. The poet is quietly but firmly realistic.

The final two stanzas change the measure to alternating pentameter and dimeter lines in symmetrical stanzas of five lines:

>   She looks like a young maiden, since her brow
>   Is smooth and fair;
>   Her cheeks are very smooth, her eyes are closed,
>   She sleeps a rare,
>   Still, winsome sleep, so still, and so composed.
>
>   Nay, but she sleeps like a bride, and dreams her dreams
>   Of perfect things.
>   She lies at last, the darling, in the shape of her dream;
>   And her dead mouth sings
>   By its shape, like thrushes in clear evenings.
>
>   (7–16)

Rhyming increases as we move through the stanzas (from $a\,b\,c\,b\,d\,b$ to $a\,b\,c\,b\,c$ to $a\,b\,a\,b\,b$) to an assured and less tense closure. Thus the form emphasizes the tension in the first stanza and allays it in the second and third. The second stanza is devoted entirely to the illusion of youth (asserted in line 1), balancing the denials of lines 2 to 6. The long lines quieten the tone and the short ones are easefully regular; the marvelously alliterated lines 10 and 11 ("She sleeps a rare, / Still, winsome sleep, so still, and so composed") soften further, so that when the denial comes again in line 12 ("Nay"), we are not ready to take it too seriously, and the *s* sounds continue ("but still she sleeps") and the "like" is not at all emphasized (placed as the first syllable in an anapest)—contrast this with the very emphatic "like" of line 1 (at the end of an alliterated series and a foot) and of line 7 (also alliterated, and this time the stressed syllable of a trochaic inversion). By this third stanza we are less concerned with that curious but not uncommon appearance and more with its proposed and resolving meaning for Lawrence. There is an irony in "She lies at last, the darling, in the shape of her dream," but Tom Marshall perhaps overstates and overgeneralizes it: "The poem develops the exquisite irony of the appearance of felicity in the fact of ultimate defeat":[68] "exquisite" does not say enough and "ultimate defeat" too much. By this time the voice is too gentle: he wants neither to use her example to note a universal failure nor to bewail her personal failure, but rather to register, at some respectful distance (respectful of her dreams and her failures), that he cares about that life, unfulfilled as it might have been.

> And her dead mouth sings
> By its shape, like thrushes in clear evenings.

Lawrence will not ease or sentimentalize the last hours of Mrs. Morel's life; one horrific fact characterizes those hours. When she falls into her final sleep, her mouth falls open, we are told again and again, and out of it "the great, snoring ... rasping breath," "the great harsh sound" that haunts and horrifies Paul and his sister as they wait for her to die (395–98). The horror is only implicit in the poem, in the suddenness of the word "dead" and of the flat rhythm that accompanies it ("And her dead mouth sings"). Finally the poem is a tribute, a consolation too, perhaps, but foremost a tribute to her indomitable spirit beneath the appearance. A thrush is a plainly colored and unobtrusive bird, but it is an excellent singer; and its song is best not at glorious and romantic sunrises or at cloud-dappled sunsets, but "in clear evenings." This is the only full figure in the poem, all the more forceful and poignant for being alone. It concludes, rather than substitutes for, an understanding.

An even plainer poem is "Sorrow"—its one figure, "soft-foot malady," although itself unobtrusive, seems almost in such a spare context to intrude. Like the previous two poems it records a double view, but this time with an echo. There are two structural principles at work here: question (stanza one, which is one sentence), and answer (stanzas two and three, which comprise one sentence), and this coincides perfectly with a move from present to past.

> Why does the thin grey strand
> Floating up from the forgotten
> Cigarette between my fingers,
> Why does it trouble me?
>
> Ah, you will understand;
> When I carried my mother downstairs,

> A few times only, at the beginning
> Of her soft-foot malady,
>
> I should find, for a reprimand
> To my gaiety, a few long grey hairs
> On the breast of my coat; and one by one
> I watched them float up the dark chimney.

We are rarely free of a sense of loss; even a distracted moment, like the stronger "gaiety" before the mother's death (this is one of the few poems that actually mentions his mother directly), is "reprimanded." The word is important: the loss of a loved life leaves as well as memories an obligation, and to break it brings a formal rebuke. It is almost public (the reason, I suppose, for the otherwise awkward fifth line). The criticism of his weakness takes the form of a reminder of vulnerability (the strand of thin grey smoke and the thin, long grey hairs), the grey dispersing upwards into darkness—again darkness (in "The Bride" its equivalent was "uncanny cold" and the "dead mouth," out of which, according to long tradition, the soul departs upwards into the void). It is the loving survivor's obligation to continue knowing that nothing can be quite the same. Unlike the other poems, there is no overt resistance here, except if one wishes (as I tentatively do) to consider the obligation suggested by "reprimand" as a kind of moral stay: certainly forgetfulness or a forced innocence is no adequate response. The loss is a real one when the life continues to be regarded as itself and irreplaceable. To chide himself for however briefly putting that absence out of mind is a sign not of weakness but of the strength of this love.

The tone again is suitably subdued but not in the least severe, because of the delayed and faint rhymes (there are only two rhymes: the first lines of each stanza and the last lines of each stanza), the frequency of feminine endings in the first two stanzas, and the gradual lengthening of the lines in the final stanza: instead of roughly trimeter-tetrameter-trimeter, we get three tetrameter lines after the opening trimeter. That final lengthening nicely enacts the slow drift of the up-floating strands of hair (the last tetrameter lines have ten, ten and nine syllables, respectively).

Lawrence wrote two poems on the silencing effect the death of his mother had on him: "Silence" and "Listening," but the first is much better. The author of a stanza like this:

> And off the forge of the world
>   Whirling in the draught of life
> Go myriad sparks of people, filling
>   The night with strife,
>
> ("Listening," 17–20)

does not to justice to the talent for diction and metaphor that is manifest in "Silence." The structure is again explicity rational. Line 1 states the general condition: "Since I lost you I am silence-haunted." The remainder of the first stanza metaphorically explains "silence-haunted," but still in general terms:

> Sounds wave their little wings
> A moment, then in weariness settle
> On the flood that soundless swings.
>
> (2–4)

The next two stanzas (lines 5–12) list four particular sounds in a "whether ... or ... or ... or" series: the "pattering-ripples" of people in the street, then the "sigh" issuing from the theatre, then the wind blowing over "the dead-black river," then "last night's echoings." The list itself is ordered: from distinct if hardly loud sounds to less and less distinct or distinguishable sounds. In the last two, additional images even deflect our attention to visual and tactile sensations:

> Or the wind shakes a ravel of light
> Over the dead-black river,
> Or last night's echoings
> Make the daybreak shiver.
>
> (9–12)

So when he returns to the absorbency of the silence in the last stanza, the progress there, we feel, has been natural: the sounds diminished as they were listed. Although he concludes by recalling the introductory generality, he now, after the vivid list of particulars, closes with the most effectively vivid metaphor of all, startling in its comparison of an auditory with a visual image:

> I feel the silence waiting
> To sip them all up again,
> In its last completeness drinking
> Down the noise of men.
>
> (13–16)

The poem is thus structurally responsible to a state of mind that refuses emotionally to indulge the loss. There is even less consolation here than in "Sorrow," but it is still not absent. In addition to the ability of this mind to order its thoughts and understand its emotions, the poem itself is an answer to the silence. The moving river may absorb the social and natural sounds as it passes through the city, but Lawrence has carefully made sounds that we recreate as we read his poem. Thus the physical substance now set against the absorbing darkness, this time the "dead-black river," is his own articulateness. As he says to his mother in "The Inheritance,"

> You left me a gift
> Of tongues, so the shadows tell
> Me things, and the silences toss
> Me their drift.
>
> (9–12)

Yes, he concedes at the end of that poem, the words of others are not as substantial as they might be to him ("the night shows through / Their words as they move"), but still *he* is "clad / With words." He does remain to define and make real his grief and his love.

"Brooding Grief" offers the closest poetic rendering of the last paragraph of *Sons and Lovers*. In structure it recalls "Sorrow": a third of the poem is a question, the remaining two-thirds an answer; he recognizes the significance of sudden emotion in the present, but the movement is reversed now. Instead of retrieving the past, he lodges himself in the solid if messy realities of his present life. But this is not to say that he cancels the obligation he acknowledged earlier.

> A yellow leaf, from the darkness
> Hops like a frog before me;
> Why should I start and stand still?
>
> I was watching the woman that bore me
> Stretched in the brindled darkness
> Of the sick-room, rigid with will
> To die: and the quick leaf tore me
> Back to this rainy swill
> Of leaves and lamps and the city street mingled before me.

The tensions are fluid here. In the first three lines, it is between the yellow leaf and the darkness out of which it emerges: it is a dying leaf, but it finds a vigor ("hops like a frog") and life ("quick") nonetheless. Later, it is between the rigidity of the will of the woman and the "brindled" nature of the darkness. "Brindled" is of the same order as "yellow," but now it is placed just short not only of darkness on one side but also of the rigid will on the other, a human consciousness separated artificially from nature and time. Finally "he would not give in," but he turns to, not away from, the ungraspable real life before him (note the emphatic repetition of "before me" [2 and 9] and their placement before and after "bore me" and "tore me").

The sequence might have ended effectively with "Brooding Grief" (the title itself is somewhat ironic), and indeed the next four poems in the *Collected Poems* move off into other topics (his final breakup with Jessie Chambers, his illness of 1911, frustrated desire, and discontent). But then we find "Troth with the Dead." In its extension of the metaphor of the half-sunk moon, it is, as Sandra Gilbert correctly says, "metaphysical,"[69] but more than just generalizing his grief (her sole point about the poem), the conceit acts as his final pledge; it is the fitting close to a series of poems more about the attentiveness and continuity of love than about his own grief.

The poem begins with a personal view of the moon "broken in twain" at the horizon followed quickly by a general comparison: "The other half of the broken coin of troth / Is buried away in the dark, where the dead all lie" (3-4). The second stanza hints at the private case: "her" can refer to both the coin and his mother. The hidden shine of the moon or lustre of the coin finds its equivalent in the grave in the silver glow of her hair:

> They buried her half in the grave when they laid her away;
> Pushed gently away and hidden in the thick of her hair
> Where it gathered towards the plait, on that very last day;
> And like a moon unshowing it must still shine there.
>
> (5-8)

The next stanza reasserts the public cast of the statement: it is "a general sign / Of the troth with the dead that we are pledged to keep." There is a firmness and insistence here only hinted at in the other poems ("it *must* still shine there," "we *are* pledged"). But the "dark," present in all these poems, is also present here (the word is repeated three times in the poem). He almost defiantly faces it, because he knows how not to yield:

> And half lies there in the dark where the dead all lie
> Lost and yet still connected; and between the two
> Strange beams must travel still, for I feel that I
> Am lit beneath my heart with a half-moon, weird and blue.
>
> (13-16)

"Lost and yet still connected"—that is the general idea controlling the conceit. The reality in which he finds refuge is finally now his own heart, the strength of his love and his connection with the past. What is important about the past is not the possibility of reviving or redoing it, but our achieved continuity with it.

Although there are clear, undeniable, and serious differences between the poetry of Robert Bridges and D. H. Lawrence, the two poets share a view of love as an effortful triumph over transience, not something one is "in," but something one achieves by acts of selfless attention. Lawrence has so dignified feelings that had their origin in intense grief that in the poems they are transmuted into tributes to the beloved, in the sense that they so tenderly attest to his resolve. In warding off the darkness with graspable reality, he pledges himself to a love that cannot exist in a life half lived. Others have written on these poems about the death of his mother, most notably Tom Marshall and Sandra Gilbert, but the former's emphasis on myth and the latter's on confession do not do full justice to a resource between the abstractly public and the existentially private; it is what used to be called "character." Although the evidence is more conclusive in the great novels, I think it can be said that we see Lawrence finding, building, and sustaining "character" in these few poems. The opponent is the void, the darkness: it is always there, always threatening, not unlike Bridges's indifferent universe. But we grip down, we hold fast to life, to the good that is love in the face of that void.

Robert Graves

Robert Graves was as much a maverick as Robert Bridges and D. H. Lawrence, as much a defier of easy classification within the modern terms of acceptance. More cantankerous than the other two, he did not even see this similarity, despite the hindsight provided by his much longer perspective on twentieth-century verse (he was ninety when he died in December 1985): he could commend Bridges's "bright eye" and "abrupt challenging manner" but found his poetry, although metrically accomplished, unexciting and effete,[70] and he seemed unaware of any formal or other accomplishment in Lawrence: "sick, muddle-headed, sex-made D. H. Lawrence ... wrote sketches for poems, but nothing more."[71] Like many of his contemporaries, he seems to have been blinded by the public myth of Lawrence. Yet, as I hope to show, he shared with Lawrence particularly many ideas regarding male and female relationships; he was only less intense and certainly less zealous in advocating them. To return to my earlier insistence, all three of these poets are very English and very "unliterary" compared with the cosmopolitan, internationalist, self-consciously eclectic, even urbane poets who gained greater renown in the first half of this century. No three poets bothered less about their contemporaries, were moved less by literary movements, were more concerned with the preservation of natural English speech rhythms (even, with Bridges and Graves especially, within traditional forms); no three poets are less capable of being imitated. Each is tainted to some degree by romantic literary conventions but also at times aware of the dangers. Between Graves and Bridges especially, there are in this connection significant affinities: "Lost Acres" is Graves's version of "Low Barometer," and "Nature's Lineaments" is not far from "The Sea Keeps Not the Sabbath" or "The Evening Darkens Over." If Lawrence urged us into life, Graves and Bridges were a little detached, as C. H. Sisson says of Graves, determined not "to hug reality too closely, not to submit to it."[72] If we substitute "experience" for "reality," I think we are closer to the mark and better able to understand their strengths.

Graves himself commented to a visitor to Deyá in 1970 that "he only ever wrote love poems."[73] I conclude this chapter with Robert Graves not only because he wrote love poetry later and further into our century, but also because he is the preeminent love poet of that century; he leaves us a larger body of first-rate love poems than either Bridges or Lawrence, or any other poet of the period.

Behind my commentary on Graves's love poetry is a general agreement with his biographer, Martin Seymour-Smith, that the love theme, present from the very beginning, only emerges "uninhibitedly and robustly" with a confident and mature tenderness in the volume he published in 1946, *Poems 1938–45*, in those poems written long after his divorce from Nancy Nicholson, as he freed himself from Laura Riding's influence, and as he found a stable relationship with Beryl Pritchard, who became his second wife.[74]

There is nothing new, of course, in singling out love poetry as the central achievement of Graves's extremely wide-ranging and varied career. Such a claim is now almost a critical commonplace.[75] It is the grounds of that claim that I wish to challenge. The critics who have tried to defend Graves's reputation as a love poet have tended to do one of two things: to concentrate on the (usually pre-1938) poems centrally concerned with the problems of sex (what Ronald Gaskell calls "the savagery of love";[76] other examples are Michael Kirkham, who finds most impressive those poems "in which the contrary pulls of romantic aspiration and realistic awareness" are the strongest, or George Stade, who finds "more powerful" the poems on lust[77]); or, to see the World War II poems as simply preparing the way for and prefiguring the full-blown matriarchal myth Graves developed in the 1940s (for instance, J. M. Cohen, W. H. Auden, Douglas Day, James Mehoke, and Katherine Snipes[78]). That second and most popular view complements both the persistent contention that Graves is, despite his discipline and his reasonableness, essentially a romantic (Patrick Keane brings this to a head in *A Wild Civility* [1980]—I will have more to say of Keane and this problem later) and the insistent desire to distinguish divisions in Graves's career. Most detect three such phases: a period of conventional romanticism (1916–26); the years of Riding's influence (called a period of "conventional skepticism" by Stade and of "negatively classical restraint" by Cohen) from 1926 to 1938; then the new, tougher romanticism of the post-1938 period dominated by the White Goddess. Kirkham suggests a fourth phase, from 1959, in which Graves celebrates the Black Goddess of Wisdom. Such convenient schema encourage one to overlook or at least undervalue those poems written between 1938 and 1945 that were not directly concerned with the White Goddess and yet were a mature advance over those of the Riding years.

My aim then is to focus on that short transition period, a period in which,

I will argue, Graves could write that Cohen says the later love poetry decidely is not, "the poetry of peaceable love,"[79] which for me does not mean complacency but rather momentary acceptance and resolution, an achieved poise just short of the tension and conflicts (between head and heart, or classicism and romanticism) so valued by latter-day romantic critics. It was the period in which Graves could be a moralist as well as a love poet without the reconciling benefit of a controlling mythological system. Aware of the dangers of his romantic heritage, he could insist on revision, on a second phase of composition: "testing and correcting on commonsense principles, so as to satisfy public scrutiny, what began as a private message to himself from himself."[80] Graves seems to agree with Dr. Johnson that "of all the uncertainties in our life, ... the most terrible is the uncertainty of the continuance of reason."[81] In love it is the threat of insecurity and of the unsettling assaults of desire unaccommodated to reason and reality.

Therefore I have taken my cue from suggestions by Auden, who says that Graves believes "that in our age the Public Realm is irredeemable, and that the only thing a sensible man can do is ignore it and live as decently as he can in spite of it";[82] by Frederick Grubb, who recognizes Graves's poems as "by-products of ... the business of living, which is the quest for maturity";[83] by Ronald Hayman, who emphasizes Graves's sense "of loving in and against time";[84] and by Michael Schmidt, who says, "formal certainty is the only certainty he has. It overlies, or draws together uncertainties, clarifying areas in the confusion. From the confusion and the paradoxes he wrests the occasional poem of fitful but compelling celebration of love."[85] But, I repeat, it is the biographer Seymour-Smith who locates achievement in the context of the life, who can connect tenderness, maturity, and repose (however precarious) with poetic strength, and who is the most helpful to me. No critic to my knowledge has given thorough enough attention to that group of love poems published in 1946 and to the relationship of that group to love poems that came before and after.

The qualities that come together with such satisfying force in the 1938–45 collection are found in rather more separable and undeveloped forms in the poetry he was writing during the previous twenty or more years. Before looking closely at those more mature poems, let us survey briefly the earlier ones to understand the growth of those qualities.

He began with a critical independence of romantic and modernist attitudes. The poetry he wrote in the 1920s and 1930s often echoed his rejection of the many post-romantic attractions and comforts. He preferred the rugged landscape around Harlech in Wales ("country of my choice,/With harsh craggy mountain, moor ample and bare" ["Rocky Acres" (1920)[86]]), to the domesticated southern rural retreats of the

Georgians. But he also could indict nature's coarse indifference and meaninglessness, as in "Nature's Lineaments": there is neither grace nor peace in the seeming reflection in nature's shapes of the human face:

> The bulbous nose, the sunken chin,
> The ragged mouth in grin
> Of cretin.
>
> Nature is always so: you find
> That all she has of mind
> Is wind.
>
> (7–12)

It is, as G. S. Fraser says, "one of the rudest poems ever written about nature."[87] The subconscious also is certainly more a threat than a guide ("To walk there would be loss of sense," he says in "Lost Acres," a Blakean parable with a very unBlakean conclusion), and language is defense and properly binding (hardly a Shelleyan inadequacy), for

> ... if we let our tongues lose self-possession,
> Throwing off language and its watery clasp
> Before our death, instead of when death comes,
> Facing the wide glare of the children's day,
> Facing the rose, the dark sky and the drums,
> We shall go mad no doubt and die that way.
>
> ("The Cool Web," 13–18)

Language civilizes and keeps us sane, and yet it does restrict experience: that is the price we pay for sanity ("We spell away the overhanging night"). It is typical of Graves to introduce that conversational "no doubt" in the last line, undercutting whatever tendency there may be toward vatic pretentiousness in the preceding rather somber lines and rhythms ("Facing ... Facing ... "). Yes, he says, with not quite enough irony in "The Devil's Advice to Story-Tellers," leave

> Motive and end and moral in the air;
> Nice contradiction between fact and fact
> Will make the whole read human and exact,
>
> (20–22)

and be proud of your "flying-crooked gift" ("Flying Crooked," 10); but these are injunctions not against closure and directness but against arrogance and especially pomposity. The literary virtue he most prizes is thrift: it is a defense against the soporific and the sprawling, the careless and the inaccurate. Just as dangerous as the presumption of the visionary is the confidence of the scientist and, I think, the imagist:

> He becomes dull, trusting to his clear images;
> I become sharp, mistrusting my broken images.
>
> Trusting his images, he assumes their relevance;
> Mistrusting my images, I question their relevance.
> . . . .
> He in a new confusion of his understanding;
> I in a new understanding of my confusion.
> ("In Broken Images," 3–6, 13–14)

His criticisms of other poets are therefore predictable and in many instances quite well known. But I cannot resist repeating some of them here; they coincide with many of my own judgments, but Graves speaks with the authority of a very professional practicing poet, and I only as a disappointed reader. Milton, he thought, corrupt; Browning, Kipling, and Swinburne vulgar; but he reserved his harshest comments for the modernist "idols," as he called them.[88] Yeats "had a new technique, but nothing to say." As for Pound, "remove the layers and layers of cloacinal ranting, snook-cocking, pseudo-professional jargon and double-talk, ... and what remains. Only Longfellow's plump, soft, ill-at-ease grandnephew remains!" Eliot, unlike Pound, "had no grudge against the world, but only a shyness of it." Auden is a plagiarist, whose only real talent is for light verse. Dylan Thomas "kept musical control of the reader without troubling about the sense." One of the few poets he loved unreservedly was Thomas Hardy. When he placed himself in a tradition, it was one that went through Hardy, from Skelton, Dunbar, Wyatt, Jonson, Campion, Herbert, Rochester, and Landor.

Graves's mastery of the love theme is the result not only of that temperamental independence, but also of a threefold development: in his poetic humor (from jocularity to a gentle wittiness), in his treatment of sex (from a somewhat Puritanical fearfulness to an urbane acceptance), and in his generalizing voice (which softens as public and moralistic warnings are replaced by more personal—but still not private—and tender pledges). The brief survey that follows, touching on each of those tendencies in turn and offering examples of each, will provide us with a context for a fuller appreciation of his best love poems.

"Call me a Catholic," says Graves in a late poem, "so devout in faith / I joke of love, as Catholics do of God, / And scorn all exegesis" ("The Ample Garden," 11–13). Graves began his career as a love poet on a jocular note. In one of the school poems published in his first volume, *Over the Brazier* (1916), he announces ironically his Petrarchan idealism: in mock recoil from the "loutish he" and "sluttish she" who in "loathsome love together press,"

> I walk aloof,
> Head burning and heart snarling.
> Tread feverish quick;
> My love is sick;
> Far away lives my darling.
>
> ("Oh, And Oh!" 15–19)[89]

Sometimes the tone in these very early love poems is jaunty and folksy, as in "Advice to Lovers," in which an old man clambers onto a cider cask to declare Love a vengeful gossip; or caustically bemused, as in "The Troll's Nosegay," in which courtly love games are the target; or subversively whimsical, as in "Lost Love," in which a seemingly sympathetic view of the grief of the lover whose perceptions are thereby intensified is undermined by the increasingly hyperbolic list of the range of his hearing:

> The groan of ants who undertake
> Gigantic loads for honour's sake
> (Their sinews creak, their breath comes thin);
> Whir of spiders when they spin,
> And minute whispering, mumbling, sighs
> Of idle grubs and flies.
>
> (15–20)

The implication in the conclusion to this poem ("He wanders god-like or like thief / ... Without relief"), that relief only will be found in a social mean between the extremes, is drawn out in "Vain and Careless" (which follows it in the *Collected Poems*). One of his earliest poems about incompatibility, it warns wryly against two other extremes: vanity and carelessness. The humor reaches almost to bitterness in "Sea Side," a criticism of the social habit of coupling ("in search of symmetry") in appropriately rhymed couplets:

> The beast with two backs is a single beast,
> Yet by his love of singleness increased
> To two and two and two and two again,
> Until, instead of sandhills, see, a plain
> Patterned in two and two, by two and two—
> And the sea parts in horror at a view
> Of rows of houses coupling, back to back,
> While love smokes from their common chimney-stack
> With two-four-eight-sixteenish single same
> Re-registration of the duple name.
>
> (7–16)

Such humor kept the inflated solemnities of so much love poetry at bay, but it also could veil what early on at least was a real and discomforting uncertainly in Graves about the place of sex in love. "Down, Wanton, Down!" is one of the most exuberantly witty of his mock-satires, but although he may enjoy his lust, there lurks a possible fear of its single-minded purpose:

> Tell me, my witless, whose one boast
> Could be your staunchness at the post,
> When were you made a man of parts
> To think fine and profess the arts?
>
> Will many-gifted Beauty come
> Bowing to your bald rule of thumb,
> Or Love swear loyalty to your crown?
> Be gone, have done! Down, wanton, down!
>
> (13-20)

Seymour-Smith goes on rather a lot about Graves's "persistent sexual puritanism,"[90] especially during the years of his first marriage and his subsequent partnership with Laura Riding. "Ulysses" deals with that hero's inescapable sensuality ("Flesh set one purpose only in the mind—/.... love-tossed/He loathed the fraud, yet would not bed alone" [18, 24–25]). Elsewhere he distinguishes true love, or "friendship," from the "twinned helplessness/Against the huge tug of procreation" ("At First Sight," 2–3).

Whereas the theme in these poems may be a trifle overstated (the obsession showing through), in at least two instances, within more adequate contexts, it generated two of his finest poems, comparable to but not quite matching the power of Bridges's "Eros." "Leda" also reminds us of Yeats's idiosyncratic treatment of the myth, but how more relevant and sane is Graves, castigating the heart's potential beastliness, than is Yeats, speculating on whether sexual intercourse transfers knowledge or not. Graves extracts human significance from the myth; Yeats imposes a private myth on an aestheticized public one. Here I am disagreeing categorically with Douglas Day who contends that "For Yeats, Leda's rape is terrifying, yet beautiful; for Graves, it is only a sordid and disgusting exhibition of lust."[91] Day only quotes the second stanza:

> Then soon your mad religious smile
> Made taut the belly, arched the breast,
> And there beneath your god awhile
> You strained and gulped your beastliest.
>
> (5-8)

But Graves has one more quatrain. He is, remember, addressing the heart.

> Pregnant you are, as Leda was,
> Of bawdry, murder and deceit;
> Perpetuating night because
> The after-languors hang so sweet.
>
> (9-12)

Graves wants to suggest the unique power of lust (Yeats wants rather to discuss the power of a deity), and we may place Graves's poem alongside Shakespeare's sonnet 129, "Th' expense of spirit in a waste of shame." Quieter and broader still in its implications is "Love in Barrenness" from the early 1920s. The poem is structured on a descriptive contrast between a barren, austere landscape, described in the first stanza, and the beautiful form of the woman addressed in the second stanza:

> The North Wind rose: I saw him press
> With lusty force against your dress,
> Moulding your body's inward grace
> And streaming off from your set face;
> So now no longer flesh and blood
> But poised in marble flight you stood.
> O wingless Victory, loved of men,
> Who could withstand your beauty then?
>
> (11-18)

In transforming her into a triumphant symbol, the poem compliments and celebrates her beauty. But "inward grace" (a Petrarchan commonplace) is "mould[ed]" by a "lusty force," and the face, where the windows to the soul are, is rigid and passive (we have to remember the title). Lovers do turn their all-too-human mistresses into goddesses, but the motive is often sexual, and the result submissiveness. The question at the end takes away as much as it gives: "Who could *withstand* your beauty then?"

The other love poems of the period (abstracting this personal fear) tend to be cautionary fables, in which Graves's understanding of the power of a generalizing language and his consequent grasp of moral categories are more in evidence than any priggishness. In the very early "The Finding of Love" he looks forward to the values of a mature love, "With end to grief, / With joy in steadfastness" (22-23). The titles attest to his allegorical purposes. "Vanity" is about the dangers of complacency: as soon as lovers declare the absoluteness of their love ("Here, here is certitude") the dragon (or toad) of vanity awakens to dry up "the fountains of the heart." That love is an ephemeral, paradoxical emotion that intensifies rather than alleviates despair is the message of "Song of Contrariety," a poem of Graves's most disillusioned period, the period of *Whipperginny* (1923) and *Mock Beggar Hall* (1924). Day calls it a "period of detachment" and regrets the pursuit by this "romantic lyricist" of abstractions and generalizations[92]. I perfer to see it as a journeyman phase in which he developed that control of moral language that made possible the more personal but also more universally appealing love poems of a later period. After all, in 1965 he could still state, "My main theme was always the practical impossibility, transcended only by a belief in miracle, of absolute love continuing between man and woman."[93] The caution so strongly advised in the early 1920s thus can become, in the early 1930s, a realistic plea in the face of mortality:

> Time is Time's lapse, the emulsive element coaxing
> All obstinate locks and rusty hinges
> To loving-kindness.
>
> ("Time," 13–15)

Here he comes close to the wisdom of the elder Hardy in "A Broken Appointment": a "time-torn man" finds lacking in the woman he was meant to meet "That high compassion which can overbear / Reluctance for pure lovingkindness' sake" (5–6).

These tendencies (a humorous perspective, a wariness before the temptations of physical love, and a dedication to public meaning within a generalized language), so evident in the early poetry, are gradually refined and harmonized. Let us now consider the fruits of that development. Graves had published more than fifteen volumes of poetry between 1916 and 1938, and in that year he put together his first *Collected Poems*, and, except for *No More Ghosts*, a retrospective selection published in 1940, his next collection was *Poems 1938–1945* (1946),[94] and it generally attests to a new, more mature, stable, and happy situation. Although we see evidence of his diversifying and wide-ranging poetic interests, the collection is weighted more significantly with positive love poems. Of the forty poems in the volume, the first twenty-five are on and around the theme of love, then a group of six deal with mythological subjects, and the last nine are set apart as "Satires and Grotesques." My concern is with the first group. I will highlight what I believe are the better love poems and comment on related and complementary poems that are interspersed between them and that provide them with a somewhat philosophical context.

The first poem in the volume is appropriately "A Love Story." It indeed may be inspired by his growing love of Beryl and a consequent long and critical look back at his relationship with Riding, but the narrative is plain and universal enough not to depend on our precise knowledge of this. It traces the failure of an affair within a bleak landscape and denies finally the pathetic projection of human moods onto nature. It opens with a present scene reminiscent of a past one:

> The full moon easterly rising, furious,
> Against a winter sky ragged with red;
> The hedges high in snow, and owls raving—
>
> (1–3)

but even before the general summary in the next line ("Solemnities not easy to withstand"), we are prepared by "furious" and "raving" for the imposition. The rest of the poem charts the phases of a love life up to the ability "to withstand." In boyhood he internalizes the scene, suffering "horror" in adolescence; but then he falls in love, making "a lodgement / Of love on those chill ramparts" of his soul, and consequently snows melt, hedges sprout, the moon shines tenderly, and owls trill like nightingales. But it was only, he realizes, an imposition ("These were all lies")—she turns "beldamish," and the winter scene returns. The last stanza draws the moral:

> Dangerous it had been with love-notes
> To serenade Queen Famine.
> In tears I recomposed the former scene,
> Let the snow lie, watched the moon rise, suffered the owls,
> Paid homage to them of unevent.
>
> (21–25)

Love will not assuage Queen Famine, which I take to be his previously undeveloped character, his paucity of resources, in the absence of which he filled the space with emotional reflections of external scenes. Now he can see them for what they are ("of unevent")—such recognition is the first step in learning to withstand, the next step from "Love in Barrenness." So from the warnings and intimations of the earlier verse, he begins here with some conviction, on firmer ground. He is not denying the older theme of love's transitoriness, only mollifying his earlier more emotional insistence.

"The Thieves," the seventh poem in the volume, like "A Love Story," is a reminder of those early cautionary fables, but just as "A Love Story" could gain authority by not being so detached, by being more personal but also more roundly and less bleakly conclusive, so "The Thieves" can bring in some of that earlier humor (now more pointedly witty than playful) to effect a result similar to that of "A Love Story." It is about the greed inherent in the sex act; D. H. Lawrence himself could agree with Graves's criticism of lovers who seek to deny each's identity: they "dispense" with "meum-tuum sense" until they cancel "I and you." The result is confusion:

> After, when they disentwine
> You from me and yours from mine,
> Neither can be certain who
> Was that I whose mine was you.
>
> (7–10)

The establishment in the first stanza of the / ⌣ / ⌣ / ⌣ / rhythm helps greatly to keep the emphasis of this passage right, the sense clear, giving us an extra pause at the beginning of each line as we draw breath to tackle those pronouns and especially to find the stress necessary for "I" in line 10. Again, the poem concludes with calm authority, drawn partly from the skillful extension of the original metaphor into the old proverb:

> Theft is theft and raid is raid
> Though reciprocally made.
> Lovers, the conclusion is
> Doubled sighs and jealousies
> In a single heart that grieves
> For lost honour among thieves.
>
> (13–18)

The urbanity of the tone here marks an advance over his earlier antisex poems (with the possible exception of "Down, Wanton, Down!"), and even makes "The Beast," which comes between "A Love Story" and "The Thieves," a leftover from the Riding years, seem out of place in the 1938–1945 volume. Compare those last lines from "The Thieves" with these from "The Beast": "Before the meal was over sat apart / Loathing each other's carrion company" (7–8).[95]

Greater significance is found in two other poems between "A Love Story" and "The Thieves." "A Withering Herb" is about the dangers of ambition, of unrooted idealism. Yearning to be "all flower, and to star the sky—/True brother to the moon," the herb "denied his root," denying the sun and its generative powers. It cast off its protective "cloak of leaves" as it tried vainly "to float upward," but only in the end "withered staunchly." That final word carries both Graves's criticism of its stubbornness and his respect for its faithfulness. That breadth characterizes these poems. "The Shot," one of Graves's finest moral poems, brings directly into this volume the ideas of "The Cool Web" and "Lost Acres," here in a direct injunction against courting our fears, seeking extremes of experience for their own sake. As so often in Graves, the finely drawn metaphor concedes to a straightforward, but not less poetic, abstract conclusion. I quote the complete poem:

> The curious heart plays with its fears:
> To hurl a shot through the ship's planks,
> Being assured that the green angry flood
> Is charmed and dares not dance into the hold—
> Nor first to sweep a lingering glance around
> For land or shoal or cask adrift.
> 'So miracles are done; but madmen drown.'
>
> O weary luxury of hypothesis—
> For human nature, honest human nature
> (Which the fear-pampered heart denies)
> Knows its own miracle: not to go mad.
> Will pitch the shot in fancy, hint the fact,
> Will bore perhaps a meagre auger hole
> But stanch the spurting with a tarred rag,
> And will not drown, nor ever ride the cask.

Sanity in a world like ours is a miracle of human nature. That wonderful "weary" in line 8 and the consequent tone of one who has seen too much foolishness in the past to waste his anger anymore—this again is the newly secured Graves whose voice of prudence is growing admirably close to that of the genial George Crabbe.

The lessons of all these poems then gather just before midway in the group into five of his most touching poems. The application is now quite personal without being private: they are five of the finest poems on married love in our century that I know: "To Sleep," "Despite and Still," "The Oath," "Mid-Winter Waking," and "She Tells Her Love While Half Asleep," which completes the first section of twenty-five poems. The first and last two deal significantly with lovers asleep or just waking in bed, that frequent refuge and place of rest secured by the loving presence of the other.

Let me go to "Despite and Still" first, in which the need for refuge is foremost.

> We have been such as draw
> The losing straw—
> You of your gentleness,
> I of my rashness,
> Both of despair.
>
> (5-9)

"Despair" is perhaps a little melodramatic, but we welcome the more moderate extremes of "gentleness" and "rashness" over the vanity and carelessness of an earlier poem about incompatibility. The difference now is that there is a will and mutual confidence:

> Yet still might share
> This happy will:
> To love despite and still.
> Never let us deny
> The thing's necessity,
> But, O, refuse
> To choose
> Where chance may seem to give
> Loves in alternative.
>
> (10-18)

Rarely have such coupleted short lines been made to serve such a gentle seriousness. We might say the assuredness of the technical accomplishment is a product of the same strength that makes the love possible. There is the usual caution, this time against overconfidence: that they can love, that love is indeed necessary, is no invitation to promiscuous plural loving ("Loves

Modern Love

in alternative"). "The Oath" follows on from "Despite and Still" and is also another answer to "A Love Story": they can, by more properly "reading" nature, disperse the restraints of doubt and the confusions of passion:

> The doubt and the passion
> Falling away from them,
> In that instant both
> Take timely courage
> From the sky's clearness
> To confirm an oath.
>
> (1-6)

Their shared love and trust, he says in the second stanza, give them meaning, else they are "lost ciphers / On a yellowing page." The owl of "A Love Story" reenters in the third stanza, but with "no more terror," or, for that matter, trilling either; it simply calls.

The three poems about sleep and awaking presuppose this notion of signified, fulfilled love as defense against the past, present, and even future (after the "yellowing page" is "Death overleaf"). These recorded moments of avowed protection are tender but not fragile, firmed up by a shared realism. "To Sleep" mixes together the concern for otherness in "The Thieves" and for the dangers of "flesh-enraged" confusions in "A Love Story" and "The Beast," and of presumptuous searches after experience for its own sake in "The Shot" ("as dawn-birds flew blindly at the panes / In curiosity rattling out their brains"). Now that he loves her, his mind is clear and she can be herself:

> Now that I love you, as not before,
> Now you can be and say, as not before:
> The mind clears and the heart true-mirrors you
> Where at my side an early watch you keep
> And all self-bruising heads loll into sleep.
>
> (18-22)

The powerful last stanza of "Mid-Winter Waking" continues with the image of the watch. His love makes him know himself once more a poet "guarded by timeless principalities / Against the worm of death" (3-4). The splendid hyphenated series and subtle modulation of rhythm wind the thought to one of his most graceful conclusions:

> O gracious, lofty, shone against from under,
> Back-of-the-mind-far clouds like towers;
> And you, sudden warm airs that blow
> Before the expected season of new blossom,
> While sheep still gnaw at roots and lambless go—

> Be witness that on waking, this mid-winter,
> I found her hand in mine laid closely
> Who shall watch out the Spring with me.
> We stared in silence all around us
> But found no winter anywhere to see.
>
> (6–15)

The inner reserves, missing in "A Love Story," are there, so now he can do more than pay homage to "them of unevent," but ask them to witness his gratitude for the hope latent in their cycles and active in her comfort. (To support and balance the comments on the healthful view of nature, he surrounds "Mid-Winter Waking" with "Language of the Seasons" and "The Beach.")

The sequence closes as delicately as possible with this:

> She tells her love while half asleep,
>   In the dark hours,
>   With half-words whispered low:
> As Earth stirs in her winter sleep
> And puts out grass and flowers
>   Despite the snow,
>   Despite the falling snow.

The use of and imposition on nature that began the volume is by the twenty-fifth poem replaced with a simple comparison: nature's fortitude can be a model for man's love. Nature does not sing our songs, it gets on with its own business. In getting on properly with ours, we realize the common law to which it is bound and to which we can choose to be bound (as Adam chose against Milton's other law).

The poems that conclude *Poems 1938–1945* point to the directions Graves will take in post-war years. What are so broadly suggestive as "Timeless principalities" in "Mid-Winter Waking" shrink down in "To Juan at the Winter Solstice" to "one story and one story only" as Graves delves obsessively deeper and deeper into the White Goddess myth. Thereafter he "stands ready, with a boy's presumption,/To court the queen in her high silk pavilion" ("The Face in the Mirror," 14–15). As with so may poets, like the one he so disliked, W. B. Yeats, when his studies become mythic, his exemplary technical skills serve less human interests. The poems become doctrinaire and single-visioned as he pursues The Muse in her several nymph-like incarnations. "Theseus and Ariadne," for instance, is about love, but is not a love poem in any meaningful sense; his concern is to tarnish a hero, to debunk a legend and replace it with a thesis on its way to becoming a full-fledged theory of superior and dominant matriarchies. The socially critical bent of "Satires and Grotesques" presage an Olympian disillusionment in later love poems. The "intractability of love" is bemoaned "Prometheus"; "the heart being obstinate" is an easy parenthetical remark in "Spoils." The assumption behind "The Straw" and "The Window Sill" seems to be that it is impossible for any woman to be constant, not to deceive. The caustic tone only increases as do the years for Graves: in the 1950s and 1960s we get such lines and sentiments as these:

> Take courage, lover!
> Could you endure such grief
> At any hand but hers?
> ("Symptoms of Love," 13–15)

> Thus the hazards of their love-bed
> Were none of our damned business—
> Till as jurymen we sat upon
> Two deaths by suicide.
> ("Call It a Good Marriage," 21–24)

> I'd die for you, or you for me,
> So furious is our jealousy—
> And if you doubt this to be true
> Kill me outright, lest I kill you.
> ("I'd Die for You," 1–4)

> Gratitude and affection I disdain
> As cheap in any market. . . .
> ("Lion Lover," 11–12)

This is not to mention "She is No Liar" or "Ecstasy of Chaos." In these he seems to recover the ironies and bitterness of those modernists from which he so successfully separated himself in most of his writing. Occasionally one finds signs of the tenderness of the *Poems 1938–1945*, for example in "Song: Dew-Drop and Diamond" and "Joan and Darby" with its fine, echoing line, "In loving-kindness we grow grey together."

The good poems are numerous and morally weighty enough to tip the balance against these later ones, as well as against continuing assessments of him as "minor" and "Romantic." He is, as Thom Gunn rightly points out, neither "eccentric nor difficult."[96] He is too serious to treat reality, especially that of love, in fragments, or to subordinate it to a set of arbitrary beliefs, and too serious about love not to be mildly humorous about sex. If he never came to terms with sex, as Colin Wilson attests,[97] he did find a way, for a while, of coming to terms with love and giving it significance; and is not that, finally, what we most require? He stayed old-fashioned enough to withhold what a New York critical weekly called "his 100%

approbation" from "contemporary poems that favour sexual freedom"; he stood by the "monosyllabic days," by the old words: "*tilth* and *filth* and *praise*" ("Tilth," 5). He got on with saying what he wanted to say, keeping "The choreography plain, and the theme plain" ("Dance of Words," 8).

Patrick J. Keane's assessment is the most obtuse: "Even in poems with few or any mythopoeic pretensions, failure results when Graves is too rationally reigned in or when he succumbs to abstraction. Too often he tells rather than shows—and despite his deserved reputation as a love poet, the later lyrics only sporadically make us feel the passion Graves asserts."[98] Throughout his book, Keane tries too hard to keep Graves romantic, and when he finally cannot even fit him into an expanded mould (he redefines romanticism to include civility as one of its chief attributes), he calls him no poet at all. The very strengths and restraints that give his verse such suppleness and ease, such wit and penetration, such ability to say durably "something durable about human experience"[99] in glorious and commendable defiance of literary fashions, are enough to make us question Keane's criteria and perhaps our romantic tradition itself. Better a poet who can in this century remind us of Jonson than another Yeatsian visionary who goes out of his way not to appear "too reasonable, too truthful."[100] Graves succeeds, says Keane, where there is "a genuine balance between wildness and civility."[101] But that may be Keane's problem: his poles are too widely apart. I perfer the Renaissance balance between reason and passion, or between rule and energy. Bridges may lean too much toward rule and Lawrence too much toward energy; among them only Graves came nearest to the balance Thom Gunn ascribed to the greatest poet:

> But sitting in the dusk—though shapes combine,
> Vague mass replacing edge and flickering line,
> You keep both Rule and Energy in view,
> Much power in each, most in the balanced two:
> Ferocity existing in the fence
> Built by an exercised intelligence.[102]

Too many post-romantic readers see only the fence and not the ferocious intelligence that maintains it and that makes civilized (not just civil) speech within it possible.

I have tried not to underestimate the very real differences among three poets. But coming from different directions, with different backgrounds and aims, this aristocrat on Boar's Hill, this rebellious miner's son from Nottinghamshire, and this shell-shocked veteran did in some love poems recolonize higher, common, and older ground. With different mixtures and proportions, they again brought together traditional craftsmanship, a seriousness softened by an informality reaching to humor and wit, a respect for intelligibility (in two senses: for the reader a plain style, for the objects of their love an acknowledgment of their separateness), a desire never to leave morality in tension with feeling, and a belief in marriage as the guarantee of love's significance. Each laid his trust in the saving capacity of loving another, "despite and still."

5
Social Consolations

> There are any number of signs showing that men of our age have now for a long time been starved of obedience. But advantage has been taken of the fact to give them slavery.
> —Simone Weil in 1943

One of the positive contributions of the challenge to modernism mounted by British poets in the 1930s was an intensifed demand that poetry once again be a public affair. This means, in the widest sense, as D. J. Enright has said, a return to poetry as "a mode of communication with other people on matters of mutual consequence."[1] Fifty years later, the return still has not been generally effected. In 1980, Enright placed much of the blame for the diminished public standing of poetry on the postwar prevalence of a "Doing-your-own-thing" or "Noble Savagery" approach by poets (who ignore the past and therefore repeat and condone their own weaknesses), and the "rough-and-ready schematism" and theorizing by recent academic critics who care little about the distinction between good and bad writing.[2] We could also see a problem in the program for re-politicizing verse promoted by the most influential thirties poets, or, more generally, in the narrowing of the very notion of the political. The latter was not a process that began in the thirties, of course, but the inability of most poets of that period to recognize the debilitating consequences of the narrowing is simply a symptom of the real limits to their challenge to modernism.

The central dictum of the experimentalists of the previous two decades was that the situation of "modern" man was entirely unprecedented, calling for unprecedented responses. Political science emerged in this climate shortly before World War I, marking the final victory of a scientific, relative, and theoretical approach (concerned with description and understanding) over classical political philosophy, which was ethical (teleological), normative, and practical (concerned with right guidance). Leo Strauss, a leading antagonist of the new approach in this century, aptly characterizes the loss:

> The attempt to replace the quest for the best political order by a purely descriptive or analytical political science which refrains from "value judgments" is, from the

point of view of the classics, as absurd as the attempt to replace the art of making shoes, that is, good and well-fitting shoes, by a museum of shoes made by apprentices, or as the idea of a medicine which refuses to distinguish between health and sickness.[3]

The connection with the developments in literary criticism noted by Enright is obvious. My immediate point about the practice of poets is that with diminished respect for older notions of "ought," and still impelled to find unique solutions to unique conditions, the politicized poets were similar to the new political scientists who sought what Strauss elsewhere calls "a judicious mating of dialectical materialism and psychoanalysis to be consummated on a bed supplied by logical positivism."[4] Such mating, if on a bed supplied by a less unpoetic host, sounds like the project of Auden and some of his followers.

Aristotle's famous assumption that man is naturally a political animal (*The Politics,* 1253al) was resumed in the thirties, but the political arena could no longer be considered the complete community (which had *naturally* developed from the family through the village); such a community facilitates man realizing his destiny by living the good life of moral and intellectual activity, is the great limiting and fulfilling condition of human existence, the environment for self-realization, and the provider of the conditions for the growth of virtue. Instead, politics had descended to what the Greeks thought the reserve of the private household, the provision for the survival of the individual and the continuity of the species, the preservation of physical sustenance and comfort.[5] As a result of the Machiavellian reduction of politics to a technique for acquiring and retaining power and of the later, even narrower dogmas, whether Lockean or orthodox Marxist, of the priority of economic conditions, by the mid-twentieth century economic "growth" was the prime political motive, economic management the central political activity, and expediency the only possible value.

Thus when poets were ready to allow politics and social concerns back into their poetry, most took what was immediately available, which amounted to what Hayden Carruth has called a "specialized" vision, a constriction of "the larger vision of humanity," that grand, ennobling, and essential view that had prevailed in earlier times when poets could still think of themselves as spokesmen and advocates rather than, or at least as much as, oracles or secret agents.[6] This specialization is only an extension, not a denial of modernism's concern with technique: whereas modernist poets placed technique over and sometimes against content, the political poets of the next generation technologized their content to make it acceptable and harmonious once again with an inherited specialized style.

The antidote here is the simple reminder that technology and value are incompatible, or that they can meet "only on the ground of restraint," almost an impossibility because technology has a necessary commitment to keep up "the momentum of innovation." Wendell Berry has forcefully articulated the causes and the dangers:

> The technological determinists have tyrannical attitudes, and speak tyrannese, at least partly because their assumptions cannot produce a moral or a responsible definition of the human place in Creation. Because they assume that the human place is any place, they are necessarily confused about where they belong.
> Where does this confusion come from? I think it comes from the specialization and abstraction of intellect, separating it from responsibility and humility, magnanimity and devotion. ...[7]

The confusion breeds not only a dead, generalized, glib language devoted to public relations rather than public responsibility, but also despair—"the despair always implicit in specializations: the cultivation of discrete parts without respect or responsibility for the whole." The connections are inclusive: acknowledgment of one's place within the concentric circles of family, community, and nature secures language's precision and vitality ("if one wishes to promote the life of language, one must promote the life of a community,"[8] its ability to tell the whole truth, and tell it in good, common English.

Poetry as a public affair, then, should not simply be what we have come to think of as protest poetry, which is too often, as Enright says, "the self-regarding exploitation" of truths.[9] It needs to recover selflessly a defensible and unspecialized view of social humanity, in a value-laden, unspecialized language. The attempted fullness of the vision may not lead necessarily to optimism or even a proffered hope, but neither does it allow its unself-regarding witness to rest with opposition and indignation. This broader view should not be confused with the cosmopolitan one: to oppose the enemy of social verse, the confessional mode that locks us in solipsistic shells, we must not internationalize man—find him a place in some self-created "Mind of Europe" or homogenized proletariat—but see his full self in his real limiting and therefore liveable spaces. Roy Fuller reminds us that the thirties had its own political version of the Eliotic and Poundian cosmopolitanism: "The Thirties were a time when the brotherhood of man was not only believed in but seemed capable of practical achievement. The labour movement, despite its weaknesses, divisions and confusions, couldn't be regarded as other than international in scope."[10] In countering that modernist impulse to embrace the universe within, that "withdrawal of allegiance to the idea of man-in-society,"[11] the poet must be careful to embrace that which is embraceable—commitment to too general a notion of the universe without, society with a capital S, can drive a writer into the specializations of which Berry warns us.

Thus in the spirit of the traditional refusal to distinguish between the spheres of the social and the political (*politikos* conveyed the meaning of both to the ancient Greeks), we might best call the writers of this unspecialized public poetry not "political" or "committed" poets, but poets of civic virtue or citizen-poets, terms I draw from Nathan Scott, Jr. and Reginald Gibbons, respectively.[12] I also would be tempted by Carolyn Forche's "poetry of witness,"[13] with its implied union of observation and judgment ("We must answer for what we see"[14]), if it were not too broad. The other terms carry more explicitly the requirement of a concern that includes and transcends the political and social (even in their modern senses); that is, publicly responsible moral intelligence that can complicate and challenge as well as strengthen our commitments to specific political doctrines and social programs. If ideology is, as Irving Howe could say in 1957, "a hardening of commitment, the freezing of opinion into system,"[15] and therefore the promoter of cliché (and not all and any belief, as so many of our contemporary "human scientists" or determinists would have it), then the kind of poetry with the kind of vision that I think is still possible by twentieth-century poets is the persistent test of ideology, the testimony to a moral order beyond ideology, and therefore the mediation between the past and present and between the witness and any, however polemical, call to action. At issue for the reader is not whether the poet's position is conservative-reactionary or progressive-radical or whether it adheres closely or loosely to a party line, but rather how responsible it is, the quality of the engagement, the exchange, and the obligation. Then we might be able to see through the obfuscating and highly inaccurate polarity of right and left, Communist and Fascist that has bedeviled our political thinking since the mid-thirties.[16] We might be able more readily to realize again that the greatest poets, those spokesmen for our complete social selves, are always both conservative and radical at the same time.[17]

The test of these general speculations must be W. H. Auden, who was easily the most accomplished of the newly socialized poets of the thirties. He was undoubtedly under the influence of Eliot when he wrote in the preface to the 1927 *Oxford Poetry*, "all genuine poetry is in a sense the formation of private spheres out of a public chaos."[18] But two significant differences from Eliot should be noted. Although Auden's generation accepted that twenties's assumption of "public chaos," Eliot's wasteland sensibility was the result of a postwar separation from a coherent past and culture, and Auden's was a more intense and more immediate prewar sense of impending disaster, the second phase of the catastrophe myth that developed into the Marxist apocalyptics of the thirties. Also, whereas Eliot's "private spheres" were fragmentary constructions from a personal sense of the literary traditions of Europe, Auden's impulses always looked forward rather than backward ("Auden always faces the future, however vague that may be"[19]). Socialism was the contemporary ordering system he found to give a public dimension to his poetry. But even before then, in the 1927 poem "Who stands, the crux left of the watershed," the industrial wasteland—an almost derelict lead mine, probably near Birmingham,

> ... dismantled washing-floors,
> Snatches of tramline running to the wood,
> An industry already comatose,
>
> (3–5)[20]

is relieved by remembered images of the heroic struggles of a few men against the forces of nature. Those forces were replaced in the next few years by economic ones, but what is significant is that socialist views satisfied the same yearning for heroic action in the face of impending danger, some vague substitute for the communication with the land (21) that has been frustrated and vexed.

He tells us, looking back in 1973, that

> When pre-pubescent I felt
> that moorlands and woodlands were sacred:
> people seemed rather profane.
>
> Thus, when I started to verse,
> I presently sat at the feet of
> *Hardy* and *Thomas* and *Frost*.

But after a stint of love poetry with the help of Yeats and Graves,

> ... without warning, the whole
> Economy suddenly crumbled:
> there, to instruct me, was *Brecht*.
>
> ("A Thanksgiving," 1–6, 10–12)

"Thus" in line 4 reveals a shallow understanding of that particular rural tradition. What is peculiar is that as nature's sacredness became less accessible, the once "profane" people were poetically and rather too neatly divided into the easy targets of blunt criticism or their victims:

> ... the insufficient units
> Dangerous, easy, in furs, in uniform
> And constellated at reserved tables
> Supplied with feelings by an efficient band
> Relayed elsewhere to farmers and their dogs
> Sitting in kitchens in the stormy fens,
>
> ("Consider this and in our time," 8–13)

or (and here is where the sacredness was transferred) a small elite who could criticize the first, pity the second, and feel superior to both: the "helmeted airman" with a hawk's-eye view, the pseudo-prophetic poet, and the "truly strong man" ("It was Easter as I walked," 26). Such a prophet is also "easy," but in his verbal rather than social gestures: "It is time for the destruction of error" and for the "Death of the old gang" ("It was Easter," 134, 161), "The game is up. ... It is later than you think" ("Consider this," 45, 52). This is the bluster of a young man with the confidence of one who sees by means of an all-inclusive system and who feels with the urgency of the historic moment.

In these early poems the symptom is more evident than the cure, and the analysis is curiously Marxist and psychological at the same time: the appropriate fate of the corrupt financier, who creates but does not share wealth, is a nervous disorder.

> ... the prey to fugues,
> Irregular breathing and alternate ascendancies
> After some haunted migratory years
> To disintegrate on an instant in the explosion of mania
> Or lapse for ever into a classic fatigue.
> ("Consider this," 59–63)

The call to arms in this poem is both vague (14–41) and self-satisfyingly fashionable.

When the fate becomes in his mind more publicly violent (by 1933), it is still the result of a kind of determinism, now an impulse in history rather than the psychological inevitability of repressed natural instincts, a determinism that like his urgency continues to relieve any pressure on him to detail the social ills and upheavals he gestures toward. In the 1933 poem, written in the same month as the Polish riots in Galicia, "Out on the lawn I lie in bed," we get only metaphoric nods to "Where Poland draws her Eastern bow,/What violence is done" (50–51) and ominous warnings of mass unrest closer to home:

> Soon through the dykes of our content
> The crumpling flood will force a rent,
>   And, taller than a tree,
> Hold sudden death before our eyes
> Whose river-dreams long hid the size
>   And vigours of the sea.
> (73–78)

The poem centers on the leisured, protected life of the guilty, self-conscious, ironic speaker, but the motive for the apprehension that drives the argument is never given life in the poem. It is as if he is more excited by the idea of social abuses and revolution than troubled by the reality of them, so we only get a rendering rather than an interpretation of the feeling of social issues. G. S. Fraser has said, Auden's was "a powerful but not a very scrupulous intellect."[21] Earlier in the poem we have "gathering multitudes outside/Whose glances hunger worsens" and "traces of/Intentions not our own" (56–57, 62–63), but the only image is the sea metaphor of the quoted thirteenth stanza. The revolutionary flood retreats just as quickly and mysteriously in the fourteenth stanza, and the poem ends with a prayer that love survive to soften the postrevolutionary world. This is one of Auden's least tendentious political poems, notable for the pervasive sympathy he accords all sides, but even so his movement of thought seems as inexplicably determined as history in the poem; his intentions are not his own or his art's.

"Spain," from April 1937, seems to mark a backing away from that determinism, that helplessness before inevitable historic forces. The poem places the Civil War in an urgent present ("But to-day the struggle") flanked by hawk-like and almost comic views of historic change in the past ("The construction of railways in the colonial desert;/Yesterday the classic lecture/On the origin of Mankind" [18–20]) and by examples of the freedom to be insignificant in a possible future ("the enlarging of consciousness by diet and breathing. . . . the bicycle races/Through the suburbs on summer evenings" [80, 91–92]). In the central thirteen-quatrain section dealing with the present, the first eight quatrains establish individual and then collective calls ("the nations combine each cry" [37]) for an intervening life force ("O show us/History the operator, the/Organiser" [34–36]), and then deny its existence: life is not so much an overwhelming force as the need for and results of moral choice ("I am whatever you do" [50]), and the pressure for such choice now: "I am your choice, your decision. Yes, I am Spain" (56).

But if the poem's message is the need to accept this consciousness of choice (an always noble and relevant message), it is never realized or given body in the poem. The voice is too detached, too enamored of its own clever manipulation of details in the flanking sections, and of its own topicality, political knowingness, and studied unsentimentality in the central section:

> Many have heard it on remote peninsulas,
> On sleepy plains, in the aberrant fishermen's islands
>   Or the corrupt heart of the city,
> . . . .
> They clung like burrs to the long expresses that lurch
> Through the unjust lands, through the night, through the alpine tunnel;
>   They floated over the oceans;
>   They walked the passes. All presented their lives.
>   (57–59, 61–64)

("It" in line 57 refers to life's answer to the nations' call). There is the suggestion of an I've-been-there-so-I-speak-with-authority tone. But how sincere is his witness? Can the strikingly irrelevant detail of "aberrant" followed so closely by the vague and facile "corrupt heart of the city" and "unjust lands" give us confidence in the speaker's responsibility? In addition, in lines 62 to 64 a glamorizing impulse regally confers heroic status on the volunteers, and the attending impulse (in the deflating comparison of them to clinging "burrs" [61]) qualifies what he's about to confer, as if he is slightly embarrassed by it.

Undermining the pretense at a historically full and prophetically sweeping view is the lurking reductiveness in his persistent faith in (or play with) psycho-analytical explanations:

> ... For the fears which made us respond
> To the medicine ad. and the brochure of winter cruises
>   Have become invading battalions;
> And our faces, the institute-face, the chain-store, the ruin
>
> Are projecting their greed as the firing squad and the bomb.
> Madrid is the heart. Our moments of tenderness blossom
>   As the ambulance and the sandbag;
> Our hours of friendship into a people's army.
>
> (69-76)

Psychological states have become external realities. If there is no longer an obvious organizing march of history, there is a ready metamorphozing of innocuous inner states of feeling into momentous and substantive political realities (a simple reversal of the process invoked at the end of "Consider this"). In this poem Auden wants to make us conscious of our freedom of moral choice, but the potentially freed man is not seen fully. It may be that individual fears of poor health or poor weather may develop on a mass scale into invading battalions, but in the absence of some commentary on the surely decisive intervening steps, the proposition remains comically speculative and perhaps inadvertently suggestive of an alternate determinism. The intentional comedy in this poem resides elsewhere. There is also a hint of determinism in the portentous implication, only an implication because it lacks political context, that "to-day" the struggle must be Spain. (Here I am not so much blaming Auden as the myth-making apparatus of the intellectual left in 1936-37: as Hynes says, early on "Spain was not so much a place as the name of a cause, and the war being fought there was the Good War, a crusade in which the issues were unambiguous. ... But even then it was *literary* propaganda."[22])

The observations of the poem are piecemeal and in the service of "poetic" not moral construction: Auden's engagement is only with his controlling idea, not with reality, which he has not confronted very thoroughly. He calls for moral choice but does not exemplify (in his own serious playfulness) the credentials for making this choice, and even suggests it will take care of itself, especially when the choices are phrased as they are: either "to build the just city" or "the suicide pact, the romantic / Death" (53–55). George Orwell is referring to the twenty-fourth stanza, in which Auden characterizes party activists and talks of "necessary murder," when he makes his famous criticism: "Mr. Auden's brand of amoralism is only possible if you are the kind of person who is always somewhere else when the trigger is pulled. So much of left-wing thought is a kind of playing with fire by people who don't even know that fire is hot."[23] Perhaps it is not so much "amoralism" that damages the whole poem as a kind of moralistic presumption, both too playful and too serious.

These extremes are even more evident in a group of socio-political poems about suffering published in *Another Time* (1940). The withdrawal of his concern from active struggle to an almost passive observation of pervasive suffering was announced in the sonnet sequence at the end of *Journey to a War* (1938). In sonnet XIV the transition and attendant recognition of the evil ("little natures") in all men is asserted:

> Yes, we are going to suffer, now; the sky
> Throbs like a feverish forehead; pain is real;
> The groping searchlights suddenly reveal
> The little natures that will make us cry,
>
> Who never quite believed they could exist,
> Not where we were.
>
> (1–6)

Unfortunately, his detachment continues even when he concentrates this new pathos on an individual case, such as "Miss Gee," the repressed spinster who dies of cancer. Stephen Spender detected "a certain callousness in portraying the suffering of the inhibited."[24] The mocking tone, intensified by the tripping ballad measure, never justifies itself; the finally irrelevant details defend themselves only as contributions to that tone:

> She'd a slight squint in her left eye,
> Her lips they were thin and small,
> She had narrow sloping shoulders
> And she had no bust at all.
>
> (5–8)

A redundancy evoking the Simple Wordsworth prepares for another cheap shot, this time at her piety:

> Miss Gee knelt down in the side-aisle,
> She knelt down on her knees;

> "Lead me not into temptation
> But make me a good girl, please."
>
> (49–52)

There is as much detail here as one finds in John Betjeman's social portraits, but there is no sign of the latter's depth of disinterested understanding and consequent sympathy. Betjeman is more concerned with the truth of the observation and its capacity to draw us into contact with the fullness of life. Auden's motive is selfish in comparison; he wants to promote an eccentric idea, in this instance Groddeck's theory of "disease self-induced as compensation for a starved creative instinct,"[25] and therefore is incapable of respecting his observations—he is still adolescently proving himself along with that idea. At the end of the poem when he returns to those pious knees, recording the insensitivity of the medical students dissecting the body of Miss Gee, he inadvertently exposes his own complicity while attempting to broaden the criticism:

> They hung her from the ceiling,
> Yes, they hung up Miss Gee;
> And a couple of Oxford Groupers
> Carefully dissected her knee.
>
> (97–100)

Auden is simply a hypocritical version of those who turn away "quite leisurely from the disaster" in "Musée des Beaux Arts," written the following year, in 1938. The political crisis of these years made him more, not less selfish, indicative perhaps of the shallowness of his earlier social commitments. He wrote of Rilke's influence in 1939:

> It is, I believe, no accident that as the international crisis becomes more and more acute, the poet to whom writers are becoming increasingly drawn should be one who felt that it was pride and presumption to interfere with the lives of others (for each is unique and the apparent misfortunes of each may be his very way of salvation); one who occupied himself consistently and exclusively with his own inner life. ....[26]

But I detect little but pride and presumption in his avowed detachment from an outer life that he nonetheless cannot leave alone poetically. We should not be surprised that his cynicism brought him back to Eliot's solipsism by 1939 ("each in the cell of himself"), and Yeats's antisocial view of poetry: it "makes nothing happen ... it survives, / A way of happening, a mouth," a mouth that with its "unconstraining voice," unrestrained itself by a discriminatory conscience, can only "sing of human unsuccess / In a rapture of distress" ("In Memory of W. B. Yeats," 27, 36, 40–41, 68, 72–73). At a time when right thinking was more and more demanded of social man,

Auden rediscovered that nineteenth-century way of excusing false thought as long as it was aesthetically pleasing ("Pardons him for writing well," 67). Hynes may be right that "this does not mean ... that art is a value in itself, but rather that to write well *in such a time* is to preserve the human imagination, and thus to defend a human value against the forces of inhumanity."[27] But those forces also could be imaginative in their inhuman programs (Hitler was passionate and innovative): they had detached imagination from morality just as Auden was proposing we do to combat them. Auden appears here just as willful in his confessed powerlessness as a poet as Yeats does in the pathetic final lines of "Easter, 1916."

"Rapture of distress" is the imaginative product of the too easily accommodated extremes we have detected in Auden's earliest verse:[28] the overstated conviction and the playful hesitations, propaganda and escape, the vague and the trivial. The only way he could resolve the difficulties of such an accommodation was either to place his art in the service of a Kierkegaardian Christianity (which also sharply divided the aesthetic from the ethical) or to isolate his talent for the frivolous. Indeed, the best work of the later years just may be the unassuming light verse. In such poems as "After Reading a Child's Guide to Modern Physics," "Ode to Terminus," "A New Year Greeting," "Moon Landing," and "On the Circuit" a certain humaneness finally emerges; almost because he avoids profundity the breezy brightness cannot so obviously undermine a residual common sense.

The obscurity of so much of Auden's early verse was offset by the later colloquiality, but even that was too often affected; he never stopped being stylish. One might even say that, like so many of his politicized intellectual friends, he had little respect for the plain and ordinary, what Orwell referred to as "their severance from the common culture of the country."[29] It was indeed an age of extremes: the other popular alternatives for intellectuals were fascism and surrealism. Auden's style was simply a version of that uneasy combination of individualistic and global views that marked the literary and political culture of the thirties. It had different effects on different writers. The leftist poets with less talent than Auden relied on a shirt-sleeve sincerity. The voice is less cautiously polemical and the diction more loosely metaphoric and general:

> You above all who have come to the far end, victims
> Of a run-down machine, who can bear it no longer;
> . . . .
> Need fight in the dark no more, you know your enemies.
> You shall be leaders when zero hour is signalled,
> Wielders of power and welders of a new world.
> (C. Day Lewis, *The Magnetic Mountain* #32 [1933], 25–26, 30–32)[30]

We might detect a dim imitation of Auden's playfulness in the alliteration of that last line. The hesitations can be even more self-conscious and blithely set aside, the need for action overcoming all:

> None of our hearts are pure, we always have mixed motives,
>   Are self-deceivers, but the worst of all
> Deceits is to murmur 'Lord, I am not worthy'
>   And, lying easy, turn your face to the wall.
>   (Louis MacNeice, "Autumn Journal III" [1939], 65–68)

But the action rarely rises above the indignation and rejection; the targets are the usual, obvious, and clichéd ones:

Come with us, if you can, and, if not, go to hell
with your comfy chairs, your talk about the police,
your doll wife, your cowardly life, your newspaper, your interests in the East,
You, there, who are so patriotic, you liar, you beast!
Come, then, companions. This is the spring of blood,
heart's hey-day, movement of masses, beginning of good.
         (Rex Warner, "Hymn" [1933], 25–30)

Easy generalizations abound in this poetry of political feeling devoid of political thinking:

> In these houses men as in a dream pursue the Platonic Forms
> . . . .
> And endeavour to find God and score one over the neighbour
> By climbing tentatively upward on jerry-built beauty and sweated labour.
>   (Louis MacNeice, "Birmingham" [1934], 13, 15–16)

> Religion stands, the church blocking the sun.
>   (Stephen Spender, "The Landscape near an Aerodrome" [1933], 31)

That last line, which could constructively be the beginning of a poem, an idea worthy of close and careful investigation, is the first mention of religion and the final line of the poem; the gesture is complacently pompous. These are the more restrained poems of the period. I have stayed away from the versified slogans inspired by the Spanish Civil War, such as John Cornfield's "We are the future. . . . Raise the red flag triumphantly/For Communism and for liberty" ("Full Moon at Tierz: Before the Storming of Huesca" [1936], 15, 66–67).

What we miss in such verse is the middle ground, the province of what I have referred to as the citizen-poet, who can be both alertly aware and thoughtful, who brings loving observation to the service of moral conclusiveness, whose poetry can compute the cost of social and political pressures on the individual soul and place "what to do" within the larger "how to live." It is more than art politicized; their poems are sustaining, engaged contributions to our will to endure. It is also poetry that recognizes that the enemy need not be simply another political creed or the State. In our own time, the most celebrated political poets and those presented as models for English and American writers are Eastern European or Soviet: for example, Czeslaw Milosz, Osip Mandelstam, and Anna Akhmatova. Terrence Des Pres is typical: during an American symposium on "The Writer in Our World" in 1984, he justified his invocation of those foreign models of open challenges to the State by assuming that "the threat of cultural extinction" was "the small core of shared values which ... might well be universal."[31] Tom Paulin, in the introduction to the *Faber Book of Political Verse* (1986) in which he complains about the lost art of political verse in England today, lauds the Polish, Czech, and Russian poets over the likes of Philip Larkin, whose "lament for lost imperial glory is a deliberately drab, formal gesture of futility and resignation," and of Donald Davie, that "conservative literary puritan who was ... to join the Church of England and support the reactionary Anglicanism of *Poetry Nation Review*."[32] So there has been an even further narrowing of the notion of what is acceptably "political" or "social" in a poem. As George Steiner says in his *TLS* review of Paulin's thesis, "the simplifications are numbing."[33]

One way to resensitize ourselves is to recognize that protest poetry is not the only kind of viable public poetry, that the state can be too easily a target, that the maintenance of a healthy, critical respect for the past and for certain human and locally manifest traditions can be as, if not more, effective a bulwark against "the treat of cultural extinction," and that growth and liberation are never themselves humanly and socially adequate goals if pursued in the absence of final sanctions against anarchy and crime. Today the conservation of certain forms and the acknowledgments of certain allegiances are the last true radical acts. Tolerance and compassion in a moral vacuum can enslave us as surely as blind faith in a reductive creed. This brings me back to Simone Weil's point about obedience, which is how I began this chapter. "Obedience," she argues, "is a vital need of the human soul."

> It is of two kinds: obedience to established rules and obedience to human beings looked upon as leaders. It presupposes consent, not in regard to every single order received, but the kind of consent that is given once and for all, with the sole reservation, in case of need, that the demands of conscience be satisfied.[34]

That last clause is crucial, as is the context of the statement: the needs she lists are arranged in antithetical pairs that "have to combine together to form a balance." Balanced with the need for obedience is that for responsibility, to feel one is useful and even indispensable. Balancing the need for order is that for liberty, understood properly not as a plentitude of choices but as a real ability to choose: "When the possibilities of choice are so wide as to injure the commonweal, men cease to enjoy liberty." Other pairings are equality and hierarchism, security and risk, private property and collective property. She ends her list with an unpaired need, the most sacred of all—"yet it is never mentioned"—the need of truth. This is especially relevant to the social writer, who must not simply "act in good faith," but must do all that is possible "to avoid error."[35] An intense sense of that responsibility is what the four poets I now wish to discuss have in common: it gives their work a seemingly modest or cautious bearing, but also allows for the breadth and depth of their relevancy. George Orwell's argument, written two years before Weil's, is a more specific and perhaps more concretely acceptable version of hers: declaring a need for an alternative to ruling-class stupidity on the one hand and high-brow shame with one's own nationality on the other, he proposes that "patriotism and intelligence will have to come together again."[36] In "Notes on Nationalism" (1945), he defines patriotism (as distinct from nationalism, which is the desire for power for a group) as "devotion to a particular place and a particular way of life, which one believes to be the best in the world but has no wish to force upon other people."[37] It is naturally defensive.

Edgell Rickword

Edgell Rickword was born in 1898, saw active service in France in 1917–18, attended Oxford University after the war, but did not obtain a degree. Most of his active public life thereafter was devoted to literary journalism: he reviewed for the *Times Literary Supplement* and the *New Statesman* before becoming editor of the *Calendar of Modern Letters* from 1925 to 1927, of the defiantly anti-fascist *Left Review* from 1934 to 1938, and *Our Time* from 1944 to 1947. He published three thin volumes of verse: *Behind The Eyes* (1921), *Invocations to Angels* (1928), and *Twittingpan and Some Others* (1931). Although his latest volume, *Selected Poems* (1976), contains nine poems written after 1931—one from 1938 and the rest from the 1960s on—his poetic career for the most part ended just as Auden and his group were getting started. John Lindsay makes the suggestive judgment that gives impetus to my decision to include Rickword in this study: if Rickword "with his strong Baudelairean sense of the City, had continued to compose and develop" from the early 1930s, "we should not have been left defenseless against the take-over by the Audens and Spenders in the Thirties. As a result of that dereliction we in England had lacked the rich development of a true political poetry."[38]

Rickword's commitment to Marxism began in his late teens with his readings of the *New Statesman,* Wells, and Morris, and has remained strong if relatively undoctrinaire. I being with a Marxist poet partly to emphasize that my complaint with most thirties' poetry is not simply ideological. I also do not wish to suggest that Rickword is comparable to Auden in the range and polish of his poetic achievement. But, as I shall try to show, the direction of his development from 1921 to 1931 is exemplary of a potential for a public poetry quite different from and in important ways more responsible than that of most of the other more famous Marxist poets of the next decade.

Of the thirty-six poems in his first collection, *Behind the Eyes,* not one can in any full sense be called social, much less political. Except for four plain, unaffected war poems, and despite a preference for Donne at the expense of Tennyson in one of them ("Trench Poets"), most of the poems are Tennysonian laments over the transience of beauty and love amidst dim landscape imagery (flowers, hills, setting suns); the titles themselves warn us: "Foreboding," "Desire," "Passion," "Reverie," "Beauty Invades the Sorrowful Heart," "Lament," "Regret." But there are hints of social concerns in a few poems. "Intimacy" is perhaps the most sophisticated poem in the volume: essentially a celebration of reciprocated love, it deals with the power of familiarity. Because he has seen her do "intimate things" (combing her hair, tying "bows that stir on [her] calm breast," and putting on stockings), "all other girls dull as painted flowers." The description of that third action illustrates his witty, extravagant tone and his acute eye:

> ... I have seen your stocking swallow up,
> A swift black wind, the flame of your pale foot,
> And deemed your slender limbs so meshed in silk
> Sweet mermaid sisters drowned in their dark hair.
>
> (6–9)[39]

Michael Schmidt rightly calls it a poem of "extrovert wit, not introvert irony."[40] A less developed instance of this side of his talent is detectable in the opening stanza of "The Tired Lover," where the play with proper names in the first stanza creates an expectation of social comedy that is too quickly and unfortunately submerged in the romantic wistfulness of the next stanzas:

> Sheila and Pam and you, Olive, and Joan,
> Your laughter wearies me and the old tricks fail.
> I love one now who is quiet and very pale;
> Her hair is of dark gold and her name Yvonne.
>
> (1–4)

Finally, within the compass of his general nostalgia there are brief intimations of his regret for the passing of rural community life. In "Regret for the Passing of the Entire Scheme of Things," we find one unexpected critical detail: "drone of mowers on suburban lawns," and in "Regret for the Depopulation of Rural Districts" a delicate and realistic evocation of the class strata of village life:

> And in the fields strong women bending
> Down to coarse toil to nourish unborn women.
> Whilst in close gardens, languid with flowers' fragrance,
> Girls linger on close lawns for unknown happenings,
> Tearing a petal in long shinning fingers.
>
> (4–8)

Such a juxtaposition in the next decade in other poets would harden into propaganda, but here it remains a telling but not insistent observation, which gives some vitality to an otherwise predictable sentiment.

The poems written during the next seven years and collected in *Invocations to Angels* in 1928 mark the growth of that regret into bitterness, still mostly in response to love's vagaries, but occasionally in response to urban settings. "Luxury" rests on his broadest theme: "Time has no pity for this world of graves/nor for its dead decked out in feathery shrouds" (21–22), but at least it starts with a less grandiose vision on its way to a Baudelairean nightmare:

> The long, sleek cars rasp softly on the curb
> and twittering women rise from cushioned nests,
> flamingo-tall, whose rosy legs disturb
> the mirror-surface where creation rests.
>
> Aconite, Opium, Mandragora, Girl!
> Essential phials exquisite array!
> Poisons whose frail, consumptive fervours whirl
> the stony city to a fierce decay.
>
> (1–8)[41]

With the impatience of youth he fails to substantiate the motive for that exclamatory flight—those first metrically regular four lines are suggestive in their detached restraint, but even "disturb" is not enough to prepare us for the "fierce decay." Like many thirties poets, he comes with an Eliotic assumption about modern life that was too authoritatively (his generation seemed to think) embodied in *The Waste Land* to need defense. "Circus," a companion piece, calms the vision, this time of the dreary respite from "day's abysmal vow" offered by whores, but still there is no local specificity. He gives abstractions some concreteness by using eighteenth-century figures (he makes better use of Augustan models later) in the third stanza:

>   In sordid Games the martyrs of desire;
>   Shame's proselytes, exempt from banal fears;
>   they mock Solicitude heaping up their fire,
>   whilst Pity gluttonously licks her tears.
>
>   (9–12)

But the scene remains general to keep the world-weary tone as broad as possible.

Other poems echo that easy swipe at the routines of daily work (with none of the duplicities of, for instance, Larkin's "Toads"). In "Poet to Punk" it is "the light's grim daily duty," and in "Prelude, Dream and Divagation" the dutiful workers on the streets become (recalling Eliot's befogged crowd flowing over London Bridge in *The Waste Land*) "the loutish mass with lingering moonish smiles/on vast cod-faces swimming crowded lanes" (21–22). "Poet to Punk" is the glaring exception to the complete absence of place names in these intensely metaphoric poems: there is one brief mention of "London" and of "the Thames," significantly in the one poem that tries explicitly (like *The Waste Land*) to mythologize its subject, and, like the Auden to come, to stress the bardic role of the poet: "'I am the Noah of the final Flood/and preach precaution to an ironic Park'" (21–22). The generalizing urge that keeps the settings so vague, accompanying the personal bitterness that keeps the language so intense, is exemplified in the way he characterizes his lover in "Beyond Good and Evil": "it is a part angelic beast/sleepily smiling at my side" (15–16), a version of those dichotomized extremes that so restrict the social aims of the later poets.

I spend this time on Rickword's early verse in part to highlight the persistence of the Eliotic atmosphere into the late 1920s; Auden and some others of his generation were equally bred on Eliot, and even as they became more explicitly political were not able to break sufficiently with those poetic habits. But Rickword did, and the first substantial indication of this is in four poems ("Provincial Nightpiece," "Apostate Humanitarian," "Divagation on a Line of Donne's," and "Ode to a Train-de-luxe") presumably written just after 1928 and added to the *Invocations to Angels* section of the *Selected Poems* of 1976. In the pre-Depression poems, the traditional forms (a preponderance of rhymed pentameter quatrains—the only concessions to modernism being the dropping of capital letters at the beginning of lines and frequent trochaic substitutions in unexpected, usually medial positions) are barely able to contain the youthful anger and cynicism of his views of the modern city. There is little or no moral ballast to stabilize the formal control, and the phrasing is adolescent (e.g., "our blanket of despair," "our sheet of disgust," "streets of pain," and "theatres of despair") and the diction too intensely metaphoric without being sharply imagistic. But in those four poems we note a move toward plainer and less personal attention to social realities, the subject becoming more important or at least more determinant of the emotional response. The four poems, published in the order given, chart the stages of his transition: a new plainness that clarifies the earlier bitterness and brings the love theme into a more public context; followed by a purgation of past fancies and a dedication to the real world and the possibilities of revolt; then, through a commentary on Donne's changes, an indirect and depersonalized announcement of his move from self-centered love concerns via an intensified awareness of mortality, to religious (and political) concerns; and a full-fledged (perhaps his first) political poem that is self-critical and unpolemical.

"Provincial Nightpiece" is a satiric look at the thin veneer of romantic sentiment overlaying mundane domesticity. Still a bitter love poem, the clarity renders it considerably less personal, the jaundiced voice in the service of a pointed social criticism.

> When girls return from tennis on
> slim bicycles of hollow steel
> through their veins' colder channels steal
> the sentiments of Tennyson.
>
> Those censers of impurity
> infect the air with vulgar dreams
> of lovers by exclusive streams
> and plages of rich fatuity.

(1–8)[42]

The punning rhymes of the first stanza are clever enough to call attention to themselves, which together with the cleanly moving iambs set us up for the full force of "fatuity" in the second stanza. "Exclusive" and "rich" are the products of a much matured sense of diction. The next two stanzas display a wry sensitivity toward detail that looks forward to Betjeman and Larkin.

> Or otherwise they long to bear
> ten children to some honest John;
> content, whilst he is getting on,
> to darn and patch their underwear.
>
> In cardboard hats and plastic shoes
> and art-silk impudence they glide,
> all substitute. Could beauty ride
> Godiva-like, and use no ruse?

(9–16)

The unesoteric allusions to Tennyson, the Lady Godiva story, and Proust (in the fifth stanza) now do much of the work previously left to metaphors that did little to limit the readers' private associations.[43] In the fifth stanza he reminds us that idealistic love depends on subterfuge, and in the sixth and last the "I" enters for the first time and only to include himself in the hypocrisy and thereby strengthen the closure:

> Yet I have bedded, I protest,
> the paragon of elegance;
> when Night with his star-dripping lance
> feathered our solipsistic nest.
>
> (21–24)

That penultimate line, of course, is a sexual joke (and also perhaps another allusion—to Blake's more ominous and also sexual stars in "The Tyger," that "threw down their spears, / And water'd heaven with their tears"). The bedding is in the dark to preserve the public, daylight judgment of "elegance."

In an interview in 1973, Rickword called "Apostate Humanitarian" "essentially reactionary," not as a warning against a coming revolution, but "the attitude that if you say, 'To Hell with everything!' 'Stamp on everybody!' then the Gods will come back."[44] The poem announces both his rejection of an imaginative world distinct from the external, sensory one and his dedication to the "hard facts":

> Those are the figures fancy bred
> to people voids behind the eyes;
> but hard facts revolutionise
> the population of the head.
>
> (13–16)

He then predicts a new "dawn" when trams will become "the tumbrils of revolt" and "crash down with every cherished dolt" (17–19). Whatever suggestion there might be of a Communist revolution in the line "red laughter waving maddening flags" (20), the ambiguity of "maddening" is heightened by the final characterization of the returning gods:

> as shams and shibboleths collapse
> swift forms replenish our tired earth,
> of bouncing goddesses and mirth-
> mad gods with wine-and-oil smeared chaps.
>
> (25–28)

The ending is an indulgence, as I think Rickword's comments in the interview suggest. He still has not overcome or harnessed tightly enough his bitterness, but at least now the motive has a more precise reference outside of himself—"pimp and parson, prude and whore, / those shadows in a dead town" (3–4).

Social Consolations

In "Divagation on a Line of Donne's" (the line is "My verse the strict map of my misery") he restates the renunciation in terms of Donne's famous move from sensuously witty love poems ("That tangled growth of intellect and passion" [5]), through meditations on mortality ("Time's handiwork on the bodies of men" [10]), to amorous religious verse ("He wooed God" [13]). The final and only vaguely reproachful comment on the failures of a complete enough corresponding change in Donne's style,

> ... but sometimes the more faithful pen
> revived a metaphor that had trapped a wench
> and shames the dandy in the wimpled shroud,
> (14–16)

may be a caution to himself as he prepared to bring his Depression-stirred conscience more poetically into the temple of a new social and economic religion.

"Ode to a Train-de-luxe" reveals that caution as he writes his first explicitly political poem. He begins by emphatically (for the first time, I think) identifying himself with the lower classes as he addresses a luxury train carrying the privileged classes to Brighton:

> On your sprung seats the Faithful glide
> oblivious of the world that is,
> O Pullmans where we never ride
> to Brightons of remoter bliss!
> (1–4)

In the subtitle he identifies "the Faithful" as "our public idealists" and proceeds to analyze the foundations of their idealism: from a native obliviousness to what he later calls the "grossly real" (17), they gain a certain ease and unflappable certainty about their place in the unalterable scheme of things, emphasized nicely by the capital letters in line 12: "Perhaps such phlegm is natural when/one sees Relations as they Are?" (11–12). Their imaginations then are set free by such assurance ("They seem to one another's gaze/mighty adventurers at least" [13–14]), so they can afford their comfortable and unstrained idealism, which will bring them natuarlly face to face with the deity who sanctions their privilege. At the seaside

> through Nature's Absolute they stroll,
> and nimbly chase the untamed Ideal
> through palm-courts of the *Metropole*.
>
> Rapt in familiar unison
> with God, whose face must soon appear.
> (18–22)

But the "fat-cheeked moon" (24) they look upon is to the poet and his "coatless" companions simply "dead rays" (27). From that neat transition, Rickword turns to a similar adventurism among some utopian-socialists and rejects its appeal:

> What rocket-plane shall pierce this fate
> and hurl us past doom-destined space
> where we might found the virile state,
> Pious Aeneas of the skyward Race?
>
> Delusion theirs'; ours' duty. Choice,
> suspended, eyes the dense star-ranks;
> yet, Sirened, leans to your husky voice,
> O Dido-city on Thames' banks!
>
> (29–36)

This refusal to abandon his duty to the here and now, the suffering of London, for the sake of some dim millennial vision of a new state, places him on moderate but socially responsible ground between the extremes of reactionary as well as revolutionary idealism.[45]

The grounds for the conversion of Rickword's poetic style and the maturing of his content are found in his critical prose of the twenties. Three recurring themes are relevant here: the deficiencies of anti-social aestheticism, plain speaking within traditional forms, and the need for more thorough and whole poetic concerns, for a poetry of fact *and* ideas. Like only a few others at the time, Rickword recognized a link between romanticism and modernism. In one of his earliest contributions to *The Calendar of Modern Letters,* which he edited, he bemoaned that "effect of the triumph of the romantic movement in the last century," the separation of the poet from "the subjects which abound in ordinary social life."[46] As a consequence, "the modern poet is to his audience an author, not a man. It is interested in his more generalized emotions, not in his relations with the life and people round him."[47] There was, he acknowledged in 1931, a resurgence of interest in social man among the Edwardian writers (with the exception of J. M. Barrie and other "apostles of loveableness,"[48] but the newer writers have, because of the loss of a common point of interest, reemphasized the individual. "At the same time," he continues, "more energy is released for the consideration of technical problems."[49] Rickword's attitude toward one area of his age's attention to style indicates the depth of his concern for socially engaged poetry. "Colloquialism may be good," he says reviewing Abercrombie in 1929, "especially as a defense against Miltonic mannerisms, and by rejuvenating idiom, but when it threatens the dominance of metre verse becomes a drawl."[50] As I have shown, only gradually did plain speaking become a goal for him in verse as well as prose,[51] but he always respected tradition (the temporal context of social man). In the early twenties he wrote, "what a man can do with words depends so much on what has been done with them before him,"[52] but he was careful to distinguish the conventional from the traditional: the former refers to "the approved stereotypes," the latter to "real vigour of expression."[53] That vigor was rarely possible outside of meter, which is what keeps poetry from being too individualistic, too unique. With formal precision as necessary control on expression, the poet could concentrate once again on his subject and see it with adequate thoroughness. On the subject of colloquialism, he insisted again, contrary to many of the new American poets of the 1920s, that it is "a means and not an end in itself; it is a stage necessary to the realization of the poetry of fact, which must precede the ultimate poetry, that of idea."[54] From the other end, wary of theorists and intellectual systems, he was continually concerned that a writer "be obliged to bring his ideas into closer touch with actuality," as he said of Wyndham Lewis in 1931. It was possible and desirable to have fact and ideas in the same poem: "Only the structures in which reason and the senses coalesce can stand the test of age."[55] This finally is what he means by poetry as a "socialized medium":[56] it is one that will see and understand man as a whole social being.

Rickword's quite perceptive review of *The Waste Land* in *TLS* (1923) brings together most of his critical and poetic interests. The allusive method, he says, is the wrong kind of reserve, which ultimately "will defeat the poet's end," preventing us from hearing "the poet's full voice."[57] Eliot too often "declines to a mere notation, the result of an indolence of the imagination." Thus in evading too vigorously the grand manner, he sometimes walks "very near the limits of coherency."[58] This manner just may be the result of what Rickword two years earlier detected as Eliot's "dandyical scepticism."[59] It is a too easy skepticism that takes Eliot to the borders of coherency. Rickwood makes similar but positive point about E. A. Robinson in the same year: Robinson knew too much to be an easy optimist. The gentle melancholy characteristic of his later attitude is "the sadness, not of despair, but of a man who probes too deeply to hope greatly."[60] The clarity and "analytic subtlety"[61] of Robinson's style cannot but be a result of that scrupulousness.

In the 1976 interview for *Poetry Nation,* Rickword elaborated on his differences in the 1920s with modernists such as Eliot and Lewis. The poet, he thought, should be committed to his own time: one could condemn modern civilization for its uniformity and mass mediocrity without cutting oneself off from common humanity, which is after all

> a condition of living, isn't it? We have to live with one another. It's very Swiftian. Swift was the most vigorous hater we've ever had in our literature, but he's not like Eliot and Lewis [who had a wrong sort of elitism]. He never despised common humanity as individuals, though he hated many things about it in the mass.[62]

Because literature is basically communication, he goes on, "you can't communicate what isn't in some sense common: in sympathy *with,* not *for*!" The kind of elitism he objects to is just that from which Auden was unable to break clearly enough, and not because Rickword was any more doctrinaire a Marxist. In the twenties, in fact, he did not think that that necessary commitment by the poet should be necessarily to a social program. Later, when his Marxist sympathies were more forward in his writings, he avoided the extremes of Marxist aesthetics. His criticism in 1934 of the "sinking-ship psychology" of Auden and others hints at his natural resistance to any historic or social determinism.[63] This is confirmed when he asserts against "some Marxists," as he calls them, that what a writer writes is not determined (although it might be elucidated) by "the background."[64] In addition, he cannot share with the likes of Philip Henderson, for instance, that simple-minded socialist view that formal diction in a poem "is proof that its emotions are unreal and affected."[65] As he explains, for him Marxism is more an analytical tool than a messianic mission: "I am a Marxist in the sense that I try to relate public happenings to the tissue of cause and effect which he [Marx] divined in the interplay of material and economic forces.... But one does not think that a sympathy with Marxism makes anyone an oracle."[66] Again, the difference from Auden is obvious.

This sensitivity toward the excesses and extremes of others carries over into his poetry in the 1931 volume, *Twittingpan and Some Others*. If the bittterness of love was his major theme in his twenties' poetry, the dangers of idealism (and the extremes it encourages) that we saw in "Ode to a Train-de-luxe" overtakes it in his increasingly less personal, more dramatic and satiric, but still admittedly not very explicitly political, verse.

Several poems do comment on love, but now with detached humor. "The Lousy Astrologer's Present to His Sweetheart" parodies not only the inflated promises of pastoral lovers:

> I owned no marble throne to raise
> your grace above the stumbling crowd;
> no vast horned herds had I at graze
> to make your passion proud,
>
> (9–12)

(all he can offer are lice), but also the sense of predestination that inspires the lover's faith in purified love. The mistress answers her speculative lover, who watches the stars for signs of their souls' remove from the House of the Crab (!) to that of Libra:

> She: Sky-ecstasies seem so austere,
>   Dearest! my novice ardour fails.

> Can't we assay love's richness here?
> Let my breast be the Scales!
>
> (37–40)

Rickword characteristically brings them down to earth.

One ironic love sonnet seems to announce openly the poet's own immunity to his earlier style:

> But having run so long in grooves of hate,
> beaten the bounds of metre choked with spleen;
> desired, despaired, despised, and in-between
> flattered mere melancholy for a Fate;
> we dodge affliction in a shell-fish state;
> though rumours reach us of might-have-been
> and suspect messages from joys not seen,
> a re-creation seems a shade too late.
> ("Answer to an Invitation to Love Delayed in the Post," 1–8)

It is as if an older Prufrock, whose disillusionment at the end of Eliot's poem had hardened into a caustic cynicism, were tempted once again by an idealized love. Such an allusion (suggested, of course, by the echo in "a shell-fish state" of Eliot's "pair of ragged claws") and the public "we" keep the poem from being simply a personal confession. A companion piece, "The Contemporary Muse," refers more directly to his former obsessions (he was once so "glamoured" by the smile of this muse, figured as "a simpering, baby-faced suburban trull" [3], that he "trailed her sad buttocks nearly half a mile" [8]), but here he places the idealism in the distortions of Tennyson (who "laboured all a vernal day / crowning a snotty brat Queen o' the May" [11–12]). Although he opts at the end for a new, and we gather more legitimate, "sweetheart," he does consider another, but expensive option: his lady says in the final lines, "'Why stir the wasps that rim Fame's luscious pot?/Love costs us nothing, satire cost a lot!'" (19–20).

Regardless of the price, Rickword did venture into satire, and thus separated his socio-critical intelligence even further from both the doomsters of the twenties and the prophets of the thirties. In "The Handmaid of Religion" and "Hints for Making a Gentleman," he rescues the tetrameter couplet from generations of neglect. In the first he attacks pious moralists (the Cardinal Archbishop of Westminster and the Home Secretary, Viscount Brentford) who, with a singled vision worthy of Freud, "annex / all blame to the one sin of sex" (37–38). He defends himself and the Queen (to whom this mock epistle is addressed) as a writer of books and a woman of fashion, respectively—two targets of the moralists—by invoking an older and broader perspective, in fact a Thomist one:

> Churchmen, when manners were more genial,
> found fleshly lapses almost venial;
> at least when measured side by side
> with sins of spiritual pride;
> but now it's safer to blaspheme
> than to revive a classic theme.
>
> (39–44)

Of the many hints for making a gentleman, one of most important is the protection of the young man from the real world. Here is a perverted idealism serving a class interest:

> Let library shelves sustain from reach
> the facts experience may teach;
> and Swift and Schopenhauer be banned
> past grasp of most inquiring hand;
> such pessimists are all suspect
> for they might teach him to correct
> the blind insurgent ego-lust
> that goads this paladin of dust
> and gives him in his rage for pelf
> rule of all creatures but himself.
>
> (5–14)

The most accomplished of the satires is "The Encounter." For this justly famous portrait of Twittingpan, a fashionable and gay man of letters, Rickword went back not to the slightly more playful tetrameter couplet but to the more sweepingly judicious and discriminating heroic couplet. On the whole, Rickword has none of Pope's poise, point, and definition—his models are more likely Byron (especially for outrageous rhymes: "show-day"—"foyer," "Prudhomme"—"Sodom," "topical"—"it at all") and Charles Churchill, whom Rickword commended in 1925 for his handling of "negative emotions":

> Churchill has little verbal delicacy and none of the fatal wit of Pope; he stuns his opponent under the cumulate blows of the obvious. But he is also capable of varying the tone of his anger, ... it is really sensitive, and so poetic, indignation. [The "Epistle to Hogarth"] is a poem of the repulsion one personality may exert on another, the expression of emotion with which one sophisticated *social being* may regard another.[67]

We may apply the same judgment to "The Encounter."

Although many of the couplets lack definition, the caesurae not always inevitable and the lines frequently enjambed, there are occasional signs of eighteenth-century balances and especially antitheses. One is suggested in the opening line, but taken away quickly when the first word of the next line denies an opposition:

Social Consolidations

> Twittingpan seized my arm, though I'd have gone
> willingly. To be seen with him alone,
> the choicest image of the present age,
> flattered my vanity into quite a rage.
>
> (1–4)

But it does announce a duplicity that brings forward the irony of the following lines. The poet is able to underline the moral discontinuities and failure of proportion in Twittingpan's butterfly sensibility:

> His mind was in a turmoil and overshot
> immediate objects in transcendent aims,
>
> (18–19)

(here the statement overlaps two couplets).

> Tokyo is down, but dancing's on at Prince's.
>
> (32)

> Luxury, cleanliness and objets d'art,
> the modern Trinity for us all who are
> freed from the burden of the sense of sin.
>
> (45–47)

> not now from mystic but hygienic motives.
>
> (51)

> They flaunted gay shirts and a grand old vice.
>
> (118)

There are even a few hints of the kind of quick deflation only the heroic couplet can effect with its patterns of internal balance:

> 'You must meet Iris, she who lives serene
> in the intense confession of the obscene
> and drags her tea-time sex-affair all fresh
> to the dinner-table, like a cat with flesh.
>
> (63–66)

The poem is unusual in Rickword's poetry for using so effectively so many proper and place names: the context is enriched, a period is kept alive, intensifying the credibility of the portrait, which remains representative. A few of the names may require footnotes for today's reader, such as the British physiologist John Scott Haldane, *Sunday Express* high-brow baiter James D. Douglas, and Shanks the sanitary engineers, but they are few.

Most are readily available to anyone familiar with literary sophistications and pretensions of the period. In passing Rickword offers us one of the finest parodies of one of the products of such: the word-obsessed free verse that only barely disguises facile and self-regarding thought.

> With that he handed me a deckled sheet
> where these lines staggered on uncertain feet:
>
> you the one onely
> not more but one than
> two is superfluous two is
> i reminds you of me
> me reminds i of you
> i is another
> identity unidentifiable
> then say is love not
> the word
> all love is perhaps no love
> or is perhaps luck
> or no luck is no luck rather.
>
> 'Chaste, isn't it? And yes, I must explain
> that I inspired it, at risk of seeming vain.'

(71–86)

"Chaste" is exactly the problem with the intellectual systems this "lank oracle of modern thinking" (94), this "intellectual athlete" (27), adopts with all the scrupulousness that his fluttering sexuality allows. If the positivists, like Lord Russell, have "freed us from the burden of the sense of sin," then other "modern" schemes will, Twittingpan preaches, free us even further from our earthly, "grossly real" selves:

> 'But look, in Shanks's shop the Past still lives;
> those gross utensils symbolically bind us
> to the brute part we soon shall leave behind us,
> for Haldane promises in the world-to-come
> excretion's inoffensive minimum.'
> . . . .
> He saw my red cheeks, and with kindly air
> proclaimed sophistication everywhere.

(52–56, 61–62)

"The Encounter" is not, of course, a political or even very social poem; nonetheless, beneath the charm of its jokey surface it implicates within its satiric compass the seriously fashionable poets of the next ten years.

Rickword could not go on joking. His energies were almost devoted exclusively thereafter to critical and political journalism. The only poem he has allowed to be reprinted from the later 1930s was written in response to

England's refusal to help arm the Loyalists in Spain. "To the Wife of a Non-Interventionist Statesman (March 1938)" is, as he himself confesses, "crude in places,"[68] possibly because its motive was too intense and immediate an anger against the leaders of his own country. But despite the bluntness, the lack of his usual subtleties, it comes across as more sincere than similar protests by the higher flying and more sophisticated Auden.

>   The grim crescendo rises still
>   at the Black International's will.
>   Mad with the loss of Teruel
>   the bestial Duce looses hell;
>   on Barcelona slums he rains
>   German bombs from Fiat planes.
>   Five hundred dead at ten a second
>   is the world record so far reckoned;
>   a hundred children in one street,
>   their little hands and guts and feet,
>   like offal round a butcher's stall,
>   scattered where they were playing ball—
>   because our ruling clique's pretences
>   rob loyal Spain of its defences,
>   the chaser planes and ack-ack-guns
>   from which the prudent Fascist runs.
>   (63–78)

Therefore, if the best of the public, socially conscious poems by Rickword from 1928 to 1931 are only promises, as Lindsay says, of what might have developed into substantial defenses against the Audens and Spenders, they do point in the right direction, setting new standards for a kind of public poetry that could avoid excesses. These poems are ground clearers rather than exemplars; they point to rather than embody the characteristics that only emerge in quieter poets in either quieter quarters or quieter times.

Elizabeth Daryush

Of all the poets neglected and overlooked because of the inordinate attention given then and now to the Audens and Spenders of the thirties, the most talented was perhaps Elizabeth Daryush (1887–1977). Rickword was usually silent as a poet after 1931, but Mrs. Daryush reached her poetic maturity during the 1930s. It may seem odd to include in this chapter this retiring daughter of Robert Bridges and of the English gentry, who spent the first twenty years of her life in a Berkshire village, and, except for four years in the mid-twenties in Persia with her Persian husband, all the rest in or near her father's house on Boar's Hill near Oxford. But, as at least two of her few commentators have noted, in the 1930s she did become increasingly conscious of social injustice and the extent of human suffering outside her class. Yvor Winters, her earliest and most vigorous champion, however, thought this discovery of new matter a temporarily disrupting influence.[69] Donald Davie hesitantly disagreed with Winters, paying a little more attention to those poems in which she "came quite suddenly to the perception of what her relatively privileged birth committed her to, or excluded her from," but not enough attention; his more pressing aim was to suggest that Winters (and Roy Fuller) gave "disproportionate emphasis to her experiments with syllabics" and that she is just as successful writing in more orthodox meters.[70] It is my purpose here to press Davie's disagreement a bit further, to give more and closer attention to Daryush's socially conscious poems and to propose that, especially in the context of this chapter, she offers, with Rickword, another responsible and positive, if quite different, alternative to the more forwardly engaged verse of this period. If Rickword is important for his warnings against idealisms and for his attentions to the realities of the external social world, Daryush is distinguished by what was most significant in her so-called privileged background, her education in traditional moral values, which provided a context and a language within which she could understand and deal with (sometimes successfully) the emotional disruptions caused by her social conscience.

Daryush suppressed her first three books of poems, published in 1911, 1916, and 1921. Her next, *Verses,* was published in 1930. That decade saw five more volumes: *Verses, Second Book* (1932), *Verses, Third Book* (1933), *Verses, Fourth Book* (1934), *The Lost Man & Other Verses* (1936), and *Verses, Sixth Book* (1938). When she agreed to publish her *Selected Poems* in 1972, she included only poems from those six volumes. *Verses, Seventh Book* had been published in 1971. *Collected Poems* (1976) included only poems from the 1971 and 1972 volumes and one long later poem called "Air & Variations."[71]

In Winters's essay on Daryush and Bridges that appeared in the *American Review* for 1936 to 1937, he said, "Her talent . . . although it was obviously formed by her father's influence, appears to have borne fruit only after his death [in 1930], and to have developed very rapidly within a very short period, after a long period of stagnation."[72] Several of the poems from the 1932 and 1933 collections indicate that she was quite self-conscious of her own maturing, moral as well as poetic. In a sonnet from *Verses, Second Book,* "From day to converse night," she states the problem generally: how best respond to life's extremes and especially how reconcile the need for "rest" and retreat with the desire for engagement and "rapture." The day (the social) brings both glory and torment, the night (the solitary) both peace and dreariness:

> ... know I not from which I now should pray
> For rescue, strenuous plight or stagnant plight,
> Nor whether angry right or easy right
> Be better, how to balance way with way.
>
> (5–8)

A narrower version of the problem is the subject of "Fresh Spring" from the 1933 book; although the adult feels intense loss of and longing for her childhood's easy imaginative converse with nature, she is aware at the same time that it was rather too easy. In the "deep woods" of spring the child sought only "phantoms" of what are after all "childish thought" and "spirits of the faery shade" (3–4); in the "fields of summer," when her imagination was "small," she met her "fancy's every fond device" (6–7). What is "fond" may be cherished, but remains also foolish. The "raptures" may be "lost beyond recall" (11), but the gain, despite "longing's fiercest flame" (14), is a "cloudless" sense of what is mortal and what not.

What she denies is that romantic view that maturity is a cause of despair. This is even clearer in another poem from *Verses, Third Book,* also untitled as most of her poems are:

> Thou say'st: *The clear stream is a troubled river grown* ...
> Would'st then confine it to one field's level alone?
>
> Thou say'st: *The flowery sward is ploughed and heaped with stone* ...
> Would'st then the treed garden's high perfection postpone?
>
> Thou say'st: *the hard woman doth the maiden dethrone* ...
> Would'st rank, O mortal, what's but to heaven's ruler known?

The compensations and reliefs here are mostly spiritual, but if we consider her use of the word "hard" in other poems from the early thirties, one can see just how a spiritual defense can be converted into a moral strength. In "Exile," for instance, which is explicitly about her matured poetic ability to discipline with "caging words" her once "wild thoughts," she compares her tamed thoughts to "hooded hawks" "whose eager eyes/See only their hard lord's intended prey" (5–6). Such hardness is a stay against the false attractions of either nostalgia or escape. The present, she says in the final lines of the sonnet, has similar and less extreme satisfactions (and we note how the opposition in "From day to converse night" has been tempered): "Here, too, may needy spirit find again/Cheer's morn, mercy's night, in the hearts of men" (13–14). Cheer and mercy may not be quite what ecstatic youth had in mind, but they are finally more productive. As she says in a slightly later poem about the hazards of unchecked freedom: there is reason to praise the Lord or whatever "keeps me from the stress,/The anguished dangers, of unhinderedness" ("You who are blest," 13–14). "Blind" (from

1934) is a cleverly sustained allegory in which "Patience" is a servant who, although she "wearies" the speaker "to death," is yet indispensable, for she often mutters "the hard text" that is a consoling, "grey comfort" for the speaker's unspecified sorrow: "'All highest wealth is won from lowest lack'" (11–12). What is "hard" here is difficult to accept (be it a religious or simply a social perspective—I suspect the former is intended, but the latter is not ruled out), but to accept difficulty is the first test of virtue. Patience does not replace the darkness ("my soul's dark room") with light, but it "Ranges the thought that hangs where light should be" (2–3); it can bring us back from the brink of an indulged pessimism.

These "hard" internal adjustments (mostly avoidances) then make possible a difficult external task, as virtue proves itself socially. In an extremely plain aphoristic poem in syllabic meter (placed beside "Exile" in the *Selected Poems* as if to draw out the relation), the poet lists what one needs "to perform your task/of hard forgiveness":

> A morsel of good,
>   a dole too of wrong,
> is the simple food
>   that make mercy strong;
>
> of joy a small sip,
>   of trouble a share,
> is all that friendship
>   takes to make her fair.
>
> ("Wherefore solicit," 9–16)

"Wherefore solicit" belongs to a group of bare, didactic, impersonal poems in *Verses, Fourth Book*; usually in the imperative mood, they draw out into a social code the moral implications of those earlier more personal poems. "You should at times go out" brings into the open the submerged message of "Wherefore solicit," that is, the need for breadth of social imagination. But Daryush characteristically does not leave it simply at that: understanding of and sympathy with the less privileged are not preludes to social revolution so much as moral exercises that strengthen one's own reserves. In the first three quatrains, she issues three parallel and progressively more difficult commands: "You should at times" (that last repeated phrase is an important qualifier) visit the domains of the doubters, the scorned, and the criminals (the language is restrained to keep the social implications moral rather than political). The last stanza explains the consequence of not doing so:

> or ever, suddenly
>   by simple bliss betrayed,

> you shall be forced to flee,
> unloved, alone, afraid.
>
> (13–16)

Although the poem is written in syllabic meter, the strong rhymes combine with unexpected accentual regularity in this quatrain to effect a particularly emphatic close. "The Warden's Daughter," one of the few poems in the 1934 volume to offer a detailed social portrait (here of a beautiful and beautifully dressed girl who parades her external charms against the background of a "squalid July street" and "sweaty crowd" [1]), is an instance of bliss's possible betrayal. The sestet is the observer's response and correction of that response:

> I thought: 'Such beauty were a magic boat
> Whereby a woman's heart might make its truce
> With fate, idly, in its own bliss afloat'—
> Forgot how even as honour has no use
>
> For honours, beauty, too, that's of the mind
> Sees only tasks, is to its mirror blind.

The opposition between "idly" and "tasks" is, again, typical of Daryush's insistence on moral effort (goodness is never natural). "Well, and what of it? What if you are beautiful?" deals with the same subject and is also a sonnet, but with twelve-syllable syllabic lines. Here the drama is more active: the poet addresses, bluntly and, initially at least, idiomatically, the beautiful specimen, this time a seductress intent on attracting "faithful thirsty lovers" (5). Rhetorical questions in the third quatrain prepare for the couplet's caution:

> Is this achievement? Is this what shall make you glad?
> Is this a gift for others bought with your life-blood,
> a sweet truth that shall warm men's starving hearts, shall add
> to weal, this cold, corroding misuse of rich good?
>
> Out on you, woman: quit your beauty, ere the day
> when what's within it shall have eat'n it all away.

Note how the social diction ("starving," "weal," "rich ") unobtrusively extends the message. Finally, "For my misdeed I blame my erring friend's" brings the "I" back, but the poem is no less public for that. As Michael Schmidt has said, "Her use of the first person ... is not encumbered by autobiography."[73] Now the issue is responsibility for one's imperfections ("Call then a halt/To visiting of blame: take home thy fault" [13–14]). Particularly interesting here is her swipe at those who blame (not infrequently in the thirties), with deterministic gusto and unrestrained imagination, some larger system—the past, evolutionary forces, the cosmos, or even heaven—for present ills and misdeeds:

> ... then fancy, winging free,
> Bears it on, till, beyond earth's blackened past,
> On blameless power primordial lies the blame,
> Till on eternal shores my times are cast,
> And glory immortal heaped with mortal shame.
>
> (4–8)

In most of these poems, Daryush tentatively circles social issues, more explicitly concerned with inner strength and moral defenses. But when she deals with the responsibilities of one human being to another, hinting occasionally at class privileges and distinctions in her self-satisfied targets as in the last four poems discussed, the circle narrows. At the center of this circle, are three poems in the 1934 collection that are openly social. In this volume Yvor Winters detected "a crisis and collapse of form ... as a result, it would seem, of the discovery of new matter to which she found her style ill adapted."[74] He is to some extent right: one might detect a slackening in her usually assured cadences and austere (even if sometimes archaic) diction. But we can still commend her attempt as she ventured into this area to avoid the usual temptations, especially intemperate generalizations and dramatics and class sentimentality. Her aim after all is to suggest an adjustment of outlook based on a reaffirmation of traditional and still defensible values, not to call for an overthrow of her own class at the expense of those values.

Two of the three poems ("The servant-girl sleeps" and "It is pleasant to hang out") are deflations of too easy, too solemn social reactions (one rather sly, the other caustic), and the third ("The woman I'd revere") presents the social ideal. The adjectives in the first part of the octave of "The servant-girl sleeps" invite the reader's sympathies rather too obviously:

> The servant-girl sleeps. By the small low bed,
> On the mean chest of drawers, are carefully
> Arranged her poor belongings—photos spread
> Cross-wise, a box of tawdry jewelry.

The next four lines enflame those sympathies with ominous (and inflatedly theatrical) hints of a coming, and more than just literal, storm:

> Outside the airless attic looms the vast
> Of sultry night; huge clouds are mounting, fraught
> With lurid flashes. ... Look! A tremor passed
> Over the tired face, as of anxious thought.

The intention may be satiric, but the effects are too crude here to condone bad writing (the ellipsis and exclamation are especially intrusive). The screw is turned further as we are set up for the bathetic correction:

> Is it of lightning tragedy she dreams?
> Is it of darkly louring pain and care?
> What profound unrest to her pent soul seems
> To gloom the world? *'On Sunday shall I wear*
>
> *The white?. ... It's less becoming ... but the blue*
> *Is last year's fashion now ... and faded, too.'*

Proletarian sentimentalists might wish to blame the servitude itself for the similarity of the servant-girl's anxieties with those of her masters, but it is unlikely Daryush (especially if we consider her other poems) would so complacently allow the social to replace the moral. Individual souls will have to be freed one by one before radical social changes can even begin to take effect.

Although no more subtle, "It is pleasant to hang out" at least has the virtue of uninterrupted sincerity. The hostility is as real as the hypocrisy is identifiable:

> It is pleasant to hang out
> this sign at your open gate:
> "*Succour for the desolate*"—
> your neighbours praise you, no doubt;
>
> but woe to whoe'er in need
> at the inner door has knocked,
> found the snug room barred and locked
> where alone you fatly feed.

In the first stanza she succinctly gives us the motive both for the advertised charity and for her anger, with much of the exposure accomplished directly using the pompous diction of the professional do-gooder, rather than subversively using her own contrived ironies and mock inflations (as in "The servant-girl sleeps"). The alliterated final phrase and rhyme of line 8 barely but sufficiently hold in and define her anger.

It is difficult to know just how to take "The woman I'd revere." Its idealistic picture of the perfect woman and perfect man verges on, if it does not actually cross over into, the sentimental. The woman, meant to oppose the Warden's Daughter (the poem by that name comes directly after this one in the *Selected Poems*), is a "warm hearth-fire," not "a chilly taper / posed for all to admire" (6, 3–4), but a "life-giver, thoughtless / how its own life appear" (9–10). The man, to balance the woman's warmth, is "a sure light / in the house," and, in addition, to balance her life-giving function, is an instrument of justice (possibly meant to oppose the hypocrite in "It is pleasant to hang out," which precedes this poem in the *Selected Poems*):

> one who'd be now and then
> o'ercharged with primal power,
> a sudden, a rushing
> flash in oppression's hour,
>   wrath's lightning, rightly hurled,
>   the dread of wrong's dark world.
>
> (19–24)

Without a hint of irony, this time the diction goes too far in line 20 as well as elsewhere. The fire-light metaphor is handled carefully throughout the poem, helping to substantiate the moral categories, but it cannot bring any life to the moribund political generalities, "Oppression's hour" and "wrong's dark world."

In her next book of poems, *The Lost Man and Other Verses* (1936), she brings part of this material under control in two ways. One is to return to her bare, allegorical style. The unrealized "wrath" of the previous poem then can become this:

> Anger lay by me all night long,
>   His breath was hot upon my brow,
> He told me of my burning wrong,
>   All night he talked and would not go.
>
> He stood by me all through the day,
>   Struck from my hand the book, the pen;
> He said: 'Hear first what *I've* to say,
>   And sing, if you've the heart to, *then*.'
>
> And can I cast him from my couch?
>   And can I lock him from my room?
> Ah no, his honest words are such
>   That he's my true-lord, and my doom.

The personal and dramatic also return, but the plainness (not unlike that of Blake's lyric parables in *Songs of Experience*) keeps the thought publicly relevant. The language of love also raises the social implication of the private and internal struggle. Of course, her concern is not with the cause of the anger but with its dual effect on her character.

The second way, and this is a true progression in her craft, is to rely on complex tones, created out of symbolic images, to project her social and class conscience. The result is one of her most distinctive poems that ranks among her best.

Still Life

Through the open French window the warm sun
lights up the polished breakfast-table, laid
round a bowl of crimson roses, for one—
a service of Worcester porcelain, arrayed
near it a melon, peaches, figs, small hot
rolls in a napkin, fairy rack of toast,
butter in ice, high silver coffee-pot,
and, heaped on a salver, the morning's post.

She comes over the lawn, the young heiress,
from her early walk in her garden-wood
feeling that life's a table set to bless
her delicate desires with all that's good,

that even the unopened future lies
like a love-letter, full of sweet surprise.

The principal advantages of syllabic meter, Daryush believed, are first its ability to avoid the "often unavoidable distortions of the natural speech rhythm" caused by the "stress-restrictions" in accentual-syllabic meter, and second (and therefore) its ability to create through a dramatic variety of rhythm, through its unexpectedness, a sense of tension and perhaps even uncertainty. As she says in her "Note on Syllabic Metres,"

> the fixed element is no longer time but number, the integrity of line and syllable is challenged by the stress-demands of sense or syntax. The aim of the artist will be so to balance these incommensurables as to reflect his own predicament of thought or feeling, thereby enhancing his consciousness of an imagined relation with the unattainable.[75]

But, she goes on to insist, great artistry is required and certain principles must be followed to keep that freedom within bounds: for instance "rhyme is almost indispensable," and "stress-variations are more effective in fairly short lines, and more easily obtained from those with an odd syllable-count."[76] Winters is more negative: unless such meter at least approximates accentual-syllabic regularities, there is nothing to vary from, and therefore there can be no precision of intention.[77] But then he thought that poets should have the discipline to be more certain about the relationship between thought (content) and feeling (style) than most, especially modern poets thought they were able to be in such "uncertain" times. The effort may have to be greater in this century, but it still needs to be made. As we have seen, Daryush would not have radically disagreed with this latter sentiment. Her experiments, like Winters's own with even freer verse in the 1920s, were very closely controlled.

In "Still-Life" she keeps the rhythms fairly firm by approximating a sonnet: there are fourteen lines, divided into three independently rhymed quatrains and a couplet, and each line has ten syllables. The number of stressed syllables is five for eight of the lines and never less than four or more than six in the remaining six lines. Except for the couplet, all the rhymes are monosyllabic with only one unstressed (line 9). The disyllabic rhyme of the couplet is thereby particularly effective in closing the poem. Also, many of the lines have strings of iambs: lines 2, 5, and 11 have four consecutive iambic feet, and at least five other lines have three consecutive iambic feet, often in the final three positions. Thus regularity is present if not dominant.

Daryush uses the formal divisions to structure the thought of the poem. The octave describes the breakfast table: the first two lines establish the pictorial situation—sunlight coming in through the window lighting up the laid table; the next two, completing the quatrain, give us the centerpiece and the porcelain service at the edge; and the second quatrain details the other "arrayed" items. The sestet describes the heiress's feelings as she "comes" from her walk toward that table. Michael Schmidt claims that most of Daryush's poems "take a point in time . . . and draw to it its past and its future, setting it in a context. The body is 'present', the soul 'past' or 'memoried', and the imagination 'future', the enchantress."[78] This accounts for another structural principle that follows the sonnet form, especially the divisions highlighted by the spaces between lines 8 and 9 and lines 12 and 13. The only real present action (and it is not very active) in the poem is the heiress's coming and feeling in the third quatrain. Before that the scene is still, but the many participles ("polished," "laid," "arrayed," and "heaped") indicate the past actions of the servants, and in probable chronological order. The couplet then deals explicitly with the future.

The poet's judgment of the scene begins to emerge as we recognize these formal and structural properties of the poem. The past has brought wealth into the present (the money is inherited), a wealth that is hardly unobtrusive: the slight ostentation suggested by the adjectives ("crimson," "Worcester," "fairy," "high silver") and the abundance and possible waste suggested by the isolated phrase "for one" at the end of line 3. The phrase also introduces a note of melancholy, but melancholy in an unsympathetic social context: the woman's lack of self-sufficiency and dependence on servants—the participial evocation. If the past is the soul, as Schmidt contends, this is a deficient one; one, we might say, stilled by comfort. The third quatrain reinforces that phrase in line 3: "from *her* early walk in *her* garden-wood." The repeated possessive (although Daryush has avoided the dramatic temptation to stress the two syllables), after the "over" of the previous line, brings forward and further qualifies this

Social Consolations 239

melancholy: she carries her loneliness almost imperiously. This then becomes explicit in her unchallengeable conviction of being favored. The last four lines, we note, are the most regular in the poem; lines 12 and 13 have exactly the same rhythm: her feelings and expectations are certainly not uncertain. "Bless" and "good" within this context cannot rise much above the kind of ready satisfactions offered by the polished table. We are ready then for the ominous, threatening note struck by the comparison of her future with a love letter. Love letters to a lonely heiress must include the possibility, to which she seems oblivious, of the suit of a fortune hunter—there may be many, because the salver is "heaped" with mail. Her imagination is as blinkered as her soul is constrained and her body pampered. Those windows, allowing in the exposing light of the sun, open onto a back, enclosed, and wooded garden. Her invulnerability is not at all assured or certain, and her future perhaps one of the incommensurables—the quality that Daryush wished to reflect through her very carefully crafted syllabic verse.

Other poems in the 1936 volume and in the next, *Verses, Sixth Book* (1938), bring the social threats to the surface, but none has the subtlety and delicate power of "Still-Life." In "Aeroplanes," which she chose not to reprint in the *Collected Poems,* the roar overhead is openly a "threat" that will soon "darken" the sky above "our homes forlorn," and reminds us, she concludes,

> Of what man-thought has made—
> The wheels of loveless might
> That never now are stayed,
> Keep turning, day and night.
>
> (9–12)

In this general poem, we see her sharing Rickword's apprehensions about the course of industrialized society. At the other end of the scale, "Along the narrow cottage-path he wheeled" (also never reprinted) has the poet watching from a gate, "almost motherly," a "bent old labourer" whose "goodwife died only a week ago": it is a simple, affecting, detailed portrait full of fellow feeling toward one doubly unfortunate. "Children of wealth in your warm nursery" (from 1938), in some ways a companion sonnet to "Still-Life," offers a direct criticism of those who are all too fortunate and all too ignorant. Cushioned behind and "guarded invisibly by" clear double panes of glass, they watch the "volleying snow":

> . . . you cannot tell
> What winter means; its cruel truths to you
> Are only sound and sight; your citadel
> Is safe from feeling, and from knowledge too.

> ... and yet perhaps this very night
>
> You'll wake to horror's wrecking fire—your home
> Is wired within for this, in every room.
>
> (5–8, 12–14)

With a more generalized target than the heiress, Daryush returns with her more explicit judgment to the firmer accentual-syllabic line. The thought in the final lines that luxuries bring with them attendant risks, although blackishly humorous in its use of the mundane—electric lighting—to symbolize this, is less socially relevant than it might be with a different, less mechanical (and now dated), more subtle example. Compare it with the heiress's love letters. One might also compare "I am your lover now, once awful Enmity" with the earlier poem on the same subject, "Anger lay by me all night long": the combination of "purity of style and richness of meaning" (Winters's judgment) in the latter has been replaced by a prosaic bluntness and a purity of meaning to express less ambiguous conviction:

> Mildness is no more, Tolerance is done to death,
> Pity is buried deep, even Pardon is shut down
> Among the shadows, starved of all but ghostly breath;
> You alone live, their slaughterer grim, now lovely grown.
>
> (7–10)

The poem is addressed to Enmity and was written "(After a massacre)," which at least hints at the motive. This may be her only poem in direct response to the Spanish Civil War.

She offered even more direct political commentary in later poems, gathered in *Verses, Seventh Book* (1971). She discusses the motives of war in "Dutiful volunteer," the "martial canons of uprightness" in "War-Tribunal," and the ageless feud between wrath and mercy in "Jerusalem, September 17, 1948." They are all curiously inconclusive and lacking in the poignancy of the thirties' poems that implicate her own social position. The most memorable poems perhaps are the elegies, on the death of older values ("He said: I left it in the porch" and "Moored in the shallows") and of a spouse ("This is the last night that my love is here"). That last poem reminds one of Hardy's "After the Last Breadth" and "The Walk," both in subject matter and in the delicate plainness of the treatment of that matter. It deserves mention in this context because it is about the individual's reliance on companionship and community. But let me close this discussion of Elizabeth Daryush with one of her last poems in that last volume, in which she returns to the theme of the 1932 poem I began with, "From day to converse night": the avoidance of extremes, "how to balance way with way," be they the individual and the social or the natural and the cultural. It is a problem of morality and poetic style, of how to tend one's garden.

For P.W.

Nor field nor garden—nor the wilful growth
Of utter wildness nor the mannered grace
Of formal husbandry; what once was chase
Unkempt, he of whom tell I, nothing loth
To image in his home his happy mind,
Turned first to even grass, then cut free-hand
The winding beds, massed there a wealth unplanned
Of all earth's flowers, the fairest he could find.

Yet still, moulding the smooth lawn, you may see
The wold's weak hollows and strong-grounded swell
Scarce altered; and he, too, of whom I tell,
Gentle, a full-crowded epitome

Of culture, yet keeps his loved gifts and flaws
As God made them, unlevelled by man's laws.

John Betjeman

To move from the world of Elizabeth Daryush to that of John Betjeman is to move from one in which social concerns only barely break the surface dominated by austere moral investigations, to one in which moral implications must be sought below a highly textured and adorned social surface. Also, to move from Rickword as well as Daryush to Betjeman is to leave behind preliminary probings and corrections and to enter a fully engaged social verse. Betjeman weaves together the two strands represented by those two somewhat older poets. Rickword's attempts to temper idealistic extremes by insisting on a sobering contact with the real world is in Betjeman the plentitude of topographical and other details, all the minutiae of social living in England from the late twenties to the late seventies. Daryush's class conscience and defense of traditional moral values is in Betjeman an intense respect for the communal conventions of the past and a passion for their preservation. When these strands combine in single poems, we have a complex elegiac protest poetry that in some ways answers Orwell's call for a reunion of patriotism and intelligence.

It is customary in critical discussions of Betjeman to worry about his public status: his immense popularity among nonprofessional readers of verse, the laureateship, the seeming lack of intellectual profundity, his disregard of continental fashions (these last two often connected), his intense Englishness. Let me approach the question of reputation and popularity as it affects Betjeman from his tone, or, in other words, the quality of his seriousness. One must be careful here; I certainly do not wish to suggest that Betjeman is a better poet than he really is, that he is more than the obviously, but solidly, minor poet that he is. I do want to stress that our age could do with more minor poets of his calibre (in place of the large number of mediocre poets with the pretensions and ambitions of major poets). I also want to question the definition of what constitutes significant poetic talent in our century. Betjeman is not a cosmopolitan, visionary, or prolific poet. He may indeed often seem, as he himself wryly said, a "funny man" of English verse,[79] and social observation may be the basis of his art. But it is wrong to conclude that, because he deals with the ordinary human world and does not promote a new and private vision or intellectual system, his intellect and imagination are deficient; that, because he did not speak directly to the great issues of his day (mass unemployment or the rise of fascism), he is therefore "personal rather than political"; that, because he does not express "a sense of metaphysical outrage at the futility, rootlessness and cultural dislocation of the century in which he lives," he is "merely nostalgic" and only temperamentally melancholic.[80] There are other ways of being intelligently, imaginatively, politically, and critically serious in this century.

Perhaps I can make this initial point with the help of an early poem, "Death of King George V," from his 1937 collection *Continual Dew*. John Press, for instance (who finds the overtly satirical poems "feeble," not serious enough, because they do not "exude an overpowering loathing of humanity" or "touch of savagery" necessary for true satire—marks of the great masters of satire) senses the seriousness or what he calls genuineness of the poem, but the only other category he has for it is "lyric": Betjeman "is stirred to write genuine poetry only when affection and compassion arouse the lyric impulse."[81] The poem opens on a comic note, lightly qualified by a superficial pathos residing in the mundane detail of line 4:

> Spirits of well-shot woodcock, partridge, snipe
> Flutter and bear him up the Norfolk sky:
> In that red house in a red mahogany book-case
> The stamp collection waits with mounts long dry.
>
> (1–4)[82]

The comedy of the first two lines is both literary and social. There is the likely allusion to the ascension of a king who had presided over a previous Georgian era as described fulsomely and solemnly by Robert Southey in *A Vision of Judgment* (1821) and satirically by Byron in *The Vision of Judgment* (1822), in which George III's soul is accompanied by an "angelic caravan." Betjeman replaces this with the souls of the game birds sportingly and efficiently shot by the country-loving George V. "Well-shot" is typical of Betjeman's only slightly ironic good fellowship. The humor is then softened considerably in lines 3 and 4, and even more in the second stanza where the pathos is thickened by a new, ominous note struck in lines 7 and 8, developing in the last stanza into direct sympathy with a passing world of firmer, surer values:

> Old men in country houses hear clocks ticking
>   Over thick carpets with a deadening force;
>
> Old men who never cheated, never doubted,
>   Communicated monthly, sit and stare
> At the new suburb stretched beyond the run-way
>   Where a young man lands hatless from the air.
>
> (7–12)

"Suburb" evokes the blurring of boundaries, and the wonderful detail of line 12, "hatless," quietly makes the point about a cherished and passing propriety, and we begin to reconsider the mildly parodic opening, preferring perhaps those natural spirits to their mechanical replacement bringing this replacement king down to earth in the final line. We recall that the Prince of Wales was called to his new responsibility from his liaison with Mrs. Simpson. The seriousness of the ending is as light as the humor of the opening—a lightness of touch made possible that deft transition of moods. Betjeman (inspired by a newspaper healine: "New King arrives in his capital by air . . .") is subtly considering the social significance of a political event. The poem does not quite have the pressing conviction of satire (even a less venomous kind than Press allows), but it also is a little more forceful than the "lyric" label would suggest.

What makes categorizing much of Betjeman's poetry difficult is the absence of explicit and generalizing messages (political or otherwise), and of readily recognizable and unqualified emotional stances. This is due to the combination of the two strands I mentioned earlier. He is able to particularize as well as personalize his public concerns without refusing their general and universal import. But because the poems abound in detail, this side of his talent is sometimes overstressed. All that the jealous Auden wants to talk about in his introduction to *Slick But Not Streamlined* is Betjeman's topophilia.[83] John Sparrow characterizes Betjeman as "the painter of the particular, the recognizable landscape."[84] Derek Stanford, in the first book-length study of Betjeman, in 1961, sees him rather too exclusively as the poet of "present English living," stressing his "localizing imagination": "this is what makes him insular and immediate, parochial and concrete, time-bound and period-loving."[85] This emphasis opens Betjeman up to criticism, implicitly acknowledging limitations: he is then essentially only a recorder of middle-class life, a writer of light verse who is memorable because of the unique blend of the flippant and the nostalgic.[86] In addition, too much emphasis on his nostalgia can give some critics, sometimes already annoyed by his resistance to modernism, the sanction to dismiss him as a reactionary snob.[87] I am not denying that these limitations are evident in some poems in which these strands are isolated, but when he brings the two together, we get poetry that places present living in a temporal context, in which particulars can measure continuity and time can be redeemed as well as remembered.[88] Each dimension (the attention to present details or the elegiac defense of older values) makes the other acceptable; the latter gives critical poignancy to the former, and the former an urgent relevancy to the latter. There is no doubt that he finds the present sorely wanting, but also no doubt that he cares enough about it to urge its reclamation. In 1952 he offered this severe prose analysis of our plight:

> Too bored to think, too proud to pray, too timid to leave what we are used to doing, we have shut ourselves behind our standard roses; we love ourselves only and our neighbours no longer. . . . We prefer facts [to the Incarnation]. . . . The Herr-Professor-Doktors are writing everything down for us, sometimes throwing in a little hurried pontificating too, so we need never bother to feel or think or see again. We can eat our Weetabix, catch the 8.48, read the sports column and die; for love is dead.

This is followed by a quote from the Book of Common Prayer, and with that the essay ends: "O Lord, who hast taught us that all our doings without charity are nothing worth; Send thy Holy Ghost, and pour into our hearts that most excellent gift of charity, the very bond of peace and of all virtues. . . ."[89] Without being "over solemn" (always a mistake with a poet like Betjeman[90]), we can see many of his poems as reminders that the social, and not just religious, attitudes and principles of a nation have much to do with the conditions that encourage or discourage neighborly love and charity, and that we can only fully live in our present if we know the past well enough to know what is missing and what value it had and can have. We must recognize the force of "no longer."

In redeeming time, then, Betjeman's aim is to revitalize our sense of tradition. It obviously is not Eliot's "tradition," that sum of European culture, now fragmented, ruined, lost, and therefore uninheritable ("if you want it you must obtain it by great labour"[91]). For Betjeman as for Hardy, tradition is local and inheritable.[92] We may, of course, give it up by ignoring or blinding ourselves to the meaning of what surrounds us ("we have shut ourselves behind our standard roses"), much of which is only there because of what was done before us. Betjeman, like the poets in the line of which he is so much a part, is inevitably descriptive and elegiac; he also was a man "who used to notice such things."

The politically sensitive reader also blinds himself to the breadth of Betjeman's vision if he detects only the supporter of the class system, an escapist, and an anti-communist. Betjeman's earliest prose work on architecture, *Ghastly Good Taste* (1933), should caution the reader of his poetry against such facile labels. Betjeman recognizes the dangers of the age: "Perhaps we are rushing towards annihilation," he says, in the course of a book otherwise devoted to telling, as the subtitle states, "A Depressing Story of the Rise and Fall of English Architecture."[93] But with his larger historic view he sets the blame not on current totalitarian systems so much as on middle-class industrialism ("the knowledge of the machine, a harder and more cruel learning than that of Latin and Greek"), which has fostered the "present state of intense individualism": "intense" because the age has lost, or in the interests of some vague belief in Progress given up, the various faiths that provided some communal cohesion, either "the religious unity of Christendom . . . [or] the reasoned unity of an educated monarchic system."[94] The virtues of ubiquity and restraint, last seen he thinks in Regency architecture, have been replaced by specialization and self-consciousness.[95] He ends the book claiming that "architecture [perhaps art and culture as a whole] can only be made alive again by a new order and another Christendom," freely admitting that he does "not know what form that Christendom will take."[96] But it is clear what orders will not do: capitalism with its commercial competition only exacerbates the problems of individualism, and Communism "seems to be going too far."[97] He is quite dismissive of any simple escape to a pastoral retreat: William Morris's project was "impossible" and "cowardly," while the latter-day "arty escapists," moving into the cottages vacated by those seeking work in the towns, are "trying to blind themselves with the past."[98] His desire for a revitalized sense of community is in some sense "conservative," but that is not to be confused, he makes clear at one point, with "class consciousness."[99] If he is wary of "the democrats and the free thinkers"[100] and (elsewhere) attacks that modern creation, "the average man,"[101] it is, as Patrick Taylor-Martin says, "not because of [the average man's] remoteness from a supposed classical tradition but because of his denial of what is human and his elevation of what is efficient, hygienic or just plain 'good for you' in its place."[102] It is because of the dulling of the faculty of discrimination; as he says in *Ghastly Good Taste*,

> To-day with regard to architecture the average man is a fool and the average architect is a snob. . . . in the eighteenth century, when the average man did not exist, every gentleman of property felt himself in a position to criticise, and every person without it felt himself in a position to admire.[103]

This must be taken in the right spirit: although its reference can stretch beyond the immediate context (the discussion of changing architectural taste), everything else in the book makes it clear he is hoping, not for a return to rigid class distinctions and unearned privilege, but for a unifying effort in perhaps a single consciousness to sustain true criticism and genuine admiration. (Is not that what his best poems enact?) Behind the social bric-a-brac of the surface is, as he says of his favorite Regency buildings, "a solid British brick wall."[104]

There is no dramatic development in Betjeman's poetry from his first volume, *Mount Zion* (1932) to his last, *A Nip in the Air* (1974), other than the expected growth in technical sophistication and the common tempering of his humor and the frequency of poems about death as he aged. My discussion therefore will center on the various kinds of social poems he wrote.[105] I propose five categories, each representing a slightly different relationship of the two strands (those primarily descriptive of social life in the present and those primarily in defense of threatened and passing values): topographical poems with a social dimension, mostly sympathetic portraits of social types, critical attacks (sometimes satiric) on certain particularly "modern" groups, general elegies of passing traditions and customs (including many on religion), and finally more personal elegies. Poems in the first two categories are more descriptive and those in the last two are more elegiac; the third category marks a transition in which the two strands are cooperating more. I will discuss the best examples in each category to delineate the ways in which social criticism informs his poems and especially how the interdependence of the descriptive and elegiac modes (regardless of the particular emphasis in any one poem) accounts for Betjeman's distinctive successes.

Before we look at these categories, we should note, as an initial restraint on our reading, two poems—the only two I have found—about poetry or himself as a poet. As expected, he presents himself as a modest humorist. In "To the Crazy Gang" (from *Uncollected Poems*), written in 1962 to commemorate the last performance of some London music hall comics, he is almost describing his own achievement: he offers a toast as one with no more pretensions than they ("The toast of a rhymer, for I'm no Milton"), and as one who is in the verse equivalent of their tradition:

> Goodbye old friends of the great tradition!
>   From the serious thirties of slumps and tears
> Into this age of nuclear fission
>   You kept us laughing for thirty years.
>
>   (17–20)

The "Preface to 'High and Low'" (1966) offers a more direct and still modest self-assessment. Verse has been to him

> ... the shortest way
> Of saying what one has to say,
> A memorable means of dealing
> With mood or person, place or feeling.
>
> (3-6)

He then pays tribute to the flexibility of the language (which he has exploited): "For endless changes can be rung/On church-bells of the English tongue"(23-24). Self-deprecation (even if a bit overstated—he calls himself in the latter poem "A buzzing insubstantial fly" [28]), economy, variety, and humor—these are the poetic virtues he at least avows publicly. But, although we should guard against distorting what we read to make him seem a different and larger poet, we also must recognize the seriousness of poems with those characteristics.

Betjeman wrote many topographical poems in the tradition of Crabbe, Barnes, Tennyson, Hood, Praed, and Hardy, describing with loving care his favorite haunts, either Cornwall or less rural sites: "I love suburbs and gas-lights and Pont Street and Gothic Revival churches and mineral railways, provincial towns and Garden cities."[106] Occasionally in those poems, almost wholly given over to describing the external natural or at least unsocial scene, he introduces parenthetically a social note. These notes draw out the other than photographic or even atmospheric value of the abundant surrounding details. Sometimes the note may seem intrusive, as in "Tregardock." His comparison of the cliffs ("Gigantic slithering shelves of slate/In waiting awfulness") to "journalism full of hate" (6, 8) is startling and not quite justified by the concluding stanza, which gives us a somewhat too personal and at the same time too unspecified motive:

> And I on my volcano edge
> Exposed to ridicule and hate
> Still do not dare to leap the ledge
> And smash to pieces on the slate.
>
> (25-28)

It only works if it can be considered as a subdued criticism of man's petty social travails in contrast to larger and more enduring threats, as brilliantly exemplified by a sea curiously weak and menacing at the same time. At one point the whole scene seems to announce "the final end of sea and land" (24). "Cornish Cliffs," also from *High and Low* (1966), builds more appropriately to a similar note, but this time referring to more positive resistances to threats, both from other men (gun emplacements and forts on the Cornish coast) and the more general one from our own precarious placement in time. The poem is all description except for the suggestion of two kinds of defensive relationships of man with nature: in the fourth stanza we have the Cornish hills "long-defended" (for the sake of the "wealth of heather, kidney-vetch and squills"—this poem's many details are a defense or preservation of those natural beauties and that wildness), and in the last stanza the ancient solace of religion within small isolated villages:

> Small fields and tellymasts and wires and poles
> With, as the everlasting ocean rolls,
> Two chapels built for half a hundred souls.
>
> (28–30)

Betjeman's powers of observation were put to even more forward social effect when he turned from portraying landscapes to portraying people. Yet although the portraits are fully particularized, the authenticity resulting from the closeness of the view and the aptness of the details establishes the individual as a type, recognizable and, after Betjeman's treatment, better understood. The presentation is usually fairly free of direct, general, evaluative comment. The accumulating descriptive phrases and sometimes the person's own words are allowed to make the case for or against.

In some of those poems spoken in the poet's voice, the tone verges on the savage, and no class escapes. In the very late "County," he scorns the landed gentry, and in the very early "The City" his target is the commercial family:

> Business men with awkward hips
> And dirty jokes upon their lips,
> And large behinds and jingling chains,
> And riddled teeth and riddling brains,
> And plump white fingers made to curl
> Round some anaemic city girl,
> And so lend colour to the lives
> And old suspicions of their wives.
>
> (1–8)

The playfulness in the pun of line 4 and the understatement of line 7 are complicated slightly by the worldly wise "old" of line 8 that sets us on our way for the conclusion of the second stanza, the first six lines of which describe the young men (and sons) who work under these bosses, and who are on their way to becoming like them. The last couplet punctures both the pretense of the quickly sketched office power structure and the potential pretense of the poem's own critical stance: "But father, son and clerk join up/To talk about the Football Cup" (15–16). When less blunt, such playfulness can become sly impishness, as in "The Wykehamist," also in tetrameter couplets. The punning continues: this quaint specialist in Norman fonts, who is "Broad of Church and broad of mind/Broad before and broad behind" (1–2), yet remains "the very slightest kind of don" (8). But Betjeman will not leave it at that, giving flight to his sexual metaphors:

"The evening stretches arms to twist/And captivate her Wykehamist" (19–20), but he blocks out such allures with his "heavy baize" (one of those Betjemanesque specifics that help to sum up a character). He has reduced and specialized his "fleshly wants" to those easily satisfied by Ovaltine and a "petit beurre" (23–25). Then there is the almost callous "Exeter," in which the death of the intellectual woman's doctor-husband is treated almost farcically:

> They brought him in by the big front door
> And a smiling corpse was he;
> On the dining-room table they laid him out
> Where the *Bystanders* used to be—
> The *Tatler, The Sketch* and *The Bystander*
> For the canons' wives to see.
>
> (19–24)

Betjeman has little sympathy, even at the most pathetic times, with pretentiousness. If he is conscious of class distinctions, it is because of the civilizing demands of decorum and propriety and not the selfish demands of privilege.

Some poems internally qualify the nonetheless harsh judgment—Betjeman can be poignant without blurring his vision. "In a Bath Teashop" is uncompromising in its assessment of "a very ordinary little woman" and "a thumping crook," whom the poet observes holding hands in the corner of a teashop, yet "for a moment" both are "little lower than the angels." He exposes the illusion as an illusion while sympathizing with it. Similar is the portrait in "On Seeing an Old Poet in the Café Royal." We are almost urged in the first stanza to make fun of this relic of an older, grander, less "modernistic" time, but in the second stanza, in one clever move, Betjeman has the old poet see someone else as he is himself seen, and the tone softens instantly so that the final details are as nostalgic as they are revelatory:

> "Where is Oscar? Where is Bosie?
> Have I seen that man before?
> And the old one in the corner,
> Is it really Wratislaw?"
> Scent of Tutti-Frutti-Sen-Sen
> And cheroots upon the floor.
>
> (7–12)

The most moving portraits tend to be of lonely, ordinary people nursing dreams that will never be much more than that, in which the poet's voice is gentle and sympathetic without being maudlin—the details are too harshly real for that. There is "Eunice," the London typist who longs for "her lonely cottage by the lonely oak" in Kent, and especially there are all those unloved "Business Girls" in dingy bedsitters. Here is a perfect example of the power of well-selected details to universalize:

> From the geyser ventilators
>   Autumn winds are blowing down
> On a thousand business women
>   Having baths in Camden Town.
> . . . .
> Early nip of changeful autumn,
>   Dahlias glimpsed through garden doors,
> At the back precarious bathrooms
>   Jutting out from upper floors;
>
> And behind their frail partitions
>   Business women lie and soak
> Seeing through the draughty skylight
>   Flying clouds and railway smoke.
>
> (1–4, 9–16)

We find the same range and variety of tones in the largest group among these portraits, the dramatic monologues. Usually the speaker inadvertently exposes himself, like the pretentious, Georgian academic in "A Hike on the Downs," and the overzealous literary scholar in "A Literary Discovery"; at one extreme members of the horsey county set in "Hunter Trials" and "How to Get On in Society," and at the other extreme ambitious or at least class-conscious members of the lower classes, like the social climbing "Wembley Lad" and the mechanically climbing "Lift Man." Even those with a threatened place in society are viewed—the public relations officer ruined by a sexual offense against a minor in "Shattered Image" and the potentially homosexual boy in "Narcissus." Betjeman's ear is as attentive as his eye: as Hillier has said, he "always catches the exact tone of voice and diction of his characters no matter from what class they come,"[107] whether from the young and gentrified,

> Oh wasn't it naughty of Smudges?
>   Oh, Mummy, I'm sick with disgust.
> She threw me in front of the Judges,
>   And my silly old collarbone's bust,
>
> ("Hunter Trials," 29–32)

or from an old retired postal clerk:

> Since the wife died the house seems lonely-like,
>   It isn't quite the same place as before;
> . . . .
> Out to Carshalton Beeches for a spin
>   And back by Chislehurst and Bromley town,
> Where Mum would have her lemon juice and gin

> And I would have a half of old and brown.
> ("The Retired Postal Clerk," *Uncollected Poems,* 1-2, 17-20)

Betjeman never writes dialect poems and never, even when he captures the rhythms of everyday speech of people different from himself, deviates from the metrical requirements of his line. That perfect blend of form and speech is particularly notable in the last example, communicating as it does the widower's controlled grief without the slightest hint of formal artificiality or dramatic sentimentality.

Two of his most memorable dramatic monologues are prayers representing the poles of his social purpose. "In Westminster Abbey" is obviously under the influence of Robert Burns: the very structure of this harsh satire on self-serving religious hypocrisy is almost the same as that of "Holy Willie's Prayer," as a snobbish middle-class woman after asking God to destroy her enemies ("bomb the Germans") and to protect the "gallant blacks" fighting for the Empire, "and, even more, protect the whites" (7, 15, 17), gradually moves to secure her own almost elect status:

> Although dear Lord I am a sinner,
>   I have done no major crime;
> Now I'll come to Evening Service
>   Whensoever I have the time.
> So, Lord, reserve for me a crown,
> And do not let my shares go down.
>   (25-30)

Along the way we have one of Betjeman's famous lists, this time revealing her decidedly weak sense of proportion (reminiscent of Burns's master, Pope):

> Think of what our Nation stands for,
>   Books from Boots' and country lanes,
> Free speech, free passes, class distinction,
>   Democracy and proper drains.
>   (19-22)

At the end she deflates religion into therapy: "Now I feel a little better" (37). In striking contrast is the delicate and touching meditation by the lonely nun of "Felixstowe, or The Last of Her Order." The security she seeks is far different from that of the wealthy woman in the Abbey. The first stanza, displaying Betjeman's topographic skill at its best, sets the scene as well as introduces us to one of the threats from which she hopes for relief (we recall the sea in "Tregardock" and "Cornish Cliffs"):

>   With one consuming roar along the shingle
>   The long wave claws and rakes the pebbles down
>   To where its backwash and the next wave mingle,
>   A mounting arch of water weedy-brown
>   Against the tide the off-shore breezes blow.
>   Oh wind and water, this is Felixstowe.
>
>   (1-6)

Remembering the chilling winters, this final member of a small order of nuns, who once ran an orphanage and school, is momentarily warmed by "the whisper of a summer sea" (20) in the city gardens and by the sight of a "cushioned scabious ... A sun-lit kingdom touched by butterflies" (21, 23); but the evening brings a strong breeze, "And all the world goes home to tea and toast" (28). She requires finally a securer kingdom. This is the last stanza:

>   "Thou knowest my down sitting and mine uprising"
>   Here where the white light burns with steady glow
>   Safe from the vain world's silly sympathizing,
>   Safe with the Love that I was born to know,
>   Safe from the surging of the lonely sea
>   My heart finds rest, my heart finds rest in Thee.
>
>   (31-36)

If our sympathy is tested by her retreat from "the vain world's silly sympathizing," we must remember her life of sympathetic service and teaching and cannot but admire the strength present even in her refusal of that worldly offering.

 The third category of social verse obviously overlaps somewhat with the second category. We have noted occasional satiric thrusts in those social portraits, but in this third group the attack is more sustained and focussed on representatives of recent progressive ways of thinking, or not thinking as is sometimes the case. When the stress is on the new, the past can be the only measure of adequacy, and Betjeman's essential conservatism begins to admonish his enormous sympathies. Betjeman is most famous for his attacks on city planners and developers for creating new towns and suburbs and destroying old towns and old ways. I emphasize that his interest in architecture has little to do with abstract design, aesthetics, or antiquarianism, and much to do with the human associations and uses of buildings; architecture is essentially a social art. Betjeman believed that, like a political or economic system, our physical surroundings, man-made as well as natural, provide the conditions that can facilitate or discourage the living of the good life of moral and intellectual activity. In an early poem he claims that Slough has been so modernized that "It isn't fit for humans now":

> Come, bombs, and blow to smithereens
> Those air-conditioned, bright canteens,
> Tinned fruit, tinned meat, tinned milk, tinned beans
>   Tinned minds, tinned breath.
>
> ("Slough," 5–8)

We are, indeed, what we eat, and then we exhale our artificiality. The blame is on those with power to "mess up" the town, on the bosses not the clerks: "It's not their fault that they are mad, / They've tasted Hell" (23–24); they belch instead of looking up at the stars (31–32). Derek Stanford is surely right when he says that this did not spring from any "party-line propaganda concerning the oppressor and the oppressed. Mr. Betjeman did not need to read Marx in order to learn sympathy with those inhumanly done by or neglected."[108] But we can stretch the point even further; more than an expression of sympathy it is an expression of loss: the disposal of traditional environments and with them traditional ways of knowing and acting. The poem attacks the presumption of those so intent on changing things. The powerless clerks, far from being neglected, are being brought down because of their lack of defenses against such change, to the same level of diminished vision as their leaders.

"The Planster's Vision," an ironic monologue, uses the sonnet structure to emphasize just what must be given up for this brave new world. The octave is the planner's list of what must be cleared away—communal meaning itself, dependant as it is on continuity. First, "cut down that timber" through which church bells "have pealed the centuries out with Evensong" (1, 4), and then the cottages where too many people have been born and died. The sestet then presents the future: workers' flats in homogenized towers ("score on score") and announcements over the "microphones in communal canteens" of the end of progressive time (and of moral distinctions in a latter-day Deism): "'No Right! No Wrong! All's perfect, evermore.'" The implication is that community rituals that mark and commemorate the important stages of our lives (part of the defenses lost by the clerks) are connected intimately with the moral measurement of those lives. This planner presumes that perfection is possible only if we forget. (Ten years later Philip Larkin is to make a very similar point with regard to the loss of religion in "Church Going": "what since is found / Only in separation.") The message is stated more directly in another poem, also from *New Bats in Old Belfries* (1945):

> Oh brick-built breeding boxes of new souls,
> Hear how the pealing through the louvres rolls!
> Now birth and death-reminding bells ring clear,
> Loud under 'planes and over changing gear.
>
> ("On Hearing the Full Peal of Ten Bells from Christ Church, Swindon, Wilts.," 9–12)

These new souls need a new language so that they will not be tempted by older values and so that they will be assured that they really do control their lives (and nature). As we hear in "The Town Clerk's Views" from 1948, they will start with nonutilitarian county names—Devon will become "South-West Area One," and Cornwall "South-West Area Two" (48, 51)—and move on to rename each old cathedral "an Area Culture Centre" (87). This will be allowed because of the softening of our moral distinctions: this same town clerk, this "cool careerist," has a "lust for power," that "is not a weakness, people think,/When unaccompanied by bribes or drink" (9, 6-8). What is uniform is manageable, and what is quantified is easily managed; the town clerk's plans have been realized by the 1970s:

> Now houses are 'units' and people are digits,
> And Bath has been planned into quarters for midgets.
> Official designs are aggressively neuter,
> The Puritan work of an eyeless computer.
> ("The Newest Bath Guide," 23-26)

Once the new language is in general circulation and it has done its initial work of blotting out the past, it can be used as a weapon against any rearguard action by the now eccentric enemies of progress:

> And if some preservationist attempts to interfere
> A 'dangerous structure' notice from the Borough Engineer
> Will settle any buildings that are standing in our way—
> The modern style, sir, with respect, has really come to stay.
> ("Executive," 21-24)

Although planners get the most intense attention from Betjeman, other poems are the pillories for a variety of progressive types, who are isolated and held in place by his undiminished historic memory. Before the war, his victims were the self-expressive utopists who reduce community to promiscuity ("Group Life: Letchworth"). After the war, when atomic energy replaced nature and God, he looked at village life: its new land-speculating farmers, the up-to-date schoolmaster teaching "civics, eurhythmics, economics, Marx,/How-to-respect-wild-life-in-National-Parks," not to mention plastics and gymnastics, the brewer's P. R. O. promoting the newly sanitized inns, and the obligatory sociologist ("the Mass-Observer") drawn from one of the new red-brick academies to gather his data in just such an inn from the locals, whose tales grow longer and taller the more rounds he buys ("The Dear Old Village" and "The Village Inn"). By the 1960s, the age no longer has a "new soul," it has no soul at all ("Inexpensive Progress," 3). The modern farmer has progressed further:

> We spray the fields and scatter
> The poison on the ground

> So that no wicked wild flowers
> Upon our farm be found.
>
> ("Harvest Hymn," 1–4)

New creatures have come forth: the irritated motorist venting his marital frustrations on the highway traffic ("Meditation on the A30"), the completely amoral ad man ("Advertising Pays"), the hypocritical civil servant who knows how to manipulate an expense account ("Thoughts on a Train"), the earnest and so very eclectic members of provincial culture clubs and their circuit lecturers ("Before the Lecture"), and new women, with their sights on either "well-selected Poles" ("A Romance") or the commercial offerings of Oxford Street ("Civilized Woman").

Even many of those few who believe they have souls and decidedly Christian ones have succumbed to the new age and its priorities. In "Bristol and Clifton," Betjeman bemoans an unfortunate trend in the Church of England: the only real ritual left is the passing of the collection plate, and as for private worship, one of the interlocutors notices a woman praying and the other exclaims,

> "Praying? The service is all over now
> And here's the verger waiting to turn out
> The lights and lock the church up. She cannot
> Be Loyal Church of England...."
>
> (55–58)

"The Diary of a Church Mouse," from *Poems in the Porch* (1954), is a charming if unsubtle satire on the more casual churchgoer whose motives are compared to those of the opportunistic mice and rats who suddenly appear, attracted by the "altar's sheaf of oats" at Harvest Festival time.

The fourth category is distinguished from the third only by an increase of attention to the past and therefore somewhat more pathos and less humor. Whatever nostalgia we detect is not, I insist again, a simple desire to return to the cozy gas-lit Victorian world of his childhood. Although he often laments the passing of that less crude, less "chintzy" world and criticizes the deficiencies of the present, his lament is usually for that previous time because it was a time when life understood, at least more than it can today, its place in an eternal scheme. There are three players in his elegies: the present, the past, and eternity. Note, for instance, "Pershore Station, or A Liverish Journey First Class." The opening lines record a moment when the past and present come together momentarily:

> The train at Pershore station was waiting that Sunday night
> Gas light on the platform, in my carriage electric light,
> Gas light on frosty evergreens, electric on Empire wood,
> The Victorian world and the present in a moment's neighbourhood.
>
> (1–4)

But that juxtaposition is then placed suddenly in a larger temporal context:

> When sudden the waiting stillness shook with the ancient spells
> Of an older world than all our worlds in the sound of the Pershore bells.
> They were ringing them down for Evensong in the lighted abbey near,
> Sounds which had poured through apple boughs for seven centuries here.
> (7–10)

Church bells are persistent symbols for Betjeman not only of religious faith but also of the sense of continuity that such faith sustains. (They are for him what the birdsong in "Adlestrop" is for Edward Thomas, who has a similar experience at a train station.) Betjeman characteristically will not leave it at that: it is not the presence of faith that is important but the effect of that faith on human action. The poem finally announces its real subject: the need of one, who feels guilty for mistreating another, for comfort unavailable in our modern world:

> With Guilt, Remorse, Eternity the void within me fills
> And I thought of her left behind me in the Herefordshire hills,
> I remember her defencelessness as I made my heart a stone
> Till she wove her self-protection round and left me on my own.
> . . . .
> Evesham, Oxford and London. The carriage is new and smart.
> I am cushioned and soft and heated with a deadweight in my heart.
> (11–14, 19–20)

The intimation of eternity does not itself bring comfort, but it can revive our sense of responsibility and therefore render us less comforted by modern conveniences.

This then is the spirit in which he laments the loss of continuities. What has been lost by our obsessive concern with change and progress is our place in a complex whole that includes nature and the remnants of our past, be they customs or buildings. Culture has gone indoors; humans have lost contact with the earth:

> ... pastel-shaded book rooms bring New Ideas to birth
> As the whitening hawthorn only hears the heart beat of the earth.
> ("May-Day Song for North Oxford," 15–16)

The wonderfully detailed portrait of Elaine the bobby-soxer in "Middlesex" is flanked on one side by a vision of her county's recent past, when humans cooperated with rather than used nature, a time which the poet can just recall and from which Elaine is separated totally:

> ... the elm-trees misty
> And the footpaths climbing twisty

> Under cedar-shaded palings,
> Low laburnum-leaned-on railings,
> Out of Northolt on and upward to the heights of Harrow hill.
>
> (23–27)

On the other side of the portrait are those "few surviving hedges" that "keep alive our lost Elysium" (7–8), to which the hurrying ("with a frown of concentration" [6]) Elaine is also oblivious, concentrating no doubt on the cultural evening before her, when she will settle "down to sandwich supper and the television screen" (18). In "A Lincolnshire Church" after nine introductory lines describing the green marsh and the church tower, Betjeman observes

> ... around it, turning their backs,
> The usual sprinkle of villas;
> The usual woman in slacks,
> Cigarette in her mouth,
> Regretting Americans, stands
> As a wireless croons in the kitchen
> Manicuring her hands.
>
> (10–16)

England has not only turned its back on its own heritage but has turned toward the lure of a historyless West. Meanwhile the Church must go East to recruit Christian priests: the poem ends with Betjeman setting aside the obvious question why an Indian priest is here in Lincolnshire and concentrating, desperately hopeful, on the ubiquity of a mysterious godhead. But earlier the summary tone was more characteristically down-to-earth and bemused:

> Dear old, bloody old England
> Of telegraph poles and tin,
> Seemingly so indifferent
> And with so little soul to win.
>
> (17–20)

The complex whole that one could know in the past is referred to unobtrusively in the third stanza of "Thoughts on 'The Diary of a Nobody.'"

> And only footsteps in a lane
> And birdsong broke the silence round
> And chuffs of the Great Northern train
> For Alexandra Palace bound.
>
> (9–12)

Even the machine has a place in this human and natural world. At first this may seem no more than an affecting but slight, lyrical celebration of another of those sunny, "buttercuppy" Sundays of which the late Victorian years appeared in hindsight to be so full. The nostalgic gesture at the end may seem too easy:

> Dear Charles and Carrie, I am sure,
>   Despite that awkward Sunday dinner,
>   Your lives were good and more secure
>   Than ours at cocktail time in Pinner,
>
>   (21–24)

until we recall (as I am sure Betjeman intends us) the actual scene in chapter 19 of George and Weedon Grossmith's 1892 novel, *The Diary of a Nobody*. "The local dogs" may have been "curled in sleep" (6) as the Pooters walked from Muswell Hill Station to Watney Lodge to dine with the Finsworths that "hot and uncomfortable" Sunday; but one of the dogs is roused as the finely dressed guests approach the Lodge, pouncing forward and landing its muddy paws on Carrie's light skirt. So a string of awkward occurrences begins. Charles comments, quite innocently, when shown some paintings but before he is told they are portraits of recently dead loved ones, that one face has a rather unpleasing expression and another must be of a "jovial" gentleman whom "life doesn't seem to trouble" much. What is important is that Charles Pooter feels "absolutely horrified at [his] own awkwardness." But his scrupulousness is not shared by his hosts, who condone the verbal crudities of another guest, "Mr. Short," with "Oh! he is privileged you know." So Charles is made to feel apologetic again. Even the dogs are privileged in this household; the one that had earlier pounced on Carrie growls and snaps at Charles's boots under the dining-room table—"It is only his play," says the unapologetic Mrs. Finsworth, and another licks the blacking off his boots—"Oh! we are used to Bibbs doing that to our visitors," Mrs. Finsworth indulgently allows.[109] The novel is, of course, a comic but loving account of the somewhat pretentious but well-meaning and innocent Pooters. Bernard Bergonzi is surely off the mark when he complains that Betjeman has no authority as a social critic when his "cultural heroes are vulgarians like the Pooters."[110] What gives their lives whatever goodness and security they have is their old-fashioned sense of propriety, their sensitivity and politeness toward others, for which they are constantly victimized, however humorously, throughout the novel: the modern age was just beginning. Again, intimately involved in that complex and threatened social unity was the possibility of moral sanctions.

    That unity has been made all the more cohesive by the Church. In a late poem about moving homes, Betjeman imports the term "fellowship" and can still joke about its disappearance. Church bells suddenly "clash out":

> ... It seems a miracle
> That leaf and flower should never even stir
> In such great waves of medieval sound:
> They ripple over roofs to fields and farms
> So that 'the fellowship of Christ's religion'
> Is roused to breakfast, church or sleep again.
> ("On Leaving Wantage," 18-23)

What he regrets in leaving are all those components held together in his knowing:

> ... we now are whirled away
> Momently clinging to the things we knew—
> Friends, footpaths, hedges, house and animals.
> (25-27)

Religious architecture also can be a reminder of continuities:

> And countless congregations as the generations pass
> Join choir and great crowned organ case, in centuries of song
> To praise Eternity contained in Time and coloured glass.
> ("Sunday Morning, King's Cambridge," 16-18)

Containment is important to Betjeman: it makes human meaning possible. The closing of an inner London railway station can be a "desecration," for example, because a social fabric is being rent:

> Snow falls in the buffet of Aldersgate station,
>   Toiling and doomed from Moorgate Street puffs the train,
> For us of the steam and gas-light, the lost generation,
>   The new white cliffs of the City are built in vain.
> ("Monody on the Death of Aldersgate Street Station," 25-28)

The twist on the American cliché of that third line (his generation is lost because it remembers in an age that has no respect for the past, unlike Hemingway's generation that felt itself separated by the Great War from the past) prepares us for the reference to the Dover cliffs in the last line. Against those new commercial walls that act as a barrier against an external threat (instead of a sea carrying an invading fleet, long memories carrying moral reproach), we are to set the poet's vision of the older "walled-in City of London" (15). The phrasing is important: these walls contain rather than repulse. This elegy to a railway station is devoted mostly to description of the many churches surrounding the station, all held meaningfully within those securing walls.

It is no wonder then that Betjeman should so value various social rituals that contain, however momentarily, our need to be serious, to have meaning, that is, to be placed. This is a theme that, as we shall see, is developed more seriously by Philip Larkin. But we are on our way in a poem like "Beside the Seaside" to Larkin's "To the Sea," published more than twenty-five years later. In Betjeman's much longer, more episodic, narrative piece, as Taylor-Martin claims, he has mounted and preserved "a whole chunk of English social history."[111] But it is also more than a historic record of "what England was like in the late nineteen-forties"; while preserving, the poem is about a necessary preservation, as annually "England leaves / Her centre for her tide-line" (18–19)—necessary because each return signals and marks change and aging more emphatically. The incidents Betjeman recalls deal with children outgrowing the previous year's obsessions and either resisting their recognition ("And I'm the same, of course I'm always ME"[1. 129], says the incredulous Jennifer when replaced in the affections of the seaside-games organizer, Mr. Pedder, by a new, younger golden-locked Christabel) or jumping with too dim a memory into a new and apparently permanent obsession:

> A single topic occupies our minds.
> 'Tis hinted at or boldly blazoned in
> Our accents, clothes and ways of eating fish,
> And being introduced and taking leave,
> 'Farewell,' 'So long,' 'Bunghosky,' 'Cheeribye'—
> That topic all-absorbing, as it was,
> Is now and ever shall be, to us—CLASS.
>
> (154–160)

Betjeman never in his regrets tries to freeze time, but he does cherish those rituals that help us understand and deal with our changes by reminding us that they are not unique. Even these defining social patterns are themselves defiend by cosmic ones. The poem ends with these lines:

> And all the time the waves, the waves, the waves
> Chase, intersect and flatten on the sand
> As they have done for centuries, as they will
> For centuries to come, when not a soul
> Is left to picnic on the blazing rocks,
> When England is not England, when mankind
> Has blown himself to pieces. Still the sea,
> Consolingly disastrous, will return
> While the strange starfish, hugely magnified,
> Waits in the jewelled basin of a pool.
>
> (191–200)

He similarly honors another ritual in his capacity as poet laureate. In "A Ballad of the Investiture 1969" he begins with a minor rite, acknowledging the "sure clarity of mind / Which comes to those who've truly dined" (5–6), in this case with Charles and exalted members of Trinity College's high table. He is much more serious as he informally describes in this "rhyming letter" (18) the Investiture itself. The ending of "Beside the Seaside" is echoed in the analogy of the closing lines here, as loneliness is consoled by understanding:

> You know those moments that these are
> When, lonely under moon and star,
>   You wait upon a beach?
> Suddenly all Creation's near
> And complicated things are clear,
>   Eternity in reach!
> So we who watch the action done—
> A mother to her kneeling son
>   The Crown of office giving—
> Can hardly tell, so rapt our gaze
> Whether but seconds pass or days
>   Or in what age we're living.
>
> You knelt a boy, you rose a man.
> And thus your lonelier life began.
>
> (55–68)

Other poems in this category that offer variations on this theme of time and continuity are "Hymn" (one of the best of his poems attacking church restoration), "Before Invasion, 1940" and "Margate, 1940" (unsentimental reminders of what the war was being fought to preserve), "From the Great Western" and "Delectable Duchy" (descriptions of changes in the West Country), "Meditation on a Constable Picture" (a plea for the preservation of "the London we knew"), and "Shetland 1973" (on the coming of oilmen to Scotland).

In poems on the death of close friends and family members, which I place in a fifth category, Betjeman simply personalizes the concerns he had in discussing the death of an older, more secure age. Death frightened him because whatever religious faith he had, for all its cohesive force ("conversion," he writes, is "turning round/From chaos to a love profound"), could not keep out doubt. "Mortal eyes," he goes on in that same poem, "The Conversion of St. Paul," "can never scan" God's "enormous plan"; there is not for him Paul's "blinding light," rather "a fitful glow/Is all the light of faith I know"; he stumbles on and blindly gropes "upheld by intermittent hope" (41–42, 55–56, 64–65, 81). His doubt even extends to the possibility of resurrection. Our own death too often promises only a longer and vaster version of our earthly isolation ("Loneliness"). The death of others is an absolute end to what we loved in them: there is no easy separation of body and soul for this poet who relished the social particulars of our lives. So, at a crematorium,

> ... little puffs of smoke without a sound
> Show what we loved dissolved in the skies,
> Dear hands and feet and laughter-lighted face
> And silk that hinted at the body's grace.
> ("Aldershot Crematorium," 3–6)

Religious faith for Betjeman is never doctrinaire; it is another of those not quite finally adequate consolations that he needs, for he cannot get rid of "a faint conviction that we may be born in Sin" ("Huxley Hall," 16). He will not condone dogmatism, because it disrupts social harmonies, therefore preferring the "moderate" worship in the Church of England of both God and the State: "Conservative and good and slow" ("Church of England Thoughts Occasioned by Hearing the Bells of Magdalen Tower from the Botanic Garden, Oxford on St. Mary Magdalen's Day," 17, 19).[112]

If religion is more a social institution than an all-inclusive explanation, death for Betjeman is primarily a social loss. In this Hardyesque elegy on his father, "On a Portrait of a Deaf Man," Betjeman looking upon the body of his dead father sees not a saveable soul but only "decay" (32), but even more memorable is his summing up of his father' life as a complex of likes: "old City dining-rooms,/Potatoes in their skin," "long silent walks/In country lanes," "the rain-washed Cornish air/And smell of ploughed-up soil," "a landscape big and bare." And "He would have liked to say good-bye,/Shake hands with many friends" (25–26). "Variations on a Theme by T. W. Rolleston" amplifies this idea. The death of a mother of five causes a social vacancy:

> But her place is empty in the queue at the International,
>   The greengrocer's queue lacks one,
> So does the crowd at MacFisheries. There's no one to go to Freeman's
>   To ask if the shoes are done.
> (9–12)

Such vacancy directs us not to metaphysics but to the past social failures of the survivor:

> Protestant claims and Catholic, the wrong and the right of them,
>   Unimportant they seem in the face of death—
> But my neglect and unkindness—to lose the sight of them
>   I would listen even again to that labouring breath.
> ("Remorse," 9–12)

At least once Betjeman in lamenting the loss of valued qualities in another (unintentionally, I am sure) memorialized the basis of his own social successes: his own humility and lack of "high-mindedness."

> Sky and sun and the sea! the greatness of things was in you
>   And thus you refrained your soul.

> Let others fuss over academic detail,
> *You* saw people whole.
>
> ("The Commander," 21–24)

After such a life and body of work, how can we regret Betjeman's popularity as so many academics have? We should, on the contrary, celebrate it as a sign of hope. Can not we agree that he should be popular, that his vision is just what modern England cannot afford to lose if it hopes to have vision at all? The English could do worse: a more difficult poet, of course, could not be as popular, but one with a different sensibility perhaps should not be popular.

Philip Larkin

In an obituary tribute to Philip Larkin in December 1985, Peter Levi wrote, "His friendship with John Betjeman ought not to have surprised anyone. When that remarkable man became Laureate, he wrote me a note saying 'It should have been Philip.'"[113] They were good friends partially because there were many similarities in their poetry, their poetic careers, and their poetic character. But, of course, when the time came Philip Larkin declined the offer of the Laureateship, and that was indicative of a signficant difference.

The qualities that Larkin shares with Betjeman have been the cause of very similar problems for the contemporary reader. Critical opinion of both men is sharply divided. Both have been very popular and conservative when most of the English literati were alienated and left-wing; neither, as an admirer of Hardy, is intellectual or visionary enough to satisfy readers who still draw their view of the modern poet from the example of W. B. Yeats; neither can be said to have developed very markedly during his career; and both were highly praised by that very changeable poet, W. H. Auden.[114] The differences between Betjeman and Larkin probably have as much to do with age an native temperament. Betjeman, as we have seen, was social in practically everything, refusing to separate the public from the private world; his concern with continuities included, along with that between the past and the present, that between the individual and the social. His Anglican faith may not have been absolute, but he managed to be hopeful much of the time. His indignation in many of his poems is with missed and overlooked opportunities, not with their absence. Larkin, however, without even the older poet's tenuous faith, was more disillusioned and resigned. He had a more intense awareness of the discontinuity between the spirit with its will to purity and nature as a realm of change, obscure forces, decay, and death. Betjeman still had his own vivid memories of Victorian and Edwardian London; Larkin spent his formative years in the depressed Midlands (what he himself called "the peculiar insecurity of pre-war England"[115]).

Because Larkin had less hope, his desperation was deeper and the need greater. He also wished to preserve, but he could not be content with recording the social minutiae of the past and present. His preservation project had to reach, occasionally at least, further down, below the surface that usually contented Betjeman, to more anciently established customs and rites, even those in which he could not himself participate. This is not to say that he was a despairing idealist. His simply sought ways of making his grasp on reality firmer. Suspicious of easy consolations, he nonetheless sought others, even if extremely difficult ones. Larkin, like Betjeman, was a social observer, but in place of Betjeman's detailed and sympathetic portraits we have Larkin's acknowledgments of limits and deprivations, poems in which he, like Rickword, attacks idealizations. But deprivation is a stimulus, not a resting place. "Deprivation is for me what daffodils were for Wordsworth," he said in an *Observer* interview in 1979.[116] And he said of Hardy: he "associated sensitivity to suffering and awareness of the causes of pain with superior spiritual character."[117] Suffering is a maturing experience, and sadness gives one authority.[118] Also, in place of Betjeman's elegiac laments (gentle as well as angry) on passing traditions, we have Larkin's probing investigations of the possibility of life in the present forms of those continuities. In a sense, Larkin was concerned less with remembering and reminding and more with getting on, with the chances for moral survival. There was a little of Daryush in Larkin, but the categories that were still if barely available to her as a poet and social being were retreating for Larkin. He needed social crystallizations of those ethical abstractions. His reliance on traditional poetic forms analogizes the need. This, I think, is what he meant when he said, "I think one would have to be very sure of oneself to dispense with the help that metre and rhyme give and I doubt really if I could operate without them."[119] Taking this a step further, one could say that free (freed) verse is an assertion of uniqueness, of unattached individuality: it separates one from one's audience and from the ability to be efficiently communicative. Modernism cannot, consequently, help us endure.[120]

The defeat of illusion requires moral effort. If reality is the coherence we find in present events (as history is the sense we make of past events), and art is the assurance of our capacity to confirm reality, then Larkin's art revivifies our capacity for preserving the social forms of that coherence. Or, more accurately, in his verse he studies the possibility within the remnants of once lively rituals—what they can still provide, what the rejection of them leaves us with. Seamus Heaney rightly claims that in Larkin's poems

> there is enough reach and longing to show that he does not completely settle for that well-known bargain offer, 'a poetry of lowered sights and patently diminished expectations.'[121]

Social Consolations

But he emphasizes Larkin's gestures "toward a realm beyond the social and the historical"[122]; my purpose here is to point out gestures toward consolations still (if not quite fully enough) within the social realm. Even in his darkest, most unrelieved poem on the absoluteness of death as an ending of life, he still can define death as an absence of linking—

> ... this is what we fear—no sight, no sound,
> No touch or taste or smell, nothing to think with,
> Nothing to love or link with,
> The anaesthetic from which none come round,

and he can close not with despair but with the need to keep in contact:

> Work has to be done.
> Postmen like doctors go from house to house.
> ("Aubade," 27–30, 49–50)[123]

Social efforts may themselves be consolations.

I should stress here that I do not presume to be uncovering hidden depths or saying anything startlingly new about Larkin. He is not that kind of poet, and his readers have been fairly thorough in their excavations. What I do hope to do is point to an area of his accomplishment that perhaps shows up a bit more positively for being placed in the context of this chapter, and even this book: that is, his often implicit recommendation of certain customs and rituals as one means of getting through, intelligently and well, modern life.

Although some critics have been aware of this dimension in his poetry, they usually do not go far enough. Three recent studies of Larkin have attempted to rescue from neglect the affirmative aspects of his work: one is Heaney's, to which I have already referred. The others are by Andrew Motion and Terry Whalen. Motion mentions in passing that "rituals offer some comfort in the face of death" but is too interested in Larkin's promotion of "the power to choose" and in his reliance on symbolist strategies ("removal from the apparently inevitable frustrations that accompany rational discourse") to consider fully those rituals.[124] Whalen is content to see the positive side in terms of Larkin's undervalued Romantic impulse, his sensitivity to beauty and mystery, "the beauty of the past," "the beauty of community life," "the mystery of the living world." His thesis in the chapter on "Family and Nation" is stated thusly: Larkin's "contribution to the social literature of the post-war period lies in his ability to notice, and record, that there is a beauty in the commonplace which persists, and also a delicate and spontaneous unity which can sometimes preside."[125] I think much more needs to be said to draw out the full meaning of that "unity." Two earlier and shorter studies are a little more helpful. J. R. Watson's "other Larkin" is *homo religiosus*, a man in search of the sacred and primitive in a profane world, of "forgotten patterns of belief and ritual."[126] I wish to stress Larkin's concern with what has been remembered, with civilizing rituals, not primitive ones. Dan Jacobson comes closest to the spirit in which I approach Larkin; at the very end of his rather general profile he notes something "new" in *High Windows,* a Larkin who, having sought before "to find a point of rest in the idea of a repetition from generation to generation of certain collective acts and gestures," finds in the early 1970s that "the continuity of such social forms.... [is] more threatened that ever before." Larkin as a result, says Jacobson, "feels impelled to speak out directly as a moralist ... to warn people of what they stand to lose."[127] I will attempt to track down the implications of this statement.

Some critics are blind to this side of Larkin's social verse. Usually they cannot get pass that first stage—the acknowledgment of limits. Alvarez, for instance, can detect "only negatives" in this statement by Robert Conquest of Movement priorities: "It submits to no great systems of theoretical constructs or agglomerations of unconscious commands. ... [It refuses] to abandon a rational structure and comprehensible language." He is unable to realize that rejecting a negative is positive. He has little to say of Larkin, except to characterize the speaker of "Church Going" as "the image of the post-war Welfare State Englishman: shabby ... hopeless, bored, wry."[128] Other critics have gone further, equally blank to the possibility that rejecting an illusion can be positive, can put one in a better position to detect whatever coherence might exist. Colin Falck claims that Larkin believes in "the necessity of life's meaninglessness." Yet he himself, even more than Alvarez, does not seem to believe in the values of civilized community life; whereas Alvarez calls for a "new depth poetry" (confessional, urgent, naked, decidedly not polite or decent), Falck wants "lucid barbarism," like the "'right-wing' violence to which D. H. Lawrence was sometimes led."[129]

I certainly do not want to deny that Larkin is usually skeptical and can be pessimistic, and that his view of postwar British life is usually dreary, but I would like to put that dreariness in context. As we know, Larkin resented this emphasis on his "miseries," on his "uniquely dreary life": "I'd like to know," he said to Ian Hamilton, "how all these romantic reviewers spend their time—do they kill a lot of dragons, for instance?"[130] The reports on Larkin's character all testify to what his prospective biographer calls "a very social man": "an obvious gift for conviviality" (Dan Jacobson), "a particularly engaging host" (John Haffenden), "a delightful companion ... urbanity verging on courtliness" (Noel Hughes), "the most enlivening companion" (Kingsley Amis), "an enhancer of life to his friends ... profoundly decent" (Peter Levi).[131] There are times when this man, unseparated from the poet who may suffer, is present in the poems.

We have to search hard for that man in the first collection, *The North Ship* (1945). Larkin was neither mature nor confident enough in a period too dominated by Yeats, Auden, and Dylan Thomas to challenge prevailing modes. Most commentators agree that the kind of poet he is to develop into, after the discipline of writing two novels, is first detectable in poem "XXXII," which he wrote a year or so after 1945 and added to the 1966 reissue of *The North Ship*. But there are at least two earlier poems in the original collection that show Larkin stepping away from self-concerned dreamy expressions of vague emotions to confront a specific social situation.

Despite the Audenesque metaphor that opens "Conscript" ("V"),[132] there follows a fairly plain (if never quite clear enough) consideration of patriotic commitment in wartime: at least that is the accessible subject of the sonnet.

> And he must help them. The assent he gave
> Was founded in desire for self-effacement
> In order not to lose his birthright; . . . .
>
> (9–11)[133]

One cannot be sure, because of the opening geographical description of the ego, that this subject is not the vehicle of a more privately psychological tenor. We do, however, detect in the very last lines a rhetorical habit he was to exploit effectively later, the quick qualification of an indulged, somewhat inflated or idealized, emotion:

> . . . brave,
> For nothing would be easier than replacement,
>
> Which would not give him time to follow further
> The details of his own defeat and murder.
>
> (11–14)

We note a similar nod toward social requirements and a similar movement in the even plainer "VI." The first seven lines describe an attempt to keep a guest from leaving late at night in fear of the desolation that seems to come too easily when the poet is alone. The poem ends:

> Who can confront
> The instantaneous grief of being alone?
> Or watch the sad increase
> Across the mind of this prolific plant,
> Dumb idleness?
>
> (8–12)

The very unobtrusive correction is here in the form of the less inflated alternative to "grief" with which he prefers to end the poem.

In "XXXII" he offers many more situational details, as he looks out of a hotel window onto a dull, misty early morning scene. An assured management of unexpectedly appropriate participles is particularly evident:

> ... Cobblestones were wet,
> But sent no light back to the loaded sky,
> Sunk as it was with mist down to the roofs.
>
> (3–5)

A qualification comes quite early in the poem as he realizes that his initial assessment of the scene ("Featureless morning, featureless night" [8]) is a "misjudgment" (9) and moves to contemplate the opposition of what appears in the final lines to be his muse to the real woman with whom he has just spent the night.

> ... Are you jealous of her?
> Will you refuse to come till I have sent
> Her terribly away, importantly live
> Part invalid, part baby, and part saint?
>
> (22–25)

Like "VI," he ends weakly with a question, but it leans toward a defining self-adjustment in a more regular blank verse and away from the "generalised sadness," as Roger Day calls it[134], and looser rhythms of the other poems in the volume.

Poems written over the next few years and published in *The Less Deceived* (1955) continue to record his personal adjustments to necessary limits, most importantly the absences in his childhood. The negative autobiography he offers in "I Remember, I Remember" (his childhood in Coventry was decidedly not like that of Dylan Thomas or D. H. Lawrence) is summed up in "Coming": his childhood was "a forgotten boredom" (13). The second poem is about something else, about what he relies on in place of that missing personal heritage. This very ordinary, short-sighted, stammering boy, who did not like other children very much and whose parents were shy, awkward, and "not very good at being happy,"[135] as he matured had to rely on public forms to structure and define his life, in contrast to those who were more privileged, with richer family or school experiences (such as Chris Warner in *Jill* and Robin Fennel in *A Girl in Winter,* each envied, even if inappropriately, by the lonely protagonist of each novel). Ostensibly, in "Coming," the structure he can make his own is the simple natural one of seasonal return: he can feel happy at the thrush's song announcing "It will be spring soon." But, as usual with Larkin and like Hardy, nature is not an adequate guide by itself. He must use a common social analogy to clarify his emotional response to a natural event:

> And I, whose childhood
> Is a forgotten boredom,
> Feel like a child
> Who comes on a scene
> Of adult reconciling,
> And can understand nothing
> But the unusual laughter,
> And starts to be happy.
>
> (12–19)

The poem has the effect of reconciling reader and poet in a sensitive response, rather than calling attention to the uniquencess of the poet's sensitivity. A common, shared experience can have the same status for the otherwise deprived poet as a natural cycle. We must not overlook the additional humility suggested by the allusion to Hardy's "Darkling Thrush": that older poet also could not understand—in his case the "blessed Hope" of a frail but optimistic bird.

This sets the tone for his other poems on various potential social consolations: this sometimes shy and often retiring poet may himself not understand through direct experience religious faith or marriage, for instance, but as a spokesman for more than himself he can invoke them. Such reliances may be rather ordinary or customary, but they prevent us from being pulled off balance. As he says in "Born Yesterday" (wryly answering, I think, Yeats's "Prayer" to his daughter that she live, in a very different sense, an "accustomed, ceremonious" life in an aristocratic house):

> In fact, you may be dull—
> If that is what a skilled,
> Vigilant, flexible,
> Unemphasised, enthralled
> Catching of happiness is called.
>
> (20–24)

Skilled, vigilant, flexible, unemphasized, yet enthralled: surely those are the qualities Larkin wishes for himself and achieves frequently in his strongest poems. Those are the characteristics of Larkin's strongest reaching after whatever happiness is possible.

The catching, however, "exacts a full look at the Worst" (as Hardy might say). The fullness of Larkin's look is what has drawn to him so often the charge of pessimism, but it might more accurately be considered the firm grounding of his feet so that he can securely without illusion determine "if way to the Better there be." Three consecutive poems in *The Less Deceived* set the ultimate limits. "Next Please" gives new life to the old saying "waiting for one's boat to come in": the only boat that actually anchors, that "is seeking us," is death, "a black-/ Sailed unfamiliar" towing a huge silence. The poem, however, is not simply a reminder of this; it is more directly a caution against being "too eager for the future" and having "bad habits of expectancy."

> We think each one will heave to and unload
> All good into our lives, all we are owed
> For waiting so devoutly and so long.
> But we are wrong.
>
> (17–20)

He attacks the unwarranted expectation, the unjustified hope in an automatically responsive universe, in which the hopeful are rewarded according to the intensity of their hope. The poem also touches on the delusion that on the rare occasions when desires are satisfied, they will be lastingly so: "it's / No sooner present than it turns to past" (14–15). (This theme is treated more fully in "Deceptions," in which a victim is declared "less deceived" than her Victorian rapist, who stumbled "up the breathless stair / To burst into fulfilment's desolate attic" [15–17].) "Going," immediately following "Next Please," develops the latter poem's final point about death's inevitability. Figured as the final evening "that lights no lamps" (3) and as a silken sheet, death nonetheless, Larkin clearly states, "brings no comfort" (6). This must be kept in mind as we read the next poem, "Wants," which even in this context is certainly one of Larkin's bleakest poems. The first stanza opens and closes with "Beyond all this, the wish to be alone," and the second with "Beneath it all, desire of oblivion runs." Roger Day reads it as a straightforward expression of Larkin's pessimism, of a "basic human desire to escape from life and awareness," with the wish for solitude concealing a wish not to exist.[136] Larkin is just as likely, I think, setting such wishes up as themselves deceptive, as deceptive as the optimistic ones in "Next Please." Neither solitude nor suicide will bring solace. It may be that the various social, sexual, and familial attempts to cheat time (as listed in the intervening lines of each stanza) are finally "the costly aversion of the eyes from death" (9). But because there is nothing beyond life, Larkin believed, the only thing beyond all these forced communal gatherings is a death-in-life that is not necessarily recommended, even if it is acknowledged, as an alternative.

Larkin's next volume, *The Whitsun Weddings* (1964), continues with reminders of the nature of our human limitations, but again they are reminders, gentle and sympathetic adjustments to our presumptions, to our longings for those ships ("Flagged, and the figurehead with golden tits" ["Next, Please," 13]). I stop short of calling them defeatist, nihilistic "dismissal[s] of the world," as readers such as Calvin Bedient do.[137] The most categorical statement from Larkin of his general outlook on time and death appears at the end of "Dockery and Son":

> Life is first boredom, then fear.
> Whether or not we use it, it goes,
> And leaves what something hidden from us chose,
> And age, and then the only end of age.
>
> (45–48)

D. J. Enright thinks Larkin is here promulgating his "homespun melancholia at its most explicit and least appealing."[138] But just how "homespun" is it? Except for the first part of the first line, which is so clearly a momentary grouse (and therefore not intended as a superior generalization), we cannot deny the obvious truth of the bare statement. It *is* bare—there is much more to say, and Larkin does say more elsewhere—but although we may wish life to be otherwise, these are the ground conditions. Note that Larkin does not say we *cannot* use it, for better or ill, to make our passage more or less tolerable. He is not disillusioned so much as unillusioned, because there is no sense that he alone has discovered this, no enactment of metaphysical disappointment. This is just the way it is, and he wants us all to be clear about it.

Two other poems about time, "Days" and "Nothing To Be Said," make equally blunt statements. In the first he says simply, where else can we live but in time; it is our limit but also our opportunity: we find happiness there or nowhere ("They are to be happy in"). The doctor and priest of the second stanza offer two answers to the question "where can we live but days?" To be out of time is either to be dead (the doctor's answer) or to be in some bodiless spiritual state (the priest's answer). This *poet's* concern, however, only can be with the possibilities for happiness in our natural state. That is, the answers are finally irrelevant, so the priest and doctor are made to seem a little awkward, hardly distinguished,

> In their long coats
> Running over the fields.
>
> (9–10)

"Nothing To Be Said" repeats the truism, "Life is a slow dying": it is for everyone (1–6), and there are different ways of spending the days that inevitably advance toward death (7–15). But Larkin's final concern is how we react when reminded:

> And saying so to some
> Means nothing; others it leaves
> Nothing to be said.
>
> (16–18)

Of course, there is a third possibility: Larkin himself, who goes on writing poems. There may be nothing more to say about the nature of death, but there is more to say about how we slowly die.

Some of the other things to be said are that we cannot be certain of very much ("Ignorance"), that youthful ideals are rarely realized ("Home is So Sad"), that the promises of ideal love—"to solve, and satisfy,/And set unchangeably in order"—are usually disappointed ("Love Songs in Age"), and that childhood is rarely the idyllic state the romantic poets told us it was ("Take One Home for the Kiddies"). That other romantic standard, nature, also cannot offer much solace:

> And the countryside not caring:
> The place-names all hazed over
> With flowering grasses, and fields
> Shadowing Domesday lines
> Under wheat's restless silence.
> ("MCMXIV," 17–21)

> Outside, the wind's incomplete unrest
> Builds and disperses clouds about the sky,
> . . . .
> None of this cares for us.
> ("Talking in Bed," 5–6, 8)

How can we hope to rest in that which itself is restless? Whatever is left of the natural in us, unidealized love, or even sex, for instance, we have made "synthetic, new,/And natureless" ("The Large Cool Store," 19–20).

Mindful of these limits, we are tempted to retire into ourselves. It was a real temptation for Larkin— "Beneath all this, the wish to be alone." We should go back to the last poem in *The Less Deceived,* "At Grass," and compare it with the first poem in *The Whitsun Weddings,* "Here." Both poems deal with solitude and chances for anonymity. I agree with David Timms that the retired racehorses of "At Grass" represent a model of the oblivion humans can imagine, "but it is no longer within our expectations."[139] I would add: it never fully was, principally because we are human beings with different, longer, more substantial, more meaningful memories. The memories Larkin gives us of the past of these now "anonymous" horses cannot be theirs:

> Yet fifteen years ago, perhaps
> Two dozen distances sufficed
> To fable them: faint afternoons
> Of Cups and Stakes and Handicaps,
> Whereby their names were artificed
> To inlay faded, classic Junes—
>
> Silks at the start: against the sky
> Numbers and parasols: outside,
> Squadrons of empty cars, and heat,

> And littered grass: then the long cry
> Hanging unhushed till it subside
> To stop-press columns on the street.
>
> (7–18)

It is not just that horses do not have a conceptual language; with the exception of "heat," "grass," and "the long cry," only humans could register these details. The very process by which fables and ceremonial prizes are made into insistent daily pressures ("stop-press") to invigorate our slow dying is a distinctly human way of getting on. The poem may be "pastoral," as Timms says,[140] but it is not nostalgic, because its subject is the inaccessibility of such a state: "they/have slipped their names, and stand at ease" (24–25). "Here" is structured similarly, but rather than a temporal it is a geographic journey into isolation, with a detailed look at the crowded, busy, social world in the middle of the poem. This time the "pastoral" is obviously ironic:

> A cut-price crowd, urban yet simple, dwelling
> Where only salesmen and relations come
> Within a terminate and fishy-smelling
> Pastoral of ships up streets, the slave museum,
> Tatoo-shops, consulates, grim head-scarfed wives.
>
> (17–21)

The port of Hull is one terminus; the other is the unspoiled beach beyond the "isolate villages" outside the reaches of the large town:

> And past the poppies bluish neutral distance
> Ends the land suddenly beyond a beach
> Of shapes and shingle. Here is unfenced existence:
> Facing the sun, untalkative, out of reach.
>
> (29–32)

Just as the anonymity and seeming joy of the retired horses is unavailable to man, so existence here is immaturely "unfenced" (see "Wires" in *The Less Deceived*). Loneliness does clarify the "removed lives" of those who live in isolation, but only the self is clarified: other people become merely "shapes." "Out of reach" is effectively ambiguous; it can suggest the impossibility of this dream of a purified self.[141]

"The Importance of Elsewhere," which comes later in *The Whitsun Weddings,* is a brief autobiographical meditation on how for him loneliness clarifies. "Lonely in Ireland," he could make sense of strangeness, the measurements of difference were all around him; they proved him separate. The subject then turns naturally to the complex nature of belonging:

> Living in England has no such excuse:

> These are my customs and establishments
> It would be much more serious to refuse.
> Here no elsewhere underwrites my existence.
>
> (9-12)

He may feel "unworkable" (8) at home; he may need to be away from his full customary self to be comfortable, indeed to work (we know that he was able to write much and well while in Belfast in the early 1950s[142]). What is significant in the poem is that he appears to say that the weakness is not in being at home but in being Philip Larkin. Our existence should not need to be underwritten (secured or guaranteed) by that which is alien to what we are.

Several years later he takes that theme of belonging a step further in a less personal poem, "High Windows." Just as in "The Importance of Elsewhere" freedom is treated ironically; there he was free to be himself only if he separated from his full self, here the sexual freedom of the younger generation is compared to the freedom from religious authority of his generation. In both cases, everyone goes "down the long slide / To happiness" (8-9). But when the movement is up instead of down, he finds not the opposite of that superficial happiness, but nothing:

> The sun-comprehending glass,
> And beyond it, the deep blue air, that shows
> Nothing, and is nowhere, and is endless.
>
> (18-20)

As Larkin explained in his conversation with John Haffenden, "the end [of the poem] shows a desire to get away from it all. . . . One longs for infinity and absence, the beauty of somewhere you're not."[143] One longs for it, but it means nullity: the diction if not the tone insists on that. In between the slide downward and the idealistic gaze upward is that which was by those who dream too much of freedom perhaps too hastily "pushed to one side": "bonds and gestures" (6), not unlike the "customs and establishments" of the other poem. Implicit in the poem is the recognition that in finding and placing our human selves above the lower animals ("free bloody birds") and below the eternal, unseeable, bodiless angels ("sun-comprehending"), we can realistically liberate ourselves, not from our real selves but from error. The limiting place is our chance for realization.

I grant that this notion is very implicit in the poem. In the poems in which they appear, poems primarily concerned with our necessarily deprived or foreshortened state, phrases like "customs and establishments" and "bonds and gestures" remain general, in contexts not always clearly flattering, but never shrilly dismissive. If, however, we remember those other poems in which he closely observes the social customs and gestures of those around him, we see that the care he gives such description moderates the criticism with a hint of reverence (as in the second and third stanzas of "At Grass" and of "Here"). Let us now move to two other groups of poems in which the reverence is more forward: first those also with ostensibly negative views that nonetheless hint at consolations to be found in more specified customs, and second those that celebrate certain rituals.

That social gatherings in general are palliatives is part of the thought of poems like "Mr. Bleaney," "Vers de Société," and "Ambulances." From another poem we know that he thought of himself as a socially responsive poet. After a wonderfully detailed description of preparing a gin and tonic in "Sympathy in White Major," he toasts himself: "He devoted his life to others." It is Larkin's characteristically self-deprecating version of Hardy's "Afterwards," the poetic accomplishment for which he hopes to be remembered.

> While other people wore like clothes
> The human beings in their days
> I set myself to bring to those
> Who thought I could the lost displays;
> It didn't work for them or me,
> But all concerned were nearer thus
> (Or so we thought) to all the fuss
> Than if we'd missed it separately.
>
> (9–16)

Refusing to use other people in the service of whatever is fashionable at the moment, he perhaps is less immediately involved with the present, hoping rather to recover the past for himself and others ("the lost displays"). Such a poetic recovery can have no lasting effect, but at least (like his much admired Betjeman) he can share the feelings of those who can care about the loss. He hopes his poems can gather people together, even if these gatherings challenge his essentially solitary, withdrawn, shy nature. He closes with another toast, "Here's to the whitest man I know" (23), the idiom designating a thoroughly straightforward, honorable man, but he immediately follows it with: "Though white is not my favourite colour" (14). Bruce Martin puts too much stress on that last line, seeing mainly disillusionment, regret, and self-doubt.[144] Like other readers of Larkin, he misses the important point, the point I have been making throughout: the regret is a given; it is what we can find to console and support us in spite of that that is important. There is some hope in Larkin, but it is rarely up front, probably because of his dedication to the truth:

> I suppose I always try to write the truth and I wouldn't want to write a poem which suggested that I was different from what I am. In a sense that means you

have to build in quite a lot of things to correct any impression of over-optimism or over-commitment.[145]

"Mr. Bleaney" also ends with the poet's doubt ("I don't know" also suggests the impossibility of entering another's mind) and stresses the replacement in the rented room of Bleaney by the poet. But the former resident had his resources and routines: he took in hand the landlady's bit of garden and had his relatives to visit in Frinton and Stoke during his holidays. The poet in "Vers de Société" has friends who occasionally invite him to dinner. Although he will not give the pious commonplaces ("All solitude is selfish" and "Virtue is social" 19, 24]) a free ride, the question is finally a real and serious one: "Are, then, these routines/Playing at goodness, like going to church?" (24–25). He recognizes that the sense of the social has diminished: we may be bored and ill at ease at such gatherings, but they just may show us "what should be" (29), and besides "Only the young can be alone freely./ The time is shorter now for company" (31–32). The sudden appearance of an ambulance (in "Ambulances") can force us into realizing what life amounts to—"the unique random blend/Of families and fashions" (23–24), and what in that life that is most significantly being lost by the dying: "the exchange of love" (26).

When this bachelor poet confronts marriage, then, his all too clear understanding of its weaknesses will not let him overvalue its alternatives, the individualistic dedication to "art, if you like" in "Reasons for Attendance," or the "unfingermarked," semantically unconfused virgin of "Maiden Name," or an equally ignored childlessness:

> For Dockery a son, for me nothing,
> Nothing with all a son's harsh patronage.
> ("Dockery and Son," 43–44)

Then there was 1963, which by separating defined the opponents, or at least the contemporary, debased versions of them: before "a sort of bargaining,/A wrangle for a ring," after the easy, guiltless, undemanding sex of the liberated sixties, when "Everyone felt the same,/And every life became/A brilliant breaking of the bank,/A quite unlosable game" ("Annus Mirabilis," 7–8, 12–15). A game that cannot be lost also cannot be taken seriously. The slide is indeed downward.

God may be more dead for Larkin and his generation than for Hardy's, but Larkin, like Hardy, still could bring into the wide circle of his regret a need for something like the seriousness Christian faith used to provide. The last two stanzas of "Church Going" are too well known and discussed for me to dwell on them here. I only will point to two implications of the respect he expresses toward that dying institution. The first is that it is the social institution of the church and not any comforting theological and metaphysical explanation that he misses. Like Betjeman's old walled City of London, the church could contain and concentrate and so give coherence to our natural needs and most universal of routines:

> ... it held unspilt
> So long and equably what since is found
> Only in separation—marriage, and birth,
> And death, and thoughts of these. ...
> (48–51)

The second implication is that the gathering and enclosing that the church encouraged provided a means of preserving human memory, of keeping contact with, and therefore not having to repeat the trials, errors, and findings of the past:

> ... this ground,
> Which, he once heard, was proper to grow wise in,
> If only that so many dead lie round.
> (62–64)

One is hard pressed to find any irony here. For one of the few times in Larkin, the last word is the most important word. Several years later he even made the connection between a meaningful solitude and God:

> ... No one now
> Believes the hermit with his gown and dish
> Talking to God (who's gone too); the big wish
> Is to have people nice to you, which means
> Doing it back somehow.
> ("Vers de Société," 19–23)

Belief in a God used to sanctify loneliness. Now as he talks to himself in the poems about his isolation, Larkin often recognizes reluctantly the need to talk to others, not simply with the forced conviviality of today's dinner parties, but where possible in the old and customary ways on the old and customary occasions, when meeting with others had an object other than filling in spare time or self-promotion ("Asking that ass about his fool research").

We come finally to poems that actually celebrate such meetings that in their recurrence have found meaning as rituals, those ceremonies that have managed to survive their more religiously inspired originals. Their future is also threatened—all the more reason for the poet's attempt to preserve the displays. If Betjeman, as Larkin says, came to the Christian religion by means of church architecture and formal ritual,"[146] Larkin came to rituals, even less formal ones, by means of the absence left in community life by the decline in religious faith. Significantly Larkin could value Betjeman so much because the older poet did not just bemoan and elegize. He found poetry in something more advanced than pity:

> Betjeman is serious because he has produced an original poetry of persons and surroundings in which neither predominates: each sustains the other, and the poetry is in the sustaining.[147]

So too, the less vivacious, less accepting, less comic, less sociable Larkin looks to sustain as best he can, given his temperament. The wry detachment is never quite absent, but in a few poems it does seem to withdraw in favor of other, more constructive possibilities that range across the many attempted bondings: of large groups with nature, of citizens with their homeland, and (most basic and importantly) of men with women in marriage.

I already have noted that Larkin has no illusions about nature either as a place to which one might go to retreat from the burdens of modern urban life or as an alternative faith and moral guide. What he does value occasionally are those customary human gatherings in natural surroundings that reaffirm dimly our place in anciently conceived natural laws and more vividly our links with less distant generations. Larkin opens and nearly closes his last volume, *High Windows,* with two such poems: "To the Sea" and "Show Saturday." Both are explicit pleas for the continuance of these mid-summer and end of summer rites. He does not offer an argument, but he does recreate, with some of his finest descriptive passages, to make his case. The tone of both poems is encapsulated in a line from the first: in a rare moment of wondrous joy, he exclaims after returning to the seaside after many years of absence: "Still going on, all of it, still going on!" (10). Much of the pleasure results from the concentration of people seeking pleasure: "The miniature gaiety of seasides./Everything crowds under the low horizon" (4–5). The same is true of "Show Saturday," that celebration of husbandry and cooperation of natural and human resources with every event and display carefully placed and confined, as in the nearly symbolic wrestling matches: "The wrestling starts, late; a wide ring of people; then cars;/Then trees; then pale sky" (17–18). At the center of this particular circle are sets of two young men in civilized competition:

>   ... One falls: they shake hands.
> Two more start, one grey-haired: he wins, though. They're not so much fights
> As long immobile strainings that end in unbalance
> With one on his back, unharmed, while the other stands
> Smoothing his hair.
>
>   (20–24)

More than pleasure, however, is to be won. Visits to the seaside may not show us physically at our best, but they are occasions when our duties to each other are somehow easier to perform:

> ... If the worst
> Of flawless weather is our falling short,
> It may be that through habit these do best,
> Coming to water clumsily undressed
> Yearly; teaching their children by a sort
> Of clowning; helping the old, too, as they ought.
>
> (31–36)

At the end of "Show Saturday" he is even more serious about these Antaean rites. People must disperse at the end of the day,

> Back now to autumn, leaving the ended husk
> Of summer that brought them here for Show Saturday—
> . . . .
> Back now, all of them, to their local lives.
>
> (47–48, 53)

The work, whose products were honored on that one day, calls them back to business and routine. The poem ends with a kind of prayer:

> ... the dismantled Show
> Itself dies back into the area of work.
> Let it stay hidden there like strength, below
> Sale-bills and swindling; something people do,
> Not noticing how time's rolling smithy-smoke
> Shadows much greater gestures; something they share
> That breaks ancestrally each year into
> Regenerate union. Let it always be there.
>
> (57–64)

The message of "The Trees" is "Last year is dead, they seem to say, / Begin afresh, afresh, afresh" (11–12). In annual, semiritual gatherings like "Show Saturday," Larkin is trying to find the human equivalent. The final rhyme of the poem emphasizes the localized sharing that is able to measure the perhaps too "local" lives insisted upon by the workaday world. (It is evident beneath the humorous surface of that notorious pair "Toads" and "Toads Revisited" or on the surface of the unusual "Livings" that Larkin takes work seriously.)

A different kind of measurement is provided by the Remembrance Day service mentioned briefly in "Naturally the Foundation will Bear Your Expenses." The opportunistic academic who speaks the poem exposes the depth of his selfishness in the way he dismisses the patriotic event that delayed his taxi to the airport.

> That day when Queen and Minister
> And Band of Guards and all
> Still act their solemn-sinister
> Wreath-rubbish in Whitehall.
>
> (13–16)

J. R. Watson puts his finger precisely on the defect: "it is the complacency with which it is done, the satisfied sense of separation from other people, which makes the speaker so monstrous."[148] Larkin, as I have said, sometimes wants such separation for himself, but he is rarely satisfied with it. Patriotic sentiments (as publicly attested to in Cenotaph ceremonies) do not often find their way into Larkin's poems, but they are not surprising when they do, as they do faintly in "MCMXIV" and bluntly in "Homage to a Government": in the former such sentiments are mixed in with a nostalgia for more innocent times, in the latter with despair at the reduction of our political values by economic priorities. The two come together in "Going, Going," an occasional poem commissioned by the Department of the Environment in 1972. It is a Betjeman-like elegy on the loss of the essential England, a little more despairing than Betjeman usually was. It is not going to last, he says: "greeds / And garbage are too thick-strewn / To be swept up now" (50–52). But his definition of his birthright as an Englishmen is similar to the older poet's: it is not either countryside alone or customs or buildings, but the mutually sustaining union—"The shadows, the meadows, the lanes, / The guildhalls, the carved choirs" (44–45). The order of this list is extremely pertinent, suggesting that same natural hierarchy Betjeman somtimes invoked.

Two of Larkin's most moving and deservedly popular poems are about marriage, the title poem and the last poem in the 1964 collection: "The Whitsun Weddings" and "An Arundel Tomb," the first about the beginning of several wedded lives, the second about the legacy of a wedded life. In "Church Going" we noted Larkin's echo of Betjeman's preference for purposeful containment that can at least analogize coherence and therefore comprehensible meaning, a restriction that actually promotes growth (a defined "ground, / Which . . . was proper to grow wise in"). "The Whitsun Weddings" is structured to highlight this notion so central to any proper appreciation of traditional rituals. Two events are narrated in the poem: the speaker's train journey from Hull to London and the wedding day of about a dozen couples. The progression of the first event is followed closely and is the dominant structural principle; the second event is gradually and unchronologically reconstructed by the observing speaker: he sees the couples boarding trains, leaving the wedding guests behind, and he imagines the prior receptions and the future lives of the couples. Significantly, the religious or legal center of the actual marriage ceremony is not recounted, but rather the immediate social consequences, and even those only from the perspective of a somewhat detached, passive, bookish traveller who only gradually becomes interested. When the two narratives touch, there is an increase, a kind of freedom *and* cohesion: "Free at last,/And loaded with the sum of all they saw,/We hurried towards London" (55–57).

Enclosing the two narratives is a pulsing imagistic movement: an expansion, then contraction, then expansion again. It is not a simple symmetry, however; the second expansion is metaphoric and not just sensory and is contained and controlled in a way the opening movement is not. The poem opens with an atmosphere of relieved, empty, warmish, inactivity:

> Not till about
> One-twenty on the sunlit Saturday
> Did my three-quarters-empty train pull out,
> All windows down, all cushions hot, all sense
> Of being in a hurry gone.
>
> (2–6)

The rest of the stanza widens the view: the rhythm of the lines eases and relaxes as the landscape spreads out:

> ... We ran
> Behind the backs of houses, crossed a street
> Of blinding windscreens, smelt the fish-dock; thence
> The river's level drifting breadth began,
> Where sky and Lincolnshire and water meet.
>
> (6–10)

As the train passes through the closely juxtaposed rural and industrial areas of the midlands, with one exception everything the poet observes out the window is plural, as the slow, expansive movement continues, slowed atmospherically as well by the "tall heat that slept/For miles inland" (11–12):

> A slow and stopping curve southwards we kept.
> Wide farms went by, short-shadowed cattle, and
> Canals with floatings of industrial froth;
> A hothouse flashed uniquely: hedges dipped
> And rose ...
>
> (13–17)

The significant exception, the one particular among the generalities, is the hothouse, which artificially produces and contains that "tall heat" experienced by the train passengers: it is a sign of man's productive attempt to control nature. The emphasis is not yet on that productive control; Larkin makes it clear in the following lines that the open and natural is preferred to the enclosed and man-made—the "smell of grass" over the "reek of buttoned carriage-cloth." The new towns he passes through are not very attractive: "new and nondescript," bordered by the refuse of dismantled cars. But "nondescript" does oppose one kind of human production to another—the "uniquely" flashing hothouse. As usual, Larkin will not indulge the sentimental dichotomy of country and city or nature and society, particularly here because he wants to celebrate an instance of the union of the natural with the social.

If the towns are "new and nondescript," the wedding parties he begins noticing on railway platforms are self-consciously out of place and unordinary (uniquely descriptive: "whoops and skirls" disrupt the "long cool platforms," the girls "grinning and pomaded" are dressed in "parodies of fashion" and are "posed irresolutely" [25, 28–30]). The speaker is roused from his book by this mixture of the old and the unique, and by its corollary, the separation from an old grouping and the initiation of a new one, which is also a survival:

> As if out on the end of an event
>   Waving goodbye
> To something that survived it. Struck, I leant
> More promptly out next time, more curiously,
> And saw it all again in different terms.
>
> (31–35)

"Again" but "different"—a new container for an old communal desire.

The descriptive catalogue that follows (just before the climactic meeting of the two narratives in line 56) offers versions of the imagistic and structural motifs introduced earlier. First he describes two distinct groups on the platform—the officiating elders and the "unreally" dressed girls:

> The fathers with broad belts under their suits
> And seamy foreheads; mothers loud and fat;
> An uncle shouting smut; and then the perms,
> The nylon gloves and jewellery-substitutes,
> The lemons, mauves, and olive-ochres that
>
> Marked off the girls unreally from the rest.
>
> (36–41)

The old are recognizably typical and the young, being more ostensibly fashionable, are momentarily distinct; yet at the same time old and young

Social Consolations 283

are customarily this distinguishable. Another complementary principle ordering the details here is the decline in the nature of the observer's awareness: from the fuller view, noting the clothes, faces, shapes, and sounds of the yet common fathers, mothers, and uncles, to more restricted views of only the outer trappings of the girls, then only the colors of their attire. What is new is immediate and superficial. A slight expansion of that fairly static scene follows as it is placed in a temporal context, where they all probably came from:

> Yes, from cafés
> And banquet-halls up yards, and bunting-dressed
> Coach-party annexes, the wedding-days
> Were coming to an end. All down the line
> Fresh couples climbed aboard: the rest stood round.
> (42–46)

The view of the past is followed quickly by the next event (now generalized) in the continuing present, so we might say there is a slight contraction as the separation is emphasized. Larkin then pauses to list the meaning this separation has for each age group in the wedding party—and defining, of course, is a narrowing of possibilites.

> ... each face seemed to define
> Just what it saw departing: children frowned
> At something dull; fathers had never known
>
> Success so huge and wholly farcical;
>   The women shared
> The secret like a happy funeral;
> While girls, gripping their handbags tighter, stared
> At the religious wounding.
> (48–55)

The order now is from those least to those most affected by the event, and from the dull to the comic to the pathetic to the tragic. It is significant that he ends with the girls, those who have most interested him throughout, for they feel the separation most acutely because they know they will soon be separated from their own virgin youths (this was, after all, the 1950s[149])—they will be the next subjects of this ritual. This ritual, as I have said, is not simply the marriage ceremony but the social custom of holding such weddings on the Whitsun weekend.

After the couples have boarded the train, concentrating and increasing the passengers ("loaded with the sum"), the poem hints at a now contained expansion: while shadows lengthen outside as the sun declines, "a dozen marriages got under way" (63). "*I nearly died*," as some of the embarrassed brides say to the grooms, is a comic touch that also echoes the "religious wounding" intimated to the envious, fearful, awe-struck girls on the platform. First a near death, then an altered life. As they move into an increasingly urban setting, their restricted futures are yet less under their own imaginative control:

> They watched the landscape, sitting side by side
> —An Odeon went past, a cooling tower,
> And someone running up to bowl—and none
> Thought of the others they would never meet
> Or how their lives would all contain this hour.
>
> (64–68)

They have agreed to other controls and moved beyond certain options. The poet can metaphorize the gains of this new ordering:

> I thought of London spread out in the sun,
> Its postal districts packed like squares of wheat:
>
> There we were aimed.
>
> (69–71)

"We": the solitary poet has been brought momentarily into this communal understanding of productive containment: "spread out" yet "packed." What the train has "held" will soon "be loosed" (75–76). All is not positive; the "backs of houses" and "blinding windscreens" as he left Hull are replaced as he enters London by "walls of blackened moss." But that image brings together man's world and nature's world. The complex attitude is summed up brilliantly in the feeling the passengers share as the train slows down: "as the tightened brakes took hold, there swelled / A sense of falling" (78–79), and the complex fate of the newlyweds is summed up in the simile that clarifies that feeling: "like an arrow-shower / Sent out of sight, somewhere becoming rain" (79–80). Although the full consequences of these reorganized lives cannot be known (the arrows will fall out of sight, "somewhere"), transformation is assured and generation is possible ("becoming rain"). Recalling the poem's title, we also can think of pentecost, the season for another sacrament, baptism, and for the celebration of the descent of the Holy Ghost to the Apostles.

The form of "An Arundel Tomb" differs significantly from that of "The Whitsun Weddings" in ways appropriate to their different subject matters. The six-line tetrameter stanzas of the former have a simpler and therefore more emphatic rhyme scheme ($abbcac$), containing more firmly the poet's less personal, less conversational, more evenly solemn and reverential attitude toward his ancient and literally static subject: the sepulchral images of an earl and countess of the Howard family, once Earls of Arundel, in Chichester Cathedral. In investigating the image, Larkin deals with the importance of two ritualized events—marriage and death—and how by means of ceremonial effigies the meaning of a shared life can be divorced from historic reality after death and still not lose its value.

The poet begins like other recent observers of the tomb, indeed like the other passengers on the Whitsun train, by just vaguely looking (not reading the Latin inscription, or even looking closely, his eye is moving but not focused), until he notices with a shock (we remember the "struck" of the other poem) one detail:

> Such plainness of the pre-baroque
> Hardly involves the eye, until
> It meets his left-hand gauntlet, still
> Clasped empty in the other; and
> One sees, with a sharp tender shock,
> His hand withdrawn, holding her hand.
>
> (7–12)

The observer is thus engaged, also in a kind of survival, this time not of an event ("The Whitsun Weddings," 31–33) so much as of a completed relationship. The tomb itself is a separation from time, a memorial freezing and generalizing of a more vivid past ("faces blurred," "habits vaguely shown": "such plainness of the pre-baroque"), and what vividness there is, the detail of the held hands, is a separation from even the reality of that particular marriage. The ever-realistic Larkin believes it symbolizes a faithfulness that probably did not exist so firmly in the earl and countess: "They would not think to lie so long" (13). The couples in "The Whitsun Weddings" separate from their former lives to enter into a productive relationship with their future. But what is separated in "An Arundel Tomb" is an idea from a reality: a particular history is sacrificed for an ideal of faithfulness. Originally at least, the gap was not very wide; the ideal may have been separated from the details of the lives, but not from their reputation, the lives as they wanted them to be remembered, or the better lives they had hoped for themselves (not unlike the Latin that dignified lives otherwise conducted in the vernacular):

> Such faithfulness in effigy
> Was just a detail friends would see:
> A sculptor's sweet commissioned grace
> Thrown off in helping to prolong
> The Latin names around the base.
>
> (14–18)

Time, however, has blurred the past and debased our teleologies. As the "tenantry" of the cathedral changed from the faithful to the curious to the tourist, the gap widened: the ideal was isolated from even a real hope; it is now no more than an "attitude" (36) in our now "unarmorial age" (33). The only comforting absolutes we have now are seasonal, he suggests in the fifth stanza, rather than ethical: at least we have the fact and the motive of persistence, and the natural version of that persistence in cyclical rather than progressive or linear or historic time:

> ... Rigidly they
>
> Persisted, linked, through lengths and breadths
> Of time. Snow fell, undated. Light
> Each summer thronged the glass. A bright
> Litter of birdcalls strewed the same
> Bone-riddled ground.
>
> (24–29)

But there might be a commonness to our human nature, as there is much more clearly in nature's patterns. What might be an instinct might just be true, even if we can no longer share an understanding of why it should be, so separated are we now from a time when there was an agreed upon truth to measure reality against:

> Time has transfigured them into
> Untruth. The stone fidelity
> They hardly meant has come to be
> Their final blazon, and to prove
> Our almost-instinct almost true:
> What will survive of us is love.
>
> (37–42)

If it had not been for the survival of the sculpture, which was itself the product of art serving age-old human custom, we might not even know that much.

Notes

Introduction. Sorting Out Modern Poetry

1. A curious blend of these two extremes, extraliterary exegesis constitutes the most recent threat to the integrity of literature and of the kind of unspecialized (usually moral) knowledge it expresses. The new theorists and "human scientists" find more interesting the knowledge generated by more specialized studies, like structural psychoanalysis, linguistics, cultural anthropology, and response theory, and so would elicit these kinds of knowledge from literature by applying the methods of these studies. Needless to say I do not intend to "reread" poems; I simply will read them as thoroughly as I can in the way that their authors (and poetry itself) demand they be read, with the aim of establishing their value.

2. Postmodernism has, of course, also questioned modernist assumptions, but from the other side, asserting that the early twentieth-century experimentalists did not go far enough, did not defy enough authorities vigorously enough (such as the author himself, or language itself).

3. Ezra Pound, "The Approach to Paris," *The New Age,* 2 October 1913, as quoted by Graham Hough, *Reflections on a Literary Revolution* (Washington, D.C.: Catholic University of America Press, 1960), p. 16.

4. Ezra Pound, *The Fortnightly Review,* 96, September 1914, p. 466.

5. Graham Hough, *Image and Experience: Studies in a Literary Revolution* (London: Duckworth, 1960), p. 15.

6. T. S. Eliot, "Isolated Superiority," *The Dial*, January 1928, p. 6.

7. The inconsistencies and contradictions in Eliot's critical and theoretical writings are now legendary. See Donald E. Stanford's summary of the problem in *Revolution and Convention in Modern Poetry* (Newark: University of Delaware Press, 1983), pp. 39–52.

8. Hugh Kenner, *The Invisible Poet*: T. S. Eliot (London: Methuen & Co., 1965), pp. 4, ix.

9. T. S. Eliot, "Preface to Anabasis" (1930), in *Selected Prose of T. S. Eliot,* ed. Frank Kermode (London: Faber & Faber, 1975), p. 77.

10. Hough, *Image and Experience,* pp. 19–20.

11. Can we not see the spectre of David Hartley (whose ideas once transformed and narrowed by the English romantics must have found their way to the French symbolists) behind Ford Madox Ford when he says, "poetic ideas are best expressed by a rendering of concrete objects" ("Those Were the Days," *Imagist Anthology 1930* [London: Chatto & Windus, 1930], p. xiii), and behind T. E. Hulme when he says, "Thought is prior to language and consists in the simultaneous presentation of two different images" (quoted by Michael Roberts, *T. E. Hulme* [London: Faber & Faber, 1938], p. 281)?

12. Robert Graves, *Collected Poems* (London: Cassell, 1975), p. 13.

13. Ezra Pound, *Collected Shorter Poems,* 2d ed. (London: Faber & Faber, 1968), p. 119. All further citations from Pound's poems will refer to this edition. Numbers in parentheses after citations are line numbers.

14. Ezra Pound, "A Few Don't's by an Imagiste," *Poetry: A Magazine of Verse* 1 (March 1913): 201.

15. Kenneth Fields, "The Rhetoric of Artifice: Ezra Pound, T. S. Eliot, Wallace Stevens, Walter Conrad Arensberg, Donald Evans, Mina Loy, and Yvor Winters" (Ph.D. diss., Stanford University, 1967), pp. 88–89.

16. H. D., *Collected Poems 1912–1944,* ed. Louis L. Martz (Manchester: Carcanet Press, 1984), p. 55.

17. Ezra Pound, "The Later Yeats," in *Literary Essays of Ezra Pound,* ed. T. S. Eliot (London: Faber and Faber, 1960), p. 380. Pound commends H. D.'s poem in a note to his "Vorticism" essay of 1914 by pointing to the intensity of the emotion expressed, not to the nature of that emotion. "Vorticism," he argues, "is an intensive art."

18. N. Scott Momaday, *The Gourd Dancer* (New York: Harper & Row, 1976), p. 12.

19. Robert Frost, "The Figure a Poem Makes," *Selected Prose of Robert Frost,* ed. Hyde Cox and Edward Connery Lathem (New York: Collier Books, 1968), p. 20.

20. *The Poetry of Robert Frost,* ed. Edward Connery Lathem (New York: Holt, Rinehart and Winston, 1969), p. 269.

21. *The Collected Poems of Wallace Stevens* (New York: Alfred A. Knopf, 1968), p. 59.

22. Eliot, *Selected Prose of T. S. Eliot,* p. 35.

23. D. H. Lawrence, "Verse Free and Unfree," *Voices,* 2 October 1919, pp. 130–132.

24. Heraclitus's doctrine was being updated by the philosophers who most influenced the early modernists at the turn of the century: Bergson's "real duration," James's "stream of consciousness," Bradley's "immediate experience," and Nietzsche's "chaos of sensations" are all versions of that newly glamorized realm of immediacy—a flux of sensations irreducible to rational formulation. See Sanford Schwartz's summary of this complex of fashionable ideas in the air just before World War I: *The Matrix of Modernism: Pound, Eliot, and Early Twentieth-Century Thought* (Princeton: Princeton University Press, 1985), chap. 1 and 2.

25. Yvor Winters, "The Influence of Meter on Poetic Convention" (1937), in *In Defense of Reason* (Chicago: Swallow Press, 1947), pp. 116–125.

26. Paul Fussell argues that there are "two ultimate kinds of free verse": the oracular (for example, that of Whitman, Lawrence, and Ginsberg) and the ruminative or private (that of Williams and Creeley); poems of the first kind tend to be long with unvarying line integrity; the second are short with vigorously enjambed lines (*Poetic Meter and Poetic Form,* rev. ed. [New York: Random House, 1979], pp. 80–81). My point would be that these tend to be extremes, one too public and other too private, and that more moderate tones require more precise forms.

27. William Carlos Williams, "On Measure—Statement for Cid Corman," *The William Carlos Williams Reader,* ed. M. L. Rosenthal (New York: New Directions, 1966), p. 408.

28. Allen Ginsberg, "Notes for Howl and Other Poems," in *20th-Century Poetry & Poetics,* ed. Gary Geddes, 2d ed. (Toronto: Oxford University Press, 1973), pp. 504–505.

29. For example, G. S. Fraser concedes that "Free verse runs more risks than other kinds of English verse, in that it cannot give always such clear and definite clues as regular verse about how the poet would like one to read it" (*Metre, Rhyme*

and Free Verse [London: Methuen, 1970], p. 78). Karl Shapiro and Robert Beum claim that "without the guideline of meter, one is sometimes unable to tell exactly how a certain word or syllable is to be stressed," and that free verse "invites the prosaic" (*A Prosody Handbook* [New York: Harper & Row, 1965], p. 151). Precision is at stake as such poets seek a dubious freedom and informality, ranging freely, as Derek Attridge says, in their "search for imitative [but not analytic] devices" (*The Rhythms of English Poetry* [London: Longman, 1982], p. 300).

30. Winters, *In Defense of Reason,* pp. 150, 130. I have yet to find a defense of free verse that adequately answers or matches in clarity and sound sense Winters's fifty-year-old essay.

31. Theodore Roethke, "Open Letter," in *On the Poet and His Craft*: *Selected Prose of Theodore Roethke,* ed. Ralph J. Mills, Jr. (Seattle: Universtiy of Washington Press, 1965), p. 42.

32. *The Complete Poems and Plays of T. S. Eliot* (London: Faber & Faber, 1970), p. 13. All further citations from Eliot's poetry will refer to this edition. Numbers in parentheses after citations are line numbers.

33. One of the first objections came from F. R. Leavis, in *New Bearings in English Poetry* (1932; reprint, Harmondsworth, Middlesex: Penguin, 1963), pp. 88–89.

34. Conrad Aiken, "An Anatomy of Melancholy," *New Republic* 33 (7 February 1923): 294–95.

35. J. V. Cunningham, "The 'Gyroscope' Group," *The Bookman,* November 1932, p. 707.

36. Cleanth Brooks, *Modern Poetry and the Tradition* (1939; reprint, Chapel Hill: University of North Carolina Press, 1965), pp. 167–72.

37. Pound, *Literary Essays,* p. 11.

38. Michael Schmidt, "The Politics of Form," *Poetry Nation,* no. 1 (1973): 51.

39. I have, of course, been anticipated by such critics as Donald Davie (*Thomas Hardy and British Poetry* [London: Routledge & Kegan Paul, 1973]) and, most recently, John Lucas (*Modern English Poetry from Hardy to Hughes*: *A Critical Survey* [Totowa, N. J.: Barnes & Noble, 1986]), but, as will be plain, my argument for and my definition of a "Hardy Tradition" is considerably different from theirs. Samuel Hynes set up some of the terms of my project in his 1980 essay "The Hardy Tradition in Modern English Poetry." Although he only offered an outline, our purposes are the same: "to argue a view of modern poetry that is not often considered by critics, though it is obviously true: that much modern peotry is traditional and continuous with the past, and that the apocalyptic uniqueness of modern experience has been exaggerated" (*Sewanee Review* 88 [Winter 1980]: 36).

Chapter 1. Yeats or Hardy?

1. As quoted by Kenneth Marsden, *The Poems of Thomas Hardy*: *A Critical Introduction* (London: Athlone Press, 1969), p. 1.

2. According to David Cecil, "The Hardy Mood" (1974), in *Thomas Hardy, Poems*: *A Casebook,* ed. James Gibson and Trevor Johnson (London: Macmillan, 1979), p. 232.

3. Vernon Watkins in Dylan Thomas, *Letters to Vernon Watkins,* ed. Vernon Watkins (London: Dent, 1957), p. 232.

4. As quoted by Joseph Hone, *W. B. Yeats 1865–1939* (London: Macmillan, 1942), p. 441.

5. T. S. Eliot, "The Poetry of W. B. Yeats," a lecture delivered at the Abbey Theatre, June 1940, and published in *The Southern Review* 7 (Winter 1942): 442.

6. D. S. Savage, "The Aestheticism of W. B. Yeats" (1945), in *The Permanence of Yeats,* ed. James Hall and Martin Steinmann (1950; reprint, New York: Collier Books, 1961), p. 186. I will be referring to the essays in this collection quite frequently hereafter. I firmly agree with Elizabeth Cullingford, the editor of the 1984 casebook on Yeats, who acknowledges that the 1950 collection "marks a watershed in Yeats studies. ... Hall and Steinmann gathered many of the most stimulating and provocative surveys of [Yeats's] achievement. ... Looking at this volume thirty and more years later and many specialised studies later is like returning to first principles. The writers speak of Yeats without that mixture of awe and pedantry which deadens so much later scholarship" (*Yeats, Poems, 1919–1935* [London: Macmillan, 1984], pp. 14–15).

7. Donald Davie, "Yeats, the Master of a Trade," in *The Poet in the Imaginary Museum*: *Essays of Two Decades,* ed. Barry Alpert (Manchester: Carcanet, 1977), p. 131.

8. Michael Alexander, "Hardy Among the Poets," in *Thomas Hardy After Fifty Years,* ed. Lance St. John Butler (Totowa, N.J.: Rowman and Littlefield, 1977), p. 49.

9. F. R. Leavis, *D. H. Lawrence/Novelist* (1955; reprint, Harmondsworth, Middlesex: Penguin, 1964), p. 10. The same opposition labels, of course, do not apply to the two novelists. But the opposition is just as clear; Tom Paulin is representative in calling Yeats "Hardy's opposite" (*Thomas Hardy*: *The Poetry of Perception* [Totowa, N.J.: Rowman and Littlefield, 1975], p. 10).

10. R. P. Blackmur, "The Later Poetry of W. B. Yeats," in *The Permanence of Yeats,* p. 38.

11. Marsden, *The Poems of Thomas Hardy,* p. 68.

12. Beach, in *The Permanence of Yeats,* p. 199; Larkin, "The Poetry of Hardy," in *Required Writing*: *Miscellaneous Pieces 1955–1982* (London: Faber & Faber, 1983), p. 175.

13. Davie, *Thomas Hardy and British Poetry,* p. 3. The parenthetical comment keeps this from contradicting his 1964 statement, quoted earlier.

14. Ibid., pp. 39, 43, 134–35.

15. Matt Simpson, "Proper Place," in *PN Review 12,* 1979, p. 58 (this is a review of *Thomas Hardy, Selected Poems,* ed. David Wright).

16. W. B. Yeats, *Variorum Edition of the Poems of W. B. Yeats,* ed. Peter Allt and Russell K. Alspach (New York: Macmillan, 1966), pp. 79–81. All further citations from Yeats's poems will refer to this edition. Numbers in parentheses after citations are line numbers.

17. *The Complete Poems of Thomas Hardy,* ed. James Gibson (London: Macmillan, 1976), p. 12. All further citations from Hardy's poems will refer to this edition. Numbers in parentheses after citations are line numbers.

18. Robert Langbaum, *The Poetry of Experience* (1957; reprint, Harmondsworth, Middlesex: Penguin, 1974), p. 20.

19. George Grant, *Philosophy in the Mass Age* (Vancouver, B.C.: Copp Clark, 1966), pp. iii, 92.

20. W. H. Auden, "Yeats as an Example," in *The Permanence of Yeats,* pp. 310–11.

21. Schwartz, *The Matrix of Modernism,* pp. 50, 48.

22. Richard Ellmann, *The Identity of Yeats* (1954; reprint, London: Faber and Faber, 1964), p. 43.

23. I use Yvor Winters's convenient definition from "A Forward," *In Defense of Reason,* p. 9.

24. Edmund Wilson, "W. B. Yeats" (1931), in *The Permanence of Yeats,* p. 35.

25. Yvor Winters, *Forms of Discovery* (Chicago: Swallow, 1967), p. 210; Arthur Mizener, "The Romanticism of W. B. Yeats," Stephen Spender, "Yeats as a Realist," D. S. Savage, "The Aestheticism of W. B. Yeats," Joseph Warren Beach, and W. H. Auden, all in *The Permanence of Yeats,* pp. 133–34, 169, 184, 196, 309; Harold Bloom, *Yeats* (London: Oxford University Press, 1970), pp. 212, 210.

26. See David Daiches, Cleanth Brooks, and Allen Tate in *The Permanence of Yeats,* pp. 107, 82, 100; and *A Vision,* 2d ed. (London: Macmillan, 1937), p. 8.

27. *W. B. Yeats: Selected Criticism,* ed. A. Norman Jeffares (London: Pan Books, 1976), pp. 27, 55, 98, 130; the fourth and fifth quotes provided by Hone, pp. 86, 236.

28. Ellmann, *Identity of Yeats,* p. 143.

29. John Unterecker, *A Reader's Guide to William Butler Yeats* (New York: Farrar, Straus & Giroux, 1959), p. 137.

30. Ibid., p. 253.

31. Yeats, *Selected Criticism,* p. 94.

32. In a note to "Magic" Yeats writes, "I am . . . certain that the main symbols (symbolic roots, as it were) draw upon associations which are beyond the reach of the individual 'subconsciousness'" (*Selected Criticism,* p. 91).

33. Yeats, *Selected Criticism,* p. 228.

34. Ibid., pp. 39, 102, 38, 27, 34.

35. It is not finally clear, even to those who have studied "the system,"whether the rough beast is Christ or the anti-Christ, whether Yeats finds the beast satisfying or terrifying (see Winters, *Forms of Discovery,* p. 214, and Ellmann, *The Identity of Yeats,* pp. 257–60).

36. Yeats, "A General Introduction for My Work," *Selected Criticism,* pp. 262–63. He says there, "I was born into this faith, have lived in it, and shall die in it." His famous change then (as I shall argue later) was not ideological and therefore only superficially stylistic.

37. Yeats, *Selected Criticism,* pp. 92, 72, 50, 45.

38. Ellmann, *Identity of Yeats,* p. 251.

39. Unterecker, *Reader's Guide,* p. 140.

40. Yeats, *Selected Criticism,* p.152.

41. Ibid., p. 118.

42. Ibid., pp. 99–100.

43. Hone, *Yeats,* p. 67.

44. Yeats, *Selected Criticism,* p. 234.

45. He said in about 1909, "There are only three classes I respect, the aristocracy who are above fear; the poor who are beneath it; and the artists whom God has made reckless" (quoted by Hone, *Yeats,* p. 232).

46. Yeats, *Selected Criticism,* pp. 135, 120–21, 153.

47. Quoted by Hone, *Yeats,* p. 121.

48. Yeats, *Selected Criticism,* pp. 165, 198. That his extremism is a result of his determinism is suggested also by these changing epithets: in 1891 he sounds almost like Hardy in referring to "the indifferent stars above" (in "A Dream of Death"); by 1912 he is talking about "the injustice of the skies" ("The Cold Heaven"); and by 1918 the stars have become, dramatically,"outrageous" ("In Memory of Major Robert Gregory").

49. D. S. Savage, *The Permanence of Yeats,* p. 190.

50. Dudley Young, *Out of Ireland: The Poetry of W. B. Yeats* (Cheadle, Cheshire: Carcanet, 1973), p. 55.
51. Balachandra Rajan, *W. B. Yeats,* 2d ed. (London: Hutchinson & Co., 1969), p. 149.
52. Yeats, *Selected Criticism,* pp. 218, 244.
53. Eliot and Henry James were equally unable to appreciate Hardy; see Robert Gittings, "The Improving Hand," in *Thomas Hardy After Fifty Years,* p. 43.
54. Vere H. Collins, *Talks with Thomas Hardy at Max Gate 1920–1922* (1928; reprint, London: Duckworth, 1978), p. 19.
55. Florence Emily Hardy, *The Life of Thomas Hardy 1840–1928* (London: Macmillan, 1962), p. 335.
56. Ibid., p. 428.
57. Ibid., p. 215.
58. Davie, *Thomas Hardy and British Poetry,* p. 62.
59. He thought of himself as "churchy ... in so far as instincts and emotions ruled" (Florence Hardy, *Life of Thomas Hardy,* p. 376). See also "The Oxen," "Afternoon Service at Mellstock," "The Impercipient," and "God-Forgotten."
60. *The Athenaeum* (1902), in *Thomas Hardy, Poems: A Casebook,* pp. 52–54.
61. Hardy's view of Wordsworth is a complex one. He never could share Wordsworth's pantheism, and whereas both concentrated on common subjects, Wordsworth cast a wondrous light over them while Hardy invigorated them by allowing us to see them more thoroughly (one might recall here a similar distinction between Wordsworth and Crabbe). In his twenties, Hardy could go to the Wordsworth of "Resolution and Independence" as a possible "cure for despair" (Florence Hardy, *Life of Thomas Hardy,* p. 58). Hardy could not accept Wordsworth's distinction between imagination and fancy (*Life,* p. 306). Hardy was always a polite tourist with an almost adolescent fondness for literary shrines (for example, the graves of Shelley and Keats in Rome and Gibbon's garden in Lausanne); in July 1873, he visited Tintern Abbey. But his response is significantly different from Wordsworth's: Wordsworth's concern is with his own development, while Hardy contemplates the age of the hills compared with that of the building (*Life,* pp. 93–94).
62. *The Complete Poems of Thomas Hardy,* p. 557.
63. Florence Hardy, *Life of Thomas Hardy,* p. 406.
64. Ibid., p. 311.
65. Ibid., p. 383.
66. Jon Silkin, "Introduction," *The Penguin Book of First World War Poetry* (Harmondsworth, Middlesex: Penguin, 1979), p. 14.
67. Howard Baker, "Hardy's Poetic Certitude," in *Thomas Hardy, Poems: A Casebook,* p. 139.
68. Irving Howe, *Thomas Hardy* (London: Weidenfeld and Nicolson, 1968), p. 164.
69. R. W. King, "The Lyrical Poems of Thomas Hardy," in *Thomas Hardy, Poems: A Casebook,* p. 107.
70. "Hardy and the Ballads," *Agenda* 10 (Spring-Summer 1972): 19–46.
71. Ibid., p. 44.
72. Hardy, "Apology" to *Late Lyrics and Earlier,* in *Complete Poems,* p. 560.
73. Florence Hardy, *Life of Thomas Hardy,* p. 363.
74. Winters, *Forms of Discovery,* p. 192.
75. Davie, *Thomas Hardy and British Poetry,* p. 26.

Chapter 2. Edward Thomas and the Georgians

1. Robert Ross, *The Georgian Revolt 1910–1922: Rise and Fall of a Poetic Ideal* (Carbondale: Southern Illinois University Press, 1965), p. 189. No one now surveying this period can avoid the important contribution of Ross's primarily historic study. I acknowledge my great debt and add that I will be proposing more evaluative conclusions than he does.
2. Harold Munro, "The Future of Poetry," *The Poetry Review*, no. 1 (January 1912): 10–12.
3. John Drinkwater, "Tradition and Technique," *The Poetry Review*, no. 7 (July 1912): 296–300.
4. Harriet Monroe, "Editorial Comment: Tradition," *Poetry: A Magazine of Verse* 2 (May 1913): 67–70.
5. "The Serious Artist," reprinted in *Literary Essays of Ezra Pound*, ed. T. S. Eliot, pp. 41–57.
6. Ford Madox Hueffer, "Impressionism—Some Speculations," *Poetry: A Magazine of Verse* 2 (August 1913): 185.
7. Harold Monro, "Futurism," *Poetry and Drama,* September 1913, p. 262.
8. Alan Pryce-Jones, "The Georgian Poets" (1948), in *Georgian Poetry 1911–1922: The Critical Heritage,* ed. Timothy Rogers (London: Routledge & Kegan Paul, 1977), p. 359.
9. T. S. Eliot, "Reflections on Contemporary Poetry," *The Egoist,* September 1917, pp. 118–19; "Verse Pleasant and Unpleasant," *The Egoist,* March 1918, pp. 43–44.
10. Eliot, "Reflections on Contemporary Poetry," p. 119.
11. Eliot, "Verse Pleasant and Unpleasant," p. 44.
12. Ross, *Georgian Revolt,* p. 160.
13. Pp. 1283–85. Reprinted as "The Present Condition of English Poetry," in Murry's *Aspects of Literature* (London: W. Collins, 1920), pp. 139–149.
14. Ross, *Georgian Revolt,* p. 210.
15. Murry, *Aspects of Literature,* p. 141.
16. Nine years later Roy Campbell was more belligerent in making a similar point: in the midst of a list of obviously negative if overstated characteristics of Georgian verse ("their conversation with dogs," "their fellow-feeling for cows, sheep, dogs, and rabbits") he places this: "their bland approvals of virtue, restraint, and intellectual dignity" (quoted by Rogers, *The Critical Heritage,* p. 38). One suspects that the blandness is not the only reason for his antagonism.
17. Murry, *Aspects of Literature,* p. 149.
18. *TLS,* 27 February 1913, p. 81.
19. This and subsequent citations from the series are taken from *Georgian Poetry 1911–1912* and *Georgian Poetry 1913–1915,* published by The Poetry Bookshop in 1912 and 1915, respectively. They will be referred to as I or II followed by page numbers after each quoted passage.
20. *TLS,* 9 December 1915, p. 447.
21. Ross, *Georgian Revolt,* p. 21.
22. Edward Thomas, "Georgian Poets," *The Daily Chronicle,* 14 January 1913, p. 4.
23. Walter de la Mare, "An Elizabethan Poet and Modern Poetry," *The Edinburgh Review,* April 1913, as quoted in *The Critical Heritage,* p. 109.
24. *The Spectator,* 5 February 1916, p. 191.

25. Morse Peckham, "Toward a Theory of Romanticism" (1951), in *Romanticism: Points of View,* ed. Robert F. Gleckner and Gerald E. Enscoe, 2d ed. (Englewood Cliffs, N.J.: Prentice-Hall, 1970), p. 246.

26. Theresa Ashton, "Edward Thomas: From Prose to Poetry," *The Poetry Review* 28 (1937): 452.

27. Ralph Lawrence, "Edward Thomas in Perspective," *English* 12 (Summer 1959): 178–180.

28. Hugh Underhill, "The 'Poetical Character' of Edward Thomas," *Essays in Criticism* 23 (July 1973): 236–253; Maire Quinn, "The Personal Past in the Poetry of Thomas Hardy and Edward Thomas," *Critical Quarterly* 16 (Spring 1974): 7–28.

29. All citations from Thomas's poems are from *The Collected Poems of Edward Thomas,* ed. R. George Thomas (Oxford: Clarendon Press, 1978). Numbers in parentheses after citations are line numbers.

30. Leavis, *New Bearings in English Poetry,* pp. 52–53, 61–64.

31. H. Coombes, *Edward Thomas* (London: Chatto & Windus, 1956), pp. 199–200; William Cooke, *Edward Thomas: A Critical Biography 1878–1917* (London: Faber & Faber, 1970), pp. 190, 199; John Danby, "Edward Thomas," *The Critical Quarterly* 1 (Winter 1959): 308–317; Roland Mathias, "Edward Thomas," *The Anglo-Welsh Review* 10 (1960): 23–37; J. P. Ward, "The Solitary Note: Edward Thomas and Modernism," *Poetry Wales* 13 (Spring 1978): 71–84; Jan Marsh, *Edward Thomas: A Poet for His Country* (London: Paul Elek, 1978), 82; W. J. Keith, *The Poetry of Nature* (Toronto: Toronto University Press, 1980), p. 157.

32. Michael Kirkham, *The Imagination of Edward Thomas* (Cambridge: Cambridge University Press, 1986), esp. pp. v, 65. At one point Kirkham transfers his conclusion about Thomas's sensibility and poetic method into a general proposition about our critical reading: "Of course, where poetry is concerned there is no such thing as certainty of interpretation" (p. 200). Fortunately Kirkham, like all serious readers, cannot proceed if that proposition excludes the possibility of a distinction between certainty and stabilized conjecture. He presents his own readings with conviction and pays respectful attention to the readings of others; if he does not believe that certainty is possible, he certainly gives one the impression that he believes that progress toward less uncertainty is possible.

33. Ibid., pp. 187, 188.

34. R. George Thomas, *Edward Thomas: A Portrait* (Oxford: Oxford University Press, 1985), p. 305.

35. Quoted by R. George Thomas, *Edward Thomas,* pp. 302, 306, 309.

36. Cooke, *Edward Thomas,* p. 199.

37. Edna Longley, "Edward Thomas and the 'English' Line," *The New Review* 1 (February 1975): 9; Keith, *Poetry of Nature, p. 157;* Andrew Motion, *The Poetry of Edward Thomas* (London: Routledge & Kegan Paul, 1980), p. 76. Motion, it should be mentioned, does recognize the sense of public responsibility in Thomas's poetry; in the introduction to his book he quotes an important passage from Thomas's prose as central to his poetic credo, and it has to do with a poet's obligation to be rationally and publicly available. Motion quotes it after calling attention to Thomas's criticism of Pound's "adventurous subversions" in *Exultations:* "a poem of the old kind has a simple fundamental meaning which every sane reader can agree upon; above and beyond this each one builds as he can or must. In the new there is no basis of this kind; a poem means nothing unless its whole meaning has been grasped" (p. 3). In May 1914, Thomas wrote to Bottomley, "what imbeciles the Imagistes are" (*Letters from Edward Thomas to Gordon

Bottomley, ed. R. George Thomas [London: Oxford University Press, 1968], p. 233).

38. Notes to *Collected Poems*, p. 169.

39. Cooke, *Edward Thomas*, p. 235.

40. Although Thomas's fascination with roads and paths often has been noted by critics, none, I think, has linked it with Hardy's similar interest. Thomas himself recognized it in Hardy; in *A Literary Pilgrim in England* he says, "Mr. Hardy's feeling for roads is a good thing to come across in poem or novel. In 'The Mayor of Casterbridge,' the exiled Henchard chooses to work on the 'old western highway,' the artery of Wessex, because, 'though at a distance of fifty miles, he was virtually nearer to her whose welfare was so dear than he would be at a roadless spot only half as remote'" ([1917; reprint, London: Jonathan Cape, 1928], p. 146).

41. "Mr. Hardy must have discovered the blindness of fate, the indifference of nature, and the irony of life, before he met them in books." Thomas goes on in that same review to suggest that this "superstition," as he calls it, while unfortunate, is indicative of Hardy's extreme seriousness ("Thomas Hardy of Dorchester," *Poetry and Drama*, June 1913, pp. 180–83). I wonder if as much can be said of Eliot's early Laforgian imitations.

42. Jeremy Hooker, "The Writings of Edward Thomas: II. The Sad Passion," *The Anglo-Welsh Review* 29 (Autumn 1970): 76.

43. Quinn, "The Personal Past," p. 25.

44. Quoted by Edna Longley, "Edward Thomas and the 'English' Line," p. 7.

45. Helen Thomas, *As It Was* and *World Without End* (London: Faber & Faber, 1972), pp. 52, 114, 59. See also p. 51: he "was much more influenced by the old than the new."

46. Thomas's concern with clarity is fastidious. Usually he will in Renaissance fashion structurally distinguish the perception from the conception (for example, "After You Speak") and use more similes than metaphors, or occasionally allow the image to carry the thought implicitly, in clear, simple, and unobtrusive symbols (as in "The New Year," "Cock-Crow," "The Green Roads," and "The Path"). Thomas, of course, has none of Hardy's range and variety of forms (but his range is nonetheless extensive—see chapter 8 of Kirkham's *The Imagination of Edward Thomas*, perhaps the best chapter in the book). He uses blank verse much more often and both these and his stanzaic lines are liberally, but rarely loosely, enjambed. His control of short lines (dimeter and trimeter) in serious lyrics is unusual, I think, in his decade, and his non-narrative use of the tetrameter quatrain follows and is comparable to Hardy's experiments with the ballad. The result is in most cases a general sense of combined ease and formality, security and care, intimacy and prudence.

47. Herbert Palmer, *Post-Victorian Poetry* (London: J. M. Dent, 1938), pp. 196–97.

Chapter 3. Poets of the First World War

1. *Out of Battle* (Oxford: Oxford University Press, 1972), pp. 32–55; *The Great War and Modern Memory* (Oxford: Oxford University Press, 1975), pp. 3–8.

2. Another 1972 book on war poetry with this very title, *An Adequate Response* (Detroit: Wayne State University Press, 1972), argues that because the war itself "defied the traditional categories," literary, moral, as well as military, the only adequate response was that offered by Owen and Sassoon—what the author, Arthur

E. Lane, borrowing Robert Langbaum's phrase (and argument), calls "the poetry of experience": immediate, concrete, usually non-metaphoric, pictorial records of life and death in the trenches, which eschewed general truths and abstract ideas. Attempting to defend Owen and Sassoon against those (such as John H. Johnston [*English Poetry of the First World War*, 1964]) who charge them with lacking epic scope, Lane argues that the reality of this war demanded this particular kind of realistic poetry of protest. Lane and Johnston both represent inadequately narrow (if opposite) approaches: there is an alternative to realistic protest on the one hand and epic grandeur on the other. But it only will be recognized if we stop blinkering ourselves with the lyric vs. epic contraries of Johnston and the experiential vs. meditative contraries of Lane, and if our criticism reaches beyond literary categories to larger, more relevant ethical categories.

3. Robert Graves in *Goodbye to All That* records a meeting with Hardy just a few years after the war that offers a penetrating portrait of the essential Hardy and the commonsensical, wide, and vital traditionalism that informs the older man's poetry and to some extent guided the work of the much younger Graves. Hardy in conversation emphasizes his commitment to the virtues of duty and loyalty, and of his high regard for traditionally heroic poems, especially Homer's *Iliad* and Scott's *Marmion*; but his is not a nostalgic myopia or a blind conservatism. For instance, Hardy describes his war work as chairman of the Anti-Profiteering Committee, proud of his success in bringing "a number of rascally Dorchester tradesmen to book. 'It made me unpopular, of course,' he admitted, 'but it was a hundred times better than sitting on a Military Tribunal and sending young men to the war who did not want to go.'" It was during this visit that Hardy also told Graves that "in his opinion *vers libre* could come to nothing in England. 'All we can do is to write on the old themes in the old styles, but try to do a little better than those who went before us.'" (*Goodbye to All That*, rev. ed. [1957; reprint, Harmondsworth, Middlesex: Penguin, 1965], pp. 248–51.)

4. Silkin, *Out of Battle*, pp. 44–51, 53.

5. Hardy was aware of these weaknesses. He wrote to Arthur Symons on 13 September, four days after the poem was first published in *The Times*: "I fear [these lines] were not free from some banalities which it is difficult to keep out of lines which are meant to appeal to the man in the street, and not to 'a few friends' only" (J. O. Bailey, *The Poems of Thomas Hardy: A Handbook and Commentary* [Chapel Hill: University of North Carolina Press, 1970], p. 417).

6. *The Letters of Charles Sorley* (Cambridge: Cambridge University Press, 1919), p. 246.

7. See Plato's *Gorgias*, 473–75.

8. Silkin, *Out of Battle*, p. 54.

9. Ford's "That Exploit of Yours" and Flint's "Lament" are reprinted in Silkin's *Penguin Book of First World War Poetry*, pp. 141–42.

10. Bernard Bergonzi, *Heroes' Twilight* (London: Constable, 1965), pp. 11–19.

11. Fussell, *Great War and Modern Memory*, pp. 21, 25.

12. J. M. Gregson, *Poetry of the First World War* (London: Edward Arnold, 1976), pp. 17–18. Other examples could be cited. Leona Whitworth Logue, in one of the earliest studies of the war poets, in 1928, began with the assertion that "Among modern war poets, the lyric has conformed more and more to the complexities, the doubts, and the experimentation of our intricate modern life" (*Recent War Lyrics: A Study of War Concepts in Modern Verse* [1928; reprint, New York: Grafton Press, 1976], p. 9). Even the otherwise sensible C. H. Sisson criticizes Owen because he failed to realize that "the new material, if it could be presented

at all, needed a profound linguistic invention" (*English Poetry 1900–1950: An Assessment* [New York: St. Martin's Press, 1971], p. 84).

13. Dominic Hibberd tells us that Wilfred Owen "invented" pararhyme not for war poems but for erotic songs in the Decadent style (*Owen the Poet* [Athens: University of Georgia Press, 1986], p. 90).

14. *The Complete Works of George Gascoigne,* ed. John W. Cunliffe, 2 vols. (Cambridge: Cambridge University Press, 1907–10).

15. The *TLS* reviewer of Fussell's book makes a similar point: the obscenity in Mailer and other writers on war is not as necessary as Fussell seems to think it is; there is still human dignity "which the old literary tradition enabled those who were brought up in it to understand and to express" (*TLS,* 5 December 1975, p. 1435).

16. *South Atlantic Quarterly* 50 (January 1951): 86–95; the essay is reprinted under the title "Prince Hal, His Struggle Toward Moral Perfection," in the Norton critical edition of *Henry the Fourth, Part I,* 2d ed. (New York: W. W. Norton, 1969), pp. 245–55. The following quote from act V, scene i, of the play is also taken from this edition.

17. Shakespeare, of course, complicates matters by adding political expediency to Hal's motives.

18. Aristotle, *The Nicomachean Ethics,* trans. David Ross (Oxford: Oxford University Press, 1980), pp. 63–72 (book III, chap 6–9).

19. Occasionally there are subdivisions suggested: Silkin subdivides the second period into three parts: the protest of Sassoon, the compassion of Owen, and the combined protest, compassion, and intelligence of Rosenberg; Gregson sees an early phase of protest in the verse of Sorley; Bergonzi detects two different responses to the realities of the post-Somme period, the traditionalists who "evaded" the conditions of the Front by re-calling images of rural England (such as Blunden and Gurney), and the deliberate, uncompromising realists (such as Sassoon, Owen, and Rosenberg)—he regards Graves as a transitional figure between these two groups.

20. As we approach such public verse we should be careful neither to overvalue nor to undervalue a poet's potential contribution in time of war. "In the stress of a nation's peril," proclaims an anonymous editor of the first of the many anthologies published in the early months of the war, "some of its greatest songs are born" (as quoted by Dominic Hibberd, ed. *Poetry of the First World War,* Casebook series [London: Macmillan, 1981], p. 31). This response is just as inadequate as that of Yeats (poets "have no gift to set a statesman right"). Statesmen do not need emotional yes-men, but they should listen to clearer and fuller definitions of moral life than those offered by journalists, economic planners, and military strategists.

21. *The Collected Poems of Rupert Brooke* (New York: Dodd, Mead, & Co., 1943), p. 86.

22. *The Penguin Book of First World War Poetry,* pp. 79–80.

23. *The Poems and Selected Letters of Charles Hamilton Sorley,* ed. Hilda D. Spear (Dundee, Scotland: Blackness Press, 1978), 71. All further citations from Sorley's poems will refer to this edition. Numbers in parentheses after citations are line numbers.

24. John Press, "Charles Sorley," *Review of English Literature* 7 (April 1966); reprinted in Hibberd's Casebook, p. 209.

25. Silkin, *Out of Battle,* pp. 78–79.

26. Quoted by John Lehmann, in *The English Poets of the First World War* (London: Thames and Hudson, 1981), p. 65. Not included in Grave's *Collected Poems.*

27. *The Letters of Charles Sorley,* p. 263.
28. Nichols, ed., *Anthology of War Poetry, 1914-1918* (London: Nicholson and Watson, 1943), p. 36.
29. Bergonzi, *Heroes' Twilight,* p. 67.
30. Graves, *Goodbye to All That,* p. 157.
31. Ibid., p. 205.
32. Ibid., p. 226.
33. Siegfried Sassoon, *Collected Poems 1908-1956* (London: Faber & Faber, 1961), p. 22. All further citations from Sassoon's poems will refer to this edition. Numbers in parentheses after citations are line numbers.
34. Silkin, *Out of Battle,* 155.
35. Bergonzi, *Heroes' Twilight,* p. 106.
36. Siegfried Sassoon, *Memoirs of an Infantry Officer,* in *The Complete Memoirs of George Sherston* (1937; reprint, London: Faber & Faber, 1980), p. 357.
37. See Sydney Bolt, *Poetry of the 1920s* (London: Longman, 1973), p. 61.
38. Wilfred Owen, *The Complete Poems and Fragments,* ed. Jon Stallworthy, 2 vols. (London: Chatto & Windus, 1983), I, p. 144.
39. Sisson, *English Poetry 1900-1950,* p. 85.
40. D. S. R. Welland, *Wilfred Owen: A Critical Study* (London: Chatto & Windus, 1960), p. 47; Fussell, *The Great War and Modern Memory,* p. 291; Silkin, "Introduction," *The Penguin Book of First World War Poetry,* p. 27.
41. *Wilfred Owen: War Poems and Others,* ed. Dominic Hibberd (London: Chatto & Windus, 1973), p. 68.
42. *Collected Poems of Ivor Gurney,* ed. P. J. Kavanagh (Oxford: Oxford University Press, 1982), 41. Unless otherwise indicated, all further citations from Gurney's poems will refer to this edition. Numbers in parentheses after citations are line numbers.
43. "Appendix A: Owen's Preface," *The Complete Poems,* II, p. 535.
44. Silkin, "Introduction," *Penguin Book of First World War Poetry,* p. 44.
45. Welland, *Wilfred Owen,* p. 92.
46. Hibberd, "Introduction," *Wilfred Owen: War Poems and Others,* p. 42.
47. Silkin, *Out of Battle,* pp. 204-206.
48. Hibberd, *Wilfred Owen: War Poems and Others,* p. 37. John H. Johnston is close: the poem "seems to be an effort to reconcile the disparity between the unredeemable evil of war and the positives inherent in Christian doctrine" (*English Poetry of the First World War,* p. 173).
49. Silkin, *Out of Battle,* p. 247.
50. That Owen is very much a Romantic poet is persuasively argued by Hibberd in his 1986 study of Owen's "poethood," *Owen the Poet.* It will be very difficult after this book to repeat the standard line that from 1916 Owen tried to get rid of the Romantic elements in his poetry and under the pressure of his war experience turned himself into a "modern" poet.
51. *The Collected Works of Isaac Rosenberg,* ed. Ian Parsons (London: Chatto & Windus, 1979), p. 183.
52. Rosenberg, *Collected Wroks,* p. 291.
53. D. W. Harding, "Aspects of the Poetry of Isaac Rosenberg," in *Experience into Words* (1963; reprint, Harmondsworth, Middlesex: Penguin, 1974), p. 93. The essay was first published in *Scrutiny* in 1935.
54. Rosenberg, *Collected Works,* p. 248.
55. Ibid., p. 227.
56. Jean Liddiard, *Isaac Rosenberg: The Half Used Life* (London: Victor Gollancz, 1975), p. 176.

57. Harding, *Experience into Words,* p. 96.

58. Silkin's attempt to save these lines is, I think, rather forced: "Rosenberg is saying perhaps that when you are fighting, the enemy will always seem brutish, and that you will not notice your own behaviour. If this seems viable then the poet is re-creating, not immediate judgments, but the *responses* which he felt he and others made to the enemy's attack" (*Out of Battle,* p. 282). If this was Rosenberg's intention, he had not adequately prepared the reader for such dramatic immediacy, especially coming as it does after the heavy-handed and calculated similes of lines 3–4.

59. Fortunately Rosenberg deleted from his final version a very confused seven-line stanza (beginning "Maniac Earth! howling and flying") after line 47; unfortunately it has been kept by many anthologists. See Ian Parsons's note, *Collected Works,* pp. 111–12.

60. Liddiard, *Isaac Rosenberg,* p. 250.

61. Silkin, *Out of Battle,* pp. 83–84.

62. Bergonzi, *Heroes' Twilight,* pp. 72, 68, 88, 91.

63. Michael Thorpe, *The Poetry of Edmund Blunden* (London: Bridge Books, 1971), p. 14.

64. Edmund Blunden, "A Supplement of Poetical Interpretations and Variations," in *Undertones of War,* 3rd ed. (1928; reprint, Harmondsworth, Middlesex: Penguin, 1982), pp. 245–80. All citations from Blunden's poems, unless otherwise indicated, will refer to this edition. Numbers in parentheses after citations are line numbers.

65. Neither this poem nor "The Recovery" is included in *Undertones of War.* See Edmund Blunden, *Selected Poems,* ed. Robyn Marsack (Manchester: Carcanet New Press, 1982).

66. Blunden's introduction is reprinted in Leonard Clark's edition, *Poems of Ivor Gurney 1890–1937* (London: Chatto & Windus, 1973), pp. 15–26.

67. The excerpts in this paragraph are from *Ivor Gurney War Letters,* ed. R. K. R. Thornton (Manchester: Carcanet New Press, 1983), pp. 26–27, 32, 76, 178.

68. Ivor Gurney, *Severn and Somme* (London: Sidgwick & Jackson, 1917), p. 15. ("The Fire Kindled" and "The Strong Thing" are not reprinted in Kavanagh's edition of the *Collected Poems.*)

69. P. J. Kavanagh says that Gurney is "the master of first lines," and adds later as an afterthought, "He is also capable of magnificent, poem-saving, last lines" ("Introduction," *Collected Poems of Ivor Gurney,* pp. 13–14).

70. Michael Hurd, *The Ordeal of Ivor Gurney* (Oxford: Oxford University Press, 1978), p. 112; Thornton is closer, I think, in recognizing Gurney's love for his fellow soldiers "as a strong innocent admiration, love and respect for the calm strength, wholeness and nobility of his comrades" ("Introduction," *War Letters,* p. 13).

71. Quoted by Hurd, *The Ordeal of Ivor Gurney,* pp. 58–59.

72. Ibid., pp. 55–56.

73. Ibid., p. 109.

74. Donald Davie quite correctly emphasizes these lines: "nothing more clearly marks off Gurney in his generation. Many of that generation vowed themselves, as Gurney did, to the great Elizabethans and Jacobeans, but no one else gave pride of place to the most *laborious* of those masters. Gurney sets no store at all by 'spontaneity', except as an effect, an illusion achieved by great labour" ("Gurney's Flood," *London Review of Books,* 3–16 February 1983, p. 6; this is a review of Kavanagh's edition of Gurney's poems).

75. Hurd, *The Ordeal of Ivor Gurney,* p. 112.

76. Clark, "Bibliographical Note," *Poems of Ivor Gurney,* p. 31.
77. Quoted by Blunden in his introduction, *Poems of Ivor Gurney,* p. 25.
78. Edmund Blunden, *Thomas Hardy* (New York: St. Martin's Press, 1967), p. 277.
79. Hurd, *The Ordeal of Ivor Gurney,* p. 203.

Chapter 4. Modern Love

1. Geoffrey Grigson, ed. *The Faber Book of Love Poems* (London: Faber & Faber, 1973), p. 14.
2. James McFarlane, "The Mind of Modernism," in *Modernism,* ed. Malcolm Bradbury and James McFarlane (Harmondsworth, Middlesex: Penguin, 1976), pp. 71–82.
3. I. A. Richards, "A Background for Contemporary Poetry," in *Twentieth Century Poetry: Critical Essays and Documents,* ed. Graham Martin and P. N. Furbank (Milton Keynes, Buckinghamshire: The Open University Press, 1975), p. 145.
4. William Pritchard, *Seeing Through Everything: English Writers 1918–1940* (New York: Oxford University Press, 1977), p. 116.
5. Jon Stallworthy, ed., *The Penguin Book of Love Poetry* (London: Allen Lane, 1973), p. 26.
6. Robert Graves and Alan Hodge, *The Long Weekend* (1940; reprint, New York: W. W. Norton, 1963), pp. 101–103.
7. Ibid., p. 124.
8. F. R. Leavis, *D. H. Lawrence/Novelist,* pp. 103, 106.
9. Ibid., p. 107.
10. D. H. Lawrence, *The Rainbow* (Harmondsworth, Middlesex: Penguin, 1973), p. 133. All further citations from this novel will refer to this edition.
11. I do not mean to imply that Lawrence is simply overturning the conventional symbolic equation, characterizing "men" as one thing and "women" as another. The concreteness of his language will not allow this: these are, we cannot forget, the Brangwen men and women, "on the Marsh Farm, in the meadows where the Erewash twisted sluggishly through alder trees, separating Derbyshire from Nottinghamshire" (p. 7). But the details still carry the sense of alternative and (only potentially) complementary casts of mind, or of soul.
12. John Baxter, "The Province of the Plain Style," *The Compass,* no. 3 (April 1978): 25.
13. Ibid., p. 27.
14. Ian Robinson, *The Survival of English* (London: Cambridge University Press, 1973), p. 189.
15. Michel Foucault, *The History of Sexuality,* vol. I, trans. Robert Hurley (New York: Random House, 1980), p. 106.
16. Roland Barthes, *Roland Barthes,* trans. Richard Howard (New York: Hill and Wang, 1977), pp. 85–86, 133.
17. This is the judgment of C. Q. Drummond, with which I concur, in the last of a series of four essays in *The Compass,* entitled "An Anti-Miltonist Reprise," no. 5 (Winter 1979): 17–38. I am much indebted to Professor Drummond for recalling my attention to these passages. Much of what I say here is based on his and A. J. A. Waldock's reading of them (*Paradise Lost and Its Critics* [1947; reprint, London: Cambridge University Press, 1964], esp. chap. II and III).

18. John Milton, *Paradise Lost,* ed. Merritt Y. Hughes (New York: Odyssey Press, 1962), p. 227.
19. Waldock, *Paradise Lost and Its Critics,* p. 46.
20. Drummond, "An Anti-Miltonist Reprise," p. 20.
21. Ibid., p. 31.
22. This and most of the examples that follow I take from Stallworthy's *Penguin Book of Love Poetry.* The exceptions are Herbert Read's "Ritz: Love Among the Ruins" (*Collecterd Poems* [London: Faber & Faber, 1966], p. 91) and W. H. Auden's "In Memory of Sigmund Freud" (*Selected Poems,* ed. Edward Mendelson [New York: Vintage Books, 1979], pp. 80–83).
23. C. S. Lewis, *The Four Loves* (1960; reprint, London: Fontana, 1963), p. 90.
24. Ibid., p. 14.
25. Robinson, *Survival of English,* p. 197.
26. Lewis, *Four Loves,* pp. 94–95.
27. George Williamson, *A Reader's Guide to T.S. Eliot* (London: Thames and Hudson, 1967), p. 75.
28. George Grant, "Faith and the Multiversity," *The Compass,* no. 4 (Autumn 1978): 3–4.
29. All citations from Bridges's poems are from *Bridges*: *Poetical Works,* 2d ed. (London: Oxford University Press, 1971). Numbers in parentheses after citations are line numbers.
30. Donald Stanford, *In the Classic Mode*: *The Achievement of Robert Bridges* (Newark: University of Delaware Press, 1978), p. 10. See especially sonnet 4 for more obvious proof of that enthusiasm. Occasional imitations of Shelley's diction seriously damage Bridges's work.
31. All citations from *Modern Love* are from *The Poems of George Meredith,* ed. Phyllis B. Bartlett (New Haven: Yale University Press, 1978), vol. I. Numbers in parentheses after citations are line numbers.
32. Quoted by John Sparrow, ed., *Robert Bridges*: *Poetry and Prose* (Oxford: Clarendon Press, 1955), p. xxxii.
33. Lewis, *Four Loves,* pp. 111–12.
34. Edward Thompson, *Robert Bridges 1844–1930* (Oxford: Oxford University Press, 1944), p. 26.
35. Leavis, *New Bearings in English Poetry*, p. 25.
36. Walter de la Mare, quoted by Sparrow, ed., *Robert Bridges,* p. xxxviii.
37. Coventry Patmore, quoted by Sparrow, p. xxiv.
38. For instance, V. de S. Pinto in *Crisis in English Poetry 1880–1940*, p. 72; and David Perkins in *A History of Modern Poetry*: *From the 1890's to Pound, Eliot, & Yeats* (Cambridge: Harvard University Press, 1976), p. 172.
39. W. B. Yeats, *Selected Criticism,* p. 221.
40. Stanford, *Classic Mode,* p. 10.
41. Ibid., p. 36; Albert Guerard, Jr., *Robert Bridges*: *A Study of Traditionalism in Poetry* (1942; reprint, New York: Russell & Russell, 1965), p. 73.
42. Stanford, *Classic Mode,* p. 29.
43. Robert Beum, "Profundity Revisited: Bridges and His Critics," *Dalhousie Review* 44 (Summer 1964): 178.
44. Ibid., p. 175.
45. I also am tempted to suggest (but I realize it is a bit far-fetched) that the allusion also may carry the reference to the famous fall of Pheidias, the charges of embezzlement and impiety brought against him by the enemies of his patron, Pericles. The last charge is especially relevant to Bridges's portrayal of Eros.

Pheidias supposedly introduced his own likeness and that of Pericles into his depiction of the battle of the Amazons, on the shield of Athena. Likewise mankind exalts physical love into an idol, or gives undue reverence to a minor god. One might counter that the charge of fraud is not relevant, because in line 16 we are told that Eros is without guile, but the worshipper—Bridges's real target throughout the poem—can be said to be a self-deceiver, appropriating his own body, that which is only entrusted to his care, to his own pleasurable use.

46. Beum, "Profundity Revisited," p. 176.
47. *Nicomachean Ethics,* VIII, p. 8.
48. "A Bit about Lawrence," in *D. H. Lawrence: A Critical Anthology,* ed. H. Coombes (Harmondsworth, Middlesex: Penguin, 1973), p. 312.
49. "The Englishness of the English Novel," *Collected Essays, Volume I,* ed. G. Singh (Cambridge: Cambridge University Press, 1983), pp. 304, 317, 314, 307.
50. Ibid., p. 315.
51. Quoted in *D. H. Lawrence: The Critical Heritage,* ed. R. P. Draper (New York: Barnes & Noble, 1970), p. 345.
52. *D. H. Lawrence: Selected Literary Criticism,* ed. Anthony Beal (New York: Viking Press, 1966), pp. 83–84.
53. Ibid., 90.
54. D. H. Lawrence, *Sons and Lovers* (New York: Viking Press, 1961), 404. All further citations from this volume will refer to this edition and will appear as parenthetical page numbers.
55. All citations from the poems are taken from *The Complete Poems of D. H. Lawrence,* ed. Vivian de Sola Pinto and Warren Roberts (Harmondsworth: Penguin, 1977). Numbers in parentheses after citations are line numbers.
56. Lawrence, "Poetry of the Present," in *Complete Poems,* p. 183.
57. Ibid., p. 191.
58. *The Collected Poems of D. H. Lawrence* (London: Martin Secker, 1928). The sixteen poems are, in the order they appear in this volume (and are reproduced in the *Complete Poems*): "Suspense" ("Patience" in *Amores*), "Endless Anxiety" ("Anxiety" in *Amores*), "The End," "The Bride," "The Virgin Mother," "At the Window," "Reminder," "Drunk," "Sorrow," "Dolour of Autumn," "The Inheritance," "Silence," "Listening," "Brooding Grief," "Troth with the Dead," and "Submergence." There are a few poems intermingled with these that could, but only very generally, refer to his grief: "Malade," "At a Loose End," and "The Enkindled Spring."
59. Harry T. Moore, *The Intelligent Heart: The Story of D. H. Lawrence* (1955; reprint, Harmondsworth, Middlesex: Penguin, 1960), p. 138.
60. Graham Hough, *The Dark Sun* (New York: Farrar, Straus and Giroux, 1973), p. 196.
61. Lawrence, "Preface to *Collected Poems* [1928]," in *The Complete Poems,* p. 27.
62. Ibid., p. 28.
63. R. P. Blackmur, "D. H. Lawrence and Expressive Form," in *Language As Gesture* (New York: Harcourt, Brace and Co., 1952), pp. 299–300.
64. *Nation,* 14 November 1914, in *D. H. Lawrence: The Critical Heritage,* p. 56.
65. *Phoenix, the Posthumous Papers of D. H. Lawrence,* ed. Edward D. McDonald (London: William Heinemann. 1936), p. 611.
66. Quoted by Coombes, ed., *Lawrence: A Critical Anthology,* p. 298.
67. D. H. Lawrence, "Sex versus Loveliness," in *Sex, Literature, and Censorship,* ed. Harry T. Moore (New York: Viking Press, 1959), p. 53.

68. Tom Marshall, *The Psychic Mariner: A Reading of the Poems of D. H. Lawrence* (New York: Viking Press, 1970), p. 49.
69. Sandra Gilbert, *Acts of Attention: The Poems of D. H. Lawrence* (Ithaca: Cornell University Press, 1972), p. 63.
70. Martin Seymour-Smith, *Robert Graves: His Life and Work* (London: Sphere Books, 1983), p. 83.
71. Robert Graves, "These Be Your Gods, O Israel!" (1954), in *On Poetry: Collected Talks and Essays* (New York: Doubleday, 1969), p. 151.
72. Sisson, *English Poetry 1900–1950,* p. 188.
73. Susan Musgrave, "A Memory of Robert Graves," *The Malahat Review,* July 1975, p. 12.
74. Seymour-Smith, *Robert Graves,* p. 355.
75. Some readers go even further. In the special Graves issue of *Shenandoah,* Winter 1962, for instance, G. S. Fraser concluded that Graves "is one of the few really good love poets in the English language" ("The Reputation of Robert Graves," p. 31), and W. H. Auden asserted that "on the subject of love, no poet in our time has written more or better" ("A Poet of Honor," p. 7). By 1969, John Press could without hesitation call Graves "a master of love poetry" (*A Map of Modern English Verse* [Oxford: Oxford University Press, 1969], p. 172).
76. Ronald Gaskell, "The Poetry of Robert Graves," *The Critical Quarterly* 3 (Autumn 1961): 215. Gaskell never mentions the 1938–45 collection.
77. Michael Kirkham, *The Poetry of Robert Graves* (London: The Athlone Press, 1969), p. 10; George Stade, *Robert Graves* (New York: Columbia University Press, 1967), p. 32.
78. J. M. Cohen, *Robert Graves* (New York: Grove Press, 1960), chap. 5; W. H. Auden, "A Poet of Honor," *Shenandoah* 13 (Winter 1962): 7; Douglas Day, *Swifter Than Reason: The Poetry and Criticism of Robert Graves* (Chapel Hill: University of North Carolina Press, 1963), chap. 10; James Mehoke, *Robert Graves: Peace-Weaver* (The Hague: Mouton, 1975), pp. 132–33; Katherine Snipes, *Robert Graves* (New York: Frederick Ungar, 1979), p. 42.
79. Cohen, *Graves,* p. 116.
80. Robert Graves, "The Poetic Trance," in *The Common Asphodel: Collected Essays on Poetry 1922–1949* (London: Hamish Hamilton, 1949), p. 1.
81. Gaskell, "Robert Graves," p. 215.
82. Auden, "A Poet of Honor," p. 6.
83. Frederick Grubb, *A Vision of Reality* (London: Chatto & Windus, 1965), p. 119.
84. Ronald Hayman, "Robert Graves," *Essays in Criticism* 5 (January 1955): 38.
85. Michael Schmidt, *An Introduction to Fifty Modern British Poets* (London: Pan, 1979), p. 171.
86. Unless otherwise noted, all citations from Graves's poems are taken from his *Collected Poems* (London: Cassell, 1975). Numbers in parentheses after citations are line numbers.
87. G. S. Fraser, "The Poetry of Robert Graves," in *Vision and Rhetoric: Studies in Modern Poetry* (London: Faber & Faber, 1959), p. 143.
88. In "These Be Your Gods, O Israel!" The following quotes are all from that essay, but reflect comments he made earlier in various places.
89. *Over the Brazier* (1916; reprint, London: the Poetry Bookshop, 1920), p. 17. This poem was not included in the *Collected Poems* of 1975.
90. Seymour-Smith, *Robert Graves,* p. 74.
91. Day, *Swifter Than Reason,* p. 136.

92. Ibid., p. 69.
93. Quoted by Seymour-Smith, *Robert Graves,* p. 47.
94. Some of the poems in that 1946 volume Graves had earlier contributed to *Work in Hand,* a collection that included work by Alan Hodge and Norman Cameron, published by the Hogarth Press in 1942.
95. Robert Graves, *Poems 1938–1945* (London: Cassell, 1946), p. 5. Neither this poem nor "A Withering Herb," discussed in the next paragraph, was included in the *Collected Poems* of 1975.
96. Thom Gunn, "In Nobody's Pantheon," *Shenandoah* 13 (Winter 1962): 34.
97. Colin Wilson, "Some Notes on Graves's Prose," *Shenandoah* 13 (Winter 1962): 62.
98. Patrick J. Keane, *A Wild Civility: Interactions in the Poetry of Robert Graves* (Columbia: University of Missouri Press, 1980), p. 101.
99. Gunn, "In Nobody's Pantheon," p. 35.
100. Yeats, as quoted by Graves in "These Be Your Gods," p. 133.
101. Keane, *A Wild Civility,* p. 101.
102. Thom Gunn, "To Yvor Winters," lines 27–32, in *The Sense of Movement* (1957; reprint, London: Faber & Faber, 1968), pp. 44–45.

Chapter 5. Social Consolations

1. D. J. Enright, "Introduction to *Oxford Book of Contemporary Verse 1945–1980,*" *The London Review of Books,* 15 May 1980, p. 14.
2. Ibid.
3. Leo Strauss, "On Classical Political Philosophy" (1st publ. 1945), in *Political Philosophy: Six Essays by Leo Strauss,* ed. Hilail Gildin (Indianapolis, Ind.: Bobbs-Merrill, 1975), p. 72.
4. Strauss, "An Epilogue" (1st publ. 1962), *Political Philosophy,* p. 107.
5. The arguments of Hannah Arendt in *The Human Condition* (Chicago: University of Chicago Press, 1958) are particularly relevant here.
6. Hayden Carruth, "Poets Without Prophecy" (1963), in *Poetry and Politics: An Anthology of Essays,* ed. Richard Jones (New York: Quill, 1985), pp. 283–85.
7. "Standing By Words," in *Standing By Words: Essays by Wendell Berry* (San Francisco: North Point Press, 1983), p. 57.
8. Ibid., p. 34.
9. Enright, "Introduction," p. 16.
10. Roy Fuller, "Poetic Memories of the Thirties," in *Professors and Gods: Last Oxford Lectures on Poetry* (London: Andre Deutsch, 1973), p. 137.
11. Nathan A. Scott, Jr., *The Poetry of Civic Virtue: Eliot, Malraux, Auden* (Philadelphia: Fortress Press, 1976), p. viii. Scott is here paraphrasing Georg Lukacs in *Realism in Our Time.*
12. Scott, *The Poetry of Civic Virtue*; Reginald Gibbons, "Preface" to *The Writer in Our World: A Triquarterly Symposium,* ed. Reginald Gibbons (Boston: Atlantic Monthly Press, 1986), p. 12.
13. Carolyn Forche, "El Salvador: An Aide-Memoire" (1981), in *Poetry and Politics,* p. 257.
14. Robert Pinsky, characterizing and applauding Forche's essay, in "Responsibilities of the Poet," *Critical Inquiry* 13 (Spring 1987): 425.
15. Irving Howe, *Politics and the Novel* (New York: Horizon Press, 1957), p. 160.
16. See George Watson, *Politics And Literature in Modern Britain* (London: Macmillan, 1977), pp. 85–97.

17. Tom Paulin, in his recent *Faber Book of Political Verse* (London: Faber & Faber, 1986), believes in that spectrum theory of politics. In his "Introduction" he divides the various traditions that inform political poetry written in English into essentially three groups: rebellion and complaint against authority (including early popular and proletarian verse, and the later developments of Puritan-Republican and Scottish-Jacobite poetry), conservative defenses of authority (including the Monarchist tradition of Dryden, and the echo of this in the revisionist gaelic poetry of seventeenth- and eighteenth-century Ireland), and anti-political quietism (the poetry of so many moderns) (pp. 21–52).

18. Quoted by Samuel Hynes, *The Auden Generation: Literature and Politics in England in the 1930s* (1970; reprint, London: Faber & Faber, 1979), p. 31.

19. Richard Ellmann and Robert O'Clair, *The Norton Anthology of Modern Poetry* (New York: W. W. Norton & Co., 1973), p. 705.

20. W. H. Auden, *Selected Poems,* ed. Edward Mendelson (New York: Vintage Books, 1979), p. 1. I cite from this edition because the texts are those of first publication in book form, thereby avoiding the difficulties of Auden's many revisions over many years. Numbers in parentheses after citations are line numbers.

21. G. S. Fraser, "Auden in Midstream," *Essays on Twentieth-Century Poets* (Totowa, N. J.: Rowman and Littlefield, 1978), p. 136.

22. Hynes, *The Auden Generation,* p. 242.

23. "Inside the Whale" (1940), in *"Inside the Whale" and Other Essays* (Harmondsworth, Middlesex: Penguin, 1962), p. 37.

24. Stephen Spender, "W. H. Auden and His Poetry" (1953), in *Auden: A Collection of Critical Essays,* ed. Monroe K. Spears (Englewood Cliffs, N.J.: Prentice-Hall, 1964), p. 29.

25. Richard Hoggart, *Auden: An Introductory Essay* (London: Chatto & Windus, 1965), p. 124.

26. W. H. Auden, "Rilke in English," *The New Republic* 100 (1939): 135.

27. Hynes, *The Auden Generation,* p. 353.

28. Spender wrote of Auden in the 1930s: "his way was the way of excess" (*The Thirties and After* [Glasgow: Fontana, 1978], p. 21).

29. George Orwell, "England Your England" (1941), in *"Inside the Whale" and Other Essays,* p. 85.

30. The citations from the poetry of Lewis, MacNeice, Warner, Spender, and Cornfield on the next few pages all refer to *Poetry of the Thirties,* ed. Robin Skelton (Harmondsworth, Middlesex: Penguin, 1964). Numbers in parentheses after citations are line numbers.

31. Terrence Des Pres, "Poetry and Politics," in *The Writer and Our World,* pp. 25–27.

32. Paulin, *Political Verse,* p. 40.

33. George Steiner, "Criticisms of Life, Voices of Protest," *TLS,* 23 May 1986, p. 47.

34. Simone Weil, *The Need for Roots: Prelude to a Declaration of Duties Towards Mankind* (1st English translation 1952; reprint, London: Routledge & Kegan Paul, 1978), p. 13.

35. Ibid., pp. 12, 13, 35.

36. George Orwell, "England Your England," in *"Inside the Whale" and Other Essays,* pp. 86–87.

37. George Orwell, *"Decline of the English Murder" and Other Essays* (Harmondsworth, Middlesex: Penguin, 1965), p. 156.

38. Jack Lindsay, *Meeting with Poets* (London: Frederick Muller, 1968), p. 61.

39. Edgell Rickword, *Behind the Eyes* (London: Sidgwick & Jackson, 1921), p. 38. In the citations from Rickword's first two volumes that follow, I retain the

original versions. (Numbers in parentheses after citations are line numbers.) Rickword did revise many of these early poems for the *Selected Poems* of 1976.

40. Schmidt, *An Introduction to Fifty Modern British Poets,* p. 190.

41. Edgell Rickword, *Invocations to Angels and The Happy New Year* (London: Wishart & Company, 1928), p. 35.

42. Edgell Rickword, *Behind the Eyes: Selected Poems & Translations* (Manchester: Carcanet New Press, 1976), p. 87. All further citations from Rickword's poems will refer to this edition. Numbers in parentheses after citations are line numbers.

43. This is the point made by Wesley Trimpi about the peculiar power of the plain style: "The denotative statement defines the writer's experience so sharply that it will not admit further qualification other than his attitude toward the experience, which will itself be the context. Connotation, then, can only be preserved by an act of understanding, of insight into what the writer is saying about his experience and about his attitude toward it. It ceases to be a series of feelings evoked by association, as, for example, by means of figurative language" (*Ben Jonson's Poems: A Study of the Plain Style* [Stanford, Calif: Stanford University Press, 1962], p. ix).

44. Alan Young and Michael Schmidt, "A Conversation with Edgell Rickword," *Poetry Nation,* no. 1 (1973): 86.

45. Simone Weil from her perspective in the early Forties could condemn contemporary culture for being "entirely deprived ... of contact with the world" (*The Need for Roots,* p. 43).

46. "The Re-Creation of Poetry: the Use of 'Negative' Emotions" (1925), in *Essays and Opinions 1921–1931*, ed. Alan Young (Manchester: Carcanet New Press, 1974), p. 170. All of the citations in this and the next paragraph from the prose I take from this edition. As early as 1922, he found in Edwin Arlington Robinson a refreshing absence of an egotistical motive: "Robinson really is interested in the relations of men and women to one another and to the general scheme, and not, or hardly, in the way they affect him. This distinguishes him from most poets, who frankly or under a mask rhyme their own sentiments" (p. 33).

47. Ibid., p. 170.
48. Ibid., p. 281.
49. Ibid., p. 288.
50. Ibid., p. 254.
51. Ibid., p. 170.
52. Ibid., p. 34.
53. Ibid., p. 198.
54. Ibid., p. 48.
55. Ibid., p. 283.
56. Ibid., p. 172.
57. Ibid., p. 57.
58. Ibid., p. 44.
59. Ibid., p. 40.
60. Ibid., p. 35.
61. Ibid., p. 49.
62. Young and Schmidt, "A Conversation with Edgell Rickword," p. 79.
63. Edgell Rickword, "Straws for the Weary" (1934), in *Literature in Society: Essays & Opinions II 1931–1978,* ed. Alan Young (Manchester: Carcanet New Press, 1978), p. 40. Hereafter referred to as *Essays II*.
64. Young and Schmidt, "Conversation with Edgell Rickword," p. 84. His attitude is very sensible and indicative of his concern for a fullness rather than

rigidity of view of the poetic subject: "The meaning [of a literary work] is two-dimensional, perhaps, and the background brings in a third dimension, in which the meaning comes alive."

65. Rickword, *Essays II,* p. 58.

66. Young and Schmidt, "Conversation with Edgell Rickword," p. 82.

67. Edgell Rickword, "The Re-Creation of Poetry," *Essays and Opinions 1921–1931,* p. 171 (emphasis mine).

68. Young and Schmidt, "Conversation with Edgell Rickword," p. 85.

69. Yvor Winters, "Robert Bridges and Elizabeth Daryush" (1936–37), in *The Uncollected Essays and Reviews of Yvor Winters,* ed. Francis Murphy (Chicago: Swallow Press, 1973), pp. 272, 275.

70. Donald Davie, "The Poetry of Elizabeth Daryush," *Poetry Nation 5,* 1975, pp. 45–47. Davie fails to acknowledge Winters's comment in *Primitivism and Decadence* (1937) that "Mrs. Daryush has been more successful, in my estimation, in writing syllabics, than was her father, though her greatest work, like that of her father, has been in the traditional meters" (*In Defense of Reason,* p. 148).

71. I will be quoting from these much more available collections of the 1970s, although some of the poems were revised since their first appearance: *Selected Poems by Elizabeth Daryush from Verses I–VI* (Oxford: Carcanet Press, 1972) and *Collected Poems* (Manchester: Carcanet New Press, 1976). The only exceptions are "Aeroplanes" and "Along the narrow cottage-path he wheeled," from *The Last Man and Other Verses* (London: Oxford University Press, 1936): neither was reprinted. Numbers in parentheses after citations are line numbers.

72. Winters, *Uncollected Essays,* p. 272.

73. Schmidt, *Fifty Modern British Poets,* p. 118.

74. Winters, *Uncollected Essays,* p. 272.

75. Reprinted in *Collected Poems,* p. 24.

76. Ibid., p. 25.

77. Winters, *In Defense of Reason,* pp. 147–48. He goes on in this passage to judge "Still-Life" "one of her finest syllabic experiments.... Yet like the best free verse, it lacks the final precision and power, the flexibility of suggestion, of the best work in accentual-syllabics, in which every syllable stands in relationship to a definite norm" (p. 149).

78. Schmidt, *Fifty Modern British Poets,* p. 118.

79. Quoted by Bevis Hillier in his "Forward" to Betjeman's *Uncollected Poems* (London: John Murray, 1982), p. 4.

80. All these charges are made by Patrick Taylor-Martin (who is often summarizing and agreeing with the misgivings of other critics) in his otherwise very sympathetic treatment of Betjeman in *John Betjeman: His Life and Work* (London: Allen Lane, 1983), pp. 186, 177, 126, 56.

81. John Press, *John Betjeman,* Writers and Their Work (London: Longman, for the British Council, 1974), p. 30.

82. *John Betjeman's Collected Poems,* ed. the Earl of Birkenhead, 4th ed. (London: John Murray, 1979), p. 45. All further citations from Betjeman's poems, unless otherwise noted, are from this edition. Numbers in parentheses after citations are line numbers.

83. W. H Auden, "Introduction," *Slick But Not Streamlined: Poems & Short Pieces by John Betjeman* (Garden City, N.Y.: Doubleday & Co., 1947), pp. 9–16.

84. As quoted by Hillier, ed., *Uncollected Poems,* p. 5.

85. Derek Stanford, *John Betjeman* (London: Neville Spearman, 1961), pp. 15, 59.

86. See A. T. Tolley, *The Poetry of the Thirties* (London: Victor Gollancz, 1975), pp. 191–94.

87. John Wain and Bernard Bergonzi are two of the most notorious detractors; see Taylor-Martin's survey of Betjeman's reputation, *John Betjeman,* pp. 10–14.

88. I am grateful to Derek Stanford for the latter point (*Betjeman,* p. 47).

89. John Betjeman, "Love is Dead," in *First and Last Loves* (London: John Murray, 1952), p. 5.

90. I fully agree with Taylor-Martin on this point (*John Betjeman,* p. 66).

91. T. S. Eliot, "Tradition and the Individual Talent," *The Sacred Wood,* 7th ed. (London: Methuen, 1967), p. 49.

92. Samuel Hynes makes this valuable distinction in "The Hardy Tradition in Modern English Poetry," *Sewanee Review,* pp. 34–37.

93. John Betjeman, *Ghastly Good Taste* (London: Chapman & Hall, 1933), p. 27.

94. Ibid., pp. 47, 26, 135.

95. Ibid., pp. 134–135.

96. Ibid., p. 136.

97. Ibid., pp. 136, 50.

98. Ibid., pp. 129, 43.

99. Ibid., p. 19.

100. Ibid., p. 13.

101. Betjeman, *First and Last Loves,* pp. 1–5.

102. Taylor-Martin, *John Betjeman,* pp. 172–173.

103. Betjeman, *Ghastly Good Taste,* pp. 16–17.

104. Ibid., p. 106.

105. I am encouraged especially by the inadequacy of John Press's categories: "his poems still fall into a few categories which can be readily defined: satirical and light verse; narrative and anecdotal poems, often set in the nineteenth century and based on a historical event; personal poems about childhood, love and death; topographical poems, especially those in which he portrays landscapes, townscapes or seascapes with figures" (*John Betjeman,* p. 25). Such a list does not call attention to the dominant social dimension in Betjeman's work. I have already pointed out how it prevents Press from properly accounting for "Death of King George V."

106. "Topographical Verse," Betjeman's own note to *Slick But Not Streamlined,* p. 22.

107. Hillier, *Uncollected Poems,* p. 11.

108. Stanford, *Betjeman,* p. 69.

109. George and Weedon Grossmith, *The Diary of a Nobody* (London: the Folio Society, 1969), pp. 130–133.

110. Quoted by Taylor-Martin, *John Betjeman,* p. 126.

111. Ibid., p. 96.

112. See his criticism (comic and otherwise) of less moderate religious types: "The Sandemanian Meeting-House," "Calvinistic Evensong," and "An Ecumenical Invitation."

113. Reprinted as "The English Wisdom of a Master Poet," in *An Enormous Yes*: *In Memoriam Philip Larkin (1922–1985),* ed. Harry Chambers (Calstock, Cornwall: Peterloo Poets, 1986), p. 34.

114. Charles Monteith reports, for instance, that Auden was willing to nominate Larkin for the Oxford Chair of Poetry in 1973 ("Publishing Larkin," in *Larkin at Sixty,* ed. Anthony Thwaite [London: Faber & Faber, 1982], p. 44).

115. Larkin, "What's Become of Wystan?" in *Required Writings,* p. 128.

116. In *Required Writings,* p. 47.
117. "Wanted: Good Hardy Critic," *Required Writings,* p. 172.
118. The final sentence of his essay on Stevie Smith is "Miss Smith's poems speak with the authority of sadness" ("Frivolous and Vulnerable," in *Required Writings,* p. 158). Larkin will not have that Eliotic separation of the man who suffers from the man who creates: "we separate the petrol from the engine—but the dependence of the second on the first is complete" (in "Context," *The London Magazine,* New Series, 1 [February 1962]: 32).
119. "Four Conversations: Ian Hamilton," *The London Magazine* 4 (November 1964): 73.
120. See Clive James, "On His Wit," *Larkin at Sixty,* p. 103.
121. Seamus Heaney, "The Main of Light," in *Larkin at Sixty,* p. 138.
122. Ibid., p. 136.
123. Published in *An Enormous Yes,* p. 64.
124. Andrew Motion, *Philip Larkin* (London: Methuen, 1982), pp. 68, 70, 79.
125. Terry Whalen, *Philip Larkin and English Poetry* (Vancouver: University of British Columbia Press, 1986), pp. 24, 40, 77, 55, 91.
126. J. R. Watson, "The Other Larkin," *Critical Quarterly* 17 (1975): 357–58, 360.
127. Dan Jacobson, "Profile 3: Philip Larkin," *The New Review* 1 (June 1974): 29.
128. A. Alvarez, "The New Poetry or Beyond the Gentility Principle," *The New Poetry,* rev. ed. (Harmondsworth, Middlesex: Penguin, 1966), pp. 23, 24–25.
129. Colin Falck, "Philip Larkin," in *The Modern Poet: Essays from "The Review,"* ed. Ian Hamilton (London: MacDonald, 1968), pp. 103, 110. Falck's criteria are those of an Imagist: he faults Larkin (this believer in meaninglessness) for using "argument" in his poetry instead of "the individual moment of perception" (p. 107).
130. Larkin, "Four Conversations: Ian Hamilton," p. 73.
131. Andrew Motion, "Philip Larkin—The Biography," *The Poetry Catalogue* 1 (January 1987): 3; Haffenden, "The True and the Beautiful: A Conversation with Philip Larkin," *London Magazine* 20 (April–May 1980): 81; Hughes, "The Young Mr. Larkin," *Larkin at Sixty,* pp. 19, 21; Amis, "Oxford and After," *Larkin at Sixty,* p. 30; Levi, *An Enormous Yes,* p. 34.
132. See Roger Day, *Larkin* (Milton Keynes, Buckinghamshire: Open University Press, 1987), p. 26.
133. All citations from Larkin's poems are taken from *The North Ship* (1945; reprint, London: Faber & Faber, 1973), *The Less Deceived* (1955; reprint, London: Marvell Press, 1977), *The Whitsun Weddings* (London: Faber & Faber, 1964), and *High Windows* (London: Faber & Faber, 1974). Numbers in parentheses after citations are line numbers.
134. Day, *Larkin,* p. 27.
135. See the *Observer* interview, in *Required Writings,* pp. 47–48.
136. Day, *Larkin,* p. 35.
137. Calvin Bedient, *Eight Contemporary Poets* (London: Oxford University Press, 1974), p. 70. Bedient does go on to allow that Larkin makes the sterility of post-war life bearable: "he shows that it can be borne with grace and gentleness" (p. 71). I contend that he does considerably more than this. He shows *how* it can be borne with intelligence and some communal benefit as well.
138. D. J. Enright, "Down Cemetery Road," in *Conspirators and Poets* (London: Chatto & Windus, 1966), p. 144.

139. David Timms, *Philip Larkin* (Edinburgh: Oliver & Boyd, 1973), pp. 74–75.
140. Ibid., p. 74.
141. See Andrew Motion for a similar reading (*Philip Larkin,* p. 80). I hope the comparison to "At Grass" strengthens the point.
142. See, for instance, Bruce K. Martin, *Philip Larkin* (Boston: Twayne, 1978), p. 21.
143. Haffenden, "The True and the Beautiful," p. 94.
144. Martin, *Larkin,* p. 43.
145. "Four Conversations: Ian Hamilton," p. 75.
146. Larkin, "It Could Only Happen in England" (1971), in *Required Writings,* p. 207.
147. Ibid., p. 216.
148. Watson, "The Other Larkin," p. 349.
149. Larkin has said that the poem describes an incident that happened in July 1955 ("An Interview with *Paris Review*" [1982], in *Required Writings,* p. 75).

Bibliography

Aiken, Conrad. "An Anatomy of Melancholy." *New Republic* 33 (7 February 1923): 294-95.
Alexander, Michael. "Hardy Among the Poets." In *Thomas Hardy after Fifty Years*. Edited by Lance St. John Butler. Totowa, N.J.: Rowman and Littlefield, 1977.
Alvarez, A., ed. *The New Poetry*. Rev. ed. Harmondsworth, Middlesex: Penguin, 1966.
Arendt, Hannah. *The Human Condition*. Chicago: University of Chicago Press, 1958.
Aristotle. *The Nicomachean Ethics*. Translated by David Ross. Oxford: Oxford University Press, 1980.
Ashton, Theresa. "Edward Thomas: From Prose to Poetry." *The Poetry Review* 28 (1937): 449-55.
Attridge, Derek. *The Rhythms of English Poetry*. London: Longman, 1982.
Auden, W. H. "A Poet of Honor." *Shenandoah* 13 (Winter 1962): 5-11.
_____. "Introduction." In *Slick But Not Streamlined*: *Poems & Short Pieces by John Betjeman*. Garden City, N.Y.: Doubleday & Co., 1947.
_____. "Rilke in English." *The New Republic* 100 (1939): 135.
_____. *Selected Poems*. Edited by Edward Mendelson. New York: Vintage Books, 1979.
Bailey, J. O. *The Poems of Thomas Hardy*: *A Handbook and Commentary*. Chapel Hill: University of North Carolina Press, 1970.
Barthes, Roland. *Roland Barthes*. Translated by Richard Howard. New York: Hill and Wang, 1977.
Baxter, John. "The Province of the Plain Style." *The Compass,* April 1978, pp. 15-37.
Bedient, Calvin. *Eight Contemporary Poets*. London: Oxford University Press, 1974.
Bergonzi, Bernard. *Heroes' Twilight*: *A Study of the Literature of the Great War*. London: Constable, 1965.
Berry, Wendell. *Standing By Words*: *Essays by Wendell Berry*. San Francisco: North Point Press, 1983.
Betjeman, John. *First and Last Loves*. London: John Murray, 1952.
_____. *Ghastly Good Taste*. London: Chapman & Hall, 1933.
_____. *John Betjeman's Collected Poems*. Edited by the earl of Birkenhead. 4th ed. London: John Murray, 1979.
_____. *Uncollected Poems*. Compiled by Bevis Hillier. London: John Murray, 1982.
Beum, Robert. "Profundity Revisited: Bridges and His Critics." *Dalhousie Review* 44 (Summer 1964): 172-79.
Blackmur, R. P. *Language as Gesture*. New York: Harcourt, Brace and Co., 1952.
Bloom, Harold. *Yeats*. London: Oxford University Press, 1970.

Blunden, Edmund. "Introduction." In *Poems of Ivor Gurney 1890–1937.* Edited by Leonard Clark. London: Chatto & Windus, 1973.
———. *Selected Poems.* Edited by Robyn Marsack. Manchester: Carcanet New Press, 1982.
———. *Thomas Hardy.* New York: St. Martin's Press, 1967.
———. *Undertones of War.* 3d ed. Harmondsworth, Middlesex: Penguin, 1982.
Bold, Sydney. *Poetry of the 1920s.* London: Longman, 1973.
Bridges, Robert. *Bridges: Poetical Works.* 2d ed. London: Oxford University Press, 1971.
Brooke, Rupert. *The Collected Poems of Rupert Brooke.* New York: Dodd, Mead, & Co., 1943.
Brooks, Cleanth. *Modern Poetry and the Tradition.* 1939. Reprint. Chapel Hill: University of North Carolina Press, 1965.
Carruth, Hayden. "Poets Without Prophecy." In *Poetry and Politics: An Anthology of Essays.* Edited by Richard Jones. New York: Quill, 1985.
Cecil, David. "The Hardy Mood." In *Thomas Hardy: A Casebook.* Edited by James Gibson and Trevor Johnson. London: Macmillan, 1979.
Cohen, J. M. *Robert Graves.* New York: Grove Press, 1960.
Collins, Vere H. *Talks with Thomas Hardy at Max Gate 1920–1922.* 1928. Reprint. London: Duckworth, 1978.
Cooke, William. *Edward Thomas: A Critical Biography 1878–1917.* London: Faber & Faber, 1970.
Coombes, H. *Edward Thomas.* London: Chatto & Windus, 1956.
Cullingford, Elizabeth, ed. *Yeats, Poems, 1919–1935.* London: Macmillan, 1984.
Cunningham, J. V. "The 'Gyroscope' Group." *The Bookman,* November 1932, pp. 703–8.
Danby, John. "Edward Thomas." *The Critical Quarterly* 1 (Winter 1959): 308–17.
Daryush, Elizabeth. *Collected Poems.* Manchester: Carcanet New Press, 1976.
———. *Selected Poems by Elizabeth Daryush from Verses I–VI.* Oxford: Carcanet Press, 1972.
———. *The Last Man and Other Verses.* London: Oxford University Press, 1936.
Davie, Donald. "Gurney's Flood." Review of *Collected Poems of Ivor Gurney.* Edited by P. J. Kavanagh. *London Review of Books,* 3–16 February 1983, p. 6.
———. *The Poet in the Imaginary Museum: Essays of Two Decades.* Edited by Barry Alpert. Manchester: Carcanet, 1977.
———. "The Poetry of Elizabeth Daryush." *Poetry Nation 5,* 1975, pp. 43–51.
———. *Thomas Hardy and British Poetry.* London: Routledge & Kegan Paul, 1973.
Day, Douglas. *Swifter Than Reason: The Poetry and Criticism of Robert Graves.* Chapel Hill: University of North Carolina Press, 1963.
Day, Roger. *Larkin.* Milton Keynes, Buckinghamshire: Open University Press, 1987.
Doolittle, Hilda (H. D.). *Collected Poems 1912–1944.* Edited by Louis L. Martz. Manchester: Carcanet Press, 1984.
Draper, R. P. ed. *D. H. Lawrence: The Critical Heritage.* New York: Barnes & Noble, 1970.
Drinkwater, John. "Tradition and Technique." *The Poetry Review,* July 1912, pp. 296–300.
Drummond, C. Q. "An Anti-Miltonist Reprise: IV. Adam and Eve: or, God Hates Love." *The Compass,* Winter 1979, pp. 17–38.
Eliot, T. S. "Isolated Superiority." *The Dial* 84 (January 1928): 4–7.
———. "Reflections on Contemporary Poetry." *The Egoist,* September 1917, pp. 118–19.

———. *Selected Prose of T. S. Eliot.* Edited by Frank Kermode. London: Faber & Faber, 1975.
———. *The Complete Poems and Plays of T. S. Eliot.* London: Faber & Faber, 1970.
———. "The Poetry of W. B. Yeats." *The Southern Review* 7 (Winter 1942): 442–54.
———. *The Sacred Wood.* 7th ed. London: Methuen, 1967.
———. "Verse Pleasant and Unpleasant." *The Egoist,* March 1918, pp. 43–44.
Ellmann, Richard. *The Identity of Yeats.* 1954. Reprint. London: Faber & Faber, 1964.
Ellmann, Richard, and Robert O'Clair, eds. *The Norton Anthology of Modern Poetry.* New York: W. W. Norton & Co., 1973.
Enright, D. J. *Conspirators and Poets.* London: Chatto & Windus, 1966.
———. "Introduction to *Oxford Book of Contemporary Verse 1945–1980.*" *London Review of Books,* 15 May 1980, pp. 14–16.
Falck, Colin. "Philip Larkin." In *The Modern Poet*: *Essays from "The Review."* Edited by Ian Hamilton. London: MacDonald, 1968.
Fields, Kenneth. "The Rhetoric of Artifice: Ezra Pound, T. S. Eliot, Wallace Stevens, Walter Conrad Arensberg, Donald Evans, Mina Loy, and Yvor Winters." Ph.D. diss., Stanford University, 1967.
Ford, Ford Madox [Hueffer]. "Impressionism—Some Speculations." *Poetry*: *A Magazine of Verse* 2 (August and September 1913): 177–187, 215–225.
Ford, Ford Madox. "Those Were the Days." In *Imagist Anthology 1930.* London: Chatto & Windus, 1930.
Foucault, Michel. *The History of Sexuality.* Vol. I. Translated by Robert Hurley. New York: Random House, 1980.
Fraser, G. S. *Essays on Twentieth-Century Poets.* Totowa, N.J.: Rowman and Littlefield, 1978.
———. *Metre, Rhyme and Free Verse.* London: Methuen, 1970.
———. "The Reputation of Robert Graves." *Shenandoah* 13 (Winter 1962): 19–32.
———. *Vision and Rhetoric* : *Studies in Modern Poetry.* London: Faber & Faber, 1959.
Frost, Robert. *Selected Prose of Robert Frost.* Edited by Hyde Cox and Edward Connery Lathem. New York: Collier Books, 1968.
———. *The Poetry of Robert Frost.* Edited by Edward Connery Lathem. New York: Holt, Rinehard and Winston: 1969.
Fuller, Roy. *Professors and Gods*: *Last Oxford Lectures on Poetry.* London: Andre Deutsch, 1973.
Fussell, Paul. *Poetic Meter and Poetic Form.* Rev. ed. New York: Random House, 1979.
———. *The Great War and Modern Memory.* Oxford: Oxford University Press, 1975.
Gascoigne, George. *The Complete Works of George Gascoigne.* Edited by John W. Cunliffe. 2 vols. Cambridge: Cambridge University Press, 1907–10.
Gaskell, Ronald. "The Poetry of Robert Graves." *The Critical Quarterly* 3 (Autumn 1961): 213–222.
Gibbons, Reginald, ed. *The Writer in Our World: A Triquarterly Symposium.* Boston: Atlantic Monthly Press, 1986.
Gilbert, Sandra. *Acts of Attention*: *The Poems of D. H. Lawrence.* Ithaca: Cornell University Press, 1972.
Ginsberg, Allen. "Notes for Howl and Other Poems." In *20th-Century Poetry & Poetics.* Edited by Gary Geddes. 2d ed. Toronto: Oxford University Press, 1973.
Grant, George. "Faith and the Multiversity." *The Compass,* Autumn 1978, pp. 3–14.

———. *Philosophy in the Mass Age*. 2d ed. Vancouver, B. C.: Copp Clark, 1966.
Graves, Robert. *Collected Poems*. London: Cassell, 1975.
———. *Goodbye to All That*. Rev. ed. Harmondsworth, Middlesex: Penguin, 1965.
———. *On Poetry: Collected Talks and Essays*. New York: Doubleday, 1969.
———. *Over the Brazier*. 1916. Reprint. London: The Poetry Bookshop, 1920.
———. *Poems 1938–1945*. London: Cassell, 1946.
———. *The Common Asphodel: Collected Essays on Poetry 1922–1949*. London: Hamish Hamilton, 1949.
Groves, Robert, and Alan Hodge. *The Long Weekend*. 1940. Reprint. New York: W. W. Norton, 1963.
Gregson, J. M. *Poetry of the First World War*. London: Edward Arnold, 1976.
Grigson, Geoffrey, ed. *The Faber Book of Love Poems*. London: Faber & Faber, 1973.
Grossmith, George, and Grossmith, Weedon. *The Diary of a Nobody*. 1892. Reprint. London: Folio Society, 1969.
Grubb, Frederick. *A Vision of Reality*. London: Chatto & Windus, 1965.
Guerard, Albert, Jr. *Robert Bridges: A Study of Traditionalism in Poetry*. 1942. Reprint. New York: Russell & Russell, 1965.
Gunn, Thom. "Hardy and the Ballads." *Agenda* 10 (Spring-Summer 1972): 19–46.
———. "In Nobody's Pantheon." *Shenandoah* 13 (Winter 1962): 34–35.
———. *The Sense of Movement*. 1957. Reprint. London: Faber & Faber, 1968.
Gurney, Ivor. *Collected Poems of Ivor Gurney*. Edited by P. J. Kavanagh. Oxford: Oxford University Press, 1982.
———. *Ivor Gurney War Letters*. Edited by R. K. R. Thorton. Manchester: Carcanet New Press, 1983.
———. *Severn and Somme*. London: Sidgwick & Jackson, 1917.
Haffenden, John. "The True and the Beautiful: A Conversation with Philip Larkin." *London Magazine* 20 (April–May 1980): 81–96.
Hall, James, and Steinmann, Martin, eds. *The Permanence of Yeats*. 1950. Reprint. New York: Collier Books, 1961.
Hamilton, Ian. "Four Conversations: Ian Hamilton." *The London Magazine* 4 (November 1964): 71–77.
Harding, D. W. *Experience into Words*. 1963. Reprint. Harmondsworth, Middlesex: Penguin, 1974.
Hardy, Florence Emily. *The Life of Thomas Hardy 1840–1928*. 1962. Reprint. London: Macmillan, 1975.
Hardy, Thomas. *The Complete Poems of Thomas Hardy*. Edited by James Gibson. London: Macmillan, 1976.
Hayman, Ronald. "Robert Graves." *Essays in Criticism* 5 (January 1955): 32–43.
Hibberd, Dominic. *Owen the Poet*. Athens: University of Georgia Press, 1986.
———, ed. *Poetry of the First World War*. Casebook series. London: Macmillan, 1981.
Hoggart, Richard. *Auden: An Introductory Essay*. London: Chatto & Windus, 1965.
Hone, Joseph. *W. B. Yeats 1865–1939*. London: Macmillan, 1942.
Hooker, Jeremy. "The Writings of Edward Thomas: II. The Sad Passion." *The Anglo-Welsh Review* 29 (Autumn 1970): 63–78.
Hough, Graham. *Image and Experience: Studies in a Literary Revolution*. London: Duckworth, 1960.
———. *The Dark Sun*. New York: Farrar, Straus and Giroux, 1973.

———. *Reflections on a Literary Revolution*. Washington, D.C.: Catholic University of America Press, 1960.
Howe, Irving. *Politics and the Novel*. New York: Horizon Press, 1957.
———. *Thomas Hardy*. London: Weidenfeld and Nicolson, 1968.
Hunter, William B., Jr. "Prince Hal, His Struggle Towards Moral Perfection." In *Henry the Fourth, Part I*. Edited by James L. Sanderson. 2d ed. New York: W. W. Norton, 1969.
Hurd, Michael. *The Ordeal of Ivor Gurney*. Oxford: Oxford University Press, 1978.
Hynes, Samuel. *The Auden Generation: Literature and Politics in England in the 1930s*. 1970. Reprint. London: Faber & Faber, 1979.
Hynes, Samuel. "The Hardy Tradition in Modern English Poetry." *Sewanee Review* 88 (Winter 1980): 33–51.
Jacobson, Dan. "Profile 3: Philip Larkin." *The New Review* 1 (June 1974): 25–29.
Keane, Patrick J. *A Wild Civility: Interactions in the Poetry of Robert Graves*. Columbia: University of Missouri Press, 1980.
Keith, W. J. *The Poetry of Nature*. Toronto: Toronto University Press, 1980.
Kenner, Hugh. *The Invisible Poet: T. S. Eliot*. London: Methuen & Co., 1965.
Kirkham, Michael. *The Imagination of Edward Thomas*. Cambridge: Cambridge University Press, 1986.
———. *The Poetry of Robert Graves*. London: Athlone Press, 1969.
Lane, Arthur E. *An Adequate Response*. Detroit: Wayne State University Press, 1972.
Langbaum, Robert. *The Poetry of Experience*. 1957. Reprint. Harmondsworth, Middlesex: Penguin, 1974.
Larkin, Philip. "Context." *The London Magazine,* New Series 1 (February 1962): 31–32.
———. *High Windows*. London: Faber & Faber, 1974.
———. *Required Writing: Miscellaneous Pieces 1955–1982*. London: Faber & Faber, 1983.
———. *The Less Deceived*. 1955. Reprint. London: Marvell Press, 1977.
———. *The North Ship*. 1945. Reprint. London: Faber & Faber, 1973.
———. *The Whitsun Weddings*. London: Faber & Faber, 1964.
Lawrence, D. H. *D. H. Lawrence: Selected Literary Criticism*. Edited by Anthony Beal. New York: Viking Press, 1966.
———. *Phoenix, the Posthumous Papers of D. H. Lawrence*. Edited by Edward D. McDonald. London: William Heinemann, 1936.
———. *Sex, Literature, and Censorship*. Edited by Harry T. Moore. New York: Viking Press, 1959.
———. *Sons and Lovers*. 1913. Reprint. New York: Viking Press, 1961.
———. *The Collected Poems of D. H. Lawrence*. London: Martin Secker, 1928.
———. *The Complete Poems of D. H. Lawrence*. Edited by Vivian de Sola Pinto and Warren Roberts. Harmondsworth, Middlesex: Penguin, 1977.
———. *The Rainbow*. 1915. Reprint. Harmondsworth, Middlesex: Penguin, 1973.
———. "Verse Free and Unfree." *Voices* 2 (October 1919): 129–134.
Lawrence, Frieda. "A Bit about Lawrence." In *D. H. Lawrence: A Critical Anthology*. Edited by H. Coombes. Harmondsworth, Middlesex: Penguin, 1973.
Lawrence, Ralph. "Edward Thomas in Perspective." *English* 12 (Summer 1959): 177–83.
Leavis, F. R. *D. H. Lawrence/Novelist*. 1955. Reprint. Harmondsworth, Middlesex: Penguin, 1964.

---. *New Bearings in English Poetry.* 1932. Reprint. Harmondsworth, Middlesex: Penguin, 1963.
Leavis, Q. D. "The Englishness of the English Novel." In *Collected Essays.* Vol. 1. Edited by G. Singh. Cambridge: Cambridge University Press, 1983.
Lehmann, John. *The English Poets of the First World War.* London: Thames and Hudson, 1981.
Levi, Peter. "The English Wisdom of a Master Poet." In *An Enormous Yes*: *In Memoriam Philip Larkin (1922–1985).* Edited by Harry Chambers. Calstock, Cornwall: Peterloo Poets, 1986.
Lewis, C. S. *The Four Loves.* 1960. Reprint. London: Fontana, 1963.
Liddiard, Jean. *Isaac Rosenberg*: *The Half Used Life.* London: Victor Gollancz, 1975.
Lindsay, Jack. *Meeting with Poets.* London: Frederick Muller, 1968.
Logue, Leona Whitworth. *Recent War Lyrics*: A Study of War Concepts in Modern Verse. 1928. Reprint. New York: Grafton Press, 1976.
Longley, Edna. "Edward Thomas and the 'English' Line." *The New Review,* February 1975, pp. 3–11.
Lucas, John. *Modern English Poetry from Hardy to Hughes*: *A Critical Survey.* Totowa, N.J.: Barnes & Noble, 1986.
Marsden, Kenneth. *The Poems of Thomas Hardy*: *A Critical Introduction.* London: Athlone Press, 1969.
Marsh, Edward, ed. *Georgian Poetry 1911–1912.* 1912. Reprint. London: The Poetry Bookshop, 1923.
---. *Georgian Poetry 1913–1915.* London: The Poetry Workshop, 1915.
Marsh, Jan. *Edward Thomas*: *A Poet for His Country.* London: Paul Elek, 1978.
Marshall, Tom. *The Psychic Mariner*: *A Reading of the Poems of D. H. Lawrence.* New York: Viking Press, 1970.
Martin, Bruce K. *Philip Larkin.* Boston: Twayne, 1978.
Mathias, Roland. "Edward Thomas." *The Anglo-Welsh Review* 10 (1960): 23–37.
McFarlane, James. "The Mind of Modernism." In *Modernism.* Edited by Malcolm Bradbury and James McFarlane. Harmondsworth, Middlesex: Penguin, 1976.
Mehoke, James. *Robert Graves*: *Peace-Weaver.* The Hague: Mouton, 1975.
Meredith, George. *The Poems of George Meredith.* Vol. 1. Edited by Phyllis B. Bartlett. New Haven: Yale University Press, 1978.
Milton, John. *Paradise Lost.* Edited by Merritt Y. Hughes. New Haven: Odyssey Press, 1962.
Monroe, Harriet. "Editorial Comment: Tradition." *Poetry*: *A Magazine of Verse* 2 (May 1913): 67–70.
Moore, Harry T. *The Intelligent Heart*: *The Story of D. H. Lawrence.* 1955. Reprint. Harmondsworth, Middlesex: Penguin, 1960.
Motion, Andrew. *Philip Larkin.* London: Methuen, 1982.
---. "Philip Larkin—The Biography." *The Poetry Catalogue* 1 (January 1987): 3.
---. *The Poetry of Edward Thomas.* London: Routledge & Kegan Paul, 1980.
Munro, Harold. "Futurism." *Poetry and Drama,* September 1913, pp. 262–264.
---. "The Future of Poetry." *The Poetry Review* 1 (January 1912): 10–13.
Murry, Middleton. *Aspects of Literature.* London: W. Collins, 1920.
Musgrave, Susan. "A Memory of Robert Graves." *The Malahat Review,* July 1975, 10–13.
Nichols, Robert, ed. *Anthology of War Poetry, 1914–1918,* London: Nicholson and Watson, 1943.

Orwell, George. *"Decline of the English Murder" and Other Essays.* Harmondsworth, Middlesex: Penguin, 1965.
———. *"Inside the Whale" and Other Essays.* Harmondsworth, Middlesex: Penguin, 1962.
Owen, Wilfred. *The Complete Poems and Fragments.* Edited by Jon Stallworthy. 2 vols. London: Chatto & Windus, 1983.
———. *Wilfred Owen: War Poems and Others.* Edited by Dominic Hibberd. London: Chatto & Windus, 1973.
Palmer, Herbert. *Post-Victorian Poetry.* London: J. M. Dent, 1938.
Paulin, Tom. *Thomas Hardy: The Poetry of Perception.* Totowa, N.J.: Rowman and Littlefield, 1975.
———, ed. *Faber Book of Political Verse.* London: Faber & Faber, 1986.
Peckham, Morse. "Toward a Theory of Romanticism." In *Romanticism: Points of View.* Edited by Robert F. Gleckner and Gerald E. Enscoe. 2d ed. Englewood Cliffs, N.J.: Prentice-Hall, 1970.
Perkins, David. *A History of Modern Poetry: From the 1890's to Pound, Eliot, & Yeats.* Cambridge: Harvard University Press, 1976.
Pinsky, Robert. "Responsibilities of the Poet." *Critical Inquiry* 13 (Spring 1987): 421–33.
Pound, Ezra. "A Few Don'ts by an Imagiste." *Poetry: A Magazine of Verse* 1 (March 1913): 200–6.
———. *Collected Shorter Poems.* 2d ed. London: Faber & Faber, 1968.
———. *Literary Essays of Ezra Pound.* Edited by T. S. Eliot. London: Faber & Faber, 1960.
———. "Vorticism." *The Fortnightly Review* 96 (September 1914): 461–71.
Press, John. *A Map of Modern English Verse.* Oxford: Oxford University Press, 1969.
———. *John Betjeman.* Writers and Their Work. London: Longman, for the British Council, 1974.
Pritchard, William. *Seeing Through Everything: English Writers 1918–1940.* New York: Oxford University Press, 1977.
Quinn, Maire. "The Personal Past in the Poetry of Thomas Hardy and Edward Thomas." *Critical Quarterly* 16 (Spring 1974): 7–28.
Rajan, Balachandra. *W. B. Yeats.* 2d ed. London: Hutchinson & Co., 1969.
Review of *Georgian Poetry 1911–1912.* Edited by Edward Marsh. *Times Literary Supplement,* 27 February 1913, p. 81.
Review of *Georgian Poetry 1913–1915.* Edited by Edward Marsh. *The Spectator,* 5 February 1916, p. 191.
Review of *Georgian Poetry 1913–1915.* Edited by Edward Marsh. *Times Literary Supplement,* 9 December 1915, p. 447.
Review of *The Great War and Modern Memory.* By Paul Fussell. *Times Literary Supplement,* 5 December 1975, p. 1435.
Read, Herbert. *Collected Poems.* London: Fabar & Faber, 1966.
Richards, I. A. "A Background for Contemporary Poetry." In *Twentieth Century Poetry: Critical Essays and Documents.* Edited by Graham Martin and P. N. Furbank. Milton Keynes, Buckinghamshire: The Open University Press, 1975.
Rickword, Edgell. *Behind the Eyes.* London: Sidgwick & Jackson, 1921.
———. *Behind the Eyes: Selected Poems & Translations.* Manchester: Carcanet New Press, 1976.
———. *Essays and Opinions 1921–1931.* Edited by Alan Young. Manchester: Carcanet New Press, 1974.

_____. *Invocations to Angels and The Happy New Year.* London: Wishart & Company, 1928.

_____. *Literature in Society*: *Essays & Opinions II 1931–1978.* Edited by Alan Young. Manchester: Carcanet New Press, 1978.

Roberts, Michael. *T. E. Hulme.* London: Faber & Faber, 1938.

Robinson, Ian. *The Survival of English.* London: Cambridge University Press, 1973.

Roethke, Theodore. *On the Poet and His Craft*: *Selected Prose of Theodore Roethke.* Edited by Ralph J. Mills, Jr. Seattle: University of Washington Press, 1965.

Rogers, Timothy, ed. *Georgian Poetry 1911–1922*: *The Critical Heritage.* London: Routledge & Kegan Paul, 1977.

Rosenberg, Isaac. *The Collected Works of Isaac Rosenberg.* Edited by Ian Parsons. London: Chatto & Windus, 1979.

Ross, Robert. *The Georgian Revolt 1910–1922*: *Rise and Fall of a Poetic Ideal.* Carbondale: Southern Illinois University Press, 1965.

Sassoon, Siegfried. *Collected Poems 1908–1956.* London: Faber & Faber, 1961.

_____. *The Complete Memoirs of George Sherston.* 1937. Reprint. London: Faber & Faber, 1980.

Schmidt, Michael. *An Introduction to Fifty Modern British Poets.* London: Pan, 1979.

_____. "The Politics of Form." *Poetry Nation,* no. 1 (1973): 49–53.

Schwartz, Sanford. *The Matrix of Modernism*: *Pound, Eliot, and Early Twentieth-Century Thought.* Princeton: Princeton University Press, 1985.

Scott, Nathan A., Jr. *The Poetry of Civic Virtue*: *Eliot, Malraux, Auden.* Philadelphia: Fortress Press, 1976.

Seymour-Smith, Martin. *Robert Graves*: *His Life and Work.* London: Sphere Books, 1983.

Shapiro, Karl, and Beum, Robert. *A Prosody Handbook.* New York: Harper & Row, 1965.

Sisson, C. H. *English Poetry 1900–1950*: *An Assessment.* New York: St. Martin's Press, 1971.

Silkin, Jon. *Out of Battle.* Oxford: Oxford University Press, 1972.

_____, ed. *The Penguin Book of First World War Poetry.* Harmondsworth, Middlesex: Penguin, 1979.

Simpson, Matt. "Proper Place." Review of *Thomas Hardy, Selected Poems,* edited by David Wright. *PN Review 12* (1979): 58–59.

Snipes, Katherine. *Robert Graves.* New York: Frederick Ungar, 1979.

Sorley, Charles Hamilton. *The Letters of Charles Sorley.* Cambridge: Cambridge University Press, 1919.

_____. *The Poems and Selected Letters of Charles Hamilton Sorley.* Edited by Hilda D. Spear. Dundee, Scotland: Blackness Press, 1978.

Sparrow, John, ed. *Robert Bridges*: *Poetry and Prose.* Oxford: Clarendon Press, 1955.

Spender, Stephen. *The Thirties and After.* Glasgow: Fontana, 1978.

_____. "W. H. Auden and His Poetry." In *Auden*: *A Collection of Critical Essays.* Edited by Monroe K. Spears. Englewood Cliffs, N.J.: Prentice-Hall, 1964.

Stade, George. *Robert Graves.* New York: Columbia University Press, 1967.

Stallworthy, Jon, ed. *The Penguin Book of Love Poetry.* London: Allen Lane, 1973.

Stanford, Derek. *John Betjeman.* London: Neville Spearman, 1961.

Stanford, Donald. *In the Classic Mode*: *The Achievement of Robert Bridges.* Newark: University of Delaware Press, 1978.

_____. *Revolution and Convention in Modern Poetry.* Newark: University of Delaware Press, 1983.
Steiner, George. "Criticisms of Life, Voices of Protest." Review of *Faber Book of Political Verse.* Edited by Tom Paulin. *Times Literary Supplement,* 23 May 1986, pp. 547–548.
Stevens, Wallace. *The Collected Poems of Wallace Stevens.* New York: Alfred A. Knopf, 1968.
Strauss, Leo. *Political Philosophy: Six Essays by Leo Strauss.* Edited by Hilail Gildin. Indianapolis, Ind.: Bobbs-Merrill, 1975.
Taylor-Martin, Patrick. *John Betjeman: His Life and Work.* London: Allen Lane, 1983.
Thomas, Edward. *A Literary Pilgrim in England.* 1917. Reprint. London: Jonathan Cape, 1928.
_____. "Georgian Poets." *The Daily Chronicle,* 14 January 1913, p. 4.
_____. *Letters from Edward Thomas to Gordon Bottomley.* Edited by R. George Thomas. London: Oxford University Press, 1968.
_____. *The Collected Poems of Edward Thomas.* Edited by R. George Thomas. Oxford: Clarendon Press, 1978.
_____. "Thomas Hardy of Dorchester." *Poetry and Drama* (June 1913): 180–184.
Thomas, Helen. *As It Was* and *World Without End.* London: Faber & Faber, 1972.
Thomas, R. George. *Edward Thomas: A Portrait.* Oxford: Oxford University Press, 1985.
Thompson, Edward. *Robert Bridges 1844–1930.* Oxford: Oxford University Press, 1944.
Thorpe, Michael. *The Poetry of Edmund Blunden.* London: Bridge Books, 1971.
Thwaite, Anthony, ed. *Larkin at Sixty.* London: Faber & Faber, 1982.
Timms, David. *Philip Larkin.* Edinburgh: Oliver & Boyd, 1973.
Tolley, A. T. *The Poetry of the Thirties.* London: Victor Gollancz, 1957.
Trimpi, Wesley. *Ben Jonson's Poems: A Study of the Plain Style.* Stanford, Calif.: Stanford University Press, 1962.
Underhill, Hugh. "The 'Poetical Character' of Edward Thomas." *Essays in Criticism* 23 (July 1973): 236–53.
Unterecker, John. *A Reader's Guide to William Butler Yeats.* New York: Farrar, Straus & Giroux, 1959.
Waldock, A. J. A. *Paradise Lost and Its Critics.* 1947. Reprint. London: Cambridge University Press, 1964.
Ward, J. P. "The Solitary Note: Edward Thomas and Modernism." *Poetry Wales* 13 (Spring 1978): 71–84.
Watkins, Vernon, ed. *Letters to Vernon Watkins.* By Dylan Thomas. London: Dent, 1957.
Watson, George. *Politics and Literature in Modern Britain.* London: Macmillan, 1977.
Watson, J. R. "The Other Larkin." *Critical Quarterly* 17 (1975): 347–60.
Weil, Simone. *The Need for Roots: Prelude to a Declaration of Duties Towards Mankind.* 1st English translation 1952. Reprint. London: Routledge & Kegan Paul, 1978.
Welland, D. S. R. *Wilfred Owen: A Critical Study.* London: Chatto & Windus, 1960.
Whalen, Terry. *Philip Larkin and English Poetry.* Vancouver: University of British Columbia Press, 1986.
Williams, William Carlos. *The William Carlos Williams Reader.* Edited by M. L. Rosenthal. New York: New Directions, 1966.
Williamson, George. *A Reader's Guide to T. S. Eliot.* London: Thames and Hudson, 1967.

Wilson, Colin. "Some Notes on Graves's Prose." *Shenandoah* 13 (Winter 1962): 55–62.
Winters, Yvor. *Forms of Discovery*. Chicago: Swallow, 1967.
———. *In Defense of Reason*. Chicago: Swallow, 1947.
———. *The Uncollected Essays and Reviews of Yvor Winters*. Edited by Francis Murphy. Chicago: Swallow, 1973.
Yeats, William Butler. *A Vision*. 2d ed. London: Macmillan, 1937.
———. *Variorum Edition of the Poems of W. B. Yeats*. Edited by Peter Allt and Russell K. Alspach. New York: Macmillan, 1966.
———. *W. B. Yeats: Selected Criticism*. Edited by A. Norman Jeffares. London: Pan Books, 1976.
Young, Alan, and Schmidt, Michael. "A Conversation with Edgell Rickword." *Poetry Nation,* no. 1 (1973): 73–89.
Young, Dudley. *Out of Ireland: The Poetry of W. B. Yeats*. Cheadle, Cheshire: Carcanet, 1973.

Index

Abercrombie, Lascelles, 222; "The Sale of Saint Thomas," 71–72
Aiken, Conrad, 25
Akhmatova, Anna, 214
Alexander, Michael, 29
Alvarez, A.: on Larkin, 266; on Lawrence, 171
American Review, 230
Amis, Kingsley: on Larkin, 266
Anthony, Saint, 44
Aquinas, Saint Thomas, 35, 225
Arendt, Hannah, 304 n.5
Aristotle, 35, 94–96, 97, 100, 101, 119, 144, 161, 168, 203
Arlen, Michael, 141
Arnold, Matthew, 14
Ashton, Theresa, 72
Asquith, Herbert Henry, 88
Associationism, 15, 21, 23, 39
Athenaeum, 65
Attridge, Derek, 289 n.29
Auden, W. H., 29, 35–36, 148, 189, 203, 205–13, 215, 218, 224, 229, 263, 267; on Betjeman, 243; on Graves, 186, 187, 303 n.75; on Larkin, 308 n.114. Poems: "After Reading a Child's Guide to Modern Physics," 212; *Another Time*, 210; "Consider this and in our time," 206–7, 209; "In Memory of Sigmund Freud," 148; "In Memory of W. B. Yeats," 211; "It was Easter as I walked," 207; *Journey to a War*, 210; "Miss Gee," 210–11; "Moon Landing," 212; "Musée des Beaux Arts," 211; "A New Year Greeting," 212; "Ode to Terminus," 212; "On the Circuit," 212; "Out on the lawn I lie in bed," 207; "Spain," 208–10; "A Thanksgiving," 206; "Who stands, the crux left of the watershed," 206

Bach, Johann Sebastian, 134
Baker, Howard, 52
Barnes, William, 247
Barrie, J. M., 222
Barthes, Roland, 145
Baudelaire, Charles, 215, 217
Baxter, John, 142–43
Bayley, John, 35
Beach, Joseph Warren, 30
Bedient, Calvin, 270
Bergonzi, Bernard, 92, 94, 100, 104, 127, 128, 258, 297 n.19, 308 n.87
Bergson, Henri, 288 n.24
Berry, Wendell, 204
Betjeman, Sir John, 29, 211, 219, 241–63, 275, 277–78, 280; general elegies by, 255–61; personal elegies by, 261–63; reputation of, 241–43; social criticism in poems of, 252–55; social portraits in poems of, 248–52; topographical poems of, 247–48. Poems: "Advertising Pays," 255; "Aldershot Crematorium," 262; "A Ballad of the Investiture 1969," 260–61; "Before Invasion, 1940," 261; "Before the Lecture," 255; "Beside the Seaside," 260, 261; "Bristol and Clifton," 255; "Business Girls," 249–50; "Calvionistic Evensong," 308 n.112; "Church of England Thoughts," 262; "The City," 248; "Civilized Woman," 255; "The Commander," 262–63; *Continual Dew*, 242; "The Conversion of St. Paul," 261; "Cornish Cliffs," 247–48, 251; "County," 248; "The Dear Old Village," 254; "Death of King George V," 242–43; "Delectable Duchy," 261; "The Diary of a Church Mouse," 255; "An Ecumenical Invitation,"

308 n.112; "Eunice," 249; "Executive," 254; "Exeter," 249; "Felixstowe, or The Last of Her Order," 251-52; "From the Great Western," 261; "Group Life: Letchworth," 254; "Harvest Hymn," 254-55; *High and Low*, 247; "A Hike on the Downs," 250; "How to Get On in Society," 250; "Hunter Trials," 250; "Huxley Hall," 262; "Hymn," 261; "In a Bath Teashop," 249; "Inexpensive Progress," 254; "In Westminster Abbey," 251; "Lift Man," 250; "A Lincolnshire Church," 257; "A Literary Discovery," 250; "Loneliness," 261; "Margate, 1940," 261; "May-Day Song for North Oxford," 256; "Meditation on a Constable Picture," 261; "Meditation on the A30," 255; "Middlesex," 256; "Monody on the Death of Aldersgate Street Station," 259, 277; *Mount Zion*, 246; "Narcissus," 250; *New Bats in Old Belfries*, 253; "The Newest Bath Guide," 254; *A Nip in the Air*, 246; "On a Portrait of a Deaf Man," 262; "On Hearing the Full Peal of Ten Bells from Christ Church, Swindon, Wilts.," 253; "On Leaving Wantage," 258-59; "On Seeing an Old Poet in the Café Royal," 249; "Pershore Station, or A Liverish Journey First Class," 255-56; "The Planster's Vision," 253; *Poems in the Porch*, 255; "Preface to 'High and Low,'" 246-47; "Remorse," 262; "The Retired Postal Clerk," 250-51; "A Romance," 255; "The Sandemanian Meeting House," 308 n.112; "Shattered Image," 250; "Shetland 1973," 261; *Slick But Not Streamlined*, 243; "Slough," 252-53; "Sunday Morning, King's Cambridge," 259; "Thoughts on a Train," 255; "Thoughts on 'The Diary of a Nobody,'" 257-58; "To the Crazy Gang," 246; "The Town Clerk's Views," 254; "Tregardock," 247, 251; *Uncollected Poems*, 246, 251; "Variations on a Theme by T. W. Rolleston," 262; "The Village Inn," 254; "Wembley Lad," 250; "The Wykehamist," 248-49. Prose: *Ghastly Good Taste*, 245-46

Beum, Robert, 164, 165-66, 167, 289 n.29

Binyon, Lawrence, 120

Blackmur, R. P., 30; on Lawrence, 170, 174

Blake, William, 37, 42, 62, 69, 94, 120, 122, 188; *Songs of Experience*, 236; "The Tyger," 220

Bloom, Harold, 37, 40, 44

Blunden, Edmund, 74-75, 119, 127-31, 135, 138, 297 n.19. Poems: "At Senlis Once," 127; "Battalion in Rest," 127; "Concert Party: Busseboom," 127-28, 130; "Gouzeaucourt: The Deceitful Calm," 127; "The Guard's Mistake," 127; "A House in Festubert," 127, 128, 129; "Illusions," 128; "La Quinque Rue," 127; "Pillbox," 129; "Preparations for Victory," 129; "Recognition," 129; "The Recovery," 130; "Return of the Native," 130-31; "Rural Economy," 129; "Third Ypres," 129-30; "Trench Raid near Hodge," 129; "Two Voices," 130; "Vlamertinghe: Passing the Château, July, 1917," 128; "The Welcome," 130; "Winter: East Anglia," 130. Prose: *Undertones of War*, 127

Bottomley, Gordon: *King Lear's Wife*, 66; on Rosenberg, 119

Bradley, F. H., 288 n.24

Brecht, Bertolt, 206

Bridges, Robert, 140, 146, 154-69, 184, 185-86, 200, 229-30. Poems: "The Affliction of Richard," 164, 169; "Dejection," 160; "Elegy: The Summer House on the Mound," 162-63, 169; "Eros," 164-67, 169, 191; "The Evening Darkens Over," 163, 169, 185; "Fortunatus Nimium," 159; "Ghosts," 162; *The*

Growth of Love, 154–59; "La Gloire de Voltaire," 169; "Low Barometer," 161–62, 169, 185; "My Spirit Kisseth Thine," 168; *New Poems*, 163; "Nightingales," 160; "To Robert Burns: An Epistle on Instinct," 161; "Rondeau," 167; "The Sea Keeps Not the Sabbath," 163, 185; *Shorter Poems*, 159, 163, 167; "Since Thou, O Fondest and True," 168; "So Sweet Love Seemed," 168, 169; "Spring: Ode II," 159; *The Testament of Beauty*, 158; "When My Love Was Away," 168
Brooke, Rupert, 67, 70–71, 79, 92, 96–97, 98, 99, 100, 132, 133, 134. Poems: "A Channel Passage," 66; "The Dead," 97; "The Fish," 70; "The Great Lover," 71; "The Soldier," 97; "Tiare Tahiti," 70
Brooks, Cleanth, 25
Browning, Robert, 55, 189
Bunyan, John: *Pilgrim's Progress*, 76
Burns, Robert: "Holy Willie's Prayer," 251
Burrows, Louise, 171
Byron, Lord, 71, 94, 104–5, 109, 226; *The Vision of Judgment*, 242–43

Calendar of Modern Letters, 215, 222
Campbell, Roy, 293 n.16
Campion, Thomas, 168, 189
Carruth, Hayden, 203
Carswell, Catherine, 171
Chambers, Jessie, 171, 175, 183
Chaucer, Geoffrey, 93
Chesterton, C. K.: "The Song of Elf," 67
Churchill, Charles, 226
Clark, Leonard, 135
Cohen, J. M., 186, 187
Coleridge, Samuel Taylor, 76; "Kubla Khan," 119
Collins, Vere, 47
Collins, William, 62
Conquest, Robert, 266
Cooke, William, 75, 76, 79
Coombes, H., 75
Corke, Helen, 171
Cornfield, John: "Full Moon at Tierz: Before the Storming of Huesca," 213
Cowley, Abraham: "Dialogue After Enjoyment," 151
Crabbe, George, 48, 68, 196, 247, 292 n.61; "A Marriage Ring," 153–54, 168
Creeley, Robert, 288 n.26
Cullingford, Elizabeth, 290 n.6
Cummings, E. E.: "May I Feel Said He," 152–53
Cunningham, J. V., 25, 142

Daily Chronicle, The, 67–68
Danby, John, 75
Dante: *Inferno*, 117
Darwin, Charles, 47–48
Daryush, Elizabeth, 229–41, 264; didactic poems of, 232–34; early, personal poems of, 230–32; social poems of, 234–41; on syllabic meter, 237. Poems: "Aeroplanes," 239; "Air & Variations," 230; "Along the narrow cottage-path he wheeled," 239; "Anger lay by me all night long," 236, 240; "Blind," 231–32; "Children of wealth in your warm nursery," 239–40; *Collected Poems*, 230, 239; "Dutiful volunteer," 240; "Exile," 231, 232; "For my misdeed I blame my erring friend's," 233; "For P. W.," 241; "Fresh Spring," 231; "From day to converse night," 230–31, 240; "He said: I left it in the porch," 240; "I am your lover now, once awful Enmity," 240; "It is pleasant to hang out," 234–35, 236; "Jerusalem, September 17, 1948," 240; *The Lost Man & Other Verses*, 230, 236; "Moored in the shallows," 240; *Selected Poems*, 230, 232, 235, 236; "The servant-girl sleeps," 234–35; "Still Life," 237–39; "This is the last night that my love is here," 240; "Thou say'st: *The clear stream is a troubled river grown*," 231; *Verses*, 230; *Verses, Fourth Book*, 230, 232; *Verses, Second Book*, 230; *Verses, Seventh Book*, 230, 240; *Verses,*

Sixth Book, 230, 239; *Verses, Third Book*, 230, 231; "The Warden's Daughter," 233, 235; "War-Tribunal," 240; "Well, and what of it? What if you are beautiful?" 233; "Wherefore solicit," 232; "The woman I'd revere," 234–36; "You should at times go out," 232–33; "You who are blest," 231. Prose: "Notes on Syllabic Metres," 237
Davie, Donald, 29, 30, 49, 58–59, 137, 214, 230, 289 n.39, 299 n.74
Davies, W. H., 67. Poems: "The Bird of Paradise," 68; "The Heap of Rags," 68; "The Mind's Liberty," 68; "Sweet Stay at Home," 68–69
Day, Douglas, 186, 191, 192
Day, Roger, 268, 270
Day Lewis, Cecil, 29; *The Magnetic Mountain* #32, 212–13
De la Mare, Walter, 29, 69, 79; on Gurney, 135; "The Listeners," 66–67
Des Pres, Terrence, 214
Dickinson, Emily, 137
Doolittle, Hilda [H.D.]: "Oread," 17–18, 288 n.17
Donne, John, 44, 139, 216, 219, 221; "To His Mistress Going to Bed," 152
Douglas, James D., 227
Drinkwater, John: "Tradition and Technique," 61–62, 63
Drummond, C. Q., 146
Dunbar, William, 189

Egoist, The, 62, 64–65
Einstein, Albert, 140
Eliot, T. S., 14–15, 19, 24–25, 29, 30, 53, 189, 204, 205, 211, 217, 218, 223, 225, 244, 295 n.41, 309 n.118; discontinuous structure in, 24; on the Georgians, 64–65; on Lawrence, 170; objective correlative in the theory of, 15, 19; on Yeats, 29. Poems: *Four Quartets*, 22; "Gerontion," 24; "The Love Song of J. Alfred Prufrock," 24, 225; "Portrait of a Lady," 150; *The Waste Land*, 24–25, 217, 218, 223. Prose: "Reflections on 'Vers Libre,'" 21

Elizabeth I, 84
Ellmann, Richard, 36, 38, 41
Emerson, Ralph Waldo, 72, 148
Enright, D. J., 202, 204, 271

Falck, Colin, 266
Fargeon, Eleanor, 77
Finch, Anne, Countess of Winchilsea: "The Soldier's Death," 91
Flint, F. S.: "Lament," 92
Fletcher, John Gould, 67
Forche, Carolyn, 205
Ford, Ford Madox, 287 n.11; "Impressionism," 62–63; "That Exploit of Yours," 92
Forster, E. M.: on Lawrence, 170
Foucault, Michel, 145
France, Anatole, 58
Fraser, G. S., 188, 207–8, 288 n.26, 301 n.75
Free verse, 21–23
Freud, Sigmund, 140, 148, 175, 225
Frost, Robert, 19, 206; "The Bear," 20; and Edward Thomas, 75, 76–77; "The Wrights' Biplane," 77
Fuller, Roy, 204, 230
Fussell, Paul, 87, 93, 108, 288 n.26, 297 n.15
Futurism, 63, 64, 67

Gascoigne, George, 93–94, 157; "The Fruites of Warre," 94; "Gascoignes Woodmanship," 94
Gaskell, Ronald, 186
George V, 242–43
George III, 242–43
Georgian Poetry anthologies, 61, 65–72, 86
Georgian poets, 60–72, 74, 86, 121, 131, 171, 188; anti-intellectualism in poetry of, 68–69; formal weaknesses in poetry of, 66–67; moral weakness in poetry of, 69–72; primitivism in poetry of, 67–68; theory by, 61–65
Gibbon, Edward, 292 n.61
Gibbon, Reginald, 205
Gibson, Wilfred: "Devil's Edge," 68; "The Gorse," 67
Gilbert, Sandra, 184–85
Ginsberg, Allen, 22, 288 n.26
Godwin, William, 42
Gonne, Maud, 42, 44

Gosse, Edmund, 67
Graff, Gerald, 36
Grant, George, 35, 153
Granville, George, 147
Graves, Robert, 15, 29, 98–101, 102, 127, 140–41, 146, 185–201, 206, 297 n.19; anti-romanticism of, 187–89; on Bridges, 185; criticisms of other poets, 189; generalizing voice of, 192–93; humor in, 189–90; on Lawrence, 185; mature love-marriage poems of, 193–99; sex in, 190–92; White Goddess phase of, 198–99. Poems: "Advice to Lovers," 190; "The Ample Garden," 189; "At First Sight," 191; "The Beach," 198; "The Beast," 195, 197; "Big Words," 100; "Call It a Good Marriage," 199; *Collected Poems*, 190, 193; "The Cool Web," 188, 195; "Dance of Words," 200; "Dead Boche," 100, 117; "Despite and Still," 196–97; "The Devil's Advice to Story-Tellers," 188; "Down, Wanton, Down!" 190–91, 195; "Ecstasy of Chaos," 199; "The Face in the Mirror," 198; "The Finding of Love," 192; "Flying Crooked," 188; "Goliath and David," 100; "I'd Die for You," 199; "In Broken Images," 188–89; "Joan and Darby," 199; "Language of the Seasons," 198; "Leda," 191–92; "The Leveller," 98–99; "Lion Lover," 199; "Lost Acres," 185, 188, 195; "Lost Love," 190; "Love in Barrenness," 192, 194; "A Love Story," 193–94, 195, 198; "Love Without Hope," 15–17; "Mid-Winter Waking," 196, 197–98; *Mock Beggar Hall*, 192; "Nature's Lineaments," 185, 188; *No More Ghosts*, 193; "The Oath," 196, 197; "Oh, And Oh!" 190; *Over the Brazier*, 189; *Poems 1938-45*, 186, 187, 193–99; "Prometheus," 199; "Rocky Acres," 187; "Sea Side," 190; "She is No Liar," 199; "She Tells Her Love While Half Asleep," 196, 198; "The Shot," 195–96, 197; "Song: Dew-Drop and Diamond," 199; "Song of Contrariety," 192; "Spoils," 199; "The Straw," 199; "Symptoms of Love," 199; "Theseus and Ariadne," 198; "The Thieves," 194–95, 197; "Tilth," 199–200; "Times," 193; "To Juan at the Winter Solstice," 198; "To Sleep," 196, 197; "The Troll's Nosegay," 190; "Ulysses," 191; "Vain and Careless," 190; Vanity," 192; *Whipperginny*, 192; "The Window Sill," 199; "A Withering Herb," 195. Prose: *Goodbye to All That*, 296 n.3; *The Long Weekend*, 140–41
Gray, Thomas, 62
Gregory, Lady Augusta, 38
Gregory, Major Robert, 43
Gregson, J. M., 92, 93, 297 n.19
Grenfell, Julian, 92, 96, 99; "Into Battle," 97–98
Greville, Fulke, 109
Grigson, Geoffrey, 29, 139, 140
Groddeck, Georg, 211
Grossmith, George and Weedon: *The Diary of a Nobody*, 258
Grubb, Frederick, 187
Guerard, Albert, 154
Gunn, Thom, 54, 56, 199, 200
Gurney, Ivor, 110–11, 119, 127, 131–38, 297 n.19, 299 n.74. Poems: "The Awakening," 135; "Between the Boughs," 137; "Brown Earth Look," 137; "Butchers and Tombs," 136–37; "The Canadians," 135–36; "De Profundis," 131–32; "The Fire Kindled," 132; "First Time In ('The Captain addresses us ...')," 133–34; "Homesickness," 133; "Pain," 133; "Servitude," 133; *Severn and Somme*, 132; "The Silent One," 136; "Strange Service," 132–33; "The Strong Thing," 133; "To His Love," 110–11; "Townshend," 134; *War's Embers*, 131

Haffenden, John, 266, 274
Haig, Douglas (field marshall), 88
Haldane, John Scott, 227

Hamilton, Ian, 266
Harding, D. W., 120, 122
Hardy, Emma, 55–59
Hardy, Thomas, 26, 29–35, 46–59, 60, 65, 68, 69, 73, 74, 75, 77, 79, 84, 87–92, 93, 105–6, 113, 123, 135, 139–40, 154, 159, 163, 171, 177, 189, 206, 240, 244, 247, 262, 263, 264, 268, 269, 276, 289 n.39, 295 n.46, 296 n.3; beliefs of, 47–52; on Christianity and religion, 48–49, 51–52, 54–55; descriptive precision of, 53–54; on nature, 47–48; pessimism of, 49–51, 80; practical ethic of, 48–49; 51; provincialism of, 31, 53; social perspective in poetry of, 52–53; tonal control in poetry of, 54–59; on *vers libre*, 296 n.3; as war poet, 87–92, 95, 97, 99–100, 127; on Wordsworth, 292 n.61; on Yeats, 47; Poems: "Afternoon Service at Mellstock," 292 n.59; "After the Last Breath," 53, 240; "Afterwards," 48–49, 53, 275; "And There Was a Great Calm," 91, 106; "'Any Little Old Song,'" 51; "An Appeal to America on Behalf of the Belgian Destitute," 90; "At the Piano," 52; "The Bedridden Peasant to an Unknown God," 54–55; "Beeny Cliff," 57; "Before Life and After," 48; "Before Marching and After," 90–91; "Between Us Now," 52; "A Broken Appointment," 193; "A Call to National Service," 87, 90; "Cry of the Homeless: After the Prussian Invasion of Belgium," 90; "A Cathedral Façade at Midnight," 52; "The Darkling Thrush," 269; "Dream of the City Shopwoman," 50; "Drinking Song," 48, 49; *The Dynasts*, 46, 87, 89, 90, 135; "England to Germany in 1914," 90; "Former Beauties," 46–47; "God-Forgotten," 54, 292 n.59; "The Haunter," 58–59; "I Am the One," 48; "I Found You Out There," 57–58; "'I Met a Man,'" 90; "The Impercipient," 292 n.59; "In Time of 'The Breaking of Nations,'" 53, 80, 88, 90, 137; "In Time of Wars and Tumults," 90; "Lament," 57; "Lost Love," 55–56; "Lying Awake," 48; "Men Who March Away," 87–90, 95, 97, 99; *Moments of Vision and Miscellaneous Verses*, 87; "Neutral Tones," 31–34; "A New Year's Eve in War Time," 90; "Night in the Old Home," 49, 54; "The Night of Trafalgar," 46–47; "Nobody Comes," 53; "No Buyers," 53; "Often When Warring," 88, 117; "On the Belgian Expatriation," 90; "The Oxen," 292 n.59; "The Pity of It," 90; *Poems of the Past and the Present*, 50, 54; "The Ruined Maid," 68; "Sacred to the Memory," 50; *Satires of Circumstance*, 87, 106; "The Shadow on the Stone," 52; "A Sheep Fair," 53; "Shut Out that Moon," 50; "A Singer Asleep," 50; "Snow in the Suburbs," 46–47; "Then and Now," 91; "Thoughts of Phena," 50; "Throwing a Tree," 53; "The To-Be-Forgotten," 53; "The Unborn," 48; "The Voice," 58–59; "Wagtail and Baby," 50; "The Walk," 55–56, 240; "Weathers," 46–47; "Winter in Durnover Field," 52; *Winter Words*, 48; "Without Ceremony," 57; "Your Last Drive," 52. Prose: "Apology" to *Late Lyrics and Earlier*, 51; *The Return of the Native*, 105–6
Hartley, David, 287 n.11
Hayman, Ronald, 187
Heaney, Seamus: on Larkin, 264–65
Hemingway, Ernest, 93, 259
Henderson, Philip, 224
Heraclitus, 21, 288 n.24
Herbert, George, 189
Hibberd, Dominic, 113, 115, 117, 297 n.13
Hillier, Bevis, 250
Hitler, Adolf, 212
Hodge, Alan, 140–41
Hodgson, Ralph: "The Bull," 67; "The Song of Honour," 69
Homer: *The Iliad*, 296 n.3

Index

Hone, Joseph, 42
Hood, Thomas, 247
Hooker, Jeremy, 81
Hopkins, Gerard Manley, 135
Horace [Quintus Horatius Flaccus], 111
Hough, Graham, 15, 174
Howe, Irving, 53, 59, 205
Hueffer, Ford Maddox. *See* Ford, Ford Madox
Hughes, Noel, 266
Hulme, T. E., 23, 287 n.11
Hunter, William B., Jr., 95
Hurd, Michael, 134, 136
Huxley, Aldous, 141
Hynes, Samuel, 209, 212, 289 n.39

Imagism, 14, 15, 16, 17, 18, 19, 20, 21, 62, 64, 67, 171
Irish Times, 29

Jacobson, Dan, 266
James, William, 48, 288 n.24
Johnson, Dr. Samuel, 52, 187
Johnston, John H., 296 n.2, 298 n.48
Jones, David, 119
Jones, Ernest, 140
Jonson, Ben, 134, 189, 200; "To Penshurst," 81
Joyce, James, 30, 35

Kahn, Gustave, 22
Karl, Frederick R., 13
Kavanagh, P. J., 137, 299 n.69
Keane, Patrick, 186, 200
Keats, John, 60, 69, 73, 77, 97, 111–12, 118, 144, 292 n.61. Poems: *Endymion*, 117; *Hyperion*, 111–12; "Ode on a Grecian Urn," 128; "Ode on Melancholy," 118; "Ode to a Nightingale," 77–78, 80, 116, 160
Keith, W. J., 75, 76
Kenner, Hugh, 15
Kermode, Frank, 35
Kierkegaard, Soren, 212
King, R. W., 53
Kipling, Rudyard, 189
Kirkham, Michael, 76, 186, 295 n.46

Kitchener, Horatio Herbert (field marshall), 88

Laforgue, Jules, 22, 295 n.41
Landor, Walter Savage, 44, 189
Lane, Arthur E., 295 n.2
Langbaum, Robert, 35, 296 n.2
Langland, William, 93
Larkin, Philip, 26, 29, 30, 214, 219, 253, 260, 263–86; and Betjeman, 263–64, 278; celebrations of rituals in poems of, 277–86; limits acknowledged in poems of, 268–72; observations of social customs in poems of, 274–77; temptations to retire in poems of, 272–74. Poems: "Ambulances," 275–76; "Annus Mirabilis," 276; "An Arundel Tomb," 280, 284–86; "At Grass," 272–73, 275; "Aubade," 265; "Born Yesterday," 269; "Church Going," 253, 266, 276–77; "Coming," 268–69; "Conscript," 267; "Days," 271; "Deceptions," 270; "Dockery and Son," 270–71, 276; "Going," 270; "Going, Going," 280; "Here," 272–73, 275; "High Windows," 274, 276; *High Windows*, 266, 278; "Homage to a Government," 280; "Home is So Sad," 272; "Ignorance," 272; "The Importance of Elsewhere," 273–74; "I Remember, I Remember," 268; "The Large Cool Store," 272; *The Less Deceived*, 268, 272, 273; "Livings," 279; "Love Songs in Age," 272; "Maiden Name," 276; "Mr. Bleaney," 275; "Naturally the Foundation will Bear Your Expenses," 279–80; "Next Please," 269, 270; "MCMXIV," 272, 280; *The North Ship*, 267; "Nothing To Be Said," 271; "Reasons for Attendance," 276; "VI," 267, 268; "Show Saturday," 278–79; "Sympathy in White Major," 275; "Take One Home for the Kiddies," 272; "Talking in Bed," 272; "XXXII," 267, 268; "Toads," 218, 279; "Toads Revisited," 279; "To the Sea," 260, 278–79; "The

Trees," 279; Vers de Société," 275–76, 277; "Wants," 270; "The Whitsun Weddings," 280–85; *The Whitsun Weddings*, 270, 272, 273; "Wires," 273. Prose: *A Girl in Winter*, 268; *Jill*, 268
Lawrence, D. H., 21, 30, 140, 141–44, 146, 147, 154, 169–85, 186, 194, 200, 266, 268, 288 n.26, 300 n.11; on death of his mother, 173–85; on free verse and meter, 21–22; heterosexual love poems of, 171–73. Poems: *Amores*, 173, 174, 178; "And Oh— That the Man I Am Might Cease to Be—," 173; "Aware," 172; "Bei Hennef," 173; "The Bride," 174, 178–80, 181; "Brooding Grief," 174, 183–84; "Cherry Robbers," 171; *Collected Poems*, 173, 174, 178, 183; "Come Spring, Come Sorrow," 172; "Demiurge," 175–76; "Endless Anxiety," 178; "Excursion Train," 171, 172; "Flowers and Men," 175–76; "The Hands of the Betrothed," 172; "The Inheritance," 182–83; "Last Words to Miriam," 172; "Lilies in the Fire," 171–72; "Listening," 181; *Look! We Have Come Through!*, 173; *Love Poems and Others*, 173; *New Poems*, 173; "Passing Visit to Helen," 172; "Patience," 178; "Remainder," 173; "Silence," 174, 181–83; "Sorrow," 174, 180–81, 182, 183; "Suspense," 174, 176–78; "These Clever Women," 172; "Troth with the Dead," 174, 183–84; "A White Blossom," 172. Prose: "Education of the People," 175; *The Rainbow*, 141–44, 146, 154, 170; *Sons and Lovers*, 170, 171, 176, 178, 180, 183; *Women in Love*, 170
Lawrence, Frieda, 169
Lawrence, Lydia, 173–74, 176–85
Lawrence, Ralph, 72–73
Leavis, F. R.: on Eliot, 289 n.33; on Hardy, 51, 74; on Lawrence, 141; on Lawrence and Joyce, 30; on Meredith, 158; on Thomas, 73–76, 82

Leavis, Q. D., 170
Ledwidge, Francis: "The Wife of Llew," 69
Left Review, 215
Levi, Peter, 263, 266
Lewis, C. S., 147, 158
Lewis, Wyndham, 223
Liddiard, Jean, 121, 122, 126–27
Lindsay, John, 215, 229
Locke, John, 203
Logue, Leona Whitworth, 296 n.12
Longfellow, Henry Wadsworth, 189
Longley, Edna, 76
Lucas, John, 289 n.39

McCrae, John, 101
McFarlane, James, 139
Machiavelli, Niccolo, 203
MacLeish, Archibald: "Ars Poetica," 150; "'Not Marble Nor the Gilded Monuments,'" 150
MacNeice, Louis: "Autumn Journal III," 213; "Birmingham," 213
Mailer, Norman, 297 n.15
Mandelstam, Osip, 214
Marlowe, Christopher: translation of Ovid's "Elegy 5," 151–52
Marsden, Kenneth, 30
Marsh, Edward, 60, 62, 63, 65, 70, 121. See *Georgian Poetry* anthologies
Marsh, Jan, 75
Marshall, Tom, 180, 184
Martin, Bruce, 275
Marvell, Andrew, 118
Marxism, 203, 207, 215–16, 224, 253, 254
Masefield, John, 67; "Biography," 69
Masters, Edgar Lee: *Spoon River Anthology*, 21
Mathias, Roland, 75
Mehoke, James, 186
Meredith, George: *Modern Love*, 155–59
Mill, John Stuart, 76
Milosz, Czeslaw, 214
Milton, John, 14, 129, 134, 246; *Paradise Lost*, 145–46, 164, 167, 189, 198, 222
Modernism and modernists, 13, 19, 20, 25–26, 29, 30–31, 35, 36, 45,

53, 60, 63, 64, 65, 72, 80, 86, 87, 93, 94, 104, 139–40, 148, 149, 150, 157, 187, 189, 199, 202–4, 218, 222, 223, 244, 264, 287 n.2, 288 n.24
Momaday, N. Scott: "Buteo Regalis," 18–19
Monro, Harold, 63, 64. Poems: "Lake Leman," 69; "Milk for the Cat," 69. Prose: "The Future of Poetry," 61; "Futurism," 63
Monroe, Harriet, 61
Montague, C. E., 135
Moore, Harry T., 174
Moore, T. Sturge: "A Sicilian Idyll," 67, 71
Morris, William, 215, 245
Motion, Andrew, 75, 76, 265, 294 n.37
Movement, the, 30, 266
Murry, Middleton: on the Georgians, 65

New Critics, 36, 75, 76, 174
New Statesman, 215
Nichols, Robert, 100
Nicholson, Nancy, 186
Nietzsche, Friedrich, 139, 288 n.24

Observer, The, 264
Olson, Charles, 22
Orwell, George, 210, 212, 215; "Notes on Nationalism," 215, 241
Our Time, 215
Owen, Wilfred, 64, 79, 93, 94, 100, 101, 103, 106–18, 119, 122, 127, 136, 296 n.2, 297 n.19; didactic demands on, 111–12; pity in poetry of, 108–10; as a romantic, 298 n.50; Sassoon's influence on, 106–8. Poems: "Anthem for Doomed Youth," 113, 115; "À Terre," 117; "The Chances," 117; "The Dead-Beat," 106–7; "Disabled," 117; "Dulce Et Decorum Est," 103, 111, 112; "The End," 117; "Exposure," 113–26; "Futility," 112, 115; "Greater Love," 109–10; "Hospital Barge at Cérisy," 113; "Insensibility," 113, 116; "Inspection," 106, 115; "Mental Cases," 117; "Miners," 117; "The Next War," 117; "The Parable of the Old Man and the Young," 113; "The Send-Off," 107–8; "The Show," 113, 117; "S.I.W.," 108; "Six O'Clock in Princes Street," 113; "Smile, Smile, Smile," 106; "Spring Offensive," 117; "Strange Meeting," 113, 116–18; "To Eros," 109
Oxford Poetry (1927), 205

Palmer, Herbert, 86
Pantheism, 18, 84
Pater, Walter, 14, 21, 71
Patten, Brian: "Party Piece," 149
Paulin, Tom: *Faber Book of Political Verse*, 214, 305 n.17; on Hardy and Yeats, 290 n.9
Peckham, Morse, 71
Pericles, 301 n.45
Petrarch and Petrarchanism, 44, 79, 109, 189, 192
Pheidias, 166, 301 n.45
Plato and Platonism, 159, 161
PN Review, 30, 214, 223
Poe, Edgar Allan, 119
Poetry: A Magazine of Verse, 62
Poetry Review, The, 61
Pope, Alexander, 104–5, 147, 226, 251
Postmodernism, 24, 287 n.2
Pound, Ezra, 14, 15, 16–17, 18, 19, 25, 29, 30, 53, 62, 63, 64, 75, 91, 189, 204, 294 n.37. Poems: *Cantos*, 15, 16; *Exultations*, 294 n.37; *Hugh Selwyn Mauberley*, 19–20, 91–92; "In a Station of the Metro," 16–17; "The Temperaments," 147–48. Prose: "The Serious Artist," 62; "Vorticism," 14, 288 n.17
Praed, Winthrop Mackworth, 247
Press, John, 98, 100, 242–43, 303 n.75, 308 n.105
Pritchard, Beryl, 186, 193
Pritchard, William, 140
Proust, Marcel, 219
Pryce-Jones, Alan, 63

Quinn, Marie, 73–74, 84

Rajan, Balachandra, 46
Ransom, John Crowe: "Piazza Piece," 150

Read, Herbert, 35; "Ritz: Love Among the Ruins," 148
Rexroth, Kenneth: on Lawrence, 171
Richards, I. A., 139
Rickword, Edgell, 215–29, 230, 239, 241, 264; critical prose of, 222–24; early love poems of, 216–18; later love poems of, 224–25; social satire by, 225–28; transitional phase, 218–22. Poems: "Answer to an Invitation to Love Delayed in the Post," 225; "Apostate Humanitarian," 218–20; "Beauty Invades the Sorrowful Heart," 216; *Behind the Eyes*, 215, 216; "Beyond Good and Evil, 218; "Circus," 217–18; "The Contemporary Muse," 225; "Desire," 216; "Divagation on a Line of Donne's," 218–19; 221; "The Encounter," 226–28; "Foreboding," 216; "The Handmaid of Religion," 225–26; "Hints for Making a Gentleman," 225–26; "Intimacy," 216; *Invocations to Angels*, 215, 217, 218; "Lament," 216; "The Lousy Astrologer's Present to His Sweetheart," 224–25; "Luxury," 217; "Ode to a Train-de-luxe," 218–19, 221–22, 224; "Passion," 216; "Poet to Punk," 218; "Prelude, Dream and Divagation," 218; "Provincial Nightpiece," 218–20; "Regret," 216; "Regret for the Depopulation of Rural Districts," 217; "Regret for the Passing of the Entire Scheme of Things," 216–17; "Reverie," 216; *Selected Poems*, 215, 218; "The Tired Lover," 216; "To the Wife of a Non-Interventionist Statesman (March 1938)," 229; "Trench Poets," 216, 218; *Twittingpan and Some Others*, 215, 224
Riding, Laura, 186, 191, 193, 195
Rilke, Rainer Maria, 211
Robinson, Edwin Arlington, 223, 306 n.46
Robinson, Ian, 143, 148
Rochester, the earl of, 189; "Written in a Lady's Prayer Book," 150–51

Roethke, Theodore, 23–24
Romanticism, 14, 29, 30, 31, 35, 37–40, 48, 49, 50, 53, 57, 60–64, 66, 67, 70, 72, 76, 77, 161, 185, 186–87, 199–200, 222, 231, 265, 266, 272, 287 n.11, 298 n.50
Rosenberg, Issac, 64, 94, 118–27, 136, 297 n.19. Poems: "Break of Day in the Trenches," 122–23, 125; "Daughters of War," 122, 125; "Dead Man's Dump," 123–26, 299 n.58; "Marching (As Seen from the Left File)," 121, 122; "Moses," 120; "On Receiving News of the War," 120; "Returning, We Hear the Larks," 121–22
Ross, Robert: *The Georgian Revolt*, 60–61, 63, 64, 65, 67, 293 n.1
Ross, Ronald: "Hesperus," 69–70
Rossetti, Dante Gabriel, 119
Rousseau, Jean Jacques, 161
Russell, Bertrand, 101, 228

Sargent, Edmund Beal: "The Cookoo Wood," 69
Sassoon, Siegfried, 29, 64, 79, 93, 94, 100, 101–6, 107, 108, 111, 118, 119, 127, 128, 130, 136, 296 n.2, 297 n.19; description in poetry of, 102–3; on Hardy, 105–6; irony in poetry of, 103–4; satire in poetry of, 104–5. Poems: "Ancient History," 106; "At Carnoy," 102; "At Max Gate," 106; "Base Details," 104; "Concert-Interpretation," 104; "Counter-Attack," 102–3; "Does it Matter?" 103–4; "Dreamers," 104; "Falling Asleep," 103; "The General," 104; "Glory of Women," 108; "In the Pink," 103; "Lamentations," 103; "Memorial Tablet," 104; "On Reading the War Diary of a Defunct Ambassador," 105; "Reconciliation," 106; "Rear-Guard," 118; "Suicide in the Trenches," 108; "'They,'" 105, 106; "To an Eighteenth Century Poet," 106; "To Any Dead Officer," 104; "Villa d'Este Gardens," 104–5

Index

Savage, D. S., 29, 170
Schmidt, Michael, 26, 187, 216, 233, 238
Schwartz, Sanford, 36, 288 n.24
Scott, Nathan, Jr., 205
Scott, Sir Walter: *Marmion*, 296 n.3
Seeger, Alan, 101
Semour-Smith, Martin, 186, 187, 191
Shaftesbury, the third earl of, 42
Shakespeare, William, 81, 92, 147, 168, 170; *Henry the Fourth*, 92, 94–96; Sonnet 129: 192
Shapiro, Karl, 289 n.29
Shaw, George Bernard, 36
Shelley, Percy Bysshe, 69, 71, 119, 130, 154, 155, 188, 292 n.61. Poems: "Alastor," 118; *The Revolt of Islam*, 117; "To _____," 147
Silkin, Jon, 52, 87–92, 98, 102, 108–9, 111, 114–15, 116, 127, 297 n.19, 299 n.58
Simpson, Mrs. Wallace, 243
Sisson, C. H., 107, 185, 296 n.12
Skelton, John, 189
Smith, Stevie: Larkin on, 309 n.118
Snipes, Katherine, 186
Socrates, 90
Sola Pinto, Vivian de, 92–93; on Lawrence, 171
Sorley, Charles Hamilton, 89–90, 91, 98–101, 297 n.19; on Hardy, 89–90, 99–100. Poems: "All the Hills and Vales Along," 99; "Such, Such is Death," 91, 98–99, 100; "To Germany," 99; "When You See Millions of the Mouthless Dead," 100
Southey, Robert: *A Vision of Judgment*, 242
Sparks, Tryphena, 50
Sparrow, John, 243
Spectator, The, 69
Spender, Stephen, 210, 215, 229; "The Landscape near an Aerodrome," 213
Squire, J. C., 170
Stade, George, 186
Stallworthy, Jon, 140
Stanford, Derek, 243, 253
Stanford, Donald, 154, 164, 166, 287 n.7

Steiner, George, 214
Stephens, James: "In the Poppy Field, 69
Stevens, Wallace: "A High-Toned Old Christian Woman," 20
Strauss, Leo, 202–3
Sunday Express, 227
Swift, Jonathan, 223
Swinburne, Algernon, 50, 61, 119, 134, 189; "In the Orchard," 152–53
Symbolism, 16, 63, 265, 287 n.11
Symons, Arthur, 14, 43, 296 n.5; on Bridges, 156
Synge, John, 67

Taylor-Martin, Patrick, 245, 260
Tennyson, Alfred Lord, 69, 216, 219, 225, 247; "Tears, Idle Tears," 160
Thomas, Dylan, 29, 189, 267, 268
Thomas, Edward, 29, 60, 65, 69, 72–86, 89, 127, 135, 140, 206; on the Georgians, 67–68; on Hardy, 295 nn. 40 and 41; melancholy of, 80–81; as modernist poet, 73–76; on Pound, 294 n.37; public poetic voice of, 76–77, 82; as Romantic poet, 72–73; rural continuities in poetry of, 81–84; style of, 85–86, 295 n.46. Poems: "Adlestrop," 81, 83–84, 256; "After You Speak," 295 n.46; "As the Team's Head Brass," 80; "Cock-Crow," 295 n.46; "The Combe," 84–85; "For These," 79, 85; "The Green Roads," 295 n.46; "Haymaking," 80, 81, 82–83; "Helen," 85–86; "Interval," 80; "Liberty," 80, 85; "Lights Out," 85; "The Manor Farm," 81–82; "The New Year," 295 n.46; "Old Man," 84; "Over the Hills," 73–74; "The Path," 79, 295 n.46; "Rain," 80–81; "Sowing," 80; "Tall Nettles," 76–77; "Tears," 84; "This is No Case of Petty Right or Wrong," 79, 89; "The Trumpet," 77–79; "Two Houses," 84; "When He Should Laugh," 86. Prose: *The Country*, 84; *A Literary Pilgrim in England*, 295 n.40
Thomas, Helen, 76, 85
Thomas, R. George, 76

332 INDEX

Thompson, Francis: "Dream Tryst," 119; "The Mistress of Vision," 119
Thorpe, Michael, 127
Times, The, 88
Timms, David, 272–73
TLS [*Times Literary Supplement*], 66, 67, 214, 215, 223
Tolstoy, Count Leo, 121
Trevelyan, Robert: "Dirge," 70
Trimpi, Wesley, 306 n.43

Underhill, Hugh, 73
Unterecker, John, 39, 41

Verlaine, Paul-Marie, 119

Wain, John, 308 n.87
Waldock, A. J. A., 146
Ward, J. P., 75
Warner, Rex: "Hymn," 213
Watson, J. R., 265–66, 280
Weil, Simone, 202, 214–15, 306 n.45
Welland, D. S. R., 108, 109, 111, 117
Wells, H. G., 215
Whalen, Terry, 265
Wheels, 64–65
Whitman, Walt, 21, 22, 61, 62, 63, 135, 137, 148, 171, 288 n.26
Wilde, Oscar, 118, 141
Williams, William Carlos, 14, 22, 288 n.26
Williamson, George, 150
Wilson, Colin, 199
Winters, Yvor: on Daryush, 230, 234, 237, 240, 307 n.70; on free verse, 22; on Hardy, 51, 58
Wordsworth, William, 48, 50, 53, 61, 62, 63, 67–68, 69, 75, 76, 81, 130, 157, 168, 210, 264, 292 n.61. Poems: *Lyrical Ballads*, 68; *The Prelude*, 69; "Resolution and Independence," 292 n.61; "The Reverie of Poor Susan," 68; "A Slumber Did My Spirit Seal," 112
Wyatt, Sir Thomas, 157, 189; "They Flee From Me," 149; "To His Lute," 151

Yeats, William Butler, 29–48, 49, 51–52, 53, 54, 55, 59, 121, 157, 160, 189, 198, 200, 206, 211, 263, 267, 297 n.20; amorality in poetry of, 34, 42–43; on Bridges, 159; deterministic philosophy of, 37–40, 41, 43; disrespect for reason and logic in, 37–39; egotism in poetry of, 43–44; extremism in, 43; on Hardy, 46–47; irresolution in, 43, 45, 47; and politics, 38, 44–45, 47; symbolism of, 39, 40–41. Poems: "Against Unworthy Praise," 44; "The Apparitions," 39; "The Cap and Bells," 41; "The Choice," 42; "Crazy Jane on the Day of Judgment," 45; "Crazy Jane Talks with the Bishop," 45, 147; "The Dawn," 39; "Demon and Beast," 44; "A Dialogue of Self and Soul," 41, 44; "Easter 1916," 41, 44, 212; "Ego Dominus Tuus," 40, 45; "Ephemera," 31–34; "The Fisherman," 41; "The Hawk," 41; "An Irish Airman Foresees His Death, 43, 98; "Lapis Lazuli," 45; "Leda and the Swan," 191–92; "Meditations in Time of Civil War," 41; "Meru," 39; "No Second Troy," 42; "On a Political Prisoner," 45; "Parnell's Funeral," 44; "The People," 44; "A Prayer for My Daughter," 43, 269; "Remorse for Intemperate Speech," 46; *Responsibilities*, 47; "Sailing to Byzantium," 45; "The Scholars," 41; "The Second Coming," 40, 43; "September 1913," 38; "To a Friend Whose Work Has Come to Nothing," 38; "To a Young Beauty," 44; "Tom O'Roughley," 38–39, 41; "Under Ben Bulben," 46; "Upon a Dying Lady," 40; "Vacillation," 43; "The Wild Swans at Coole," 43; *The Wild Swans at Coole*, 47; *The Wind Among the Reeds*, 41. Prose: "At Stratford-on-Avon," 42; Introduction to *Oxford Book of Modern Verse*, 39, 46
Young, Dudley, 43
Young, Edward, 130; *Night Thoughts*, 128